COMMUNITY AND THE WORLD:
PARTICIPATING IN SOCIAL CHANGE

COMMUNITY AND THE WORLD:
PARTICIPATING IN SOCIAL CHANGE

TORRY D. DICKINSON
EDITOR

Nova Science Publishers, Inc.
New York

Senior Editors: Susan Boriotti and Donna Dennis
Coordinating Editor: Tatiana Shohov
Office Manager: Annette Hellinger
Graphics: Wanda Serrano
Editorial Production: Vladimir Klestov, Matthew Kozlowski, Tom Moceri, Alexandra
     Columbus and Maya Columbus
Circulation: Ave Maria Gonzalez, Vera Popovic, Luis Aviles, Raymond Davis, Melissa
     Diaz, Marlene Nunez and Jeannie Pappas
Communications and Acquisitions: Serge P. Shohov
Marketing: Cathy DeGregory

Library of Congress Cataloging-in-Publication Data
Available upon request

ISBH 1-59033-633-X

Copyright © 2003 by Nova Science Publishers, Inc.
     400 Oser Ave, Suite 1600
     Hauppauge, New York 11788-3619
     Tele. 631-231-7269 Fax 631-231-8175
     e-mail: Novascience@earthlink.net
     Web Site: http://www.novapublishers.com

For Robert Schaeffer,
who is there for the next generation

CONTENTS

PREFACE

Dear Reader,

This book is for you.

It contains accessible, activist scholarship on local-to-global change. *Community and the World* features articles and presentations written from multidisciplinary, women-inclusive and feminist perspectives. In a personal way, peer-reviewed and scholarly writings explore social change projects in Women's-Studies related areas, including in science, education, cultural studies, history and the social sciences. Additional writings and artistic contributions explore contemporary change and politics through popular and emotional art. Readers will learn new ways for democratic, community-based and global scholars to carry out egalitarian *community development education*, or the women-inclusive, research-based process of identifying needs, designing and starting projects, learning from group efforts, and building sustainable, community to global connections.

The particular emphasis in this book is on *inclusive* community development education, which engages members of diverse and sometimes marginalized groups in research and education for social change.

This book was conceived of as an academic project that would speak to all community development educators who possessed applied research expertise and good interpersonal communication skills, whatever license or degree they held. You may notice, as you look at each article, that authors' names are not followed by the "top" degree they hold. To learn more about the diverse group of writers, turn to the "Contributors" section at the end of the book. There you will find descriptions of the writers' scholarly activism, and you will learn about their interests, concerns, and commitments. You may not, however, always learn about the writers' academic degrees; for the most part (with some editorial changes) writers chose what they wanted to say about themselves, and the degree status issue was not always at the top of the list. In some fields, too, the M.A. is the terminal degree. And, of course, there are some intellectuals and forceful educators around the world who have little formal education, but extensive informal education and on-the-job-training.

On the other hand, this is a scholarly book. Two formal "calls for papers" went out on Women's Studies and World-System list services, and these were distributed widely to scholars in various disciplines and multidisciplinary areas. All academic articles included in this book went through an extensive peer-review process, and all articles went through one or more revisions. Many university educators represented here do this kind of work as part of their academic research; we wanted to be sure that strict academic standards were met and that scholarly contributions could be counted for tenure, promotion, and other markers of university accomplishment. The academic review and revision process took a year and a half.

Other contributions were included in the collection, too. These examine social change education in multiple venues: in culture, music, art, community, and work. These participatory, research-based pieces may take the form of an essay, an interview, or an arrangement of artwork.

This is a multicultural, cross-over collection. One goal of the book was to encourage university scholars to recognize the value of scholarly work done by research-based educators in non-university contexts, and to encourage social change makers in non-profit organizations and social movement settings to work more closely with university-based social change researchers. By putting our heads and our resources together, more progress will be made on local to global levels.

This is a cross-over collection in other ways, too. The contributions all serve as personalized invitations to begin living life in ways that work for everyone. This includes: to work with others as equals, to join democratic social projects, to talk to people you "wouldn't have talked to before," to value self-education that we have been encouraged to replace with formal classes, to value the contributions made by unpaid workers, to invent ways to be nonviolent, to challenge passivity, and to use democracy as a way to make our community and world better. The book's cover invites us to travel, to experience new places and people, and to walk through new doors, which we once might have chosen not to cross through.

As editor, I was surprised at how much I became involved with the writers and artists as they developed their pieces, went through the review process, and revised their articles. By working closely with writers, I got to know them and their ideas, which created a more holistic book. Together the chapters give an overview of related aspects of community development education. Contributions also stand firmly on their own, without any assistance from others. Each piece included in this collection contains diverse themes, comes from multidisciplinary research, and speaks to the subject of education for social change in many personalized and intellectual ways. I will say that all contributions focus on the importance of self-education, self-defined group education, and sometimes classroom-, program- and university-centered group education. In other words, contributions suggest that research-based education (and not finding the correct organizing strategy) is the starting point for social change.

I salute the writers and contributors and the work that they have done! Thank you for working with me and with each other. I have enjoyed this experience immensely, and I will always value the interactions that we had. In fact: I would like to bring all of the contributors together sometime soon, and see where we can go from here.

All of the book's contributors make choices about what they will do with their workday and with their time on earth. We all do. We all benefit when we learn more about our individual and collective choices, and when we listen to each other more carefully. If we do this, maybe we can learn how to work together better. I may not agree with all of the ideas expressed in this collection (and I'm sure that most writers disagree with some of my ideas), but I do appreciate all the approaches to using education as a means to make research-based decisions together. You, the reader, will probably find yourself agreeing and disagreeing with specific ideas and approaches, but I hope that the "dialogue" you have with each contributor will help you learn more about your own choices and what you would like to do with others. This is a diverse collection of writings that, I hope, will help you begin to appreciate more about our social choices and how we can work together across cultural and organizational divides.

We all became involved in community development education in different ways. Most of the volume's contributors share how they became engaged in specific projects. For me, it happened in U.S., state-funded, public schools, a place where democracy and cultural renewal can thrive, if public schooling is cultivated. Because I have seen how invigorating public education can be—when people choose to develop it and to participate in it—I am one of the strongest defenders of public education you may ever encounter.

In an urban junior high in the mid-1960s, I saw how important it was for students to relate to learning, and to guide it. Many people of my generation did not learn about Women's Studies, Black Studies, or the student movement until they were in high school or college. I personally felt the impact of the Free Speech and Black Power Movements filter down to adult teachers and to my junior high school in Detroit, where our curriculum became enhanced as a result of alternative-vision movements.

I began appreciating how good education encourages a change in power relations when I was placed in Mrs. Ruthie Nelson's eighth grade English class, and when I signed up for Mrs. Nelson's after-school class in Afro-American Studies. In English class, we read Margaret Walker's *Jubilee*, Frederick Douglass' autobiography, and a story about a teen boy in Spanish Harlem; and, in Afro-American Studies, we got to read Richard Wright's *Uncle Tom's Children*, which gets readers to value Black people's telling of history in Black English. When we studied etymology with Mrs. Nelson, we learned that we spoke words that came from many languages (African, European, Latin American, and Asian). As junior high students, this helped us value our own power as knowledge-holders, thinkers, and writers, and we became connected to the world and its history.

English lessons, taught from "a bottom up," historical perspective at my junior high, were followed by Mr. Hammond's world history class, where we learned the de-colonized countries in Africa and were introduced to the Mexican Revolution. The following semester, in Mr. Westveer's history class, we met in a magical room that was encircled by wooden banisters and magnificent hanging lights, which our teacher had carefully removed from neighborhood homes before they were razed for "slum clearance." We students saw we were valued, and so were the neighborhood and its people.

In this learning environment, we were encouraged to see struggle as a positive, dignified social force. Not surprisingly, within a few months we began to engage in struggle ourselves. After one classmate asked me to start a reading group with her, we began walking to the downtown Gratiot library on a regular basis and reading every "insurrectionist," Afro-American history book in the library (there were not many, and librarians granted access to only the most headstrong). Changing your own thinking, of course, often leads you to challenge others about theirs'.

In our ninth grade class, one strong, visionary girl led the way as some students challenged our world history teacher to go beyond a European-centered perspective, and to include African history before European expansion and conquest. This teacher was open to change initiated by students. As a result of student initiative, our school ordered a supplementary textbook that covered many African civilizations and their largely unknown achievements and contributions.

Because our class prepared the student newspaper, we also started writing and publishing political editorials. Two brave teen boys in our class wrote an appreciative commentary on the two U.S. Olympic track athletes who, in 1968, raised their fists in a Black Power salute. I remember co-writing, with a classmate, an editorial that criticized society's coldness and social brutality. Because of my teachers at Miller, because of the leadership of my Detroit classmates, I have looked for good ways to learn, teach, and prepare people to make the world a better place.

Ultimately this interest in participatory democracy took me to the study of sociology and Women's Studies, eventually to Kansas State, and then to this book project.

Community and the World is about social change projects that have come about because of the concerted work of dedicated groups, whose work (in financial terms) was often uncompensated or under-compensated. It is important for those of us in academia to recognize that we receive faculty and research salaries to write about world happenings, including activities carried out by "volunteer" and non-profit projects like these. Sometimes we even get small royalty checks after our books are published. I would like to recognize the work done by non-profit organizations (501c3 organizations) that carry out inclusive community development education. Once book royalties cover expenses, my editing income will be contributed to a non-profit, women-inclusive, community development project. By redistributing income that comes from social change writing, community development educators can help promote equality, democracy, and sustainable living.

As I was working on this book, I appreciated the administrative and research support provided by Patricia Swanigan and Summer Lewis. Donna Dennis, Nova Science editor, was helpful, kind and innovative. Thanks to my university for providing a sabbatical, which enabled me to focus on this project. As always, I appreciated the spirited discussions, constructive advice, and loving support provided by my family: Robert, Jazz and Jeffree.

This book really is for you, the reader. I hope you enjoy it and jump into some new educational and community projects with gusto!

Torry Dickinson, Editor
April 9, 2003

PART I: INTRODUCTION TO COMMUNITY AND THE WORLD

Chapter 1

Reunifying Community and Transforming Our World: Inclusive Community Development Education and the University

Torry D. Dickinson

Abstract

Educators for social change strive to meet local to global human needs by participating in democratic, multicultural, multidisciplinary, research groups that design and implement new projects. Making collective decisions with others, community researchers plan and initiate work-related, political and cultural relationships that promote egalitarian community-based, regional, and global development. Today, learning centers organized by civil societal groups are taking the lead in initiating egalitarian development processes. Non-profit and non-governmental organizations, alternative educational projects, social movement projects, and independent-minded unions for the disenfranchised often emerge as intellectual leaders in the search for better ways to meet human needs.

This article examines the recent history of gender- and ethnic-inclusive community development education in the United States, and analyzes some of the field's key writings, educational theories, and organizing ideas. Feminist and non-racist community development education, a scholarly and multidisciplinary research methodology, helps build new theories of social change through democratic engagement. This collaborative research method, it is argued, has the potential to redefine and link community and worldwide development processes in ways that could promote equality in our world community.

Here research for social change is analyzed in relation to: the impact of social movements on the university, theory-making in history and the social sciences, and community development methodology as it relates to diverse learning centers that promote social change. The value of peer learning groups is shown through the author's inclusive community development work in four different settings, including: a displaced homemakers' center, a Cooperative Extension Service's community service and employment project for low-income elders, an urban university that builds theoretical understandings from community research, and the writer's Women's Studies teaching and community development work at a land-grant university.

INTRODUCTION

Today's most promising efforts to improve and transform society often start with open, democratic discussions and problem-solving sessions that become sustained, research-based, educational projects. Open talk is central to this process. According to Lois Gibbs, who helped fight toxic dumping at Love Canal, women organizers stressed the importance of "talking to people, getting them together, reaching a decision and taking action—for the survival of our children and ourselves" (quoted in Kaplan 1997:77).[1] According to Temma Kaplan, "Dialogue—talking things through and talking to everyone—is the basis for the new democracy" (Kaplan:77).

The best educational, social-change practices involve much more than traditional adult education techniques (which are often called community development education, too). Traditional community development education addresses the immediate needs of small groups of community residents, but it typically has not been inclusive education. Without culturally diverse learning groups, and without intentional intervention that tries to prevent the ongoing reproduction of unequal social practices, community development projects may just provide short-term solutions for the few. By connecting local problem solving to broader *social transformations, and by extending and transforming the meaning of community development, inclusive research teams can strengthen social relations and help end conflict.*

This article explores the establishment of educational projects that include members of social groups who may have been marginalized within our society.[2] These projects recognize that women and disenfranchised ethnic or other groups have been denied social benefits and social respect, even though they have been major social contributors, as underpaid paid and unpaid workers, and as hard-working neighborhood and family members who have shaped affirmative, cultural traditions. The working assumption here, which is derived from applied community research, is that those who have been internally marginalized within our communities and within global society often know the most about how community problems manifest themselves, and how they can be addressed in effective ways.

Educational, change-oriented, participatory research processes that are fully inclusive and egalitarian can be called *feminist and anti-racist community development education.*[3] This

---

[1] Temma Kaplan found this quotation in: Lois Marie Gibbs, "Some Thoughts on Women Who Move from Being Local Grassroots Leaders to Full-time Organizers," in Robbin Lee Zeff, et al. eds.,1989, *Empowering Ourselves: Women and Toxics Organizing*, Arlington, VA: Citizens Clearinghouse for Hazardous Waste, Inc., pp. 37-41; 37.

[2] Earlier writings on my participatory action research appear in: (1) Torry D. Dickinson, 1995, *CommonWealth: Self-Sufficiency and Work in American Communities, 1830 to 1993*, Lanham, MD: University Press of America, Inc., especially the "Introduction: History and Social Change" (ix-xvii); Chapter Seven on "Class Formation and the Emergence of New Social Identity Movements" (167-191); and Chapter Eight on "The Reorganization of Work and the Social Hierarchy" (pp. 193-212) and (2) Torry D. Dickinson, 1999, "Reunifying Community and Transforming Society: Community Development Education and the University," in ed. Dan Chekki, *Research in Community Sociology*, Vol. 9, Stamford, CN: JAI Press, pp. 41-63.

[3] Participatory, change-oriented education is called different things: liberatory education, popular education, community-based education, education for social change, community-action research, applied experiential

educational model may be most effective when it is guided by members of historically locked-out groups who build development processes by creating new cooperative networks that link local areas to regions, and regions to global, economic- and cultural-democracy projects.[4] By participating in open global forums[5] (and not just conferencing with other holders of doctoral degrees), university scholars can begin to connect with scholarly activists who have taken the lead in developing these effective, educational projects for work-based and cultural change.

Through its multiple, far-reaching impacts, inclusive community development education greatly extends and changes the meaning of "adult education." Suddenly populations that have "dropped through cracks" are making decisions, addressing specific barriers, and coming up with innovative solutions. The inclusion of locked-out groups helps to concretize and transform group educational processes through: the targeted assessment of needs, the designing and selecting of multi-purpose program models, the implementation of projects at community and trans-regional levels, and the striking effectiveness of ongoing evaluation processes. Members of groups that have been excluded from social resources really care about evaluation because they *need* their community projects to work for them and others. Rather than being an avenue for grant renewal, evaluation means determining whether the needs of different target groups are being met in the short- and long-term.

Inclusive evaluation typically leads to the creation of social solutions that go beyond addressing an existing problem to developing broad social solutions that prevent the emergence of a series of related problems. When feminist and anti-racist community learners implement an effective community project, it usually meets many critical social needs, and provides a social-relational base for future community redesign efforts. This broadens the meaning of democratic participation, and opens up possibilities for achieving economic equality.

Based on my twenty-years of involvement with community-based and globally oriented social change projects, I argue that university classrooms and community-based social change environments often share common educational processes. Peer learning circles have been found in diverse community settings, including the university, secondary educational

---

community education, participatory action research, applied research informed by feminist and anti-racist pedagogies, methods from the margins, critical pedagogy and border pedagogy, global pedagogy and neo-abolitionist pedagogy, community development education, and related names (hooks 1994; Smith and Willms 1997; Arnold et al. 1991; Thomas-Slayter et al.; Park et al. 1993; Kirby and McKenna: 1989; Gillespie et al. 2002; Dlamini 2002; Leonardo 2002).

[4] Although many educational projects push for nation-states to change priorities and reallocate resources, civil societal projects typically bypass the bottleneck of state politics by initiating new relationships between the local, the regional, and the global (or cross-border connections). Because unequal social relations are promoted through the global institutions of the dominant, integrated world-system that shapes work and culture, social projects become most effective when they introduce equal social models at local to global levels. For example, racism and white privilege appears throughout the world, linking "the local with the global processes of racial privilege"; this makes it necessary to consider a global pedagogy, if long-lasting social change is to take place (Leonardo 2002: 36). However, scholars and activists sometimes reject a global approach, choosing to focus on instabilities within regions and nation-states. For example, Deborah Gordan argues that feminist ethnography needs to focus on the "nexus of nation and class," and not become lost in "diasporic identities" that ignore the nation-state (Gordon 1999:67). Actually, both approaches can help advance change, and both are employed today. Ultimately, however, most major social problems have global-historical roots; social change agents are more effective when they confront the global dimension right from the beginning.

[5] This includes women's, ecological and South/North forums.

institutions, non-profit and non-governmental organizations, social movement groups, cultural groups, health care organizations, government agencies, worker cooperatives, and local to global micro-enterprise and equivalency-oriented marketing networks. Many projects rebuild social relationships on multiple levels, such as through education and housing innovations. By becoming inclusive learning groups that implement equitable solutions to short- and long-term problems, research-informed, social-change groups can improve the social welfare of individual communities and their encompassing social networks. Engaged, research-based, educational learning groups like these are considered "scholarly activism." Social transformations are fostered when people crossover intellectual boundaries and rejoin historically separated groups of thinkers and change agents. The majority can benefit greatly when democratic, egalitarian border-crossings and collaborative, visionary, social-change projects develop between different organizations and key social institutions.

Examined here are efforts to advance changes through the development of civil society, and through institutions found in communities and in global society, including the workplace, the state,[6] ethnic groups, gender groups and households. Inclusive community development education is seen as the methodology that links practical social action with key sets of contemporary, holistic, and multidisciplinary theories of global society and social change. Key, contemporary theory sets include: world-system, cultural and post-structural, ethnic and post-colonial, and feminist perspectives (Dickinson 2003).

Although these perspectives have been cast as oppositional, together they help build a framework that provides community researchers with social change tools. World-system analysts study the development of historical capitalism since 1500, identifying patterns and structures of the dominant global system, and exploring anti-systemic movements (Wallerstein 1996: Schaeffer 2002). This global, systemic research helps to explain cultural and post-structural research.

Cultural Studies researchers look at the social construction of culture and the emergence of fragmented forms of cultural resistance within regions and nation-states. Research subjects often include feminist, sexuality, youth, elder, anti-racist, anti-colonial, anti-ruling class, and sometimes anti-middle class movements. These movements, which grow out of a stratified world-system with unequal work and cultural relations (see world-system research), constitute many of the fragmented cultures that try to transform society.

Feminist researchers and anti-racist/post-colonial scholars stress that our society reproduces gender and racialized hierarchies (as well as age, sexuality and other divides) as part of its workings. Feminist and anti-racist movements respond to, and attempt to transform our unequal society and create social relationships that foster equality and democracy.

As these four theory sets are put together in different ways, these new convergences, which are based on the combination of theoretical frameworks, will help community action researchers develop different models of social change and implement more egalitarian relationships. This multi-dimensional, convergence process will be informed by knowledge

---

[6] State-related popular education projects include: the open hearings sponsored by the post-apartheid, South African Truth Commission, and Chile's truth and reconciliation process that followed dictatorship and led to the researching of detained-disappeared citizens (Aguilar 2002). Other recent public educational and compensation processes are Europe's holocaust compensation procedures (involving banks and manufacturing companies, governments, and civil societal groups) and the various research-based attempts in the United States to obtain educational compensation for the ancestors of enslaved Americans of African descent.

gained from participatory action research, or feminist and anti-racist community development education.

ADDRESSING BARRIERS AND CROSSING BORDERS BETWEEN LEARNING COMMUNITIES

Of particular interest to contemporary social-change makers is the combination of scholarly analysis with problem solving activism, which can be described as scholarly activism. The line is blurred between educational, intellectual, research, applied and activist activities. Critical thinkers border-cross.

Identifying barriers that have inhibited past research points to ways to improve educational work. We usually fail to see how our work is connected to the efforts of others, and this limits our ability to be effective scholarly activists. Most social projects carried out by governments, educational organizations, and non-governmental or non-profit organizations started because social movements pushed for certain changes to be made, but applied thinkers often overlook the role of social movements. It helps to search for connections among various efforts to end social problems, especially those advanced by governments, non-profit organizations, schools, and social movement groups. Local initiatives often relate to social-change efforts in other parts of the world, and participatory action researchers often can learn from social movement projects. Educators, social scientists, and historians have studied similar problems from different angles, but they typically avoid doing research outside of their fields and on comparative geographies. Those who address global problems and world policy issues can also gain insights from researching both case studies and bridges between local and broader processes of change.

Members of overlapping gender, ethnic, class, and global South/North groups benefit when they practice cross-border learning and research. This is necessary if we are to appreciate how much gender, ethnic and "colonial" inequality have restricted past efforts to openly see and transform our common world community.

Multigenerational scholars increase their effectiveness when they leave their confined work, school, and residential pods. New connections start to reverse the social divides that came from specialization, bureaucratization, the growth of cities and suburbs, the rise of the "university" and "community" dichotomy, and the growth of class-related hierarchies, including those that are expressed through different consumption options and choices.

It has taken a long time for most universities to recognize the value of applied learning in community and global social change. Until about a decade ago, scholarly activism was generally restricted to "magnet social change programs." Then academics' professional associations began to endorse service learning, appreciate multidisciplinary scholarship, respond to revitalized student and community demands, and realize that departmental boundaries limited academic success for teachers and students, and restricted universities' ability to compete for a diverse body of students and outside funding (increasingly designated for collaborative projects). Even though feminist and anti-racist student movements in the 1960s had called for the university to participate in the transformation of community life, relatively few scholars joined applied research teams, even during the 1970s and 1980s, and few have continued their scholarly activism for 30 or more years.

As universities build connections with non-governmental organizations and state agencies, today's teachers generally acknowledge that education is strengthened when scholars and students partner with participatory action researchers in community and international settings. Teachers and students are now taking up service learning activities and pursuing community connections, sometimes to facilitate job-placement efforts. However, it is still fairly unusual for universities to consider carrying out the changes proposed by early proponents of Women's Studies and Black Studies: establishing an open, multicultural, student-influenced, cross-disciplinary learning environment, where students explore mechanisms perpetuating inequality and learn to value the stimulation and insights of off-campus intellectual and social life.

Democratic learning processes in the university and in other community settings often share common educational elements: learner-centered education, applied learning on social change, the development of multicultural relationships and knowledge, the naming and definition of social problems by marginalized and disenfranchised groups, the development of social solutions by cross-cultural groups, the individual and collective empowerment of community members, and the formation and implementation of social alternatives. Community development education and social change projects can either spring from the collective activity of social movements or from the expressed interest of concerned residents and scholarly activists. "Classrooms" take many forms today, including social service planning sessions, community speak-outs, community dialogues, needs-assessment teams, and non-profit board meetings.

Getting educators and learners to assume that "all spheres are theirs" is a tall order for educators in diverse learning environments. Unfortunately, the divide between the enclosed spaces of ivy-covered universities (including land-grant state universities which are mandated to serve the public) and other service organizations and groups has not always narrowed in recent years, even with federal and state initiatives to reward institutional collaboration. University teachers often are intimidated by the practical, "real-life" knowledge displayed by policy advocates and program operators. And faculty members are afraid (with reason) that they will face professional penalties if they link their scholarship with real-world concerns.

On the other hand, educators in community organizations often feel "put off by" and "not included in" activities at the university. Some of these fears about the majority's exclusion on campuses are based on negative experiences with others, and some are based on assumptions that developed simply because research-informed activists did not try to connect with the university. These tensions between teachers and practitioners often surface, demonstrating that effective collaboration requires new knowledge, new skills and a lot of practice applying them. Practice with these applications helps develop people, and this is a central part of community development.

The social change field is open, and scholarly activists and activist teachers do not have to feel constrained by rules made by others. There are no hard-and-fast rules that limit or clearly define the roles that teachers and students, social workers, volunteers, and movement activists can play in the process of conducting education for social change. Intellectuals who want to do more than talk about social change activities can start to invent new ways to help learners acquire knowledge.

A HISTORICAL PERSPECTIVE ON U.S. COMMUNITY DEVELOPMENT EDUCATION

In the last decade, the National Women's Studies Association and professional disciplinary associations have developed a renewed interest in ethnographic and service learning research, reintroducing a long-standing debate about the extent of the split between the university and the community. Journal articles, conferences, universities and departments now, once again, address the apparent divide between academic and community organizations. Many teachers may find themselves, for the first time, joining discussions about building school and community linkages. Because so many schools are just beginning to move forward with service learning and internship classes, and because most service-providing non-profits have not reached out to schools, relationships between these spheres are only beginning to be redefined.

Community development education is social change education that contains applied, historical, process-based, and theoretical elements. If one considers the integrated knowledge acquired from both classroom and "hands-on" environments, these classrooms reinforce each other. They contribute to the cumulative development of knowledge about social change, giving learners "a sense of efficacy," and "deepening commitment" (Gilbert 2000: 129, 133). Rather than seeing faculty members and students as tied to an elite-minded sphere that is outside of "real life," I see teachers and students as members of communities and global networks, and non-profit classrooms as part of our intellectual wealth.

We are challenging the identity of intellectual and activist. As we do this, we need to realize that working people around the world—whether they had formal schooling or not—have carried out decades of intellectual and social change work in their families, neighborhoods, and in their paid and unpaid jobs. The expertise of all intellectuals, artists and community activists needs to be recognized.[7] One can be a thinker and a social analyst, with or without formal school experience, and regardless if one is pre-literate or highly literate. Many of the world's most effective community educators and creative artists have not had the benefit of even six years of elementary education, but—because they address critical subject matter with knowledge gained first-hand—they may be effective public researchers, communicators, and leaders. To be an effective scholarly activist in academia, it is vital to go beyond just considering the "radical" notion of talking to and solving problems with people who have totally different educational backgrounds. Change agents jump into problem-solving teams, cross borders that separate cultures, and do everything they can to *learn* how to change society.

Cross-cultural work shows that many family and community members still provide community service as a part of everyday life, even when it has not been elevated with the name of "volunteerism." The complex and historical division of the world's work actually served to devalue social change and service efforts that all family members used to do as part of daily life. The separation of housework and community work and paid employment brought the separation of family members. And it even divided members of low-income households from each other; building huge barriers between family members, these barriers

---

[7] Poet Dana Gioia, nominee for chair of the U.S. National Endowment for the Humanities, has called for the reinvention of public literary culture through populist participation (Pogrebin: 2002, NYT Oct. 28).

were arbitrarily erected by the state and business world, and by members of those groups named as "dominant": men, whites, the able-bodied, middle-years people and, in some cultures, elders. It took a long time before all the dominant and subordinate groups that comprised households, and who represented the multitude of household and workplace divides, started to rethink their values about work (Dickinson 1995). The idea of "giving back to the community" was fostered by the cultural resistance and new self-definitions exhibited by many members of excluded ethnic and gender groups. And the commitment to community service often remains the strongest within those disenfranchised groups that need to be leading problem-solving teams.

During the global cultural revolutions of the 1960s and 1970s, many people felt that community work had the greatest impact in terms of transforming society and eliminating injustices. Working people increasingly saw themselves as thinkers and important social change makers, whether or not they had degrees or held teaching positions at the university, whether or not they learned to be critical thinkers and doers in cross-cultural contexts. This cultural shift often expressed itself through the rise of grassroots projects throughout the world, producing a bottom-up resurgence that has become a foundation for many contemporary intellectual and activist initiatives. We now see the widespread construction of democratic networks within civil society and a growing recognition that informed community work can start to rebuild global society from within local civil society. In this sense, changes made today through feminist and anti-racist community development education can help build the foundation of tomorrow's more egalitarian society.

A critical part of our global cultural heritage comes from "forgotten people's studies," which are taught in disciplines like sociology, history, political science, and English, and in multidisciplinary programs like Women's Studies, Black Studies, Chicano Studies, and Gay and Lesbian Studies (Wallerstein and Gulbenkian Commission 1996). These areas of intersectional study have been based on the understanding that academic studies, autobiography, culture, community, and applied research experiences are all useful sources for helping younger and older learners acquire knowledge about the social hierarchy and processes of social transformation.

The historical "split between knowledge and pedagogy, and between traditional and "new" disciplines" disrupted not just Women's Studies (Maher and Tetreault, 2001:13), but relationships between feminist inquiry and other elements of "forgotten people's studies." Because the related bodies of "forgotten people's" scholarship formed an important component of the pedagogy of freedom, the social division of the university slowed down scholarly activism in different learning communities.

In the 1960s and early 1970s, when Women's Studies and Black Studies were being initiated in the U.S. academy, considerable emphasis was placed on thinking about how to change the world. After that, an intellectual break impeded the creation of a common, diverse knowledge base that could have helped social change efforts in the following decades. In addition, global problems multiplied. It can be argued that the cumulative disadvantages that resulted from universities' disconnected education and laboratory-model social scientific research could have been minimized if university policy makers had directed all academics to help eliminate local, national and global social problems. Academic culture and politics stifled learning, and there was a relative absence of participatory social change work. Consequently, students and faculty have missed so much of the excitement that is associated with qualitative and quantitative research in the united community. But some of this history is beginning to be left behind today as non-university learning centers are showing academics how to be more effective community researchers.

IMAGINING SOCIETY'S GLOBAL RELATIONSHIPS, IMAGINING SOCIAL CHANGE

As learners engage in community development education in different locales and networks, they face the challenges of imagining what the operations of the system look like, and of creating a new imaginary of a better world. Inclusive community development education involves honestly exploring how the workings of the social system affect groups in unequal ways. As learners see how problems are created, they begin to develop very specific and useful ways to change societal operations so that fair, respectful social relationships replace unfair ones. This allows us to move, as novelist Rainelle Burton might say, from hope that is "based solely on want or need," and that "has no means for reasonable expectation," to faith, which is based on "some tangible outcome or measurable proof that provides the means for a reasonable expectation" (Burton 2001:5-6).

In the United States and throughout the world, ideological walls blocking free thought often seem to materialize out of the fog. Repression of free speech is sometimes reinforced by governmental violence and university complicity in the United States, in Mexico, and in other countries. As sculptor Eric Fischl says, "Right now we're shrinking away from the truth" (Fischl in interview by Rakoff, 2002). World citizens may get the message: "do not think too deeply or say too much, and definitely do not stop living in denial of material realities." But scholarly activists, who live in First World apartments and in Third World self-constructed dwellings, continue to tear down these walls, creating new mental images of society and what we can do. Scholarly activism encourages learners to use their basic human and civil rights, to their fullest extent, as people talk, think, and work together, and extend our notion of democracy.

Rigid rules about education, writing and talking constrain and prevent learners from seeing the whole, and from pulling together elements that reveal the whole society and its transformational aspects. Learners from all walks of life are discouraged from seeing institutional connections that create many of our social problems and that reproduce inequality here and abroad. If one starts with gender, a central institution of the world, and if one branches outward and explores gender relationships within other global institutions, including the household and age and sexuality, and within ethnic groups, classes and businesses, and the state, it is possible, through all of these institutional linkages, to imagine a relational construct of the entire global society.[8] In other words, because global society's institutions and people's actions are so interrelated, one can begin to see—and to learn how to affect—human relationships in our world.

---

[8] Because groups of people are placed in unequal, overlapping positions within a common world-system, "positionality helps to explain why so many alternate explanations for the same phenomenon exist" (Sattler 1997:227).

Although feminist pedagogy[9] forms a large part of what has been missing in applied efforts to transform society, feminist pedagogy only obtains and reveals its full meaning (as with other key social theories) when it is located in relationship to other equally important elements of the pedagogy of freedom, a concept developed by educator Paulo Freire (2001). Ultimately gender relations (like all other social relations) can only be understood when they are placed in relation to other perspectives and knowledge about the whole. Due to subject restrictions and a limited field-of-vision about all social elements, stand-alone theories of any sort do not lead to a comprehensive understanding of society. Feminism, anti-racism and post-colonialism, cultural analysis and world-system analysis, along with other relevant theories, cannot be understood apart from other complementary components of the pedagogy of freedom. By tracing the different groups who need and can benefit from education for social change, it is possible to construct, as Freire did, a theoretical framework that leads to the concept of the "pedagogy of freedom." But this pedagogy of freedom is much more than a social-action theory. The pedagogy of freedom grows out of concrete knowledge about social needs and visions; and this knowledge is generated through the research methodology of inclusive community development education.

As one engages in popular education, learners see how civil society touches these institutions and how these global institutions influenced the development of civil society. Learners see how there remain somewhat independent, open places for social development in civil society. In addition, a thorough analysis of any institution allows one to see links between constraining cultures and constraining paid/unpaid work relations, as well as between liberating cultures and liberating work relationships, processes that are reinforced through community action research.

Even with all of today's cultural ferment, colleges' disciplinary divides and wooden educational traditions prevent students and teachers from creating new convergences. Higher education's structure and the fiscal politics of disciplinary divides often discourage border-crossings and theoretical innovations in the university. It would be helpful if community researchers could promote and benefit from the integration of world-system analysis; Women's Studies; gender, age and sexuality studies; global ethnic and post-colonial studies; post-structural and cultural studies, and other fields, including those in formation. This would enable scholars to obtain a more complete understanding of global society and potential transformation possibilities. Applications of inclusive community development education seem to be pushing these changes, demonstrating that university knowledge often lags behind social change knowledge emerging from research projects around the world.

Global institutional arrangements, including relationships between paid and unpaid work, the state, the household, and ethnic and gender/sexuality and age hierarchies, are rarely challenged through university priorities and policies. Schools and workplaces encourage

---

[9] Path-breaking books are beginning to appear on feminist activism in relation to global politics. Here I include: Nancy A. Naples and Karen Bojar, 2002, *Teaching Feminist Activism: Strategies from the Field*, NY: Routledge (a collection that emphasizes social change and participation in local and global politics from a feminist pedagogical standpoint). In the articles, there is a strong emphasis on encouraging students to become activists, as it is defined through the perspective of feminist writings. In historical terms, sometimes the lens of feminism (and of activism) has been defined in narrow ways that limit the political and social imagination, and reduce our effectiveness. Another emphasis might be to prepare students for the life-long work of thinking about and participating in carefully considered projects that create the society we want. Also see Nancy A. Naples and Manisha Desai, 2002, *Women's Activism and Globalization: Linking Local Struggles and Global Politics*, NY: Routledge.

people to "be nice," to ignore systemic problems, and to hold society together (even if it is unequal and undemocratic), rather than to explore change through collective decision-making, participation in practical projects, long-range democratic planning, and long-term social reconstruction from within civil society and various institutional settings. Community development education provides a method for schools to: identify social problems, meet human needs, preserve the world's natural resources, redistribute and share global resources, learn from different cultures, and value each others' contributions, regardless of whether a market value is attached to work or not.

By applying the community-action method, we increase our chances of preserving our planet for succeeding generations, whose future is shrouded by cumulative gender, ethnic, cultural, economic, political and ecological violence. Applied social change work helps students understand how and why social problems are reproduced, where social barriers present themselves, how learners can intervene and eliminate one or more barriers, and what this concrete process reveals about constructing broader social-change plans and initiatives. Students imagine what society could look like, and how they could design concrete, doable ways to get there. Participatory action projects[10] can free young and older scholars from the trappings and confines of constrained academic thinking, thus energizing students, teachers and universities. Ultimately, imagining how today's society affects our world community and creating an alternative imaginary of evolving social relations may depend on the network of applied local, regional and global educators.

THEORETICAL, HISTORICAL AND APPLIED FOUNDATIONS OF COMMUNITY-ACTION RESEARCH

The democratic traditions of the world's marginalized groups have "filtered up" to shape critical education in often undisclosed ways, and the ideas of key social-change educators have "filtered down" to university and other community education settings in the United States and around the world. An examination of key educators' ideas reveals that community development education is more than a straightforward research process, more than an organizing strategy, more than an exercise in democracy, and more than an informed decision-making process leading to change. Community development education is designed to unlock the transforming power of democratic education. Feminist and anti-racist community development work is essentially an *educational* group process of researching and carrying out social change.

My work on community development education has been influenced by practical work in this field, and by research on community-based educators and researchers, including bell hooks (who was influenced by popular educator Paulo Freire). Paulo Freire conversed and debated extensively with Myles Horton, a community educator who founded Tennessee's Highlander Folk School sixty years ago (now known as the Highlander Research and Education Center). Before he met Freire, Myles Horton turned to the knowledge acquired by

---

[10] Galen Rowell, the environmental photographer who traveled all over the world, engaged in (what he called) participatory photography. By expressing his love of mountains (which led him to become so skilled at mountaineering that he climbed the Himalayas), Galen Rowell's photography became a medium

Jane Addams of Chicago's Hull House. Horton also learned from the writings of Bishop Grundtvig, who started Denmark's early cooperative movement and proposed that a "School for Life" replace academic learning (Horton, 1990:47-52). Early Western European folk schools, cultural transmission processes of subordinate ethnic groups, cultural preservation movements, and anti-landlord movements[11] in Latin America all influenced twentieth-century educators, grassroots activists, and reformers in the Americas.

Myles Horton's work at Tennessee's Highlander Folk School reflected the community organizing values of many U.S. educators involved in participatory change, and his influence is widespread. Horton stressed the importance of creating true democracy, and not false and limited political liberalism. He writes, "To have democracy, you must have a society in which decision making is real, and that means replacing, transforming and rebuilding society so as to allow for people to make decisions that affect their lives" (Horton 1990:174). Part of this, he stipulated, means ensuring that profit maximization does not take precedence over democratic decision-making. Myles Horton described the Highlander educational process as one where adults learn about their personal interests, work with others as part of a learning group, and then make democracy work for them ("You Got to Move," 1985). This early educational model contains many strands that closely resemble key elements in feminist community development education, even though women's systematic exclusion was not addressed.

The women, men and children who lived in Bumpass Cove, Tennessee in the early 1980s demonstrated the effectiveness of the Highlander's educational method. Residents of Bumpass Cove used democratic education and community research as ways to fight the secret toxic dumping that had been taking place in the landfill near their homes. Although the Highlander Research and Education Center had included some Bumpass Cove residents in their educational workshops, women began the cycle of community development education when they started to recognize that their children were becoming chronically ill. As this group of mothers began to identify and prioritize their needs, men from these households also started the process of determining whether illegal wastes were being trucked to the nearby landfill. The men videotaped the trucks' movements at all hours of the night and shared this information. The town's women conducted archival research on what toxic wastes had been buried in the landfill over a seven-year period, and on what the effects of certain chemicals were. After a huge flood sent barrels of chemicals into the creek and revealed the extent of contamination, the women, men, and children, took immediate action. Together they blocked the small dirt road leading to the landfill, stopping the dump trucks laden with a new shipment of toxic barrels ("You Got to Move," 1985).

As the Bumpass Cove community assumed more responsibility for its own destiny, the women started the long process of beginning to believe in their own abilities, and in each other. Each woman stopped seeing herself "as just a housewife, a nobody" and started to recognize that the lack of a high school education did not prevent her from establishing democratic, community-based procedures for saying what should happen in Appalachia ("You Got to Move," 1985).

---

for practicing environmental education and for promoting environmental protection. Rowell explicitly rejected gaining knowledge through an "objective," distanced viewing of nature.

[11] For a historical novel that explores the influence of a repressive, Mexican land-tenure system on culture, politics and spirituality, read Timothy J. Knab, 1993, *A War of Witches: A Journey of the Underworld of the Contemporary Aztecs*, San Francisco, CA: Harper San Francisco.

Paulo Freire's writings and hands-on work with the world's dispossessed totally re-energized the world's popular educators. In *The Politics of Education*, Paulo Freire provides a summary of how critical education for social change can be applied in various community and cross-national settings. Freire discussed and debated the merits of his method of critical education with the Highlander's Myles Horton in the late 1970s and 1980s, and with feminist learner and teacher, bell hooks. A review of Freire's educational method reveals that he was doubtlessly influenced by the century of applied education carried out by democratic Cooperative Extension Service educators in various countries, including in Third World and First World countries.

As a literacy educator in Brazil, Freire was greatly influenced by the "learner empowerment goal," a general goal often endorsed by community development educators, including those with the U.S. Cooperative Extension Service. But while many educators have hoped that individual learners would become "experts" at directing and transforming their own lives, educators like Freire and Horton envisioned the empowerment of locked-out groups. With Freire, adult education meant teaching groups to empower themselves through reading socially relevant concepts, thinking more about society, and taking social action to meet human needs.[12] And this is where peer-centered learning circles took on a new life in the academy. Brazilian rural workers, who were learning to read, became the center of the learning circles (or self-directed learning groups). The educational process began when the adults identified key concepts in their lives, which related to the land-owning class, the work they did, and their culture. As they learned to read these key words, the adults learned related concepts, contributing to the widening of their world. The learners empowered themselves by linking reading, social analysis and social action together.

A quick interjection: participating in an open, educational group like this requires a great deal of self-acceptance, and an appreciation of one's own knowledge and ideas, regardless of the social relations (agricultural day labor or office work) that produced those egalitarian insights. In learning groups, this means that learners need to listen to each other and to respect each other's knowledge bases. When learning circles are fully inclusive, they often deal with self-acceptance, mutual acceptance, and socially generated self- and group-esteem issues.[13] In order to have the most successful class sessions and community projects, learners need to feel comfortable being who they are.

A story about teacher Barbara Cook relates here. Cook, a singing teacher who once played Marian the Librarian in the film "The Music Man," tells her music students today, "I give you permission to do what you already know how to do." Then she gives another message, which also benefits members of learning circles: "It's so hard to believe that what the world wants is us. It's hard to believe, whatever you're doing, that you're enough. We are *all*, always enough" (Purdum, 2002). Being an effective learner and co-educator in an applied learning circle, like those motivated by Freire's teachings, requires self-acceptance and (for members with more power) a lot of humility.

---

[12] Many scholarly feminist activists, who are in touch with community work, emphasize a humanist vision. For example, Patricia Hill Collins writes that Black feminism is "a process of self-conscious struggle that empowers women and men to actualize a humanist vision of community" (Collins, 1994:598).

[13] Audre Lorde reminded people that, "We must move against not only those forces which dehumanize us from the outside, but also against those oppressive values which we have been forced to take into ourselves" (1994:455).

As a feminist historical sociologist and activist teacher/learner, I agree with Paulo Freire's ideas about theory making, which follow from Marx's method of political economy (Marx, ed. Dobbs, 1972). According to Freire, when a person thinks about the social world, s/he moves between the totality and its parts, seeing the general and then the concrete (or seeing the concrete and then the general). Then the learner can move from the concrete back up to general; or for those who started at the concrete, the learner can move from the general back down to the concrete (Freire, 1985:38). Learners, in other words, should start where they are at, not at one predetermined, jumping-off point (such as theory).

Within peer study circles, adult learners need to go through key learning stages, Freire writes. These include: *codification* (abstraction); *decodification* (studying and defining relationships between abstract categories); *problematizing* (comprehending codification and beginning to see dialectical movements); *comprehension* (understanding related dialectical movements and beginning to see what can be done by a group); *denunciation* (identifying negative trends); *annunciation* (knowing what is needed and defining interventions); *praxis* (attaining unity between thought and practice); and *critical consciousness* (after trying to think and act, and after learning the lessons that come from this process, acquiring an intention toward the world and bringing about cultural action for freedom) (Freire, 1985:52, 87, 160, 172).

Because he was concerned with educational processes in the classroom and in community settings, these writings on education's liberating power encouraged many social scientists, educators, and activists to consider the relationships between scholarship, teaching and social change practices. "History is made by us," and "history makes us while we remake it" (Freire 1985:199). People's reflections become real when they act, he wrote. Through critical education, the act of knowing helps to transform the real world, and it helps learners create their own world (Freire 1985:4-8, 124-125, 158).

Self-organized educational experiences encouraged the development of circles of culture, or small learning groups that engage in critical thinking. Through praxis or cultural action, these circles enable learners to experience a reintegration and to develop a new cultural synthesis (Freire 1985:34, 155, 168, 176). Because of the comprehensive scope of critical thinking, which leads to a critique of all institutions and relations, this pedagogy offers learners the opportunity to reintegrate their community life in profound ways. In particular, feminist and anti-racist pedagogies add egalitarian elements to collaborative and critical education, as researchers identify multidimensional ways to apply "their learning to social action and transformation," and as learners "recognize their ability to act to create a more humane social order" (Mayberry and Cronan Rose 1999:7).

Radical pedagogy, according to bell hooks, includes critical, feminist, and anti-colonial orientations.[14] In *Teaching to Transgress*,[15] bell hooks argues that teachers should create participatory learning experiences. To help students acquire knowledge about how to live in the world, teachers must "connect the will to know with the will to become" (hooks 1994:19). Embracing multicultural relations and focusing on who speaks, who listens and why all are important are parts of radical pedagogy. Describing Paulo Freire's work as "living water to

---

[14] Namulundah Florence relates bell hooks' method to Third World situations in: 1998, *bell hooks' Engaged Pedagogy: A Transgressive Education for Critical Consciousness*, Westport, CN: Bergin and Garvey.

[15] In all of her books, hooks invites cultural engagement.

me," bell hooks places emphasis on theory, which "helps you understand what is going on around and within you" (hooks 1994:50, 59).

Believing that social struggles must be rooted in theory, bell hooks writes, "Making theory is the challenge before us." For example, if we develop a feminist theory that addresses women's pain, she writes, "then we can make "mass-based feminist resistance struggle" (1994:65, 75). Although I agree that personal testimony contributes to theory formation, the development of feminist (or other) theories may have little to do with the development of social movements. Grassroots and global feminist struggles around the world often reflect social relations and social choices that U.S. university scholars have not begun to understand; even involved participants may not understand how their social action affects changes in the wider set of social relations. Many struggles are waged somewhat successfully even though participants started with specific reactions to concrete experiences, and not theoretical formulations.

Most activists are just beginning to understand social problems when they begin to do research and fight for change. Because considered engagement is a form of research, activists' understandings grow when they engage in the process of remaking the world. Engaging as a participatory change-maker is similar to studying human needs in the library and classroom: in both locations, successive steps need to be taken. One critical act for both groups is stepping over to "the other side": activists can push their knowledge forward with simultaneous reading and critical thought, and scholars can push their knowledge forward by engaging in social action as one form of research and knowledge acquisition. It is impossible to just act or to just study, and then to come away with the knowledge that will be necessary to resolve human conflict. Both ways of learning must take place at the same time, both ways must be valued equally by social change makers, and both scholarship and activism, like two intertwined roads with integrated pathways, must be carried out by all those interested in making a better world.

Learners from different social groups should be encouraged to talk about and transform their intimate relationships that are created by social hierarchy, as bell hooks suggests. Leading her students and readers through the needs identification and strategy development stages of the learning cycle, hooks compels learners to see that "it's all tied together"— patriarchy, racism, heterosexism, white female domination over black women, and capitalism—and that it is all part of a global system (hooks 1994:95, 53). As part of efforts to transform society, hooks argues, relationships need to develop in an integrated setting, where European-Americans accept they, too, need to deal with racism, and where all learners are involved in the collective task of breaking barriers (hooks 1994:63, 101-110).

By preparing students for learning in more informal, social change settings, bell hooks encourages educators/learners to recognize that classroom learning, dialogical learning, and social action reinforce each other and contribute to each other. Her theoretical and dialogical approach help students integrate these learning processes together. Often engaging in constructive, controversial discussions with scholars and public figures, hooks insists correctly that there is a necessity for multicultural communication and problem solving in classroom settings and in public dialogue (hooks and West: 1991). Hooks' educational work and writing helps to prepare feminists to engage in cross-cultural dialogue, which is an integral part of community development education in classrooms and in other community settings.

We learn from Horton, Freire and hooks that community development involves: democratic participation in identifying and solving problems; learner-centered change based on the connection of theory with everyday life; and the creation of social movements through multicultural interaction and multi-level social analysis of gender, ethnicity, class stratification in the community and the world.

When students are introduced to community development education in the united learning community, they should be encouraged to work in a context where many forms of social reconstruction take place, and where many innovative programs are developed to benefit people who have unmet social needs. As with previous waves of global integration and conflict, popular education has continued to spring from the grassroots level as everyday people have questioned the ongoing reproduction of major social problems. As some women and men have placed priority on family, community life, and cooperative relationships with others, popular education has provided an important way for people to understand and shape social life. Looking at the world in historical terms, sixteenth- to twenty-first century collectives and cooperatives organized redistribution and self-sufficiency networks, saving their communities and providing grassroots development models that inspire many in the global North and South today.

It is useful to study the complementary struggles of working people that develop in multiple locations, including the workplace, the state, the family, and ethnic and gender groups. Critical struggles also take place in civil society, the amorphous, "public" sphere that develops semi-outside of, but in relation to, the state and other dominant institutions of global society. Community development education initiatives and feminist projects are often carried out within civil societal realms. Civil society is often considered the social space of non-coercive human association, but we know that civil society can be despotic (for example, consider domestic violence, hate crimes, and white racism). Civil society's boundaries overlap into the "private" sphere of households, into the public sphere of the state, and—partly through state-regulated unions—into the public sphere of the for-profit business world. Household members participate in social networks (as members of informal support networks or as non-profit volunteers, for example) that form part of civil society. And non-profit organizations often involve community board members, at the same time that they receive governmental contracts and grants and do "state" work. Many local, statewide and national organizations are structured as non-profit groups, where social change partly takes place in what can be considered civil society. Community research that redefines civil society typically tries to increase people's local control by creating democratic and egalitarian alternatives to large-scale businesses and the state.

Massive global changes have been taking place in the last twenty years and students need to be prepared to understand the changing context of social change movements. The last twenty years of global history in both the global North and the South has been characterized by an intensification of working people's efforts to improve their quality of lives. As part of these civil societal and other efforts, inclusive community development education has emerged as a central learning and social change approach, partly because many activist learners have felt the need to implement long-term solutions.

During the 1960s and 1970s, social movements prepared students to think about changing work and public policy (as well as social consciousness), but today's movements often are directed at restructuring labor's reproductive relationships (Mitter 1997:171). These efforts, which partly take place in civil society, may be directed at "reclaiming the commons" or creating sustainable living conditions where considerations about economic growth do not override efforts to meet human need. Accordingly, Maria Rosa Dalla Costa writes: "women now represent the new outposts for interpretive insight, denunciation, and initiative, in a reversal of priority from production to reproduction" (Dalla Costa 1995:11). By extending the classroom outward, and by bringing the community in, we are asking our students to be ready to think about, and to even participate in, the creation of new social paradigms, new definitions of civil society, and new ways of remaking the world.

MY INVOLVEMENT WITH INCLUSIVE COMMUNITY DEVELOPMENT EDUCATION

If I had not participated in hands-on social change, my education and professional skills would have been weaker, and I would be giving less to my community and to others. And I would be lacking a method for increasing my effectiveness as a social change educator and learner. As a teenager, my interests in urban life and social inequality led me to urban sociology, and then to development in Third and First World countries, Women's Studies, world-system studies, and policy and program development for women. In college I was introduced to classroom learning that was linked to the community; as part of assigned class work, I worked for a rent control group and eventually saw a municipal rent control law passed (a law which was soon overturned). I read about colleges where students' service work was exchanged for tuition, and where students ran resident hall cooperatives.

My understanding of economics and change strategies broadened when I started studying in another country and getting professional-level work experiences. As a student, I volunteered for a Mexican self-sufficiency cooperative, which renovated and refinished furniture for resale on the informal market; from the window of our daycare's art center, I could see mothers working on furniture. I began connecting the value of this "volunteer" community work with the value created by women vendors in the urban marketplace, which was just being documented by Mexican feminists. I later received professional training in "social work" at a county welfare office, and at a state office that served mentally disabled adults whose fleeing family members had institutionalized them. In addition, I was a union member for three summers, when I worked on the assembly line at glass and make-up factories; some of my fellow assembly line workers were middle-years women who joined other women glass workers and went all the way to the U.S. Supreme Court to win equal pay for equal work (what if I thought I was "too good" to work in a factory, or "too good" to talk with these women?). Work provides a direct way to learn about society, and how to change it.

By the time I went to graduate school, I was already committed to "learning through doing," and, as a result, I supervised some sociology internships and taught for an experiential college. My Revson Fellowship in Women and Public Policy at SUNY-Albany's Center for Women in Government provided a hands-on transition from academic studies and policy analysis to program evaluation and then forward to non-profit, community-based work on employment, education, and job training for women, which led to more book-oriented research, research on downsizing and its impact on vocational students, teaching at public and non-profit universities, and community action research with diverse non-profit and non-governmental organizations.

I slowly began to appreciate the importance of extending the use of community development education, as I learned that local redevelopment through education can lead to the sharing of resources and increase people's social involvement at the same time. As a result of concrete research experiences over ten to fifteen years, I eventually started to question, at more than a subterranean level, some of the hard-and-fast rules about maintaining distance from what one is studying. Even for those critical academic thinkers around me, who argued that maintaining objectivity was a myth, there was a general distaste for mixing analysis with participation in social change projects. The "safe" position seemed to be that academic understanding comes from maintaining one's distance.

My work experience and training with Maine's Cooperative Extension Services demonstrated to me that learned-defined education could be used to develop effective diversity training programs, public policy education forums, elders' housing projects, community and economic development projects, and home-to-school and training-to-work transitions. In the past, I had almost instinctively turned to democratic discussions as a way to help women and other excluded groups. But the Extension Service reinforced my commitment to community education, at the same time it provided me with new skills for supporting community, regional and national groups.

My reliance on direct democracy and knowledge sharing became more grounded. I learned that democracy works, but not always in the ways one expects. When people examine society and make decisions together, they take unexpected twists and turns; these unforeseen pathways generally show that more people make better decisions than one or two people do. Democratic decision-making and program development by those who are most affected by problems is a far better community development approach than autocratic rule by government agencies, representative democracy run by the powerful, and "forced" consensus within the best-intended groups. Through my Extension work, I learned to do more than trust democracy-in-progress. I learned that "true democracy" can happen, and how to help it take place. This understanding eventually led me to write about how democratic and egalitarian movements around the world complement each other, releasing individuals and movements from the responsibility of having to create the "perfect" strategy (Dickinson and Schaeffer, 2001).

Teachers, researchers and educational institutions can start more of these complementary democratic projects, and help people think about and address some the world's trickiest challenges, like redistributing power, wealth and resources within and between regions, and coming up with development models that work for all groups. It is not enough to encourage and celebrate inclusive community development education, wherever it may be. Just hunkering down and attending to our own communities and regions will not stop the social processes that have created so many of our problems. It does not help to pretend that most of the world's people are not poor and that the rich do not live in gated enclaves protected by armed guards (Zwingle 2002:72-99).

It is essential for those with resources—educators, activists, government officials, business owners, foundation directors, whomever—to help turn around processes that lead to sustained, cumulative disadvantages in the workforce (Valian 1999), in schools and neighborhoods (Lipsitz 2002:61-84), in property rights than come from racism, and we can add from sexism and classism (Harris in Roediger, 2002:24), and in global society (South Centre 1993). Almost all of us are all relatively privileged in some way, at some point in our life (even if it comes in the form of middle-age authority), and almost everyone is disadvantaged in some way at some time (even if it comes in the form of disrespect we feel as youth or elders); and we can use these understandings to stand up *together* for those who are being hurt, and to use our research and resources wisely.

It is most important to deal with the cumulative and historical impact of colonialism. By dividing the world up into colonial enclaves, the powerful countries in the West and East ended up dividing our world generally into two groups: those who now have and feel entitled to material security, and those who have dealt with generation after generation of extreme poverty and material deprivation. Just imagine being members of a family, whose ancestors have been told for up to 500 years: "Well, be patient, wait a little more. Maybe, just maybe, the next generation will pull themselves out of poverty through schooling. Then, maybe they will be able to feed themselves and their children." Two broad social movements work from opposite ends to stop and reverse cumulative, work-based damages: the living wage movement—as carried out by global fair trade networks and by municipal living wage coalitions—and regional to global movements to promote worker ownership through cooperatives. In these practical ways, scholarly activists can apply community development education to the process of eliminating poverty.

In the next section, I examine peer-centered learning experiences that influenced my historical research, teaching and applied work. As a result of these experiences, I became engaged in facilitating public policy education, which is the practice of bringing all community members into a common dialogue about controversial public policy problems, such as ethnic conflict, gender issues in employment and safety, water access issues with rivers and coastlines, access to affordable and high-quality day care, and oil spill and other environmental clean-ups. Education is a democratic, lifelong process that involves everyone, pre-literate and literate, schooled and unschooled. Lifelong learning is the relating of knowledge from everyday life, which partly comes from community action, to the process of understanding and transforming the world in concrete and diverse ways.

This is, of course, part of theory building. The theory building process changed the way I related to myself and to others. I moved from seeing the world as I thought I knew it through other people's theories. I began to see and understand the world as I knew it, as learners around me knew it, and as other community members and as world-community members knew it. As I worked with diverse community-based groups in universities and in other settings, I saw that academic study, democratic education and sustained community development go hand in hand.

OAKLAND, CALIFORNIA: DISPLACED HOMEMAKER CENTER

Meeting social activists who really care about people has made a tremendous difference in my life. I like to show students how exciting it is to visit project sites, talk with project designers, and meet those who benefit from improved services. Traveling to social change projects shows me how others have carried out education on social change. Visiting other types of organizations gives me new ideas about how to convert various social change strategies to different contexts, especially to my local and global networking projects. As a teacher/learner, I want to share the joy of local and global discovery with students in my Women's Studies classes.

It is also useful to meet social movement leaders, who may talk about the personal side of movement history. After I completed some work on women and public policy advocacy, I found myself exploring San Francisco and visiting the office of the National Council on the Aging. There I meet Jo Ann Wilder, an outspoken advocate for elders and women who have faced interpersonal violence. When Jo Ann saw how much I was interested in women's economic issues, she told me that I had to meet Milo Smith, the co-founder of the first U.S. center for women who were re-entering school and the work force. Public policy makers then called re-entering women "displaced homemakers," a name that stuck with state legislators. Re-entering women now include young to older women who face barriers returning to school and work; those women who have relied on welfare to sustain their families are also considered "displaced homemakers" by lawmakers and policy implementers.

When Jo Ann Wilder introduced me to Milo Smith, co-founder of the displaced homemaker movement, my life really changed. Milo Smith became my mentor and friend, and I permanently became involved in the women's re-entry movement. My engagement led me to compile, organize and place the Displaced Homemakers' Archive at the University of California-Davis library, a fifteen-year project. Milo Smith, a fellow organizer of the archive, taught female and male feminists everything she knew about listening to women, supporting women as they conceived of social alternatives, developing long-term strategies for changing women's lives, and involving others in working with women. The women's job and school re-entry movement was a learner-centered one right from the start. And this allowed it to meet women's needs in creative ways.

Just twenty-five years ago, re-entering middle-years women were largely considered "too old to be trained" and "unproductive," as far as many employers, universities, and employment and training officials were concerned. Jobs for Older Women, which started in the East Bay, was one of the first grassroots organizations to begin helping divorced and single women who sometimes fell into poverty by the time they were 40. Milo Smith was a pioneering member of Jobs for Older Women, a group that was based on the premise that middle-years women understood their situation better than anyone else. Because they understood the multiple dimensions of their situation, the idea was that they should be the ones to design the solutions.[16] From this understanding, peer support groups emerged; this peer support group model was soon replicated when the group was reborn as Oakland's Displaced Homemaker Center. Some of the best people to help re-entering women, it turned out, were other re-entering women. These peer support groups helped women address internal barriers (e.g., lack of self-confidence, inability to set and reach goals) and external barriers (e.g., discrimination against middle-years women, lack of institutional supports).

Integrated into peer support groups were peer advisers, re-entry women who had successfully navigated their way to greater self-sufficiency. By serving as volunteer peer advisers, women gained new leadership skills and remained in a supportive environment, which enabled them to become better prepared to deal with a pressured, unequal society. They were able to give back to the organization that helped them, and to pass on the skills that they had acquired.

---

[16] Alice Walker notes the intellectual, spiritual and creative power of the "mules of the world" (to use a concept used by Jean Toomer and Zora Neale Hurston). "For these grandmothers and mothers of ours were not Saints, but Artists; driven to a numb and bleeding madness by the springs of creativity in them for which there was no release" (Walker 1994:517).

Women formed this grassroots organization and its peer adviser support system to enable them to become socially, psychologically, culturally, politically and economically self-sufficient. Many of the program elements that became incorporated into federal and state employment and training programs were developed in these peer support groups. The idea of comprehensive support services and one-stop service centers (which just became part of federal Department of Labor programs in 1996) emerged from the work carried out by Oakland's Displaced Homemaker Center. Community action agencies, youth programs, probation programs, and substance abuse programs have also turned to the peer-support model, which educators often call "peer learning circles."

The Displaced Homemaker Center became a one-stop, comprehensive service center, as much as it could, during the years it received funds from California's Economic Development Department. After that, Oakland's Center tried to pass service-provision activities to all organizations that served women, including: federal and state agencies, non-profit employment programs, industry-centered planning groups, adult education and GED centers, vocational programs, community colleges, and colleges and universities (like Mills College, the Oakland Center's first home). The idea was to help re-entering female employees and students by establishing special programs (at colleges, for example), and by creating comprehensive, learner-centered service programs.

In addition to challenges faced by other job seekers (including ethnic, class, and age discrimination), re-entering women who were headed toward wage-employment and school faced additional barriers related to gender exclusion. As women went through job training and placement programs, or met with re-entry advisers on college campuses, the upgrading of skills and remedial work often had to take place at the same time that gender-related barriers needed to be addressed. In other words, many barriers to workplace and school integration had to be confronted before women could become as independent as they could, given all the still-remaining levels of social inequality.

As California's women in transition acquired knowledge from their peers, staff assessed women's individual needs and engaged re-entering women in designing their action plans. Program staff then worked with individual re-entry women, peers, and local organizations to access the comprehensive support services, which were needed to help the re-entering woman meet individual and family needs. Because most re-entry women were responsible for taking care of dependents, it was essential that a woman's entire family needs were met. Comprehensive support services might include: housing, social service support (welfare), medical and dental care (including eyeglasses and hearing aids), individual or family counseling, drug counseling for a dependent teen, child care, transportation, job training, vocational or college education, goal identification, skills assessment, individual and family stabilization, and clothing for a job interview. The individual assessment process and the resulting comprehensive service plan addressed both external and internal barriers faced by re-entry women.

In addition to developing a broad social service and educational model, these peer support groups also identified ways that organizations needed to change if they were to meet the needs of re-entry women. Schools needed to accept middle-years students, job service offices needed to place middle-years workers, and veterans offices needed to recognize the needs of women who had served in the military. State legislatures and Congress needed to develop legislation that would recognize women's special needs that resulted from gender discrimination, and to establish educational and employment programs that were targeted to meet women's needs.

Although the displaced homemaker movement rested on peer support groups, its programs were generally directed at meeting individual women's needs. This, in fact, has been the case with almost all employment and training programs, as well as micro-enterprise initiatives; program designers, funding organizations, implementers, and participants imagine individual women becoming independent. If they do imagine changing the system and eradicating inequality for groups, as Milo Smith has, most programs are funded to create self-reliant individuals, not self-sufficient groups or communities. Ironically, one of the strengths of displaced homemaker programs—its emphasis on tailoring services to meet the needs of individual women and to address each and every barrier faced by individual women and their own families—has also turned out to be a quiet weakness. The best way to meet individual women's needs is to meet the comprehensive needs of families, communities, and social groups. This requires initiating democratically defined, economic development processes that lead to equality (not to cumulative disadvantages for most and cumulative advantages for a few). In summary, there is an urgent need to go beyond helping individuals and to start learning how to create social relations that will allow women and other groups denied full security, and their families and communities, to be self-sufficient. This means changing how we imagine and carry out economic development in communities, in regions, and around the world.

Even with its emphasis on individual women and their families, Oakland's Displaced Homemaker Center and its advocates set the stage for the development of statewide and national women's job and school re-entry movements. By demonstrating how to meet the full range of women's needs, the organization and the movement eventually transformed the ways that traditional employment and training programs and schools addressed the needs of women and men. It took more than twenty years for the federal government to set up one-stop career centers (where comprehensive support services are provided in one location); as documents in the Displaced Homemaker Archives show, these government-funded centers developed as a direct result of the displaced homemaker movement's peer-centered learning groups.[17]

And at the heart of the Center's invention of family support services was the learner-centered educational process, where women defined their individual and collective needs, and the solutions for their problems. One goal of the re-entry women's movement was to relocate service provision for re-entry women from the volunteer terrain of civil society to the state, including to its schools and universities and to its employment and training operations (Smith and Dickinson 1995).

At the same time that the Displaced Homemaker Center secured sunset legislation in California during the mid-seventies to establish a comprehensive program to meet re-entry women's needs, advocates from this women's re-entry organization traveled to other cities and helped other women establish similar centers. Re-entry women—many from Oakland's Displaced Homemaker Center—became public policy advocates in California, in Washington, D.C., and in state houses all over the United States. A major transition took place, reshaping a peer adviser and grassroots movement into a partially state-subsidized, institutionalized set of services. As a result of the women's job re-entry movement, peer-

---

[17] Displaced Homemaker Archives, Special Collections, University Library, University of California-Davis.

adviser centered support groups and comprehensive support services became hallmarks of the national model for serving women and other disadvantaged groups.

ORONO, MAINE: SENIOR COMMUNITY SERVICE PROJECT

The University of Maine's Senior Community Service Project, a statewide program that I managed in the mid-1980s, addressed the training, schooling and job re-entry needs of low-income elders over 55. Because older women tend to be impoverished more than men, over 80 percent of program participants were women. The National Council on the Aging, a national non-profit that administered about 60 similar projects for the U.S. Department of Labor, provided funding for this project, which was then run by the Cooperative Extension Service for the University of Maine. The Extension Service saw this re-entry project as consistent with its own democratic and educational mission of "educating people to help themselves."

Key goals of this service and employment project were: (1) to enable elders to become well-trained, economically self-sufficient community members; and (2) to encourage life-long learning through job training, civic participation and classroom work. Program participants were paid government-subsidized wages to receive on-job-training at non-profit organizations, where older women and men could update their job skills or develop new ones. Integral to the educational process was the idea that, in individual and group contexts, older women and men would be involved in assessing their own needs, defining their future goals, and helping to create social solutions for themselves and others. Learner-centered education for women was at the center of making social change happen.

Even though the Senior Community Service Project was constrained by bureaucratic procedures, regulatory constraints were minimized in this learner-centered educational context. The peer support group model was used, making use of "graduates" who had gone through Project training and who had been placed in job sites. These peer advisers were paid paraprofessionals whose skills had been updated at non-profit organizations. Through the peer support group model, women in Maine were introduced to Extension's group-learning process, which is intended to result in social change for the community. These peer support groups formed the heart of community development education in this project. As they worked with women throughout the state, paraprofessional peer advisers helped other low-income women assess their needs and identify ways to meet their needs. Like most other women's job and school re-entry projects, peer advisers helped to develop comprehensive support service plans to meet participants' self-defined needs.

In Maine, older women faced many of the same internal and external barriers that the re-entry women did. Women who came from lower-income ethnic and social groups included: Native Americans, African Americans, French-speaking or Acadian women, and impoverished white women (especially those from isolated, severely impoverished, rural communities). Women faced additional barriers, including some of the following: the lack of medical services in rural communities, the lack of public transportation, an inability to travel to work during the snowy months, the lack of public libraries in many small towns, and homes that were unheated or heated by wood stove (which was compounded by the discrimination directed against low-income women when their clothes carried the "woody smell" that came from wood-burning stoves).

The peer adviser group, who were elders over 55, confronted many dimensions of gender and age discrimination as they worked with other low-income, older people throughout the state. Part of their work was listening to what other women and men wanted for themselves and their families, and trying to help them meet their goals on their own terms. This was an empowerment model, one that enabled individuals develop; participants' work contributions, in turn, enhanced community development. Once again, employment and training success was measured by how well individual trainees did in a society that was still unequal and full of traps that led to impoverishment; advisory councils, federal agencies, and Congress did not consider how to create new jobs in communities, how to end group discrimination, and how to develop more sustainable work relationships that offered economic opportunities for families, communities, and regions.

What did we learn together as we tried to increase women's and men's income-earning and educational options? The inadequacy of job placement services became obvious as older workers found that they were playing musical chairs with other job seekers (who often were other elders, youth with or without high school diplomas, displaced homemakers, and other economically disadvantaged women and men). The idea behind this program was to provide low wages to older trainees as they worked at non-profits and upgraded their job skills, and then to help them make the transition to unsubsidized jobs.

Given Maine's particular labor-market configuration[18] and the compounded job discrimination faced by older women everywhere, it is no surprise that retrained and reeducated women with job placements typically did not earn living wages that covered family needs. Although some women did find administrative work in offices, older women continued to find themselves locked in minimum wage and temporary jobs, usually without health care or other benefits. This employment-focused social change model did not contribute to a healthy cycle of community development because there were few good jobs and only occasional job vacancies. In addition, elders and especially older women were very undervalued in the overall labor market.

In addition to developing a broad social service and educational model, these peer support groups also identified ways that organizations needed to change if they were to meet the needs of re-entry women. Schools needed to accept middle-years students, job service offices needed to place middle-years workers, and veterans offices needed to recognize the needs of women who had served in the military. And state legislatures and Congress needed to develop legislation and programs that would meet women's special needs that are related to gender and age discrimination. In other words, the establishment of social equality required hard, multifaceted, compensatory work that confronted and addressed how some groups have been held back by cumulative *dis*advantages, while others have continued to benefit from cumulative *ad*vantages.

As I helped women seek employment, I recognized that self-employment or micro-enterprise could expand the number of available income-earning options, as well as do away

---

[18] Maine's economic environment, where local production (including shoe manufacturing) was relocated to countries with low-cost labor, also helped to cultivate resistance to sweatshops. For example, in an effort to promote ethical purchasing campaigns, scholarly activists formed the Maine Clean Clothes Alliance in 2000. With over 60 businesses supporting the Maine Anti-Sweatshop Purchasing Law, the Maine legislature enacted and allocated a budget in 2001 for the first state law of its kind. This law requires businesses selling footwear, apparel and textiles to the Maine State government to sign an affidavit saying that the goods were not made in a sweatshop (Claeson 2002:239-241).

with the "fixed" musical chairs situation, where one worker moves out of a job and another moves in. And I started revisiting my earlier observations about the Mexican cooperative that sold remade furniture in the informal economy. And I reconsidered my later research on how partial sustainability was taken from 19th and early 20th century U.S. families and neighborhoods as they were weaned from remaining access to the global commons and reconnected to wage labor and market-driven consumption (Dickinson 1995).[19]

This historical and comparative analysis started to take my research in new directions, aligning my work more closely with the thinking of and actions taken by many of the world's feminists, anti-racists, anti-colonialists, and proponents of sustainability. I realized that it might be helpful if U.S. community members made democratic decisions about economic issues; if groups of displaced, marginalized and underemployed workers became involved in redesigning their work options; if we designed and implemented these alternative economic relationships in ways to help sustain communities; and if we worked to institutionalize this supplementary, sustainable economic layer so that working people and eventually their children would receive stable, good incomes. These insights got me started thinking about how I could help develop sustainable networks of interdependent micro-enterprises and cooperatives, especially for those workers who had been excluded from the traditional job market.

BERKELEY, CALIFORNIA: WESTERN INSTITUTE FOR SOCIAL RESEARCH

The Western Institute for Social Research (WISR) helped to ground and reshape my research and teaching (refer to WISR chapter). As I taught at the Western Institute on a part-time basis over a ten-year period, I discovered that all undergraduate and graduate teachers could benefit from sustained interaction with neighborhood people who think about and solve problems. In the early 1970s, student founders of the Western Institute for Social Research derived their original energy from an analysis of Freire's writings and from the application of his ideas about theory and praxis to social change education and research in the San Francisco Bay area. Today WISR remains one of the few higher education institutions where academic analysis is always related to real social problems and human challenges. It is the only school in the United States where students can earn a Ph.D. in Higher Education and Social Change, an educational process that requires an applied and theoretical understanding of group-defined needs identification, program development, program implementation and evaluation.

The Western Institute has many working adults as students, creating an engaged, creative, and applied learning experience for students and facilitators. All undergraduate and graduate students become involved in sustained, community action research that involves other community members. Individual students, who make their own decisions about their placements, usually work on community action research projects for at least a year. Learner-centered education at this school prepares students to help community members define and address their problems. By practicing learner-centered education in classroom learning

---

[19] A comprehensive collection of feminist writings on efforts to reclaim the global commons and civil society appears in the *Canadian Journal of Development Studies*, Volume XXII, 2001, Special Issue, "Gender, Feminism, and the Civil Commons," Guest Editors: Terisa E. Turner and Leigh S. Brownhill.

circles, students are gaining assessment and program implementation skills that they will use when they work with community members on community-action projects.

At the Western Institute, there are clear similarities between particular community-centered educational approaches (e.g., feminist education, multicultural education, and Africana, Native American, and Chicano participatory education). Some students apply this educational approach to community action projects that help to create new spaces in civil society for Native American healers, urban gardeners, young African American males, or citizens seeking more democracy in South Africa today. Other students research prisons or youth authority systems and come up with alternatives, or research and develop multicultural counseling practices. Gender analysis centers around the recognition that women and men are socially constructed in ways that have to do with much more than gender, including through racialized and class-based hierarchies.[20]

In seminars, multicultural analysis was understood as an integral part of a broadly defined participatory pedagogy. All students were encouraged to speak from their own knowledge base, and to explore how racism affected their individual research, their research with community groups, and the choices they made in their learning processes. Dialogical learning around the issues of racism, sexism, ethnic and national identity, class divides, ageism, and imperialism provided an important way for students to examine issues and to learn from each other in peer-centered learning groups. Learners in non-profits and in seminar discussions examined *how* and *where* social barriers were created; this research led to the invention and implementation of specific solutions that would undermine these barriers. I have taken this practical approach with me.

MANHATTAN, KANSAS: BRIDGING LEARNING COMMUNITIES THROUGH WOMEN'S STUDIES

As a Women's Studies teacher at Kansas State University, I have connected classroom and social-action learning experiences that prepare students to design innovative social change projects. If students are to be effective workers, scholars, and activists in the future, they need to be inventive social analysts and program developers who are prepared to work in democratic settings, where they work as group members. Since I arrived in Kansas, I have done feminist research on historical, global, and social change processes; which this examines the present and future in relation to ongoing trends and historical shifts. As I have engaged in archival, secondary, and community action research, I have applied my knowledge to curriculum development in Women's Studies and to local social change projects, both on and off campus. This Women's Studies scholarship has enabled me to go beyond well beyond supplementing world-system and feminist educational work with knowledge from community development methodologies to fully integrating inclusive community development education into a more comprehensive framework.

I have explored service learning literature and applications in a sustained way, eventually turning back to the strengths of feminist and anti-racist community development education as

---

[20] For writings that develop this theme in different ways, refer to the "Doing Theory" section of Gloria Anzaldua's 1990 collection, *Making Face, Making Soul, Haciendo Caras: Creative and Critical Perspectives by Women of Color*, San Francisco: Aunt Lute Books, especially pp. 335-402.

a means of doing any scholarly activism. Service learning typically places students in somewhat fixed community situations where observations are made (in much the same way that one reads a book in an analytical way). Service learning is typically cast as a way to help individual students become participants and leaders in established civic culture. Community development education, in contrast, focuses on learners' participation in educational learning groups and on social change made by these democratic groups.

Feminist and anti-racist community development education require learners to work as part of community groups that make decisions together. Students learn how to identify specific barriers faced by locked-out groups, and they learn to invent new program models, when existing ones are not meeting people's needs. Teaching related to inclusive community development education would probably place an emphasis on: critical thinking about society, understanding how problems are created historically, examining how various groups are marginalized from society's mainstream, considering various solutions and social-change avenues and seeing who they might benefit, and realizing that the most effective leadership comes from democratic, egalitarian groups that can work together over a long period of time.

Teachers of service learning, Women's and Ethnic Studies, and community research should be encouraged to draw on the knowledge of community development educators. This will help local, multicultural groups identify critical needs and design and carry out projects that will meet people's concrete needs. Multiple impacts can be obtained when women are included, and when their needs and ideas form part of the grounding for future development activities. For example, Women's Studies students often appreciate local, regional, and global efforts to recognize of the true value of all work, whether it was organized in large or small enterprises, in cooperatives, in family and informal market contexts, or through volunteer work. This emphasis on the equivalent value of work underlies cooperative, fair trade, bartering, and local currency practices today. When community developers value women's work and women's skills, in both paid and unpaid work contexts, they can accomplish much more than a project that accepts the market's limited valuation of human labor.

In the Kansas River Valley of the Great Plains, a loosely organized, fluctuating group of feminists and egalitarian souls (who are primarily women) have gone through various research stages that are involved in starting a women's self-sufficiency network. So far, at our land-grant university, we have: developed some university classes on inclusive, feminist change; held a mini-conference on "10 Sustainable Ways" to meet women's needs; held a discussion for women who choose to be single and self-sufficient; interviewed experts in the field of women's micro-enterprise in Kansas; conducted research on agricultural programs that can help small farm families and developed related publications; wrote two collaborative grants to start university classes on women's cooperatives and regional networks (still under development); "studied with" a rural woman who has used who has built a straw-bale house in Matfield Green, and who has started a ranching program for women; took students to Salina's sustainable Land Institute, a research and community development center that was a recipient of the worldwide "Right Livelihood Award"; took students to visit participants in the Glacial Hills women's micro-enterprise project in Holton, and to a private ranch in the Blue River Valley that practiced sustainable ranching; and helped to initiate the Developing Scholars for Kansas program, which places selected disadvantaged students in research positions, with the goal of increasing graduation rates for students of color.

On campus, feminist-and-egalitarian network participants also helped to start, and have provided leadership for, a major university project to prevent violence through education. As part of this effort, group members took the following actions: discussed economic violence against low-paid and unpaid workers as part of the University's Campaign for Nonviolence; wrote three grants to develop innovative ways to address violence against women on campus and in the nearby community (under development); showed films on non-violence and held discussions at the University and at the public library; related the lack of women's self-sufficiency and unequal education for women to pervasive sexual and domestic violence; increased Campaign for Non-Violence efforts to support students' peer learning circles and social-action groups; developed and carried out a 64-Day Season for Nonviolence, which—following the Los Angeles model—taught new ways to promote a peaceful culture on local, national and world levels; and worked with University Commission on the Status of Women, the University Campaign for Non-Violence, the Women's Center, Women's Studies, and University administrators (including our Provost) to arrange and hold a series of talks for students, staff, faculty and department heads on promoting gender equality on campus.[21]

Going beyond the realm of the university, some members of our feminist-inspired sustainability network have used popular education as a way to promote broader social change efforts. Group members have—on their own, in families, or with friends or other social-change makers—engaged in the following activities: organized a reading group on democratic economic practices; organized a fair trade buying club to connect small coffee, tea, and cocoa producers in the South with buyers in the North; organized two fair trade discussions in Manhattan, and invited a speaker from Equal Exchange; participated in the sale of fair trade Marketplace India clothes at the Lawrence food co-op, which connected women's cooperatives in India with U.S. consumers who wanted to support global living wage practices;[22] purchased a historical building to start a small business and cooperative incubator (the purchasing family recently sold this building due to the high cost of roof and building repairs); and participated in the bilingual 2002 meeting of the eighth Continental Bioregional Congress (which was organized by Lawrence's KAW Council and held on the Kansas prairie), involving bio-regional ecologists from Canada, the United States, Mexico, and Central America and resulting in the formation of a continental bioregional council and network to support sustainable development projects.[23]

---

[21] This has including bringing a number of speakers to campus who can reach out to men and women alike, including: Allan Johnson who talks about the real impact of patriarchy, Michael Kimmel who talks about men against sexism, and Virginia Valian, who has researched why women's progress has been impeded in the professions.

[22] Fair trade invites consumers to respect everyone who makes products and provides services, whether these goods and services are provided in our own region or by workers we will never meet. Purchasing one fair trade item—such as a jacket—invites consumers to examine from where all the various components of the jacket came; what the production relationships were like for the makers of the textile design, the cloth, the string, the dyes, the cotton, and the transporters of these goods; and how much these workers were paid (and whether it covered the costs of keeping a family in good health and of sending all the children to high school and college). Fair trade also invites consumers to educate others so that all goods will become fair trade goods, and so that all workers will be paid a living wage or will co-own businesses and receive a fair valuation of their collective work.

[23] At this meeting, I learned about many inspiring models of alternative development that start with regional redevelopment in a watershed or river valley. These models included: (1) Tepoztlan, Mexico's "la Montana: rancho permaculture," an educational and training project that prepares middle- and high-school students to support themselves and other community members by establishing sustainable agricultural cooperatives that have a strong base in affirmative cultural and community-health practices [project goal: to educate all regional public school students in the technical and inter-relational processes of initiating and enhancing integrated rural communities that are based on two types of related practices: planned,

The goals of our loosely organized, feminist working group have been to start new projects that establish peaceful and sustainable ways of living, and to urge others (who may have power and privilege) to start assuming responsibility for bringing about equal relationships between gender, sexuality, ethnic, and class groups on campus, in the Manhattan area, and in the state. Our group would like to include women in the process of starting a complementary network of cooperatives and fair trade consumers, which would strengthen and add to the regional economy, and perhaps even help support Third World communities. Because we are committed to minimizing the risk that small producers take when they develop their communities along alternative pathways, we have proceeded with caution. As a next step, we have considered showing films and holding public discussions on alternative economic arrangements in public locations that are accessible to people from various cultural and income groupings.

As a faculty member, I developed and began teaching a series of classes for Women's Studies that linked the global analysis of society and gender relations to community-based and social-change education. I also wrote about the connections among scholarship and activism, including writings on feminist community development education, "globalization" and changes in women's paid and unpaid work, changes in the relationships between women's work and social movements, and new approaches to theory construction and research methods.

Most feminist scholars have been concerned with showing how to expand a field or multidisciplinary endeavor by examining gender and other social divides. Women's Studies knowledge develops in relation to other sets of knowledge, and all disciplines and fields ultimately overlap. In my writings, I show how Women's Studies knowledge, when seen in relationship to other fields, changes the way that other academic research unfolds. Rather than just giving additional information about women and gender, Women's Studies provides new views of the world and human development.

I have been concerned with transforming disciplines and multidisciplinary programs, and with showing how Women's Studies and global ethnic studies is theoretically just as holistic as world-system and cultural studies knowledge. By tracing gendered relationships, I argue, it is possible to see related relationships and to eventually see the whole system; this allows peer learners to see how to change communities and global society. The same is true for other key contemporary theories. But none of these theories, I now argue, can lead to comprehensive understandings of society and change without the methodology of inclusive community development education.

My classes are designed as invitations to examine the world, our place in it, and the power that we all hold to change the world. My first teaching innovation at Kansas State

---

holistic, sustainable *agriculture* and egalitarian—stressing gender equality—democratic, collective, holistic, *community health*]: lamonranper@intertepoz.com; and (2) Mexico City's Social Ecological Collective, Tierra Viva, which involves young adults in urban, organic agricultural development; popular, political education about environmental problems in the metropolitan area; and the grassroots political empowerment of urban youth [project goal: to purchase a piece of urban land—with nearby access to the Metro subway system—where members of the Collective could establish an organic farm, permanent urban home, and a multi-media educational center (which would include a library): www.laneta.apc.org/tierraviva. To learn more about projects that have established new models for promoting regional sustainability throughout the North American continent (Mexico through Canada), contact a member of the Continental Bioregional Congress' network, such as the KAW Council, Lawrence, Kansas.

University grew out of student need. As one of my students read *Dreams of Trespass* by Fatima Mernissi, one student remarked that she had never been out of Kansas, and that she would love to travel (Mernissi, 1995).[24] This got other students talking about their limited experience inside and outside of Kansas, and their desire to see other parts of the United States and other countries, too. Some students had not been to Kansas City, and most had not been to a big city; most had not seen a subway or been on a plane. Over the next two years, students from two of my classes formed a peer-learning group to collectively plan and carry out a travel course to London and Paris, where we eventually studied how different feminist perspectives on ethnicity, gender, and history related to urban life in England and France.

This trip led to many ongoing learning experiences. A few students and I became very aware that wheelchair users were often excluded from class trips to overseas locations. We realized that this was a problem only after two wheelchair users started expressing interest in Women's Studies travel classes. In order to have a successful travel class for learners with differential abilities, it is necessary to plan the trip a year ahead of time; this enables planners to identify accessible transportation, hotels, restaurants, rest rooms, and travel sites.

I soon found myself designing and offering a series of fully accessible travel classes. A small service-learning grant enabled me to pay three students to develop an accessible travel class to Amsterdam. One teacher offered to have her publicity and journalism class develop advertising posters about feminist study in the Netherlands, and students selected the one we would use. More teachers and administrators seemed to appreciate what we were trying to do, and this helped. Eventually, two Women's Studies students who planned the course took the travel class as an independent study, learning more about designing accessible travel courses. University classes designed to include wheelchair users never ran due to unforeseen bureaucratic problems, low enrollments, advertising problems, and cost issues for working-class students who typically held part-time jobs. Student travel planners and I were not willing to settle for unsatisfactory options, such as having wheelchair users study overseas on their own. When we heard that non-credit classes do not have full accommodation requirements, we argued strongly for the expected and *planned* inclusion of all students in credit-granting classes.

We identified many widespread barriers to accessible travel. Student planners and I found that the only a few tour companies offer accessible overseas travel, but it is too expensive for most students; furthermore, these tours are not designed for students, who have particular educational needs and cultural interests. A big barrier is that the large student-travel company prefers to offer less-than-full accommodations for physically challenged students; this seems to be related to extra planning time, the possibility of additional costs (these companies have large, pre-arranged contracts with hotels, bus companies, restaurants, airlines), and the concern that other student travelers in the group will have diminished experiences, if they have to slow down and see fewer places, for example.

In general, teachers and administrators often fail to realize that accessible student travel in credit-granting classes represents a widespread educational equity issue in the United States, and probably in other countries, too; all schools can and should address this barrier right now, without legal pressure from the courts. It is important to do the right thing, even if the courts have not forced schools or companies to do it.

---

[24] Mernissi writes that travel "to faraway lands to observe foreign ways" allows one to "get closer to the strangeness" within oneself (15).

This year I have decided to explore travel options for inclusive classes by joining a social-change trip to Costa Rica, and by participating in a fair trade trip to Nicaragua. Obviously, teaching my first "Introduction to Women's Studies" class took me on this unexpected journey, and I am now engaged in this ongoing community action project.

I have developed and offered many classes that use feminist community development education as a means to engage students in scholarly activism. In the last few years, these classes have included: "Introduction to Women's Studies" (where students read about women in the global North and South, and do a multicultural community action placement that addresses inequality faced by women and girls); "Women and Global Social Change" (where students research nearby social change projects that build women's power in civil societal contexts); "Women's Studies Internship" and "Women's Studies Field Experience" (where students read social change books and work in community and university placements that address the inequality experienced by different groups of women); "Gender, Ethnicity, and Class" (where students analyze how these forms of inequality develop in relationship to each other in our society, and where students carry out their own educational outreach activity—last year's was a two-session Campus Conversation—); "Senior Seminar in Women's Studies" (where students can do book-oriented research or community-action research); and the graduate course in "Feminist Thought and Action" (where a multidisciplinary group of graduate students engage in learner-centered education that relates to scholarship and community applications).

Social change projects that use the pedagogical model of community development education take students and other learners through the entire process of making woman-inclusive, feminist, participatory social change.

Democratically initiated changes could establish inclusive development patterns that would be helpful in rural regions (like much of the Great Plains), as well as in inner-city neighborhoods and impoverished suburbs in large metropolitan areas. Models of social change might have relevance for different regions, and for different relationships between the global North and South.

If women and other economically and politically marginalized groups are to become more sufficient, it will be necessary to create new alternatives to the historically established, stratified labor market, where too many groups find themselves locked into low-paid, essentially segregated employment in the service sector. Developing relationships oriented more around use values and long-term public health, and de-emphasizing relationships oriented around profit making, may also enable more people to stay in small towns. Today small towns are disappearing partly because effective development processes have not been introduced to reverse the migration of young people to cities, to preserve the environment, to fund local public services, and to provide alternatives to absentee corporate takeovers, large-scale industrial agriculture, and "discount" corporate retailers who move to new, mid-size and large cities.

In summary, more than just "learning by doing," inclusive community development education involves "collective learning by doing together" in culturally diverse, democratic, and egalitarian redevelopment groups. It means assuming responsibility for improving society (even when learners had nothing to do with the creation of social problems). It also means taking a serious look at how learning groups today can begin to simultaneously address local problems and reverse the 500-year process of cumulatively providing advantages to a few and disadvantages to the world's majority.

Simply redeveloping local relationships (without looking at the overall global context in which we live) will tend to increase security for those who already have accumulated the most resources and wealth. Today it is also critical to: end environmental destruction and keep water a public resource (ending its privatization); introduce sustainable land, water, and life-preserving practices and nurse our global, biological system back to health; redistribute resources from North to South; provide technical and joint-planning assistance for those in different parts of the world; and establish mutual support systems (including cross-regional, educational-exchange visits) for those in rich and poor countries. Only by working together across world groupings will we begin to promote development that leads to long-term improvements in the quality of life for all. Positive development encourages the valuing, sharing and protection of common resources for the world community.

It is never possible to know, with absolute certainty, the best thing to do when one engages in participatory social-change research. But analytical work can help guide us as we make community-action choices. As we learn more by engaging with others as equals, we often see that many choices are helpful, partly because most democratic, egalitarian projects and social movement actions complement each other at some level. Of course, the best way to learn about the power of popular education and research is to start practicing inclusive community development education.

CONCLUSION: COMMUNITY DEVELOPMENT EDUCATION AND SOCIAL SCIENTIFIC RESEARCH

Knowledge gained from community development processes provides a critical supplement to other social scientific and historical research methodologies. Other research practices can help learners examine their experiences in relation to other social change projects, and in relation to changing social structures. Conducting slightly more distanced ethnographic and participant observation research on related social change efforts can provide insights into the scholar-activist's community action research (Buraway 1991; Weiss 1994). Gathering contemporary and historical archival data on related community-based efforts, state-run projects, and workplace and neighborhood changes can help place social change experiences in context, and lead to a more critical evaluation of them. Conducting preliminary surveys of major employers, service providers, and community leaders in a project's neighborhood can provide a clearer picture of structural constraints and opportunities. And conducting semi-open interviews and oral histories with some of the individuals surveyed can broaden social understandings, at the same time that learners acquire greater analytical depth. When educators, scholars, and activists look at the big picture, they should be able to imagine studying communities within a broad historical and comparative framework; this framework helps learners to understand the unintentional and intentional human elements that are involved in social transitions. Furthermore, educators can connect community problems and community-centered social change strategies with analyses of related global problems, global structures, and global social change strategies.

One way to connect the local and global is to do comparative research, where teachers and students have the opportunity to compare and contrast service learning in their communities with their study of social problems and social change models in other countries.

Participating in work camps in regions that are facing economic duress, and joining voluntary work teams in communities (where homes are renovated and built for low-income families, or where tutoring is provided to at-risk youth) provide other ways to understand social forces and how local people are responding to and reshaping them. Community solutions in one place may lead to community solutions in other parts of the world. And these innovations may help lay the groundwork for trusting, face-to-face, local to global relationships.

Even though the United States and most other countries are committed to democratic ideals and social equality, multi-leveled democratic participation and economic equality remain elusive in all countries. In structural terms, women and other disenfranchised groups have been excluded from social arenas where decisions are made about how society will develop and what the social priorities will be. Many of these key decisions have to do not so much with electoral process, but with decisions about how work is allocated and rewarded, and how groups of people are valued in relation to their work and in relation to where they live in the world. Social scientists, educators and social service workers need to examine some of these "unconscious" and largely unquestioned decisions about how we live and what we think about each other.

Peer learning groups can develop profound and personalized understandings of community and world-level relationships, and of social transformation. Scholarly activism promotes produces enriched research findings and leads to deeper democracy. Rather than making their living by observing how social movements address impoverishment and violence, educators can promote change by reconnecting learning centers. Educators can reunify the community by bringing the community into the classroom and the classroom into the community, opening up the possibility of new relationships within the world community. Our books and articles do not tell us all that much about how to change the world, and teachers and students cannot know how to do this until we broaden our understanding of what constitutes the classroom.

We all need each other, and given some of the similarities between our educational approaches, we may be closer in terms of our understandings than we think. As educators and learners, we need to reach out to each other in more conscious ways, and to think together about how we can research and transform the world around us. Engaging in the process of inclusive, democratic, community-to-world development is one of the most important contributions we can make. This is something that we learn every day from community educators throughout the world.

REFERENCES

Aguilar, Mario I. "The Disappeared and the Mesa de Dialogo in Chile 1999-2001: Searching for Those Who Never Grew Old." *Bulletin of Latin American Research*, Vol. 21:3, 413-424.

Anzaldua, Gloria. 1990. *Making Face, Making Soul: Haciendo Caras: Creative and Critical Perspectives by Feminists of Color*. San Francisco: Aunt Lute Press.

Arnold, Rick, Bev Burke, Carl James, D'Arcy Martin, Barb Thomas, eds. 1991. *Education for a Change*. Toronto: Between the Lines and Doris Marshall Institute for Education and Action.

Buraway, Michael. 1991. *Ethnography Unbound: Power and Resistance in the Metropolis*. Berkeley, CA: University of California Press.

Burton, Rainelle. 2001. *The Root Worker*. New York: Penguin Putnam.

Claeson, Bjorn Skorpen. 2002. "The Maine Ethical Purchasing Campaign." In Mike Prokosch and Laura Raymond, eds. *The Global Activist's Manual: Local Ways to Change the World*. New York: Thunder's Mouth Press.

Collins, Patricia Hill. 1994. "Defining Black Feminist Thought." In D. Soyini Madison, ed. *The Woman That I Am*. New York: St. Martin's Press, 578-600.

Dalla Costa, Mariarosa. 1995. "Introduction" to *Paying the Price: Women and the Politics of International Economic Strategy*. Eds. Mariarosa Dalla Costa and Giovanna F. Dalla Costa. London: Zed Books, 1-14.

Dickinson, Torry D. 2003. "The Feminist Face of World-Systemic Change." In Wilma Dunaway, Ed. *New Theoretical Directions for the 21st Century World-System*. Westport, CN: Greenwood Publications.

Dickinson, Torry D. and Robert K. Schaeffer. 2001. *Fast Forward: Work, Gender And Politics in a Changing World*. Lanham, MD: Rowman and Littlefield.

Dickinson, Torry D. 1999. "Reunifying Community and Transforming Society: Community Development Education and the University." In Dan Chekki, ed. *Research in Community Sociology*. Vol. 9, Stamford, CT: JAI Press, 41-63.

Dickinson, Torry D. 1995. CommonWealth: *Self-Sufficiency and Work in American Communities, 1830-1993*. Lanham, MD: University Press of America.

Dickinson, Torry and Milo Smith. 1995. "Are You Headed for Poverty? Middle-Years and Older Women and the Downward Spiral to Poverty." Unpublished paper.

Dlamini, S. Nombuso. 2002. "From the Other Side of the Desk: Notes on Teaching About Race When Racialised." *Race, Ethnicity and Education*, Vol. 5:1, 51-66.

Florence, Namulundah. 1998. *bell hooks' Engaged Pedagogy: A Transgressive Education for Critical Consciousness*. Westport, CN: Bergin and Garvey.

Freire, Paulo. 1998. *Pedagogy of Freedom: Ethics, Democracy and Civic Courage*. Lanham, MD: Rowman and Littlefield.

Freire, Paulo. 1985. *The Politics of Education: Culture, Power and Liberation*. Translated by Donaldo Macedo. New York: Bergin and Garvey.

Gilbert, Melissa Kesler. 2000. "Educated in Agency: Student Reflections on the Feminist Service-Learning Classroom." In Barbara J. Balliet and Kerrissa Heffernan, eds. *The Practice of Change: Concepts and Models for Service-Learning in Women's Studies*. Washington, D.C.: American Association For Higher Education, 117-138.

Gillespie, Diane and Leslie Ashbaugh, and JoAnn DeFiore. 2002. "White Women Teaching White Women about White Privilege, Race Cognizance and Social Action: Toward a Pedagogical Pragmatics." *Race, Ethnicity and Education*, Vol 5:1, 237-253.

Gordon, Deborah A. 1999. "U.S. Feminist Ethnography and the Denationalizing of "America": A Retrospective on Women Writing Culture." In Rae Bridgeman, Sally Cole, and Heather Howard-Bobiwash, eds. *Feminist Fields: Ethnographic Insights*. Peterborough, Ontario: Broadview Press.

hooks, bell. 1994. *Teaching to Transgress: Education as the Practice of Freedom*. New York: Routledge.

Horton, Myles. 1990. *The Long Haul: An Autobiography*. New York: Doubleday.

Hughes, Kate Prichard. 1996. "Education for Liberation? Two Australian Contexts." In *Gender in Popular Education: Methods for Empowerment*. Eds. Shirley Walters and Linzi Manicom, London: Zed Press. 102-117.

Kaplan, Temma. 1997. *Crazy for Democracy: Women in Grassroots Movements*. New York: Routledge.

Kirby, Sandra and Kate McKenna. 1989. *Experience Research Social Change: Methods from the Margins*. Toronto: Garamond Press.

Knab, Timothy K. 1993. *A War of Witches: A Journey of the Underworld of the Contemporary Aztecs*. San Francisco: Harper San Francisco.

Leonard, Ann. 1995. *Seeds 2: Supporting Women's Work Around the World*. New York: Feminist Press.

Leonardo, Zeus. 2002. "The Souls of White Folk: Critical Pedagogy, Whiteness Studies, and Globalization Discourse." *Race, Ethnicity, and Education*, Vol. 5:1, 29-50.

Lipsitz, George. "The Possessive Investment in Whiteness." In ed. Paula S. Rothenberg. *White Privilege: Essential Readings on the Other Side of Racism*. New York: Worth Publishers, 61-84.

Lorde, Audre. 1994. "Learning from the 60s." In ed. D. Soyini Madison, *The Woman That I Am*. New York: St. Martin's Press, 454-462.

Maher, Frances A. and Mary Kay Thompson Tetreault. 2001. *The Feminist Classroom: Dynamics of Gender, Race and Privilege*. Lanham, MD: Rowman and Littlefield.

Marx, Karl. 1972. *A Contribution to the Critique of Political Economy*. Ed. Maurice Dobbs. New York: International Publishers.

Mayberry, Maralee and Ellen Cronon Rose, eds. 1999. *Meeting the Challenge: Innovative Feminist Pedagogies in Action*. New York: Routledge.

Mernissi, Fatima. 1995. *Dreams of Trespass: Tales of a Harem Girlhood*. Reading, MA: Addison-Wesley Publishing.

Mitter, Swasti. 1997. "Women Working Worldwide." In *Materialist Feminism: A Reader in Class, Difference, and Women's Lives*. Eds. Rosemary Hennessy and Chrys Ingraham. New York: Routledge. 163-174.

Naples, Nancy. A. And Karen Bojar, eds. 2002. *Teaching Feminist Activism: Strategies from the Field*. New York: Routledge.

Naples, Nancy A. and Manisha Desai, eds. 2002. *Women's Activism and Globalization: Linking Local Struggles and Global Politics*. New York: Routledge.

Park, Peter, Mary Brydon-Miller, Budd Hall, Ted Jackson, eds. 1993. *Voices of Change: Participatory Research in the United States and Canada*. Westport, CN: Bergin and Garvey.

Pogrebin, Robin. 2002. "Poet is Viewed as a Calm Fit for Arts Post." *New York Times*, Oct. 28.

Rakoff, David. 2002. "Post-9/11 Modernism: Questions for Eric Fischl." *New York Times Magazine*, Oct. 27, 15.

Roediger, David R. 2002. *Colored White: Transcending the Racial Past*. Berkeley: University of California Press.

Sattler, Cheryl L. 1997. *Talking about a Revolution: The Politics and Practice Of Feminist Teaching*. Cresskill, N.J.: Hampton Press.

Schaeffer, Robert K. 2002. *Understanding Globalization: The Social Consequences of Political, Economic, and Environmental Change*, Second edition, Lanham, MD: Rowman and Littlefield.

Smith, Susan E. and Dennis G. Willms. 1997. *Nurtured by Knowledge: Learning to Do Participatory Action Research*. New York: Apex Press.

South Centre. 1993. *Facing the Challenge: Responses to the Report of the South Commission*. London: Zed Books.

Stuart, Rieky. 1996. "Understanding Difference Differently; A Canadian View." In *Gender and Education*. Eds. Shirley Walters and Linzi Manicom. London: Zed Books. 134-148.

Thomas-Slater, Barbara, Rachel Polestico, Andrea Lee Esser, Octavia Taylor, and Elvina Mutua, eds. 1995. *A Manual for Socio-Economic and Gender Analysis: Responding to the Development Challenge*. Worchester, MA.: Clark University, Institute for Development Anthropology.

Turner, Terisa E. and Leigh S. Brownhill, 2001. Special Issue: Gender, Feminism and the Civil Commons. *Canadian Journal of Development Studies*. Volume XXII.

"You Got to Move." 1985. Film produced by Lucy Phenix for the Cumberland Educational Cooperative, MacArthur Foundation.

Valian, Virginia. 1999. *Why So Slow? The Advancement of Women*. Cambridge, MA: MIT Press.

Walker, Alice. 1994. "In Search of Our Mother's Gardens." In ed. S. Soyini Madison, *The Woman That I Am*. New York: St. Martin's Press, 516-523.

Wallerstein, Immanuel, and Gulbenkian Commission. 1996. *Open the Social Sciences*. Stanford: Stanford University Press.

Wallerstein, Immanuel. 1996. *Historical Capitalism with Capitalist Civilization*. London: Verso.

Walters, Shirley. 1996. "Training Gender-Sensitive Adult Educators in South Africa." In *Gender and Popular Education*. Eds. Shirley Walters and Linzi Manicom. London: Zed Press. 23-39.

Walters, Shirley and Linzi Manicom. 1996. "Introduction." In *Gender and Popular Education*. Eds. Shirley Walters and Linzi Manicom. London: Zed Press. 1-22.

Weiss, Robert S. 1994. *Learning from Strangers: The Art of Qualitative Interview Studies*. New York: The Free Press.

Zwingle, Erla. 2002. "Megacities." *National Geographic*, Nov. Vol. 202:5, 72-99.

Part II: Creating New Educational Centers for Social Change

ACADEMIC ACTIVISTS: COMMUNITY STUDIES AT THE UNIVERSITY OF CALIFORNIA, SANTA CRUZ[*]

William H. Friedland and Michael Rotkin

ABSTRACT

Community Studies, created in 1969, is an innovative undergraduate major educating social change activists at the University of California, Santa Cruz (UCSC). This undergraduate program has flourished for over three decades, producing over 1,000 community activists, making contributions to community organizations around the world, and creating a model for engaged academic research at the undergraduate level now being emulated in other institutions of higher learning.

This paper describes the program's intellectual antecedents, the social context within which it was formed, how it was institutionalized within the University, curriculum development and evolution, the central role of experiential field study, senior projects and theses students have produced, and some of the experiences of alumni. The program is described in detail so that those interested in creating similar programs will understand the model and assess its appropriateness for their own academic contexts.

THEORY AND TRADITIONS

Community Studies (henceforth "CS") as a formal academic program and department was created in 1969. Its antecedents rest in the student rebellion, the civil rights movement, and the anti-Vietnam war movement of the 1960s, although its theoretical antecedents are even older. With the passage of almost four decades since the first major manifestation of student activism in Berkeley in 1964 (Lipset and Wolin 1965), there is often a tendency to forget the social turmoil of the period 1964-1972, when movement after movement appeared

---

[*] We are grateful for comments by our colleagues John Borrego and Deborah Woo, which have helped clarify some aspects of this paper. The authors are solely responsible for its contents and the paper is not a

on the American scene. From the student rebellion (Becker 1970; Bell and Kristol 1969; Horowitz and Friedland 1970; Wallerstein and Starr 1971 which most directly influenced the formation of CS, to movements for civil rights, antiwar movements against the Vietnam war, race and ethnicity-based movements of Blacks and Chicanos, the farmworker movement, the rise of feminism — all of which played a role in stimulating the effort that was embodied in CS, the program was conceived and stimulated with a powerful orientation toward social change.

Part of the background of its formation also rested in the ferment taking place in U.S. universities. While most universities maintained their well-established ways, new programs were beginning to be shaped exploring innovations to make their pedagogy more effective. In the founding document of Hampshire College, for example, its authors wrote:

> Hampshire College is the World... The academic program is intended to utilize field experience actively in connection with course work, to allow students time out either before or during college for extended leaves, and to use the "interim" midyear break for off-campus work and study projects (Patterson and Longworth 1966).

The first year of CS operations saw the culmination of the student rebellion in May 1970 with the killing of four students at Kent State University (Gordon 1990; Michener 1971; Bills 1982) and two students at Jackson State College in Mississippi (New York Times, May 15, 1970:1). The turmoil of this period had not been witnessed in the United States since the labor uprisings of the mid-1930s.

The CS idea was born in a period of considerable spontaneous activism best characterized by the slogan at the beginning of the rebellion in 1964-65: "Don't just stand there, do something!" This spontaneous slogan provided an explanation for what became much mindless activism. While not all American universities joined in the struggle, student movements erupted on campuses such as Berkeley, Madison (Wisconsin), Stanford, Cornell, Columbia, and elsewhere. Students searched for ways to make their activism effective, accelerating the growth of the Students for a Democratic Society (SDS), that, in turn, sought participation in local utilitarian actions. Among these was an approach that led to a focus on the complicity of universities in the war effort.[1] If nothing else came out of the student rebellion, the separation of profit-making institutes from ownership by universities was one concrete result of the student uprising.

As the rebellion expanded and grew, students and faculty members were energized and hundreds of experiments were initiated; some students sought a more immediate confrontation with the authority structures of the American university system since President Lyndon Johnson and Congress seemed too distant except for the largest demonstrations.

---

formal representation of the Department of Community Studies at the University of California, Santa Cruz.

[1] University complicity with the war effort took many forms ranging from facilitating interviews by CIA recruiters to faculty conducting research on chemical warfare and counter-insurgency. As the need for troops in Vietnam increased, student exemptions from the draft became subject to examinations, which were held on university campuses. This "conveniencing" of students by holding exams on campus brought home to many the links of universities to an increasingly unpopular war. At many universities, the long-established Reserve Officers Training Corps programs came under attack as students demanded their removal from campuses. As the war progressed, students attacked university research entities that had

Often, on many campuses, the traditional doctrine of *in loco parentis*, by which college faculties and administrations acted in place of parents in disciplining student behavior, came under challenge; within a few years, the doctrine was abandoned or significantly modified at many universities.

Almost as rapidly as students began their confrontation with campus administrators, students turned to the outside world. Upset by the abstract academicism of their professors and demanding relevance in their studies, many students turned to the "real world" by translating off-campus activity into field study, i.e., remaining enrolled but obtaining academic credit for the activity beyond the campus. Field study had been, in the social sciences, a well-established practice by anthropologists and sociologists but had been utilized almost exclusively at the graduate level. With the new activism, field study proliferated for undergraduates.

Field study, often referred to at the time as "internships," had a long-established history in many professional schools such as social welfare, business, and nursing. Such internships — periods in which students would confront "real" problems in the "real" world — were also found in a few liberal arts colleges such as Antioch and Oberlin, both of which were well known in academic circles but field study had not extended beyond small elite colleges. Liberal arts programs such as Antioch's had no explicit academic component; students were expected to learn from their off-campus field study but were never institutionally required to come to grips with their field experiences intellectually. The experience was purely internal to each student and the lessons gained were implicit rather than explicit. Nor was the Antioch model focused on social change.

There had also been earlier experiences with field study models but these exposed students to functioning institutions, preparing them for post-university employment. Business, architecture, and engineering schools had encouraged students to take internships to learn practical aspects of daily employment. Some apprenticeships had an explicit academic component, with students required to analyze their experience by writing papers or developing case studies; but just as frequently, experiences were individualized, each student being expected to somehow gain from the exposure to the "real world" without requiring academic reflection that could be examined and critiqued by faculty and community members to assess benefits to potential users of student findings.

During the 1930s, small numbers of students who became radicalized found outlets for political expression in socialist and communist youth groups. For such students the university became a distraction and they left the campus completely. Engaging in radical political activity (especially off-campus activity) while remaining within the university was still to be invented. This was to be a product of the 1960s.

As the 1960s activism became more widespread, field study with a social change focus emerged. In one sense, this innovation was well rooted in the university's Baconian tradition that the world had forms of order — that the systematic application of science and reason could transform what seemed like unformed chaos into order (Busch 2000). Baconian applications had characterized the natural sciences and, with some delay, the social sciences. Bringing together confrontations with the "real world" while seeking social change seemed a reasonable way for the university to operate. It was, of course, not this simple. While field

---

been established at Stanford, Cornell, and the University of California. The connections of U.S. universities to the government and the war, in other words, came under increased challenges.

study had been accepted in anthropology and sociology, it had been accepted only at the graduate level and was considered feasible only after long and intensive preparation.

Now, however, with students on hundreds of campuses seeking relevance off campus but wanting to maintain a relationship with the university, field study emerged as a viable solution. Many faculties had to struggle with its acceptance but field study metastasized nationally. Although it had traditions in John Dewey's educational pragmatism — his notion of learning by doing — 1960's university field study emerged more out of practical experimentation than a conscious search for intellectual antecedents. Similarly, although Paolo Freire in Brazil had developed a theory using everyday life activity for literacy instruction (Freire 1975), his work was discovered in the U.S. only after field study had spread.

What made the CS program unique or near unique were its features: First, the curriculum of the major was centered on the idea of a six-month full-time field study which, second, had to be accomplished within a social change context. Third, the field study had explicit academic objectives, including the production of a senior thesis reflecting the student's learning during the field period.

By the mid-1960s a plethora of field study experiments were getting under way. Some permitted students to go off campus either for credit or without; some offered students transcript notations so that they would have "something to show" for community work. Frequently, with no explicit academic demands (i.e., intellectually processing the field experience in some tangible way such as an analytic paper), some programs required an academic component. But experience was idiosyncratic; students might write papers and submit them to faculty members but with no extension beyond one-on-one interaction.[2] Other programs encouraged students to do field study by providing service to an organization. Again, there might or might not be an academic component; experiences were either individualized or took place in the context of service provision. With the exception of some social welfare schools, few programs had an explicit social change orientation.

What was missing were field study programs with an explicit social change orientation and institutionalized academic requirements. This was the program that developed at the University of California, Santa Cruz, taking the form of a distinct department (at that time called a "Board of Studies" at UCSC) with its own faculty and curriculum. Having our own faculty FTE (full-time equivalents) turned out to be crucial to the long-range survival of the program.

Community Studies had its most immediate origin in the Cornell Migrant Labor Program, a year-long course focused on understanding migrant agricultural labor in upstate New York.[3] The Cornell program involved recruiting undergraduates for a preparation for field study semester, largely following traditional sociology and anthropology field preparation; inserting students into migrant labor camps as agricultural workers for a summer of field activity; and

---

[2] This identifies an issue of concern to the Community Studies faculty at the beginning that has never been resolved satisfactorily: the problem *of accumulation* of individual efforts by students in some way. Once each student completed her or his field study and thesis, activity with respect to the community or organization in which the student had worked, in effect, died. Faculty struggled to develop a limited number of projects where a succession of students would provide continuity and student contributions would begin to accumulate. We were not successful in these endeavors and it has remained a source of frustration for faculty to the present.

[3] The authors of this paper were the developer and instructor of the program (Friedland) and a student participant (Rotkin).

conducting a post-field seminar in which the students wrote analytic papers. Students were "serviced" in the field by having their field notes taped and transcribed for them; these became the basis for the post-field analyses.[4]

During the 1967-8 academic year, Friedland was on sabbatical at Stanford and met faculty members from UC Santa Cruz, which had opened in 1965. UCSC students were among the earliest to move off campus into "real life" activities, but UCSC faculty were concerned about some of the exotic experiments such as raft-floating down the Mississippi (recapturing Huckleberry Finn) and redwood hugging. The worry was that the potential for experiential learning was being dissipated in uncontrolled experimentation. Friedland was invited to talk about the Cornell project, which engaged the interest of several UCSC faculty members.

Around the same time, the University of California Regents, disturbed by the urban insurrections of the 1960s, had funded an "Urban Crisis" initiative that called on campuses to create academic programs to respond to the crisis. This provided initiatory funding for new faculty recruitment and program development. Friedland was recruited to initiate CS in 1969.

While CS followed the Cornell model in establishing an integrated program of preparation, field study, analysis, its format was different. At Cornell, all students worked on migrant agricultural labor. At UCSC, students would determine their individual locus of field study. They would engage in preparation and analysis together but there would be no attempt (at least until later) to cluster students around a single area. An important aspect of the UCSC program was that each student would prepare a senior thesis out of the field experience.

One salient emphasis guided students in selecting field study sites: they were strongly encouraged to select field situations with a social change component, to find situations where change was an explicit aspect of the organization or community to which they went. For example, rather than placing students in standard schools, they were encouraged to experiment with new programs aimed at minorities or alternative educational projects. No explicit ideological commitments were made, so an occasional student would stray into CS with a conservative view of social change; such variations were acceptable to the faculty but there is little doubt that students overwhelmingly selected field locations geared at progressive social change.

In many respects, CS fitted very well with the land-grant origins of the University of California although, in the late 1960s, it was regarded as a "radical" experiment. Land-grant universities, originating in the Morrill Act of 1862, had evolved a tradition of providing instruction, research, and the extension of learning to constituent populations. CS followed this pattern, providing teaching and analysis, research (through the production of tangible products), and extension through the utilization of students by external constituencies. CS students would explicitly be oriented to working with constituencies that had traditionally been underserved by the University of California, i.e., minority communities and groups, poverty programs, social experiments.

One early issue had to be resolved: we quickly learned that turning largely inexperienced students loose to form new organizations was doubly perilous. First, students often had little idea of the complexities and difficulties of initiating new social forms. Very often their enthusiasm outran their capabilities. Secondly, when students formed a new organization, if it

---

[4]   A book, *Migrant: Agricultural Workers in America's Northeast*, was drawn from student field notes and writings (Friedland and Nelkin 1971).

was successful, students would be confronted by unsatisfactory options. Often such organizations depended for continuity on the originating student remaining with the organization, thereby subverting return to the university and completion of the degree. Accordingly, students were encouraged to find existing organizations and communities within which they could work. Existing organizations, already rooted in their communities, served to mediate between the students' idealism and the complexity and often conservative views of the communities being served.

INSTITUTIONALIZATION

The University of California, Santa Cruz (UCSC) opened in 1965 so that the campus began its fifth year with the initiation of CS as a major for undergraduates. One of three new University of California campuses – Irvine and San Diego being the other two – Santa Cruz immediately established a reputation for being explicitly oriented to undergraduate education and for academic innovation. Its founding philosophy, in the words of U.C. President Clark Kerr, was to "make the campus seem small as it grows larger" (UCSC Academic Plan 1965: 3) by emphasizing the importance of its colleges and de-emphasizing traditional departmentalism. From its opening, the campus became a magnet for the best, most innovative and experimental — and in some cases, kooky — high school graduates in California.[5]

Although the campus had been founded with the idea that faculty members would be fellows of a college, they were also attached to Boards of Study (departments). Faculty in the humanities and the social sciences were housed in the colleges; natural scientists were allocated offices in the colleges but also had laboratories in a central cluster of science buildings where most tended to spend much of their time. Although it seemed to come as a surprise, disciplinary attachments were starting an inevitable evolution in which departmentalism would become hegemonic. Still, in 1969, colleges were vibrant parts of the Santa Cruz experiment. Into this unfolding drama came CS, the first interdisciplinary department.

Departmental affiliation, however, was the prevailing organizational principle since, in their college roles, physicists hardly knew how to talk to sociologists, and vice versa. In contrast, CS was aggressively interdisciplinary, the first of the campus' interdisciplinary programs. A distinctive complication was added to faculty affiliation because of CS's interdisciplinary character. In other departments, faculty had two organizational affiliations,

---

[5] Indicative of the kinds of energies that students would bring to UCSC was a class created on the spur of the moment as the 1969 academic year opened. A community controversy had developed over the location of a proposed freeway that would come close to the downtown shopping district of Santa Cruz. The City Council favored the proposed freeway location which would eliminate approximately 400 housing units, mostly occupied by retired low-income seniors whose cause was taken up by a right-wing populist woman Council member. The California Transportation Commission was unable to effect a compromise between the Council and the seniors but left the hearing record open for 30 days for additional information. A Freeway study was organized by CS. Twenty-eight students were recruited to a hastily organized class, taught research and interview design, population sampling, interviewing and data processing. The students recruited additional students for various activities. One thousand face-to-face interviews were conducted with a random sample of the Santa Cruz population, data processed on a counter-sorter and analysed, a report written and delivered to CalTrans within 28 days. The results showed only a small minority of the citizenry supporting the City Council's position. CalTrans shelved the freeway project.

department and college. With no experience in interdisciplinary departments, CS policy required each faculty member to have a traditional disciplinary and college affiliation. This originated because the new department was staffed in part by faculty already in disciplinary departments (politics, sociology, etc.). Begun with the best of intentions, triple organizational affiliation rapidly became unviable, with CS faculty carrying the burden of operating in three demanding organizational environments as the campus shaped itself. Some departments were amenable to joint appointments of faculty with CS; others boggled at the idea and refused. With CS attempting to recruit sociologists, political scientists, historians, fiction writers with anthropological training, community organizers trained as architects, and historians, it became increasingly difficult to find departments willing to share an FTE with CS and, slowly, new faculty increasingly had a single departmental affiliation with CS only.

Highly motivated, UCSC students demanded entry into the decision-making processes of the university. CS students also wanted access to decision-making with the faculty. Initially students demanded equivalent representation with the faculty. After some debate, the faculty proposed that the students could have as many members as they wanted except equivalence. Once students decided to have one member more than the faculty, the issue dissolved. The faculty view was that it didn't matter how many members the students had; it was up to the faculty to convince the students if there was a disagreement. CS faculty accepted student participation in all aspects of running the program although, following university policy, only faculty could formally vote on personnel matters. In practice, decisions in the early years were usually based on consensus. Over the next decade, faculty and students began the institutionalization process, which was largely centered on the evolution of the curriculum, a topic discussed below.

Having initiated an academic program explicitly focused on involving students in social change activities, the faculty was acutely aware of the need to be sensitive to the administrative environment, including the Social Sciences Division, other departments on campus, the campus administration, the University as a whole, and the State of California. Not all of these external entities had to be accorded equal recognition and time, but we could not take their support for granted.

The UCSC faculty was composed of a small number of senior professors with well-established reputations and a much larger number of newly minted PhDs who, on the whole, had been classically trained in their respective disciplines but who had been recruited because of their interest in pedagogic innovation. Few, however, whether senior or junior, had any grasp as to what CS was or how its curriculum worked. Social science departments such as sociology and anthropology understood CS's mission but departments elsewhere were often puzzled by the idea of institutionalizing academic credit as part of a curriculum, especially since some considered the field experience simply as "trouble making." When some students, doing field study with the United Farm Workers union, found themselves on boycott picket lines in front of a California supermarket chain, its chief executive and a major provider of funds to one of the UCSC colleges protested to the UCSC chancellor. The chancellor defended the program on academic grounds: students chose their own field study sites and were expected to act responsibly within the organization with which they did their field study. The University's responsibility, through CS, was simply to ensure that the students were experiencing a university-level education. The chancellor diplomatically rejected the complaint.

This nevertheless served as a warning: the department could not afford to be solely wrapped up in its own work. To let other departments know about CS, it was essential that the CS faculty be active in campus affairs. This was not a problem for a campus still shaping itself, and our faculty actively sought involvement in standard campus committees involving budget, planning, personnel decisions, academic freedom, affirmative action, etc. Connections were made to other departments and CS became legitimated.

The early years through the 1970s were not easy, as cycles of boom and bust normal to California's economy visited cyclical financial crises on the University. When fiscal crises developed, established disciplinary departments looked hungrily at the CS faculty FTEs. Several such crises had deans thinking about the "consolidation" of CS into other departments (especially sociology) as a way of "streamlining."

Part of the vulnerability of CS arose from the effects of California's changing economy on the "market" of student choices of their major. In the early years, with the economy booming and with the pick of California's high school graduates, UCSC had the luxury of all kinds of experimentation. Students flocked into CS seeking outlets for their individual desire for relevance, anxious to pursue areas of interest they saw as their post-university future. As the economy tumbled into crisis in the later 1970s, students moved into a more conservative mood. Economics, for example, which languished for students during the activism period, now became a popular major. CS, in contrast, with students seeking employment in "trouble making" occupations after graduation, found the number of majors dropping. Deans of the social sciences inevitably reminded us that we were near the bottom of the social science division as far as student loading (the number of students majoring in CS and the ratio of students to faculty) was concerned. Over the years and through the financial cycles, the state of the economy has manifested itself in increases and decreases of students majoring in CS.

The relationship of universities to the larger society has been an issue since the first universities were formed in medieval Europe. Ranging from town-gown conflict over student behavior and norms to explicit concerns about preparing students for post-university employment and involvement, universities have responded to financial incentives, legislative interventions, and social pressures with a wide range of programs and activities. Beginning in the 1990s, some universities began to pay greater attention to explicit social missions by encouraging student activity in public service. Since public involvement by students is integral to the CS curriculum and the department continues to encourage field study in communities and organizations traditionally underserved by the university, in a period that also celebrates diversity, the department has emerged as a favorite with campus administrators.

While most of CS's public service activities became manifest in the field study through student placements, the consequences organizationally for many communities were profound. In the Santa Cruz area, CS students, through their field placements, were responsible for providing the basis for many community organizations such as Senior Legal Services, child care and after school programs, AIDS projects, domestic violence prevention groups, an immigration project, tutoring programs, drug and alcohol programs, neighborhood organizing projects, political advocacy and civil rights groups, to mention only a few.

EVOLUTION OF THE CURRICULUM

From the outset in 1969, the CS program had a basic curriculum for students to complete the major. Students took an initial Preparation for Field Study course, undertook a six-month (two academic quarters) internship, returned to campus to take an Analysis of Field Study course, and completed the program with a senior thesis or project.

The preparation course was intended to introduce students to field methodology as well as to raise ethical issues likely to be confronted. The primary methodology, still fundamental to the program, was participant-observation, a method in which students attempt to maintain critical perspective while committing themselves to their organization and immersing themselves in the group's daily work. The preparation course originally included an eight-hour-a-week "part-time" placement with a local community group which served both as a "laboratory" for experientially based assignments in understanding social organization, taking field notes, learning how to conduct interviews, and as an introduction to issues students would likely be confronting during their internships.

For the first decade, the preparation course was actually composed of two courses for credit, one for classroom work and one for part-time field study. The course was co-taught by two faculty to insure an interdisciplinary approach and encourage students to develop an approach to field study based on diverse perspectives from the faculty.

Because of student complaints that the two-course preparation requirement made it difficult to take a sufficient number of theory and elective courses, the preparation course was reduced to a single course and the part-time field study was reduced from eight to six hours a week. Later, because of limited faculty resources and the need to teach substantive courses, co-teaching of the preparation course was abandoned.

Initially, the only requirements for the full-time internship or field study (the terms have always been used interchangeably) were that students work with an existing community organization (not on their own), and that the organization not be located on a college campus. Full-time internships were initially mostly with organizations located in the communities close to campus, although from the beginning, one student went to Ireland to work with an intentional community serving people with mental health problems and another went to San Francisco to work with its Zen Center.

The analysis class following their return to campus was always intended to help students put their experience in the field into a wider theoretical and political context. When the program was small, the course was a combined analysis and thesis-writing course co-taught by two faculty. Later, the two courses were divided into a separate Analysis of Field Study course followed by a Thesis Writing course and the courses are no longer team-taught.

Over time, the curriculum has seen a number of changes. Most interestingly, students have consistently argued for and won faculty approval for required courses to provide more theory and background related to the kinds of fieldwork they undertake.

Fairly early, a requirement was added for a theory course taught by CS faculty. Initially, the course was offered as an introduction to social theory rooted in Marxist and neo-Marxist approaches and integrated with feminist and anti-racist concerns. While generally well received, outside reviewers of the program suggested that it had too limited a perspective. The department then experimented with a new course offering "conservative, liberal, and radical" theoretical approaches to social change. This approach was not well-received and a third approach was tried involving each of the faculty coming to the class to explain his or her approach to theory and practice, usually organized around a field study that the faculty member had conducted previously. Again, students complained that the course seemed "disjointed," "too busy," and that many of the lectures appeared unrelated to particular students' interests.

Finally, the department adopted its current approach to theoretical preparation. This involves a series of "theory and practice" seminars. Each faculty member offers a seminar related to his or her research area, teaching students relevant theory and examples of practical organizations and work. With the support of the program's field study coordinator, faculty are increasingly developing working lists of organizations they recommend to students as sites for full-time field studies. Students can either select from these lists or work with the field coordinator to develop placements related to the theory and practice seminar they have selected.

Theory and practice seminars offered by the program vary slightly from year to year and have included:

- Labor Movements and Immigration
- Health Activism
- Economic Justice
- Race, Gender, Work and Family
- Schooling, Inequality, and Social Change
- Resistance and Social Movements
- Sexual Politics
- Social Documentation
- Asian Americans and Social Change
- Youth Societies and Schooling
- Arts and Social Change
- Global Capitalism and Community Restructuring

This approach has been successful both with students and faculty. Faculty members feel that students who join the major are interested in their areas of work, and students feel their theoretical preparation is focused on areas where they will be doing field studies. Faculty attempt to be flexible and broad in how they define the topics of theory and practice seminars; however, the program only has a limited number of faculty and the foci of the seminars do not cover every conceivable student interest. Consequently, there have been students who might have majored who cannot find an appropriate theory and practice seminar and must choose other majors. Nonetheless, the theory and practice seminars are popular with students and the courses are responsible for the increase in the number of students enrolling in the major, now the fastest growing major at UCSC.

Although there was a negative impact, in increased faculty time, of having each faculty member teach a theory and practice seminar, the new format represented a welcome change. It had the consequence, however, of the faculty withdrawing from sponsoring field studies. The field study coordinator, also a lecturer in the program, now sponsors these seminars. Previously, faculty followed students through the entire curriculum; now they lose contact while on field study. This decrease in the direct supervision of field studies by faculty is creating some feeling of disconnect and alienation from the heart of the undergraduate program. Addressing this problem is currently the focus of faculty discussion.

In addition to the theory course, and to meet consistent student demand for better theoretical preparation, the program added a requirement for three upper-division elective courses which must be related to each individual student's field study. One of these electives must be taken in the CS Department, but the other two can be taken from any campus program. Students, for example, take courses in general social theory, such as a course in Marxism or urban economic issues; courses providing background on the geographical context for their organization, for example, courses on Latin American history or politics; social movements; or courses related to issues they will confront in field study, for example, courses in health care systems or adolescent development.

SPECIAL CURRICULA AND THE PROBLEM OF "ACCUMULATION"

The department continually sought to resolve the problem of "accumulation," i.e., overcoming the individual student's project "dying" when they left the field. Two experiments were notable, even if neither survived. The first was the "Second Curriculum," modeled after the Cornell Migrant Labor Program, which allowed a faculty member to plan a curriculum around a clearly defined research project. Students took group independent studies and courses with the faculty member with the expectation that senior theses would be part of the larger research endeavor. In practice, the faculty who undertook second curriculum projects found that they were unable to attract sufficient numbers of students to justify the faculty member being released from other teaching obligations.

A second more successful curricular innovation was the "Extended University" in which the curriculum was adapted to offer a BA program to community workers of a Model Cities Program in Fresno, California, and social service agency employees in San Jose. In place of the field studies of the on-campus students, Extended University students were given special preparation to make their employment locations into field study sites. New faculty were hired to teach in Fresno and San Jose and teaching exchanges were arranged to provide these students a reasonable range of course alternatives.

Ninety percent of those admitted to the Extended University successfully received Bachelor's degrees. The program was successful in getting older students, mostly people of color who had dropped out of college, to think critically about their community employment. Students were encouraged to focus on ways to empower their clients and involve community residents in the planning process for city redevelopment or as activists in structuring of social service delivery plans. Students loved the program and most learned how to navigate through the many contradictions of being simultaneously an employee and a social change activist.

Despite the success of the Extended University program, it was terminated after four years because California Governor Jerry Brown found it "inconsistent with the educational mission of the University of California to educate the *best students in the state*" [emphasis added], i.e. high school graduates in the top 12% of their class. The decision to close the Extended University may have been the result of a lost "turf battle" between the University and the State University system which had branches in Fresno and San Jose, but the real reason may never be known.

FIELD STUDY

The full-time six-month field study has always been the heart of the CS program. In exit surveys completed by graduating seniors and in an alumni survey conducted after fifteen years of the program's existence, students uniformly reported that full-time field study was what they liked most and was of lasting importance in shaping their lives.

With guidance from a faculty advisor (usually the faculty teaching the student's theory and practice seminar) and the program's field study coordinator, students select a field study based on their academic and social change interests. A major task is to direct students toward placements in which they can observe and participate in social change processes and distinguish them from other forms of social service. Although the CS program is a form of "service learning," it is distinguished from most service or experiential learning programs by its emphasis on social change. CS encourages students to locate their placements in organizations explicitly committed to social change or open to students exploring social change with or within their organizations. While many students select social service organizations whose central mission is to provide services to low-income or underserved ethnic populations, preparation and feedback students receive on their field notes push them to focus on social change opportunities.

"Social change" versus "social service" has been the subject of continual discussion and debate since the founding of the department. Faculty always recognized that service to the sponsoring organization or community was an integral part of the student's field study. At the same time, the faculty was committed to the perspective that no student should treat the field study simply as an opportunity to provide service. Students, we believe, should consciously be alert to issues, challenges, and opportunities for change aimed at making their sponsoring organization more democratic, participative, and reducing hierarchy and its privileges. Change orientations have to be introduced with great care since students are essentially "visitors" until they might become actual participants. The service-vs.-change tension is continuing and can only be resolved by each individual student during the field period.

This is, of course, not an even or uniformly successful process. Many students take positions in cutting-edge social change organizations and welcome the opportunity to become activists in the social change process. Others have views along a continuum that, at its other end, see any form of service as a form of social change — or as is sometimes stated: "If I just help one person solve one personal problem, I will have made a difference." Few students leave the program, however, without an appreciation for the distinction between the kinds of social services that reinforce existing social arrangements and activities which organize communities and/or empower their members to take more active control of the institutions affecting their lives.

CS students work for a variety of types of organizations including community-based, non-profits (or NGOs in the international context), governmental agencies, unions, political parties, alternative schools, and occasionally for-profit groups. Non-profit agencies include community health centers in inner cities or on Native American reservations, HIV/AIDS projects, drug and alcohol rehab programs serving adolescents, battered women's shelters and domestic violence education projects, family planning agencies, affirmative action advocacy groups, international development groups like Oxfam America, groups producing film and video documentaries, and community access television and radio stations.

Educational placements may include community schools, after-school programs for at-risk youth of color, schools in intentional communities, outdoor education programs for at-risk youth, or special programs for children, youth, or adults with a wide variety of disabilities. Work with youth has been a continuing area of interest, and we strive to direct students away from work as aides in traditional public school classrooms and toward placements involving the empowerment of youth in anti-racist, anti-sexist, and other movements addressing social inequality.

Governmental placements have included working in focused programs for elected officials or public administrators, regulatory agencies like the Environmental Protection Agency, environmental health departments, city and regional planning agencies, and legislative committees. Students have worked with alternative political parties or on citizen-generated electoral initiatives or referenda. Although few students work with for-profit groups, students occasionally find appropriate placements with them; one student worked with a for-profit group developing, selecting, and distributing media to schools on sex education, family planning, and HIV/AIDS.

In all placements, faculty and staff seek to ensure that students are not just doing repetitive, routine activities (mundane work that develops few skills) or serving as file clerks or receptionists. Every placement has its fair share of routine administrative work, but it is our responsibility to prepare the students for more challenging activity organizing community groups, mobilizing client action, or doing direct educational work with the broader community outside the agency. For example, in work with unions, we encourage students to look for placements involving organizing unorganized sectors of the workforce rather than just providing services to organized union members.

Students sometimes become responsible for starting new projects within their placement agencies after discovering unmet needs of clients or the broader community served by the agency. In some instances students have been responsible for creating new agencies or organizations. One, for example, used his field study as an opportunity to "field test" ideas about starting Barrios Unidos, an organization he currently directs and which has grown to 27 chapters in over fifteen states. Another student had major responsibility for creating a new Family Court system in San Jose, California, when she "discovered" the ineffectiveness of the regular court system in handing family law cases during her field study.

Field studies are currently divided more or less evenly among placements in Santa Cruz County, other places in California and the United States, and outside the United States. In the Santa Cruz area, our students provide significant contributions to local non-profits and it is not an exaggeration to say that, without their thousands of hours annually committed, the social service network would be in profound disarray. Many political changes that transformed Santa Cruz from a conservative Republican town to one of the most liberal in the country (with a string of socialist, gay, and feminist mayors, an extensive social service network, and progressive and environmental policies with local educational, business, and civic organizations) are a result of CS internships. One example is a field study in which a student organized a network of social service agencies and activist groups to redirect county financial resources from road projects, sheriff patrols, and public works boondoggles to childcare, senior, homeless, and other social service programs.

In other parts of the country, students have worked with housing projects in the Bronx; political organizations among Native Americans; unionization efforts in rural Mississippi; and socialist, gay, anti-racist, and feminist newspapers and radio and television programs.

Sometimes placements are with local grassroots organizations like a group of housewives fighting a toxic waste dump near their neighborhood; other students work to transform large corporate organizations and structures—for example, the student who got a placement writing health scripts with a feminist perspective for Dateline NBC and the one who infiltrated the Miss California (segment of the Miss America) contest to expose its sexist bias.

Outside the United States, our students tend to be concentrated in Mexico and Central America; however, students have worked on every continent: with street kids in Zimbabwe, Nicaragua, Mexico, El Salvador, and Italy; battered women's shelters and battered women's groups in Mexico, France, England, Argentina, and Chile; political parties in Quebec, Mexico, and Italy; women's cooperatives in Guatemala, China, Nicaragua, Brazil, and South Africa; midwives in South Africa, Ghana, Guatemala, and Mexico; family planning groups and health centers in every country in Central America and five countries in Africa; youth groups in fifteen countries; HIV/AIDS projects involving needle exchanges and education for sex workers in Thailand, New Zealand, Australia, Mexico, and France; arts groups working with youth throughout Latin America; unions in eighteen countries; peace groups on every continent; economic development projects in Africa and Latin America; peace groups in Palestine and Israel; gay, lesbian, and transgendered groups in Australia, France, Italy, and Mexico; and indigenous groups in a wide variety of Latin American and African nations.

While the critical skills and attitudes which CS students are encouraged to develop and carry with them to their field studies may sometimes be the source of tension between students and their organizational supervisors or other staff in the field study organizations, they are equally as often the basis for improvement in the field study organizations. Of course, teaching students how to make suggestions for change in a way that is respectful of their organizations and that they do not come across as arrogant or impatient is not easy. However, evaluations by supervisors often emphasize their appreciation for the "breath of fresh air" that students bring — fresh ideas, enthusiasm, and a deep belief that positive and meaningful change is possible.

Although a surprising number of students make significant contributions to the social change process while in field study, we understand the limits of what can be accomplished in a six-month period. We therefore emphasize the importance of students viewing the field study as a learning experience. The opportunity for critical reflection in notes students keep every day while in the field and the feedback on those notes are viewed as opportunities to refresh the students' critical approach. Students who write that "there is nothing new to write notes about" are pushed to think about the social change opportunities which present themselves in virtually all community work and to take a more proactive approach — at least in their field notes — to thinking about what might be done to more effectively deliver services or empower clients or communities. The degree to which they can realistically implement the strategies they develop in their notes, of course, varies with the placement, views of other staff, and a host of complex factors.

Although a few students return from field study with a cynical view of the possibilities for change, the overwhelming majority come back excited and energized. The analysis class places them with other students returned from internships and they quickly become aware that they are not alone in having encountered barriers to social change, limits to their ability to solve particular problems, or an inability to overcome the alienation and/or apparent apathy of the people they were trying to mobilize toward some particular goal.

Fortunately, it has been our experience that bringing students together encourages the constructive analysis of what they might have done differently to achieve more success in their social change goals. Both by reviewing the students' own self-assessment, and based upon faculty evaluations of the work following their return to campus, it appears that fulltime field study reinforces and strengthens rather than undermines students' commitments as change activists.

SENIOR THESES

A critical element in the institutionalization of CS rests upon the "tangible manifestation" of the individual student's learning, the senior thesis.

In the beginning and until the requirement was modified in 1990, all students were required to present a senior thesis for examination before being certified as having completed the major. As previously noted, the thesis could take a multiplicity of forms but it had to be tangible, transmittable, and examinable orally. Furthermore, for the first 15 years, the oral examination on the thesis included two CS faculty members and a person from the community or organization with which the student had done the field study.

Although it was not intended for these purposes, the senior thesis collection became a bulwark for the department when it was threatened during recurrent fiscal crises. When CS faced its first external review, we wanted reviewers to be exposed to our students and their products. Meeting with students gave the reviewers a sense of the enthusiasms students brought to CS. Reviewers were invited to pick half a dozen theses off the shelves and examine them overnight. Despite the occasional weak thesis that had been accepted, the overall quality was impressive and the collection proved to be a significant academic achievement on which review after review commented in the most favorable terms. One early external reviewer found the theses, "the equivalent of most master's theses in the social sciences."

The thesis collection continues to grow year by year; it now totals over 950. Approximately fifty percent of the students now choose to prepare a thesis. All senior theses (including those from other departments) are managed by the Special Collections library and are physically housed in Special Collections in McHenry Library or, for older ones, at the University's Northern Regional Library Facility. Theses do not circulate.[6] Because some theses deal with delicate topics, they cannot be photocopied except by the author's permission. Almost all theses are in English but the odd one can be found in another language where the student felt that language would make the thesis more accessible to the community where the student did fieldwork.

Student theses have included social science analyses of organizational activities; novels, collections of short stories, and poetry; handbooks for their organizations on how to access

---

[6] Senior theses are not catalogued in the University's Melvyl electronic catalog but can be accessed through the Internet. Begin at the Community Studies Web site (http://communitystudies.ucsc.edu), click on "General Information" and on the screen that opens, scroll to "Thesis Requirement Information" and click on "Thesis Data Base." This will open the Thesis Collection search screen (http://libweb.ucsc.edu/Search.html). Searches can be made by author, title, keywords, or year of thesis submission. The catalog does not contain abstracts of theses. Theses are available in the UCSC Special Collections of McHenry Library at UCSC.

services; guides to community resources for clients; and funding proposals for their field organizations. A sample of thesis titles include:

- The Role of Women in the California Agricultural Labor Force
- Training Manual for Lay Persons Handling Welfare Cases
- A Study of the Inadequate Enforcement Policies Concerning Farm Labor Codes in Santa Clara and
- San Benito Counties
- Palestinians Under Occupation
- Construction Dysfunction: The Role of the Capitalist State in Undermining Community Organization
- Otra Historia Interminable: La Historia de los Campesinos de Ixcamila y su Historia
- Virtual Organizing: Contingent Workers in the High Tech Industry
- Bar Raids and Bible Thumpers: Empowering Queer Young Adults in Dallas, Texas
- Getting the Bugs Out: A Critical History of Insect Control Technology, and Designer Genes: The Emergence of Genetic Engineering
- Liquefying Capital and Liquidating Labor: The Case of Firestone, Salinas, California

The collection draws two to three students each week throughout the academic year. Students preparing for fieldwork are encouraged by instructors to do a keyword search for theses relevant to their field interests; students preparing theses also use the collection as models for their own work.

In addition to the written theses archived with Special Collections, many theses are produced in alternative formats and stored with the Social Science Media Lab, including video documentaries on youth and drug prevention and the history of the abortion issue. One student produced an hour-long audio documentary on the international debt crisis and its impact on Latin American nations that was carried on many National Public Radio stations across the country. Another produced a slide show on the dangers and high costs associated with nuclear power. One student created a musical CD produced by kids at a Boys and Girls Club, along with a guide on how to start and fund an after-school music program for at-risk youth.

Several students each year also complete the senior requirement by teaching a student-directed seminar on issues confronted on their field studies. Some examples include:

- Filipino-American Identity and Community: Current Issues and Challenges
- Environmental Policy and the Sustainability Movement
- Zapata Vive: Chiapas in Struggle
- Critical Passage: Imploding Constructions of Teenage Sexuality
- The Idea and Practice of Cooperation
- Exploring Jewish Identity: Current Issues and Challenges
- Permaculture and Social Change
- Queer Public Health
- The Politics of Health Care in Guatemala
- Feminism and Activism

- Anti-Racist Organizing
- Grant Writing for Non-Profits
- The Web of Life, the Systems Approach to Health
- Women's Empowerment Through Reproductive Knowledge
- Sex Work, Youth Empowerment, American Poverty and Child Welfare
- Teen Pregnancy and Prevention.

Several students have written plays and others have presented theses as works of fiction or collections of short stories. The range of theses has been enormous.[7]

ALUMNI AND OUTCOMES

CS is currently the fastest growing undergraduate major at UCSC, having increased approximately 30% annually for the last four years. Beginning with an initial complement of twelve students, the program grew fairly quickly and stabilized as a major with about 50 to 60 students annually. Essentially a two-year program, this meant in practice that the program was sending out about 25-30 students a year on full-time field study and graduating roughly the same number each year during the 1970s and 1980s and into the middle of the 1990s.

Since the introduction of the theory and practice seminars five years ago, the program has grown to over 200 majors annually or a graduating class of about 100 students. The program has always had a low attrition rate, graduating over 95% of those who enter the major as juniors or sophomores.

Taken as a whole, there is every indication that CS has been successful in meeting its goal of preparing students to be active in social change activities after graduation and, it is to be hoped, for their lifetimes. Our graduates move into a wide variety of occupations. Perhaps the largest single employment category is directors and assistant directors of non-profit or governmental social service, affordable housing, or public health programs. The second largest occupational category is educators. Our alumni include large numbers of public and alternative school teachers at every level from pre-school to university. Many graduates have developed careers as school counselors, principals and other administrators, or special education teachers, while others work in social service programs serving at-risk youth.

A significant number of alumni work in the public sector as city managers, mayors of small and large cities, and middle-level managers or department heads in city, county, state, and federal government agencies. Over a dozen of our graduates work as union organizers and an equal number as community organizers for groups tackling a wide variety of social, economic, and political issues. Many graduates have positions as community or regional planners. Other alumni are self-employed as consultants in fields like environmental protection and planning, educational innovation, organizational development, and community arts development. Still others work as proposal writers.

---

[7] Since 1990, because of pressure of increasing enrollments and the stable size of the faculty, a new option, the *Synthesis*, has been offered as an alternative to the thesis. To fulfill this requirement, students submit a collection of already-written papers plus a new synthesis paper tying the papers together. Currently about one-third of the students utilize this option.

Dozens of other alumni work as medical doctors, physicians assistants, midwives, nurses, and public health educators, while others work as lawyers, most of whom are in public service sector positions as public defenders, labor lawyers, or as counsel for social service and social change organizations.

A growing number of recent graduates have found employment as reporters for print and broadcast media or managing alternative television and radio stations or alternative print media outlets. Several work as documentary filmmakers or on news production crews. Many alumni make a living as writers (fiction and non-fiction, including technical writing) and others have published novels, stories, poems, plays, or have directed or produced video documentaries.

Some of our alumni have made significant contributions in creating new organizations to respond to social needs. As mentioned earlier, Daniel "Nane" Alejandrez created Barrios Unidos, a national organization with 27 chapters around the country working to reduce barrio or ghetto warfare by providing positive alternatives to youth at risk for gang involvement. The organization now employs three of our graduates in its executive management team and others as directors or staff of local chapters. Another graduate, Christine Longaker, played a major role in the creation of Hospice, an organization providing services to terminally ill individuals and their families throughout the United States. Tony Newman, who graduated in 1998, created an advertising agency to promote peace and social justice issues. Margaret Cheap was the first director of the Santa Cruz Community Credit Union, which began with all its assets in a cigar box and currently has over $40 million in assets and is a major lender to workers' cooperatives, female- and minority-owned businesses, and affordable housing projects. She went on to help found the National Cooperative Bank in Washington, D.C. Another graduate, Ron Garcia, is the Mayor of San Jose, California, while two other graduates, Jane Weed and Christopher Krohn, have been Mayors of the City of Santa Cruz. Graduates too numerous to mention have served on advisory bodies to local, state, and national governments.

A systematic attempt to assess the program's effectiveness in meeting the goal of preparing graduates for lives as social activists was made through a mail survey in 1993, following a recommendation of an External Review Committee. We received responses from 197 of the 745 students who had graduated from the program over the first 23 years. Respondents were fairly randomly distributed across the 23 years. Those years with significantly more or less than the average level of response are randomly distributed over the life of the program with no observable concentrations in the early, middle, or recent years. Of course, respondents may be skewed in their responses to particular issues. Analysis based on cross-tabulations of two issues suggests that support for the program is not related to the length of time since graduation, while the value attributed to various components of the program (e.g., the part-time field study, elective classes, etc.) declines in direct proportion to the time since graduation. Overall, the results reflect positively on CS. They demonstrate that we have been successful in our primary goal of preparing social activists to integrate social change goals into their work and leisure lives.

Seventy-eight percent of the respondents are professional or technical workers with the remainder spread fairly evenly among the other occupational categories. Seventy-three percent were currently employed in jobs with self-described social relevance and 82% have jobs with either high or medium social relevance. Sixty-one percent of the respondents obtained a first job after graduation with high social relevance and 30% said that their field study led to their first employment after graduation.

Three-quarters of the graduates responding to the survey said they were more concerned with the creativity or social contribution involved in a job than having a high salary (5% prefer high wages and 15% rate them equally). Nevertheless, 95% of our graduates have employment histories demonstrating high or medium upward occupational mobility (61% with high vertical mobility). An examination of the jobs held by alumni since graduation is impressive, with large numbers working as agency directors of non-profit social service agencies or holding management positions in government, legal, and educational institutions. Many have received impressive honors of various kinds. Slightly over half of our graduates went on to post baccalaureate or professional degrees including M.A., Ph.D., J.D., M.D., M.S.W., Education Certificate, and others.

One set of questions on the survey asked alumni to rate their social concern at various periods since entering the CS major. In this self-assessment, those with very high and high social concern went from 66% at the time of entering the major to 87% after graduation. Most significantly, very high or high social concern only dropped to 83% at the current time. Those rating themselves with low or very low social concern went from 8% before entering the major to 5% at the current time. It appears that the CS experience not only raised the level of our students' social concern while they were in the program, but it also helped foster a lasting level of social concern after they left.

Alumni also rated themselves on their social involvement. Unsurprisingly they consistently rated their level of involvement lower than their level of concern. Only 46% rated themselves as having a very high or high social involvement before entering the major. Seventy-two percent rated themselves as having a very high or high level of social involvement after field study. At the time of the survey, 63% rated themselves as very high or highly involved. However, only 12% rated themselves as having low or very low levels of social involvement compared with 25% at the time they entered the major.

It is possible that alumni are simply displaying the high expectations they hold for themselves about social activism. When asked to combine their social concern and involvement and compare themselves with others, 82% of the alumni rated themselves as more socially or politically involved than their neighbors. Only 2% rate themselves as less concerned or involved.

Our own assessment of alumni social involvement in community, social, and political activities, as measured by the activities listed in their responses, support the alumni's views of their level of involvement as high compared to others in society. Seventy-three percent engage in some social involvement outside of work, and 61% demonstrate high or medium levels of such activity. It is possible that these numbers understate levels of involvement since alumni may not have listed all their non-work activities.

A comparison of past to current community involvement indicates that our alumni have been fairly consistent in their high levels of community engagement over time. Other responses revealed that 77% of the alumni feel positively about having chosen a non-traditional major as an undergraduate. Seventy-one percent have encouraged others to major in CS.

From anecdotal evidence based on alumni contacts in recent years, it seems clear that CS has been able to do an impressive job of creating and reinforcing a strong sense of social commitment among its graduates.

CONCLUSION

The CS program has existed as a unique and growing undergraduate program for over thirty years. The program has been through five highly successful external reviews and receives frequent public statements of support from the UCSC Chancellor and campus administrators. While, of course, many educators have succeeded in creating or reinforcing a strong sense of social commitment in their students, entire programs explicitly created to produce the kind of progressive outcomes realized by CS are rare, if they exist at all.

A critical element in supporting the program has come in every external review of the Department. Reviews have been uniformly positive in evaluating the program, assessing the faculty in its teaching and research, and being impressed with the caliber and quality of its students. Perhaps the best way to summarize the accomplishments of CS is to quote from the last two external reviews. The 1994 review committee, commenting on the academic quality of the Department, wrote: "...our assessment is very strong and definitive: the overall approach of CS is intellectually coherent, socially significant, pedagogically innovative, and organized and managed with painstaking care.... Santa Cruz should be extremely proud of what this unit has accomplished in refining a model that combines pedagogy and community service to the enormous benefit of each."

The 1999 External Review Committee came away from its campus visit "deeply impressed with the Department's high scholarly quality, pedagogic integrity and future prospects." Casting its report substantially on the increased interest in universities in experiential education, the Committee found a number of features that "stand out": the long-term fulltime field study requirement for all students majoring in CS, the "rigorous and integrated system of courses to prepare students," and the "distinctive orientation to placing students in field sites oriented to social change."

We would not want to suggest that every element of the CS model is the most appropriate for other programs. The program has gone through changes, many of which were prompted by demands or issues specific to the UCSC campus, funding priorities of the University of California, or other exigencies about which it is difficult to generalize. Taken as a whole, however, we believe that the program has done a remarkable job within existing constraints and provides a model on which to fashion future programs intending to educate social activists within the university.

There are **prospects for new programs** that build on our experience. Whereas the conditions under which the CS program was formed in 1969 and the present differ considerably, we are persuaded that possibilities exist currently for new programs modeled on our experiment. The birth and continued existence of CS was clearly advantaged by the radicalization of the 1960s and the arrival on the university scene of UC Santa Cruz, anxious to experiment. While such conditions were unique, the present situation may actually offer a context equally conducive to undertaking new programs.

First, there is a growing interest within higher education in experiential learning and "service-learning" where student interest in public service is linked explicitly to academic programs. Generally, there is an increased concern and commitment within public universities and colleges in providing public service to various constituencies, as more and more universities are "celebrating diversity," anxious to reach new constituencies previously not served or underserved by institutions of higher learning, including communities of color and low-income.

Secondly, growing intellectual movements in virtually every academic discipline, ranging from physics to the social sciences and the humanities, are challenging the model of the detached and objective scientist who was expected to approach the object of study only at a distance and avoid any pre-determined commitments to outcomes or sympathetic involvement in the needs of communities or their residents. Anti-positivist movements in the physical sciences have been paralleled by the rise of critical theory and deconstructionism in the social sciences and humanities. The new recognition by academic disciplines of the impact of point of view, the breakdown of the absolute distinction between theory and practice, and the acceptance of practical outcomes as important factors in the university's research mission are transforming the landscape on which new programs can try to plant themselves.

At its worst, it should be recognized that the transformation of the university mission to recognize a public service component and changes in the disciplines themselves to a new engagement with practical issues can lead to the prostitution of institutions of higher learning to the powerful and moneyed interests of the corporate world. At the same time, one result of these trends is a serious compromise, if not the destruction, of the "ivory tower" attitudes toward "objectivity" and insularity that formed the major bulwark against programs like CS in the early 1970s.

Currently, there is also a growing interest by foundations and other extramural providers of fund for service-learning experiments. Literally dozens of foundations as well various federal and state funding sources exist that will provide start-up funds for new programs that attempt to integrate public service into academic institutions. The key for academics with a commitment to social activism is to use these opportunities for new programs that are explicitly focused on service-learning with a social change emphasis of the kind embodied in the CS program.

In summarizing some of the key elements that led to the success of the CS program, we emphasize:

1   The importance of locating the program within the academic rather than the student service divisions of the university or college.

2   The need to establish the program as an explicit degree-granting department with regular FTE commitments for faculty rather than as a program based on soft-money which can become expendable during any and every economic crisis faced by the institution.

3   The need to gain acceptance for regular academic credit for the field study portion of the program as the first stage of program development so that faculty time and commitments are rewarded in the institutionally accepted coin of the realm.

4   The need for a structured curriculum with adequate preparation for students before field study and opportunities for structured analysis afterwards.

5   The need for a senior thesis, project, or other capstone requirement mandating that students summarize their learning experience in the program and provide tangible and transmittable evidence of their learning.

6   The need for a full-time field study coordinator to handle the logistical issues related to students' field studies upon which tenure-track faculty have little incentive to

focus (including both developing potential placements and dealing with logistical problems while the students are in the field.)

7   The need to develop a broad range of field study opportunities for students to provide them with cutting-edge social change and activist opportunities without allowing sectarian limitations on the kinds of groups with which the students work.

8   The need to have students work with existing organizations rooted in communities rather than working "on their own" or with organizations that students form themselves.

Since the year 2000, there are indications that several other universities and colleges are considering programs modeled on or borrowing from what we have accomplished. Colleges in Baltimore, Maryland, and Boston, Massachusetts, have sought our input in planning new CS programs. Given our success in achieving important political goals while maintaining academic legitimacy and developing strong institutional support within a public university, one would expect others to attempt similar experiments in the future. While some academic programs worry that they are "overproducing" graduates in their field, it is unlikely that the problem of too many social change activists is likely to constitute a serious issue for the foreseeable future.

REFERENCES

Becker, H. S. 1970. *Campus Power Struggles*. Chicago: Aldine.

Bell, D., and I. Kristol (eds.). 1969. *Confrontation: The Student Rebellion and the Universities*. New York. Basic Books.

Bills, S. L. 1982. *Kent State/May 4: Echoes of a Decade*. Kent, Ohio: Kent State University Press.

Busch, L. 2000. *The Eclipse of Morality: Science, State, and Market*. New York: Aldine.

Freire, P. 1975. *Conscientization*. Geneva: World Council of Churches.

Friedland, W. H., and D. Nelkin. 1971. *Migrant: Agricultural Workers in America's Northeast*. New York: Holt, Rinehart & Winston.

Gordon, W. A. 1990. *The Fourth of May: Killings and Coverups at Kent State*. Buffalo, New York: Prometheus Books.

Horowitz, I. L., and W. H. Friedland. 1971. *The Knowledge Factory: Student Power and Academic Politics in America*. Chicago: Aldine.

Lipset, S. M., and S. Wolin (eds.). 1965. *The Berkeley Student Revolt: Facts and Interpretations*. Garden City, N.Y.: Anchor.

Michener, J. A. 1971. *Kent State: What Happened and Why*. New York: Random House.

Patterson, F. K., and C. R. Longworth. 1966. *The Making of a College: Plans for a New Departure in Higher Education*. Cambridge: MIT Press.

University of California, Santa Cruz. 1965. *Academic Plan*. Santa Cruz: UCSC.

Wallerstein, I., and P. Starr (eds.). 1971. *The University Crisis Reader*. New York: Random House.

Chapter 3

Multicultural, Community-Based Knowledge-Building: Lessons from a Tiny Institution Where Students and Faculty Sometimes Find Magic in the Challenge and Support of Collaborative Inquiry

John A. Bilorusky and Cynthia Lawrence

Abstract

The two authors of this article, longtime colleagues at the Western Institute for Social Research (WISR), analyze and tell a story of community-based, knowledge- building at WISR in Berkeley, California. WISR was created in 1975 to provide a very small, socially progressive, and multicultural learning environment in which community-involved adults could construct individualized BA, MA and PhD programs in close collaboration with faculty. In this article, we look at WISR's history, keys to our success, how we measure our success, stories that illustrate some outcomes for our learners, and WISR's intangible qualities, including the subtle ways in which WISR faculty challenge and support our learners. Quite importantly, learners at WISR often come to appreciate that they, and indeed, most everyone, is involved in knowledge-building, to a greater or lesser degree.

Our efforts at WISR are considered in relation to the "bigger picture"—the teaching and learning of inquiry and scientific methods, other alternative programs and the conventional higher education establishment. As individuals, WISR learners find their own voices, build bridges to their desired career paths and pursue their hopes for bettering their communities. As inquiring colleagues of others, they further contribute to knowledge-building—in immediate endeavors in their local and professional communities, while directly and indirectly conveying to others what they are learning as well as how they are learning. Amidst the nuances of such collaborative inquiry, there is a special magic. That magic is the focus of this article and at the heart of why WISR continues to thrive in the face of seemingly impossible challenges to a tiny, alternative institution with severely limited financial resources.

INTRODUCTION

The Western Institute for Social Research (WISR), fondly known as "wiser" is located in a storefront with a door that opens on to the sidewalk of a busy street in a modest neighborhood on the Berkeley-Oakland border that is multiethnic and predominantly African American. People sometimes walk in off the street. As one of us came in one day to meet with students someone stopped and asked, "What do you do in there?" I was tempted to answer "MAGIC!" That's exactly what happens when learners come together for a self-directed, individualized program of learning.

WISR emerged from the dynamics of the 60s. It was included in the movement with universities without walls, free universities, ethnic studies, women's studies, student-initiated courses, and the like. WISR still exists, although many other institutions of alternative higher education from the 70s do not. WISR is still alternative. Since then, there have been alternative institutions devoted toward new age consciousness concerns, but not with the same community/multicultural/social change emphases. There are, seemingly many, programs aimed toward working adults that are very effective "money makers" for their institutions. There are also nontraditional programs aimed at some degree of flexibility and individualization, but rarely, if ever, in our view, with a similar emphasis on intellectual challenge and inquiry, along with community involvement, multiculturality, and social change concerns.

When WISR celebrated its 25th Anniversary a few years ago, we asked ourselves questions about, "what we do in here." And, why do we still exist, and continue to pursue our founding ideals, after the others have gone, or have changed drastically from the alternatives they once were, to the traditional places where adults go for degrees, licensure, advanced training, and sometimes, learning? So, what's the magic?

We certainly don't believe that WISR's ways are the only ways to promote community-based learning, but we believe we have developed some ways, with our other faculty and students, over the years that often work very well. The results are found in such recurring events as learners discovering that they know more, and can do more, than they realized they could. Learners come to express themselves in their own voice—in their talking, writing, thinking and acting—with an enthusiasm and insights that give new energy and directions to their ongoing efforts. And of course, these efforts almost always result in important contributions to the larger community, whether they are subtle and hidden from public view or dramatically noteworthy.

In this paper, we will explore this question of what's the magic in WISR's ways from several vantage points:

- The history of WISR as an institution and a distinctive learning community.
- Some keys to our success.
- How we measure our success.
- The intangible qualities underlying the learning relationships between WISR faculty and learners. These intangibles are, we believe, quite revealing and are characterized in part by the subtle combination of ways in which faculty at WISR challenge and support our learners.

- Some outcomes for our learners, including some stories that illustrate these outcomes.
- The "bigger picture"—the teaching and learning of inquiry and scientific methods, other alternative programs and the conventional higher education establishment.

HISTORY OF WISR AS AN INSTITUTION AND A DISTINCTIVE LEARNING COMMUNITY

WISR was founded in part as an attempt to improve on both conventional and alternative higher education as they had evolved into the 1970s. At that time, in the aftermath of the sixties, many educators and students were debating the merits of the university's role in the community and in social change, the "relevance" of the curriculum, and generally, the values served by higher education. WISR was founded partly as our modest but concerted response to some inadequacies in conventional education—for example, the absence of emphasis on personalized education, multiculturality, social change, and partly in response to the limitations of alternative programs of the 70s, which oftentimes were too preoccupied with simply "looking different" from the conventional.

Since then, many conventional institutions have adopted reforms which have incorporated in a partial way some of the agendas from the sixties (e.g., field studies programs, women's studies, ethnic studies), along with more recent reforms to marketing academic programs to appeal to the growing population of mature adults who have been interested in returning for further academic study and professional certification (e.g., to obtain degrees and licensing). This has resulted in a host of programs for "re-entry" adults, with flexible class schedules, credit for life experience, correspondence and study at home arrangements, and most recently, online study using the internet. Unfortunately, for a large proportion of these programs, the bottom line is to "bring money" into the educational institution (even in the case of non-profit institutions).

Most alternative institutions of higher education have failed to survive, but a few have continued. Some have changed their curricula, but have held to their initial sense of mission and purpose. Others have shifted most of their attention to institutional survival and growth. Some have ceased to offer degrees, but have continued to be involved with adult education. Larger, more established institutions have also absorbed some of these alternative institutions.

WISR was founded in 1975 to provide individualized BA, MA and PhD programs in Education and Social Change, Social Sciences, Psychology, and Human Services and Community Development for working adults concerned and involved with community improvement, social change and educational innovation. WISR was founded as a multicultural institution. We received initial approval for all of our degree programs from the State of California in April 1977, and we have continued to maintain and have that approval renewed, even as the State has "upgraded" approval standards to be more comparable to the academic expectations of regional accrediting agencies. Recently, we received four-year re-approval from the State Bureau for Private Postsecondary and Vocational Education through 2007. Because of WISR's personalized, student-centered approach, WISR is very small by design, and in recent years we have had our largest enrollments, ranging from 25 to 40 students, with plans to soon grow to 50 or 60 students, but probably never beyond 100 students. Past conversations with the Western Association of Schools and Colleges (the regional accrediting agency) suggest that they will not even consider evaluating us for candidacy status unless we are larger than 100 students. Consequently, our students are not eligible for Federal financial aid funds.

WISR's primary problem has been in developing a solid financial base. In the absence of Federal Financial Aid funds, and in the absence of private funding to WISR for student scholarships or loans, we have not been able to enroll many of the people in our target populations who would like to enroll at WISR. Most of these people are working in community agencies with modest salaries, with significant family responsibilities, often to both aging parents and children. Some are single parents.

One double bind we face is that to keep our commitment to personalized education, WISR needs to remain small (at least under 100 students), and to do so means we are disqualified from consideration for regional accreditation and from applying for Federal financial aid monies for our students.

In addition, WISR's faculty and Board has maintained few, if any, contacts with key people in the foundation world, nor do we have the funds to hire someone to develop and nurture such contacts. Oftentimes, foundations look at one of our proposals and say that we don't look like a university, but look more like a community agency. At other times, the foundation will tell us that they can't consider us because we are a degree-granting educational institution rather than a community agency. Another double bind.

In 1980, WISR obtained a three-year grant from FIPSE (the U.S. Department of Education's Fund for the Improvement of Postsecondary Education) to demonstrate how people in community agencies can use and teach others how to use practical research methods in their everyday work. That grant gave us our first big boost financially and led to our first major increase in enrollment from about 6 students to 20 students. Over the years, we have made decisions to primarily fund ourselves from student tuition. By limiting administrative and overhead costs we have kept student tuition very low (currently, $6,000/year which can be paid out at a monthly rate of $500/month). In fact, our tuition is only slightly higher than that of public universities in California. We have no scholarship funds, however, several years ago we experimented with offering about a dozen students a $100/month reduction in tuition.

Although we do not have foundation contacts, and do not have the funds to pay for a development officer, we did obtain a few grants and contracts following our FIPSE project to do other community projects in the mid-80's and early 90's. Several foundations and public agencies gave us grants and contracts to coordinate a community-based project to do AIDS education and outreach to highly at-risk populations in primarily African-American communities in the Oakland and Berkeley areas. We received small grants from local foundations and corporations to sponsor and operate a three-component project to involve Black elders in community development, self-help and community health education activities. We also received a large contract from the City of Los Angeles' Community Redevelopment Agency to do a very large study to assess needs and services available to elders living in the downtown Los Angeles area.

In 2000, 2001 and 2002, we received $55,000 from the Richard and Rhoda Goldman Fund to embark on the establishment of a Revolving Loan Fund for students in need. With the aid of these monies, we have been able to enroll two dozen learners who are dedicated to community service activities and whose incomes are insufficient for them to pay even the modest $6,000/year tuition. The students participating in this program have been paying most of the tuition out of their own pockets, with $200/month ($2,400/year) being deferred until after they graduate, when they will repay the tuition at a rate of $200/month plus 5% interest.

SOME KEYS TO WISR'S SUCCESS

So, why does WISR still exist? What are some of the conscious, and sometimes only partly conscious things we have done over the years that have resulted in WISR's continued existence and WISR's steadfast pursuit of our rather distinctive mission? Certainly, we have chosen to remain small, for better and for worse, rather than opt for an enrollment over 100 students. We could have charged more tuition and probably still attracted a number of more affluent students, and a large number of students who would have been mostly concerned with job advancement and not so much with social change, as well. We would have most likely been less multiethnic had we done so.

In recruiting students, we have tried to portray, quite vividly in our catalogue, and in our conversations with prospective students, the distinctive qualities of our students—diverse, yes, but strongly concerned with community service and most often, with social change, as well; inexperienced, in a few cases, but eager to learn and help others; very definitely, multiethnic and multicultural by intention and commitment.

A story comes to mind. About 8 years ago, a student with whom one of the authors was speaking suggested that if WISR wanted to get more students enrolled, we should change the cover of our catalogue. The student said that when she showed our catalogue to friends they got the impression, from the photographs on the cover that WISR is a Black school. In fact, WISR's cover has always shown faces of quite varied genders, skin tones and facial features. There was never any consideration given to changing the cover of the catalogue. It was a quiet choice to present the photos we do. They are photos of our students. It never occurred to us to do our catalogue another way.

Upon reflection, we are inclined to think that a few interesting "different" faces of color make the institution appear "diverse" and appealing to the masses. However, "too many" faces of color may still give the impression, even in the "enlightened" San Francisco Bay Area that WISR is a "colored school" and "not for me." Further, we have not encouraged students to enroll if they merely wanted a flexible or "easy" degree program. We continue to be pleased with the students whom we attract and enroll.

One of our current students has commented that the emphasis in our catalogue is on "social change" and the melding of the practical and the intellectual. He added, "For someone interested in social change, you can see yourself having fun in the program." He went on to say that in regards to multiculturalism, "WISR is an oasis of support where [by contrast] for many [in other institutions], the concept of multiculturalism has a lot of charge around it." One of our recent alumni told us that when he was looking for a Ph.D. program, WISR's catalogue stood out from all the others because so much space is devoted to the profiles of alumni and current learners. He could see that we are really serious about learners being the center of the institution.

WISR is to a large degree the learners (and alumni) and what they represent in their current endeavors. This has probably resulted in us continuing to attract the "kinds" of students we wish to attract—students concerned with furthering their own learning, and with social change and issues of empowerment, and with bringing imaginative and socially responsible practices into play in their chosen field and profession. Despite our small numbers, we attract a very diverse group of learners who vary in gender, age, class, sexual orientation, physical ability, nationality, and fields of special interest. The feedback we receive tells us that these enrolling students perceive that their experiences, values and concerns will be respected, appreciated, and even supported and promoted by others at WISR. The learners are the school!

We have also recruited faculty who understand and appreciate our educational and social values and philosophy. Like the learners, the WISR faculty are attracted to the institution because of the strong emphasis on social change, multiculturalism, and connecting inquiry to everyday community work. WISR's faculty members do have conventional academic skills and knowledge, but quite importantly, beyond these qualities, they have a desire and curiosity to be engaged in learning and inquiry with an impressive array of learners. Faculty are excited that students at WISR bring to the collaborative learning relationship with faculty varying experiences, talents, learning challenges, current involvements, and interests. Faculty want to nurture evocative dialogue with students, and they want to keep the learning process open-ended rather than mechanistic or abstractly formal. They are comfortable in working with students to see what will emerge, rather than feeling that the result of the learning endeavor needs to be predetermined or outlined in a clearly stated learning contract.

We have recruited Board members who also understand and are committed to our philosophy and educational approach. Some of these decisions to maintain institutional integrity and commitments have steered us away from decisions that might otherwise had been financially expedient and beneficial. For example, we have decided not to recruit Board members with paid contacts if they did not understand what we're about and if they were not committed to our core ideals, even though we probably could have enticed such people to serve. We have rejected proposals from others to enroll a large group of students en masse, if the proposal involved simply helping an entrepreneurial educator to facilitate a group of students' attainment of a degree, and in we return we would be paid well for this "you scratch my back and I'll scratch your back" arrangement.

HOW WE MEASURE OUR SUCCESS

The main ways we measure our success are by what our students learn, and in particular, how that is translated in what they are able to do during and following the learning at WISR. We get a lot of direct, informal verbal feedback from our students and alumni as to the contributions of WISR to their learning and to their community involvements. In addition, we intermittently conduct interviews of our alumni about the impact of WISR on their learning, and on their professional and other community work. Further, whenever, a student completes a project, they write at least two paragraphs of evaluative remarks about what they learned on that project and how it contributed to their job and other community efforts. At the end of their degree program, students write a several page evaluation of their experience at WISR. Here are a few remarks, typical of other end-of-program evaluations, made by two students:

- Of benefit was the warmth and patience of faculty, leading to trust and a sharing of concerns.
- The student received flexibility, support and challenge, direction.

- The student got excited about doing focused research more than in the past, because research is serving topics that interest her.
- Usually students share their papers and theses with some friends, colleagues, coworkers or students of theirs.
- The knowledge the student developed was used in her professional community, with clients, fellow professionals and professional trainees.
- Most projects increased her self-confidence in some area, e.g., in her teaching skills.
- Of benefit was faculty's non-judgmental approach and wide ranging knowledge; this enabled the student to explore unknown territory comfortably and opened up new avenues.
- A limitation is that the small size of WISR limits the number of fellow learners with similar "content" interests.

As one partial indication of the effectiveness of WISR's program, we can look at the work our students do after graduation—work that most students say was made possible to some degree (and often to a very large degree) by their studies at WISR. Keeping in mind that what our students do is much more than what their titles or job descriptions are, it is still useful to consider the positions of our alumni, which do suggest the kinds of skills, involvements, commitments and accomplishments of our alumni, as well as the kinds of individuals who choose to become involved in learning at WISR. Here are a few examples:

- Dr. Oba T'Shaka is a tenured Professor, and former Chair, of the Black Studies Department at San Francisco State University.
- Dr. Anngwyn St. Just became an internationally involved educator, author and therapist, concerned about the psychology of recovery from trauma, including the effects of global trauma. She founded the Colorado Center for Social Trauma.
- Dennis Hastings was Tribal Historian for the Omaha tribe in Nebraska, and is currently seeking to establish a reservation-based museum as part of his many efforts to restore and preserve the culture of the Omaha. His Master's thesis was the book he coauthored with anthropologist, Robin Riddington, about the Sacred Pole of the Omaha tribe and the tribe's efforts with Dennis' leadership to successfully obtain the return of the Sacred Pole from Harvard University's Peabody Museum (*Blessings for a Long Time: The Sacred Pole of the Omaha*, University of Nebraska Press).
- Dr. William Duma was an exiled Black South African journalist who was named Contra Costa Community College District Teacher of the Year in 1994, and has now returned to assist in the development of South Africa under the new government.
- Eli Rosenblatt coordinates the Prison Activist Resource Center in Berkeley. His senior thesis was a handbook of readings for educators and activists on the crisis in prisons. It has since been published by South End Press under the title, *Criminal Injustice: Confronting the Prison Crisis*.
- Ronald Mah is a licensed Marriage and Family Therapist, and consultant to numerous community-based organizations and parent groups, and serves on the Board of the California Kindergarten Association.
- Sunaree Medrala is the principal of a business college in her native country of Thailand.

- Dr. Richard Allen is a retired school teacher who served until recently as educational mentor for the Oakland Library's Second Start Literacy Program. His Ph.D. program also centered on his efforts to create a grassroots, community-based adult learning center in a low-income neighborhood on the fringe of downtown Oakland.
- The late, Dr. James Todd, II joined the faculty of the Black Studies Department at San Francisco State while working on his Ph.D. at WISR, and he then became head of the Step to College program there. He then assumed the position of Chair for the Business and Hospitality Department at Morris Brown College in Atlanta.
- Susan Wayne is Manager of the Toronto Centre for Career Education.
- Dr. Marita Davila received her Ph.D. at WISR in 1980. In 1982-83, she was granted a postdoctoral fellowship in the administration of higher education from the American Council on Education. Her postdoctoral studies built on her Ph.D. studies which included an examination of causes and prevention of dropouts in California community colleges among Spanish-speaking students. Her dissertation was an in-depth study of The Black Presence in Spanish America, and this work has been used as a resource at Stanford University and several other Bay Area colleges.
- Nadine Shaw-Landasvatter is the mother of two biracial boys and the founder of a support network for parents of biracial/multiracial children. Her senior thesis centered on the research and initiatives necessary to her successful efforts to incorporate this support network as a nonprofit organization. She is continuing on toward her M.A. in Psychology at WISR, in order to attain the State's Marriage and Family Therapy license, and augment the scope of her work with multicultural/multiethnic families.

THE INTANGIBLE QUALITIES UNDERLYING LEARNING RELATIONSHIPS AT WISR

The real "magic" that is WISR is even more intangible than the images that can be grasped from WISR's institutional history, from our institutional problems and "successes," and from the community activities of our students and alumni. In trying to articulate these intangibles, we have decided that, in part, there is something special in the ways that faculty at WISR combine challenge and support in their work with learners. Indeed, the idea that students and faculty, alike, are first and foremost learners is a basic tenant of WISR's philosophy. It is the interests of students as learners and the learning needs dictated by their community involvements that become the focus of student-faculty inquiry. Faculty members at WISR take on different roles—the mentor, the partner in inquiry, the facilitator and coach. Further, in our collaborative inquiries with learners, we are eager to become engaged in their interests and strive to assist them to center their action-research activities and knowledge-building around their interests and learning needs.

It might be magic, but it is definitely not easy. Learners, for whom WISR is the place to study, work very hard to realize their dreams. These learners are not just seeking a degree, although degrees are appropriate goals. They are challenged by their commitment to correct social wrongs and bring about needed changes in their communities-of-reference. The objectives and interests brought by learners vary, as would be expected given the diversity of our student population. As faculty, our intention is to meet learners where we find them—to support their research, to guide their process with suggested readings and questions we put forth as "food for thought," and to use our knowledge to guide the development of theirs.

WISR is an individualized program. As we write that, it is easy to conjure up visions of people sitting in cubbyholes with programmed worksheets, where they work alone, and "correct" their own work against answer sheets provided by whatever publisher has used their own perspective, their values, and their social and political views to provide. That is NOT WISR! Nor is WISR set up to award credit to students for previous life experience or current work-related activities. In contrast, we tell prospective students that if they enroll, they should expect to be actively engaged with their own learning, and actively engaged with faculty in their inquiries.

By individualized, we mean that learners choose and direct their own program. Although the program is self-paced, self-assigned and self-regulated, we, as faculty, take a major role by maintaining close contact with the learner to work with them in assessing their progress and process. Students meet often with one or several of the faculty, one-on-one, and the meeting is almost always a cooperative and collaborative learning experience. It makes us smile to note that when one of our learner's forgets to put their name on their paper, we easily recognize whose paper it is by the content and style. We are so intimately involved in student learning that we know many of the nuances of each learner's thinking, and indeed, it is interesting that students are so sure that we will know that they wrote a particular paper, that our students often "forget" (don't bother?) to put their names on the papers they hand in.

Because learners are given the opportunity, indeed encouraged, to think about what they want to learn and accomplish, they often arrive at more clarity about their ideas and the directions in which they are headed. At the same time, we as faculty actively and enthusiastically share thoughts that spring from our interests, curiosities and commitments, but as they might pertain to the interests of the particular learner with whom we are meeting.

There are some overall themes that characterize the subtle, emerging combination of challenge and support that we give to our students. These themes are not facile techniques, nor cut-and-dried formulas that we "implement" on a day-to-day basis, rather they are some of the things that we have become aware of as recurring patterns in they ways we try to work with our students, and qualities underlying the learning relationships with them. This list of themes is not an exhaustive one. The themes could have been listed in any sequence, or categorized in any of a number of different ways. This list should be read in the way that one would study a mosaic, or perhaps a kaleidoscope of patterns. Looked at in different ways, each part provides us with an additional perspective on the other parts and on the total "picture." In thinking about the items on this list, the reader may want to keep in mind such notions as exploration, reflection, creativity, engagement, inquisitiveness, social justice, collaboration, open-ended exploration, and emergence. What other qualities come to mind as you read this?

- We encourage learners to do projects they've been wanting to get around to, but haven't—for example, developing a needed, new program or writing a critically reflective autobiography on their community/work/life experience, as these experiences relate to the bigger picture.
- We encourage learners to not just study topics they want to, but also to realize that implicit in their insights are emerging theories to be communicated to others.

- We invite learners not only to write about what they're interested in, but also to write in their voice, to use the first person, to wonder and ask questions out loud on paper.

- We see learning projects as open-ended, not as "products-to-be-graded." We tell students that they may often end a paper by coming up with new questions more than definitive conclusions.

- We urge learners not to formulate thesis and project topics by what "sounds good" (e.g., not to focus on coming up with a "good" hypothesis to test, where the answer is really known in advance and can then be verified). We urge learners to search for the questions that are important to them, and to others, for the things that they are sincerely and deeply curious to learn more about.

- We try to identify with the learner and his or her concerns, and elicit from her/him some insights, questions and ideas that's interesting to them. And, we also challenge them, by asking them to read and think about how their concerns relate to the bigger social picture, what they see to be the pros and cons of theories of social change put forth by others, as they think about how those theories could be applied to their concerns.

- We even tend to encourage the reading of certain books and articles we have come to find useful for learners over the years—Paulo Freire, bell hooks, T.S. Kuhn, and action-research handouts written by WISR faculty among others. Also, we are continually learning from our learners of useful books and articles that we can suggest to other learners to read. The material is more than simply male, Euro-centric material.

- We are characterized by the diverse "politics" of the faculty, the learners, and the institution. As a group, a significant majority of us could be characterized as progressive and very much to the left of center, and yet we are diverse in our politics. As an institution and a learning community, we do not have a particular "party line" nor do we have a litany of "politically correct" behaviors or positions that learners are supposed to adhere to. Most importantly, however, unlike most institutions, we are actively hospitable and even encouraging of learning endeavors that seek to reflect on issues of racism, sexism, classism, and other forms of oppression and social injustice. We rather consciously and emphatically find ourselves supporting learning and actions which are intended to promote equality, human liberation and justice.

- We encourage learners to probe beneath the surface of things, to look concurrently at both the immediately practical tasks before us in community work and the bigger picture (society as a whole). We want learners to become more conscious of how they evaluate and judge evidence, and to be alert to get more information, to broaden their experiences. We suggest concrete research strategies for accomplishing these things.

- We also improvise and brainstorm about specific ways each student can proceed with their inquiries, when we are in the midst of thinking with them about their unfinished projects as well as their yet-to-be-formulated projects. What research methods are likely to facilitate the learner in productively addressing the questions, interests, problems, and actions with which they are engaged?

- We endeavor to help learners to do more than simply think or write about their community involvements, for we encourage them to be creative, intellectually and practically. Our students are very apt to write books and articles putting forth the insights and ideas growing out of their experience. Many work on establishing their own non-profit organization, to try to fill some unmet community need in a distinctively innovative way.

- We encourage learners to critically reflect on their community/job experience. People often get involved in routines and find it difficult to take the time and give the attention to looking beneath the surface of what they are doing, or to think about the bigger picture. We try to encourage learners to take notes on what they are doing and then write papers about their insights, and the questions, problems and challenges they encounter, what works, what doesn't work, and how their efforts might contribute to longer-term changes.

- Talking with us in one-on-one meetings is another way to get learners to reflect on what they are doing. We encourage them to talk with others, as well. In a more formal way, they often interview clients, coworkers, and others who are doing similar work, to learn about their experiences, their insights, and the concerns, questions and problems that matter to them. Often learners lead seminars at WISR to get feedback from other students and faculty on the things in which they are involved.

- We also ask learners to read what others have to say about social change, about the factors that contribute to it, and their vision of how it should happen and where it should lead. We ask them to critique these ideas and theories about social change, in terms of what they agree and disagree with, and in terms of how these ideas relate to the specific types of activities in which the student is engaged, be it work with youth, therapy with trauma survivors, health education, or job training. In this way, students can stand back from the details of what they are doing and think about it in terms of the bigger picture.

- We are always curious to learn more about what our students are doing, both from their perspective (i.e., in terms of their knowledge and experience) and from the perspective of others engaged in the kind of efforts our student is. Our work with learners at WISR leads us to want to learn more about their particular field of study, for very often our students are more expert in their specialized area (be it the development of biracial children, the psychology of trauma, community-based health education, African culture and spirituality, or providing services to homeless families) than we are. By learning more about the learner's field, we are able to ask better questions of them, to know enough about what they are doing to ask interesting questions for ourselves, and to share our wonderings and thoughts with the student, in the role of colleagues, co-inquirers who are actively interested in scratching our heads about the problems our students care about.

- Sometimes learners at WISR are changing fields, and we encourage them to do more research about the field or field(s) they are considering. This may involve doing interviews with others in the field under consideration—to learn more about what they do, what problems they encounter, and why they find it meaningful or challenging. Sometimes we encourage the learner to write an autobiographical piece on how their experiences have led them to the interests and concerns they are currently exploring or embracing.

- We encourage the learner to take his or her own ideas more seriously as a basis for developing theories about a topic in which he or she is an expert. Very often, people think theories are something developed by "other" people, by so-called famous people, and don't take their own insights seriously enough. Autobiographical writing, or at least writings about one's own experience, as they pertain to ideas, questions, concepts developed on a particular topic, is a good way to help students begin to develop their own theories, which they often have but don't realize that they have. We believe that most of us know more than we realize that we know, and we just need the right kinds of support and dialogue to help us become aware of our knowledge, as such, and then to articulate it.

- We spend a lot of time commenting on student rough drafts, and encourage our students to submit rough "drafts" that are still in the form of bits and pieces of as-yet unorganized ideas, as well as more polished drafts that have a beginning, middle, and end to them.

- We sometimes suggest that learners interweave reviews of literature with their own ideas—not so much to support their own ideas (which usually can be supported by examples and evidence growing out of their own rich experience) as to think about how their ideas fit in (or don't fit in) with the body of writings that other people have put forth on similar topics.

- We often encourage learners to interview others to test out their ideas, to see how others' experience is similar to or different from their own, and to use these interviews as a basis for involving others in taking some kind of action on the problems of concern to the learner.

- We try to put learners who have similar or overlapping interests in contact with each other, so they can support and learn from each other. We encourage learners to come to seminars to see how others, even with seemingly very different interests, jobs or involvements, may often share their deeply felt values and broader ideas about the society, where it is going, and where it should go. These seminars also serve as a basis for learners of different cultural and ethnic backgrounds to come together and learn more from each other because of both the differences in their life experiences and from the similarities than transcend the differences.

- We try to encourage learners not to accept "pat" answers or narrow, technical solutions to problems, whether those approaches are ones they are advocating or whether they are adopting someone else's recipe for success. We usually find when questioning students about these formulaic approaches, that the learner's deeper thoughts about the strategy are much more complex, and more subtle, but that the action advocated has been more simply stated, sometimes because the simply stated version sounds "acceptable" and similar to approaches validated by others in positions of high status or authority.

SOME OUTCOMES FOR OUR LEARNERS

Having considered these various, admittedly interrelated and overlapping themes, it may be worthwhile to comment on a couple of other themes that often characterize the outcomes of learning at WISR.

For many students, one thing leads to another. For example, one learner, the mother of two children, had become concerned about how the recommended treatment for head lice didn't seem to work. As a single parent, she was all too aware that when students miss school, parents often miss work, sometimes with dire financial and emotional consequences. Then, there is the stigma of having head lice. Her senior thesis on this seemingly mundane topic propelled her forward into the position of becoming an expert on natural, safe remedies for head lice; consequently, she formulated a plan of outreach and education to schools and child care centers. She came to be recognized by others as being a repository of information about head lice and its treatment, as well as a valuable resource and consultant on the effective (and ineffective) organizational (school) responses to head lice epidemics. She was then able to educate others to become more sensitive to the human and interpersonal fallout from this problem, and how to avoid some of the misguided "solutions" to the problem.

Another example is from the action-research project of a student who is the director of a large, multipurpose agency serving homeless families. She wanted to interview homeless mothers and service providers in other agencies serving homeless. Her concern is: how do these clients experience the rules imposed by the agencies serving them? In particular, she is concerned that although the rules are well-intended, the homeless mothers often experience the rules established by the service providers, who have considerable power over them, as a re-traumatizing event, as one that reminds them of an experience with say, a battering partner. The result is that these mothers take their children and flee the very places that have been created to shelter them. This project is not yet complete, but she has already learned much more than she thought she would. Further, the homeless mothers interviewed have experienced the interviewing process itself as very empowering and esteem building. Other service providers have become curious about her interviewing efforts, and now want her to interview them and their clients. She has begun to consider having some mothers discuss these issues directly with service providers, or help her in conducting some interviews.

Sometimes "the one thing that leads to another" is that a learner imparts both the content and method of their learning to others. As one learner wrote in a self-evaluation, "Not only has my knowledge base increased tremendously, but my ability to integrate and articulate disparate types of information has increased dramatically. My own learning process has given me a clear way to identify gaps in my knowledge and methodically fill them. In addition, my ability to guide [my own] students in a similar building of confidence through their own education has been much enhanced. I have begun to include research projects in their training and to help them share this learning through peer education." This illustrates how a result of participation in this kind of collaborative inquiry is that learners develop the skills and motivations to engage others in similar kinds of learning processes. In this regard, our efforts seem to have a "multiplier effect." That is, the learning of one person multiplies in the society if that person conveys in their relationships with others what, and in this case also, how they have learned.

Another example of an important outcome is when learners find their own voice in a deeper, more authentic and more powerful way than they have been able to previously.

Learners who are about to write their first paper at WISR discover that they can write in the first person, and take ownership of the knowledge they have built and wish to communicate to others. They come to realize that they are not limited by the "behaviors" of academia (e.g., writing in the third person in a neutral, indifferent-sounding way) that they have always assumed was part of professional communication and "research." For example, one student at WISR who had long been well recognized in his field and profession, and who was a very capable and accomplished writer, had a breakthrough in his own writing during his studies for the Ph.D. at WISR. He told us that for the first time, he grappled with issues involved in his "coming out of the closet" with his Marxist convictions in the way that he writes about the insights and lessons that have evolved over the years as he has taught English in Japan and has done research in various parts of the world on the topic of intercultural communication.

Learners at WISR often come to see knowledge-building as something that most everyone is involved in—to a greater or lesser degree. Through such realizations, our students become more confident to make their own paths, to embark on their own self-defined careers—be they an activist for changes in our prisons, a therapist focusing on healing the wounds of war and global trauma, a mother who wants to bring together multiracial families in a process of collective learning and support, or a Native American who wants to preserve the history and culture of his tribe. To be sure, such individuals in many cases had embarked on these distinctive paths prior to enrolling at WISR, and for others new options occurred to them in the midst of their involvement at WISR.

Indeed, WISR faculty rather consciously and emphatically help students to design learning activities—action projects, research, and writings—that help to build bridges to the student's desired career path. In most academic programs, a student first gets a degree, and then uses that degree to qualify for a particular type of job. Although WISR degrees are a source of credibility for most of our students in their professional endeavors, many WISR alumni have told us that it was much more significant that WISR gave them the intellectual, social and emotional support and impetus to develop, embark on and/or stay committed to their own distinctive career paths, while they were in the midst of their learning at WISR. They especially value the personalized assistance from faculty, to not limit their visions by the definitions of existing jobs and careers, and to enable them to be both visionary and realistic in pursuing a life path that makes sense to them.

THE BIGGER PICTURE

So, how do our efforts at WISR connect with several aspects of the bigger picture—with the teaching and learning of inquiry and scientific methods, with other "alternative" efforts, with the hopes of others to start alternative programs or institutions of higher education, and the conventional higher education establishment?

Science

Our emphasis on knowledge-building and inquiry at WISR is aimed at demystifying science and helping people to learn that science and scientific methods are not fixed abstractions but works in progress that grow out of the efforts of real human beings, with all the strengths and limitations that we as human beings bring to science and inquiry. We are not anti-science, but against the one-dimensional stereotypes of science that suggest that hard science is good because it is aloof and "objective" rather than human and open-ended. We want our learners to come to appreciate that many of the best qualities of scientific breakthroughs in the so-called "hard" sciences often involve very subjective and imaginative involvements of the scientists who often achieve fame. Einstein drew on his intuition in very important ways, as do many other creative, productive scientists. Watson and Crick made a conceptual leap to the double-helix structure of DNA based on a dream about intertwined serpents. At many points in the achievement of scientific breakthroughs, scientists engage in debate as they wrestle with theories and interpretations of evidence that are far from clear-cut and conclusive.

In ways that are very good and important, science at its best is messy and requires the active engagement of learners (including famous scholars) rather than an aloof stance of psuedo-objectivity as students are often taught to believe. One of us completed a B.A. in physics and interned in high energy physics and mathematical physics before being pulled to social activism and the field of higher education reform in the late 60s. This understanding of some of the strengths and limitations of the hard sciences from the inside out has contributed to our writing and our teaching about action-research, participatory research, the philosophy of knowledge and inquiry in the social sciences.

We teach our students that the social sciences are no more "soft" than the natural sciences. Too often, social scientists try to emulate an inaccurate view of the complex, organic, "messiness" that allows people in the natural sciences to sometimes achieve very creative and important insights. In the past couple of decades, there has been a gradual but noticeably growing awareness of "complexity theory" and its applications to many fields of study. This has been a very positive development by calling wider attention to non-linear and organic qualities of knowledge building.

More and more, people are coming to realize the severe limitations of mechanistic, formulaic versions of science that overemphasize numeric manipulations, rigid protocols and aloof, unimaginative research designs and interpretations of data. One of us once interviewed a professor of physics at the University of California who had been identified by students and colleagues as a very distinguished instructor. This professor (who was also well-respected as a scholar in the field) said that one of the challenges he had in educating his graduate students was to help them develop what he called a "qualitative understanding" of physics. He felt that all too often when students were working on a problem, they would make some numeric mistake of computation but would be unable to catch their mistake because they didn't have a good intuitive, qualitative grasp of the relationships that they were trying to study through unreflectively plugging numbers into a formula.

As learners come to appreciate this "bigger picture" of science and inquiry, they also feel more confident about their capacity to contribute to knowledge building. Partly, they develop more sophisticated skills—in designing research, gathering and judging evidence, and articulating the insights and questions that grow out of their practical experience. Beyond this, they become motivated to see themselves, as well as their colleagues, clients and/or fellow citizens, as active participants who are capable of contributing to knowledge that has the potential to improve our communities and contribute to social justice.

Alternative Education and the Education Establishment

As noted earlier, WISR was one of a number of alternative institutions that came onto the higher education scene in the 1970s. Most of these institutions have died and faded away. A few, such as the Union Institute, have accomplished much, grown, and even achieved regional accreditation status. Many of the concerns of alternative education have been adopted by established institutions—ethnic studies, women's studies, evening and weekend classes for working adults, individualized learning contracts (but within fairly tightly defined boundaries of content and process), more community experience and internships, and a larger number of interdisciplinary, community oriented programs (e.g., environmental studies).

Unfortunately, however, the "successes" of most of these efforts are limited by the constraints of the institutions that "house" them, by the unimaginative, lockstep standards and procedures of regional accrediting agencies, and by economic considerations which rather continually push for educational programs to demonstrate success by increasing their size and their budgets, indeed even their "profits" (i.e., excess of income over expenses). Although most colleges and universities are not profit making in the literal sense, some notably large and well-respected institutions such as Phoenix University are profit-making corporations. To be sure, some alternative programs within established institutions provide very important forums and learning contexts for learners and faculty who wish to pursue progressive social and community agendas.

Other programs, and sometimes entire institutions, are an excuse to make money off of the needs many adults have to find flexible programs which allow them to obtain degrees while working so that they can progress in their fields and improve themselves financially. Many of these programs exploit part-time faculty with large teaching loads, while providing little opportunity for serious inquiry either with their students or on their own, few if any fringe benefits and no job security. Students receive degrees, and are able to sign up for classes that fit in with their job schedules, and further, often without the stress of being expected to be seriously and energetically engaged in their studies. In a real sense, the students are paying for a degree, not so much for an opportunity to learn. One of us was a visiting lecturer for a class in a well-known, very large, regionally accredited institution aimed at enrolling massive numbers of mid-life working adults, and encountered students who clearly had not previously been expected to even pay attention during class, much less be seriously engaged in their studies out of class. For example, one student was clearly perturbed when the visiting instructor asked her to stop reading the magazine she probably recently purchased at the grocery store checkout stand.

How is it that these institutions are so easily accredited, while small schools with unconventional learning methodologies such as WISR are almost always required to change their fundamental institutional character in order to achieve accreditation status? Representatives of accrediting agencies often remind us that they are "voluntary associations," acting as if the powerful consequences of recognition don't much matter in the world, and we have been approached with a stance of "benign neglect." A few years ago, an accreditation official politely and respectfully informed us that unless we decided to grow to an enrollment of over 100 students, they wouldn't even know how to evaluate us. Because of our commitment to personalized education and a manageable institutional scale, it is unlikely that we will ever choose to grow beyond 100. Right now, we have less than 50 students, and would like to grow somewhat, but rather than exceeding 100 students, we would prefer to see others start institutions similar to WISR, but with their own distinctive qualities.

Unfortunately, however, some people who would be very enthusiastic learners at WISR eventually decide not to enroll because the lack of accreditation status might work against them when they are up for a salary increase in their school district (if they are a public school teacher) or a job promotion in county bureaucracy (if they are a social worker for a governmental agency, for example). Our students who do private consulting, who aim to obtain the State's Marriage and Family Therapy license, and who work in non-profit community agencies find almost always that our degree is very helpful and the absence of accreditation is not an obstacle. Not uncommonly our students and alumni are even successful in using their WISR degrees (and their learning at WISR!) to obtain professorial positions in some accredited, well-established colleges and universities. But there are times when the lack of accreditation poses limitations for our students, and drives away some prospective students who really want to pursue the kinds of learning opportunities we provide at WISR, which they consider to be superior to any they are able to find elsewhere. We consider it an injustice to our students and to some of our prospective students that "accreditation" is not truly based on a measure of the solidity of the learning going on in an institution. Arguably, it doesn't necessarily correlate with institutional stability, for despite our limited financial resources and small size, we have been around for 28 years and continue to thrive and grow (more in the quality of what we do than in our size).

So, we really wish we could be accredited—not in order to grow to be a huge and wealthy institution—to better serve our students and to grow a little bit in size, to enroll others whose learning needs could be well-served by WISR, and maybe even to offer modest amounts of financial aid monies that our students are currently not eligible for, due mostly to our lack of accreditation. Fortunately, we do have California State Approval, and that designation does lend some tangible external credibility to our institution. Fortunately, we occasionally receive other outside support, as well. Over the past three years, the Richard and Rhoda Goldman Fund in San Francisco has awarded us $55,000 to establish a revolving loan fund for students who can't afford our $6,000/year tuition. In the absence of Federal financial aid, these grants from the Goldman Fund are enabling us to enroll a number of students who are receiving a deferral of about 40% of their tuition (in effect a partial loan of tuition monies). When these students graduate and begin to repay their loans, such loans can then be given to others.

So, others who might wish to start their own distinctive institutions like WISR should realize that there may be trade-offs between affluence and integrity, and between size and qualitative success. And, it is of course quite possible that others might succeed where we have failed and create dynamic, vital learning institutions with some of the kinds of ingredients we have strived to nurture at WISR, while still achieving larger enrollments, greater institutional affluence, accreditation and the like. In fact, we hope that others will succeed where we have not.

Most of all, we hope that some of the ideas we have shared about our insights about teaching and learning will be helpful and even at times inspiring to others. Certainly, we are continually inspired by what our students accomplish and the kinds of collaborative inquiry they often elicit from us. The "magic" that is WISR is this special, rather rare, emphasis on collaborative inquiry into community-based knowledge-building. We hope that, if push comes to shove, the educators and others reading this will choose to give first priority to creating their own magic, and second priority to size, money and accreditation. These latter realities are important, and need not be shunned just to make a "political statement," but we do not believe that they should become the tail that wags the dog. After 28 years, we know that it is possible to create and sustain magic, even though accreditation and affluence still remain elusive.

CONCLUSION

WISR continues to exist, in the face of seemingly impossible challenges to a tiny, alternative institution with severely limited resources. Undoubtedly, we will continue to grapple with the matter of attaining a size large enough to be more financial viable, but still small enough to maintain our emphasis on the quality of learning through individual attention. But there is no question about what we do and in turn what learners accomplish here that is important to their intellectual growth. WISR is one of the few places where faculty and students, alike, are focused on larger social change and the immediate changes that can be made in our communities. It is also one of the few places where people consistently attend to praxis, to ways of bringing research and action together.

We suspect that there is more about the magic that is WISR that we are not yet consciously aware of. We know that there is always more to learn and new ways to make more magic. One of the authors helped found WISR in 1975, and the other has been involved here since 1984. We have learned much during our years at WISR. We are sure that it has been obvious to our readers that we are proud of our involvement in this very magical, albeit, unassuming and modest institution.

WISR continues to thrive, and we have tried to convey something of the essential spirit of WISR with the hope that WISR's story may serve as a source of inspiration for similarly minded people. We welcome opportunities to learn from your experiences, and be in dialogue with you. Please contact us (mail@wisr.edu).

AUTHORS' NOTE

After a long and fruitful life of activism and community-based leadership and intellectual creativity, our good friend and colleague, Dr. Antonia Pantoja, recently passed away. For 12 years in the 70s and 80s, Dr. Pantoja and Dr. Wilhelmina Perry created and operated the alternative Graduate School for Community Development in San Diego, which became a kind of sister institution for WISR. Dr. Pantoja's visions live on in her legacy of community development in both New York City and her homeland, Puerto Rico. Her impact is an integral part of WISR. We celebrate her life, and to her memory we dedicate our ongoing efforts to education for social change and equality.

REFERENCES

Bilorusky, John and Harry Butler, 1975. "Beyond Contract Curricula to Improvisational Learning." In *Individualizing Education Through Contract Learning*, Neal R. Berte (ed.), University, Alabama: The University of Alabama Press.

Freire, Paulo, Ana Maria Araujo (ed.) and Donaldo Macedo (ed.), 2000. *The Paulo Freire Reader*. London: Continuum International Publishing Group.

hooks, bell. 1994. *Teaching to Transgress: Education as the Practice of Freedom*. New York: Perennial Press.

Kowalski, Joanne, John Bilorusky and Victor Acosta, 1979. "Does Alternative Higher Education Need an Alternative?" *Alternative Higher Education*. Summer 1979.

Kuhn, Thomas S., 1970. *The Structure of Scientific Revolutions*. Chicago: University of Chicago Press.

Lewin, Roger, 1992. *Complexity: Life at the Edge of Chaos*. Chicago: University of Chicago Press.

Lunsford, Terry and John Bilorusky. Unpublished curriculum materials on Action-Research, 1981-83. Sponsored by a grant to the Western Institute for Social Research ("Extending the Teaching, Learning and Use of Action-Research Throughout the Larger Community") from the U.S. Department of Education's Fund for the Improvement of Postsecondary Education.

Pantoja, Antonia, 2002. *Memoir of a Visionary: Antonia Pantoja*. Houston, Texas: Arte Público Press.

Chapter 4

WORKERS' EDUCATIONAL ASSOCIATIONS: LIBERAL ARTS LEARNING FOR ACTIVE CITIZENSHIP

Wendy Terry

ABSTRACT

Workers' Educational Associations have developed the thinking ability and knowledge of individuals as citizen learners. The force of their minds and of their activism has been a source for social change. WEA's are an adult education model for delivering liberal arts learning in the community. They are community associations run by the learners but associated with universities and supported by government funding. In Nordic, European, and some Commonwealth countries, the WEA is an integral part of adult education provision. As a result, adults who would rarely take university level courses have access to a liberal arts education, and therefore develop critical inquiry skills. Study circles and tutorial methods of learning, and small group learning methods which facilitate dialogue, are used in order to link the curriculum to issues of interest to class participants. As a result, WEA's help adults better understand their life and their society. The record shows WEA students thus informed often become social activists, a force for social change.

INTRODUCTION

In countries where Workers' Educational Associations form a network of community-run learning centres for adults, the alternative to a conservative government is a labour or social democratic one. Is this coincidental or are the WEA's a social force?

The WEA's have three key characteristics. They are democratic, governed by a community board; liberal arts comprise the curriculum so partnerships with universities are often the norm; and the study method used is half lecture, half discussion. Study circles prevail in the Nordic WEA's, and tutorials are used in the Commonwealth WEA's. Adults engage in a dialogue with the teacher and other students so learners' questions and experiences are examined. As a result, knowledge is gained and critical inquiry and community development skills are developed. Thus informed and empowered, many become active citizens, catalysts for social change.

The paradox of the WEA model is this: although their purpose is not to foster social change, they do. The purpose of a Workers' Educational Association is to create a local centre where adults can learn what interests them. Nevertheless, what often interests adults is their personal engagement with larger social issues. Therefore, WEA's indirectly become a force for social change. The WEA model seems benign and has been criticized as being such by social activists. However, given that the purpose of the WEA's is to develop the critical inquiry skills and the knowledge of ordinary citizens, their members often become social change agents.

This paper examines how community access to liberal arts learning was marginalized in North America during the 1950's. It looks at how we came to see workers' education as being education for trade unionists on the one hand or for socialists on the other hand, rather than continuing education for working adults. Given that liberal arts learning fosters active citizenship and that this learning was key to the development of national citizenship, an argument is made for the need to revitalize university- community links for the development of global citizenship.

THE HISTORY OF WEA'S

The WEA's were founded in the first decades of the twentieth century and continue to be important associations for learning in this century. For example, in Nordic countries (Norway, Finland, Sweden), in some European countries (Denmark, Germany), and in some Commonwealth countries (the UK, Australia), the WEA is the largest voluntary provider of non-formal learning. The national associations of local WEA branches are members of the International Federation of Workers' Educational Associations (IFWEA), which was founded in 1947. IFWEA was formed from international networks for workers' education, as part of the reorganization of the international NGO community around the founding of UNESCO in 1947. IFWEA has continuously had consultative status with UNESCO.

In countries which sustained the development of the WEA's throughout the last century, a learning environment exists where an adult may walk into his/her local community learning association, suggest a topic that interests him/her and have it considered. On the other hand, in the USA and Canada, where workers' education was marginalized, adults pursue their interests independently through self-directed reading, or as part-time, evening credit students at a university or college. Their learning interests are pursued autonomously or as an adjunct to the main purpose of educational organizations, which is to educate youth and train academic professionals. Individuals are expected to pay pro-rated university fees for this personal interest learning. As a result, adults do not have a learning home. Human development learning (education) is not a visible sector of provision as are the sectors for human resource development (training.) This is especially true in the last decades of the 1900's as adults and nations must learn to compete for high tech jobs within a globalized labour market. In North America, although it is commonly recognized that access to a general education—history, sociology, psychology, civics— is fundamental to the development of citizenship and democracy, we have a laissez-faire attitude to adults' learning in this area. We assume what we learn about these subjects in high school will do.

To see the development of this learning environment you could draw a historical map showing the rise and fall of sectors of adult education provision during the twentieth century. On such a historical map, you would see that in the first half of the 1900's adult education was called workers' education or citizenship education—human development learning. Citizenship education was often focused on English as a Second Language courses: its purpose was to help newcomers become good citizens, and it did receive government support. Marius Hansome divided workers' education into five categories: Integrative (Scandinavian workers' educational associations), Cultural (WEA)—the UK model, Political, and Trade Union and Consumers Co-operative. In 1968 Hansome wrote *World Workers' Educational Movements: Their Social Significance*. The WEA's had roots in four out of five of these categories (1968:11). These strands of workers' education have at times been woven together and at other times have become unravelled.

The universities cooperated in developing the WEA's liberal arts curriculum often through their extension departments, but as the field of adult education developed, extension departments saw WEA students as part of their educational market. Association histories document this competition for enrollments (Shuker 1984: 123; Higgins 1953: 39; Sangster in Welton 1987: 85). Universities are still partners with WEA's. The trade unions co-operated in promoting WEA courses to their members—a market access function in today's terms. They are still partnered with WEA's. However most trade unions took ownership of their leadership training and political education in the mid -1900's. They needed their education to be political as opposed to cultural, but not radical. The socialist parties offered education to workers, as did the WEA, but the WEA philosophy was based in developing critical inquiry skills in general, not only from one political perspective. As socialist parties became distinct from social democratic and labour parties, partnerships with WEA's were possible; the Nordic models have these political links.

Fundamentally, the WEA model is a community association one. One could call it a learning co-operative. Indeed Albert Mansbridge, a key figure in the founding of the British WEA, had his roots within the Co-operative movement. Although the links with the co-operative movement are now not strong, there are clear parallels. Learning at a member-run WEA, as opposed to learning at an educational institution, is similar to being a credit union member as opposed to being a bank customer, or being a member of a housing co-operative as opposed to being a renter. To date it has not been part of my studies to trace the evolution of the relationship between the WEA's and the co-operative movement, though the co-operative movement could be a key partner in the revitalization of the WEA model in North America. The WEA of Canada did work with The Canadian Co-operative Association in a recent project that looked at developing a learning co-operative in Toronto. The Education Exchange project is described in a later section of this chapter.

By 1983, when I first became aware of the WEA of Canada, the history of workers' education was all but invisible in North America. Adult education in North America had been transformed from the sixties through the eighties from community models to professional and institutional ones. Some trade unionists and activists use popular education methods for political education, but there are few community-run learning centres that offer a liberal arts education to adults (User et al. 1997: 5). Over the course of the century, the field has moved from an environment of providers co-operating with each other, with a sense of community in mind, to one where providers compete with each other in an educational market (Stern in Alford 1980: 5). In his book titled *Learning in Social Context: Workers and Adult Education in Nineteenth Century Chicago*, Fred M. Schied presents a general academic examination of the marginalization of workers' education by adult education. In an afterword entitled: "Workers' Education and the Reconceptualization of Adult Education History," Schied asserts that it is important to look at the history of workers' education within a social context (Schied 1995: 162-63.)

Therefore, we need to look at the evolution of culture in countries that supported workers' education and those that marginalized it. In North America, the social context was the Cold War; the ideological debates about capitalist versus communist economic theories and systems were subjects of interest not only to intellectuals but also to members of the general public. However, trade union leaders and professional adult educators were concerned that workers' education, the political model, would lead workers to support doctrinaire systems as opposed to democratic ones. So the unions took over workers' education to contain the radical politics, and the profession of adult education ignored workers education in order to distance themselves from the politics. Activists persisted with a political model which became increasingly marginalized, and which denigrated the WEA cultural model as being benign. The conflicted history of McCarthyism has hampered our ability to look at our historical context. As a result, North American academic studies of the history of adult education, written in the last half of the twentieth century, seem to start mid-century, without looking at its roots in workers' education in the first half of the twentieth century (Alford 1980: 151). Fortunately, in the UK where the WEA continues to thrive, adult education histories do look at the WEA and one recent study by Johnathon Rose looks at the political effect of workers' participation in a cultural model of workers' education (the WEA).

THE WEA AND SOCIAL CHANGE

For social activists the debate has always been whether a liberal, cultural, integrating model of workers' education, as opposed to a political or trade union model is a neutralizing force or a catalyst for social activism. Even today part of the development strategy for restoring liberal arts learning in the community would include convincing social activists that supporting the general education of adults is a good social change strategy, just as effective and maybe more so than the "political education" promoted within advocate organizations. On the other hand, for conservatives the contention has been that workers' education was too radical—they tarred the WEA model of liberal arts education with the same brush that they tarred political and trade union education. Perhaps the conservatives saw more clearly than did the activists that in developing the independent thinking of workers a force for social change was also being developed.

Jonathan Rose examined this debate about liberal arts learning versus political education in Chapter Eight, "The Whole Contention Concerning the Workers' Educational Association," which is in *The Intellectual Life of the British Working Classes*. His study gains its authority from the learner's voice, a history of audience response (Rose 2001: 6). By studying documents like workers' diaries, autobiographies, letters to the editor and class evaluations, he documents how the workers themselves described their intellectual life. Rose's study of the workers' view shows that the WEA was a catalyst for social change. One of many citations that document this finding is an exchange of letters between a supporter of political education and a supporter of a liberal education in the *Cotton Factory Time* issues of

March and April, 1914. Ethel Carnie, the proletarian novelist, warned that the WEA would 'chloroform' the workingman:

> After having had the best of his strength and brain power sapped during the day in the interest of the capitalist, in his limited time and valuable leisure he is taken to look at this being exploited FROM EVERY POINT OF VIEW!

Lavena Saltonstall, a garment worker and WEA student responds:

> I say that if Miss Carnie, and those from whom she has imbibed her views concerning the WEA, insist that a working man or woman is liable to be side-tracked or made neutral or impartial because they look at all sides of the question in order to understand it fully, then they are libeling the intelligence of the working classes. (Rose 2001, 264)

Rose cites many sources, which document that WEA students appreciated learning how their life fit into the larger society. George Norris, a student of the WEA who rose to the Executive Council of Postal Workers, and who after twenty-two years of WEA classes in industrial psychology testifies in *The Highwayman* (May 1948,) the WEA newspaper, that:

> Instead of seeing my job in isolation as an individual postal worker and from that angle only, it began to take shape as a planned industry with a complex social structure: one of many in the social structures of the country I live.
>
> ....
>
> Training in the art of thinking has equipped me to see through the shams and humbug that lurk behind the sensational headlines of the modern newspapers, the oratorical outpourings of insincere party politicians and dictators, and the doctrinaire ideologies that stalk the world sowing hatred. (Rose 2001, 277)

Rose notes that the WEA provided a "haven" for workers seeking to learn (Rose 2001, 278.) Today even though formal learning opportunities for workers are more accessible, the WEA is still a home. A scanning of the WEA web site in Britain (www.wea.org.uk) shows the following:

- The Workers' Educational Association founded in 1903 aims to provide high quality learning opportunities to adults from all walks of life, but especially those who may have missed out on learning in early life, or who are socially and economically disadvantaged
- The WEA is controlled by its members. Many of our courses are planned and promoted by our network of 650 local WEA branches run by voluntary members.
- The WEA also works closely with a range of partners including Local Education Authorities (school boards to North Americans,) Universities (Oxford was the founding partner,) and other voluntary and community organizations (trade unions are key partners) [Bracketed information is my expansion]
- The General Programme covers a wide range of subjects including Information and Communications Technology (ICT), history, literature, music, visual arts, science, and natural history, philosophy and the social sciences.

- Learners say:

" I enjoyed asking questions, giving my own ideas. The course made me reason and think more deeply than I thought I could." (Licenfield)

" I came out of each session exhilarated. The course has been a tremendous leap for me." (Literature, Kenilworth)

History and current experience show that the WEA, a learner-run community organization, offering liberal arts education to working adults in co-operation with the universities, is a social power in fostering activists and social change. It does not chloroform the working person to think along establishment lines, as those who favored political education feared, and it does not brainwash the working person into becoming a radical, as the conservative forces feared. As George Norris stated, the WEA trained him in the art of thinking; it equipped him to see through doctrinaire ideologies and media sensationalism (Rose 2001: 277). The WEA gave working people the knowledge and skills to become active citizens and a source of social power.

It is clear why the WEA works for learners: it responds to the human need to understand one's self and the larger picture-the social context. But how did the WEA become an accepted, funded part of the adult learning environment if both activist and conservative forces were concerned about the WEA's?

THE WEA SUPPORTED

As the field of adult education transformed itself in the twentieth century from community volunteer models to professional market ones, the WEA was able to secure its role because many WEA members were members of the British Labour government elected in 1945. They shaped educational policy with the WEA model in mind. Rose notes that a total of fifty-six WEA supporters, teachers, and students were sitting in the House of Commons, including the new Prime Minister and Chancellor of the Exchequer. A 1938 survey of England and Wales found more than 2,300 WEA student and alumni held public office, including fifteen MP's. Of the 303 students attending the Oxford University Tutorial Classes in 1917-1918, 195 were politically and/or socially active. There were fifty-three trade union officials, twenty-six members of the trades and labor councils, twenty-five Co-operative Society officers, eleven members of local government bodies, thirty-eight people involved in the adult student movement, and twenty-six volunteer teachers (Rose 2001, 292.)

Today WEA members are found in social change roles. In 1993, when I became the IFWEA Liaison to UNESCO, the Assistant Director General of the Education Sector was a former WEA tutor from Australia. The WEA of Northern Ireland organizes cross-sector (Protestant, Catholic) historical study groups and their Executive Director is an active leader in the peace movement. The first NDP (New Democratic Party) Premier of Ontario was a WEA tutor when he was a university student in England.

Similar to what occurred in the UK, labour or social democratic governments took power in Nordic, European and some Commonwealth countries, and given these governments were liberally sprinkled with WEA students and tutors, the WEA's were sustained by government. In North America, the social context was different.

THE WEA MARGINALIZED

The WEA was not able to survive in Canada because McCarthyism shaped our North American culture. Not only was union education shaped by the Cold War but so too was adult education. Both trade unions and professional educators were concerned that workers' education was political education and as a result, they marginalized it.

Only now with some distance from the Cold War are we able to look at these dynamics. In 2001, readers benefited from the release of Jeffery Taylor's *Union Learning, Canadian Labour Education in the Twentieth Century*. Taylor documents in detail the marginalization of the WEA of Canada, founded in 1918. In Canada, workers' education was influenced by the WEA, the British model. Beginning in the 1930's it was also influenced by the American experience (Taylor 2001:5).

At first the workers' education movement in the United States was more political. Taylor notes that it dates from 1906, when the Socialist Party formed the Rand School for Social Science in New York (Taylor 2001, 5.) In 1921 the Workers' Education Bureau formed. Its first President was James Maurer, a socialist (Kornbluh 1987: 11). Later he was a lecturer at Brookwood Labour College, an independent labour college. The staff association of Brookwood survived as Local 189 up until the late 1990's as an association for labour educators. The Workers Education Bureau, WEB, founded in 1921, co-ordinated union-centered educational activities and, although independent of the American Federation of Labour, functioned as their educational arm from 1929 on. In 1954 it became the AFL education department (Kornbluh 1987:54; Taylor 2001: 5). Taylor notes that the Rand School delivered in the spirit of the British Plebs League and the National Council of Labour Colleges, political education (Taylor 2001: 4). Both were marginalized, through displacement by the labour movement as unions moved to own their educational programs, and through the communist purges of the 1950's.

It should be noted that there was a nation-wide federally supported workers' educational program in the United States during the 1930's, which started as a relief project of the Roosevelt government. Although the courses seemed benign, the program was criticized for being political and ended up being cancelled (Kornbluh 1987: 3-4).

While the British were electing a Labour government in 1945 (liberally sprinkled with WEA people) the Canadian Congress of Labour was expelling all communist-led unions in the period from 1945-1948 (Taylor 2001: 62). Drummond Wren, Secretary General of the WEA of Canada from 1929 to 1951, had prided himself on walking a fine line between the communists and social democrats (the Co-operative Commonwealth Federation, precursor to the New Democratic Party) in order to offer an independent education to the working person (Taylor 2001: 68). However, Walter Reuther, President of United Auto Workers of America, branded Wren a communist. (Taylor 2001: 66). Wren resigned in 1951 to save the WEA.

Taylor notes that Wren did not go quietly: he gave a long speech when he resigned detailing the accomplishments of the WEA (Taylor 2001: 68). In page after page he detailed the summer schools, the radio programs, the study groups, the branches all across Canada, and the support of the students. Every one that reads that speech feels the emotion crackle off the page. Wren had started out as a WEA student after the Great War. He had dedicated his life to the WEA. Wren became a victim of McCarthyism, the WEA lost its role as a key provider of adult education, and only now, fifty years later and almost twenty years after the end of the Cold War, are historians giving the WEA its due.

In Britain, the Labour government moved to democratize access to formal education, spurred on by WEA advocacy, and in those policy developments still supported informal education for adults—the WEA. In the USA and Canada we moved to professional and institutional models for adult education. Community colleges were introduced to the United States and Canada mid-century, and adults became part time evening students at institutions designed for youth going full time. Originally the community colleges were seen as community learning centres, but they are now seen as centres of excellence for technical learning (Usher 1997: 37). In these developments adult students lost a learning home: they became adjuncts of educational institutions and the nation lost a social force for active citizenship.

In Europe, the social context was different. The excesses of McCarthyism were not a key factor. The workers' education movement retained political models. For instance, the Socialist party of Belgium is a major provider of adult education and is a member of IFWEA (Bladt in London 1990: 211). Rita Bladt has been a member of the IFWEA Executive Committee. The trade unions are supporters of the WEA in the European, Commonwealth and Nordic models, as are the universities. In the United States, there is a strong link between the universities and the trade union movement through an extensive network of university labour education programs. The creators of these programs formed an association called the Universities and Colleges Labour Education Association which lasted up until the late 1990's when it merged with Local 189 to form the United Association for Labour Education. These university-union links are more informal in Canada. Internationally, the trade unions are leading the political education of workers in response to the globalization of the economy, and that activist stream has been reflected in the IFWEA International Study Circles on Globalization held during the last of half of the 1990's. For the general public at the local community level, there is also a need for a parallel program of Study Circles, so that university and community knowledge can be joined in order to support the development of global citizenship.

THE WEA- CITIZENSHIP EDUCATION FOR GLOBALIZATION

Fundamentally, the WEA is about education for citizenship. Today the concept of citizenship is so much a part of our culture we are hardly conscious of it. Yet the concept of citizenship is undergoing profound change as we become global citizens as well as citizens of our country. Along with the development of the globalization of the world economy, there is the development of the concept of global citizenship—learning how to co-operate as individuals and nations on social issues like environmental sustainability. Just as the concept of national citizenship required each individual to learn, to develop a common identity and to participate in national governance, the concept of global citizenship requires us to learn how to live in diversity locally and globally, and how to influence global politics (Castles 2000: 8).

When political communities moved from territorial states ruled by absolute monarchs to nation states ruled by citizens, adults needed to develop a national consciousness (Baylis

2001: 620). They debated the development of rights from the eighteenth century to the twentieth century: first their legal rights, then their voting rights, and finally their social or welfare rights (Baylis 2001: 623). Today we are beginning to discuss the enforcement of human rights within concepts of global citizenship. Adults need popular access to a liberal arts education to think through the development of global consciousness, just as they did when they thought through the development of a national consciousness.

Michael Mann described the cultural phenomenon of coffee houses and debating societies of the 1700's, which were the adult education communities of the day. They were the places where the emerging concepts of national citizenship were discussed, concepts that emerged from the French Revolution (Mann 1997: 225-229). In his two-volume study on the *Sources of Social Power*, he described the social power of what he called "discursive literacy," or the literate mastery of argument and debate. He described it as an extensive and diffuse social power, key to communicating ideas and organizing actions. He noted that literacy was first used in the mid-1700's to question power but, prior to that, it was used to administer it. (Mann 1993:38; 1986: 125). This informal community education for citizenship education from the 1700's transformed itself through each decade and century into associations for learning, like the Mechanics Institutes and Mutual Improvement Associations in Sweden where citizenship education is delivered through a nation-wide network of workers' educational associations.

One can examine the WEA model from the individual learner's perspective, looking at its effect on fostering social change, as Jonathan Rose did in his book on *The Intellectual Life of the British Working Classes*. Or one can examine the WEA model from a social policy perspective, looking at its effects in promoting active citizenship, as Henry Milner did in his book *Civic Literacy: How Informed Citizens Make Democracy Work*. Milner wants to "understand what makes equitable welfare states able to survive and adapt—what makes them sustainable" (2002: vii.) He concludes that the key factor is what he calls civic literacy: "the knowledge and ability capacity of citizens to make sense of their political world" (2002: 1). He identifies a number of measures that promote civic literary, such as "subsidization of newspapers, the informational activities of political parties, and the encouragement of public broadcasting and adult and civic education" (2002: 3). Sweden was his case study, though his overall study was an international comparative one.

ABF is the workers' educational association in Sweden. It organizes about 100,000 study circles a year for over a million participants, about 30% of all study Umea circles in Sweden. In the ABF at Umea they offer courses on general subjects like languages, computers, art, music appreciation and ones that address citizenship roles. They include "courses in organizing groups, cooperatives, public speaking, writing, understanding media, social and civil rights, the United Nations, war and peace, the future of democracy, feminism, various aspects of history and important contemporary books" (Milner 2002: 128). Looking at all the educational associations in Sweden, it has the most significant role in offering education to those who would be least likely to participate in adult education (Milner 2002: 123).

This popular access to adult education ensures that those who left the child-youth stream early can come back into a system for adult education that creates programs for the diversity of their adult interests. Statistical studies show that "the ratio of university graduates participating in adult education compared to those with less than nine years education is nine to one in Canada but only three to one in Sweden" (Rubensson, cited in Milner 2002: 122). Milner states that "there is good reason to believe that, when it comes to civic literacy, the content of what is learned as an adult is more important than that learned in school in one's youth" (2002: 17). In Sweden and other Nordic countries, there is no assumption that what is taught to youth in high school about citizenship will suffice for the rest of their life. Liberal arts learning is a sector of provision, equal in funding priority to the education of children, youth, literacy and training programs (Niemi 1990). Nordic countries, the most egalitarian, were high in civic literacy, as all have a Workers' Educational Association. Milner's research documents that it is no coincidence that WEA's are a force for social change.

Global Citizenship: International Call for Learning to Be

There is certainly a global call for this liberal arts learning for global citizenship. In 1998 UNESCO held a World Conference on Higher Education. On April 16 and 17, 1998, in Toronto, Canada, the United States and Mexico took part in the North American Preparatory Meeting for the UNESCO World Conference on Higher Education. The second of three sub-themes was: "The challenge of world and national citizenship in a global and multicultural society." Morris Keeton from the University of Maryland wrote the paper for Workshop 1, entitled: " The Challenge of Connection: Higher Education's Connection to Social and Economic Development." In his suggestion No. 8, "Enhance Workers by Preparing Them to Be Better Citizens," he noted the following:

- Workers, in turn, have a major effect in their role as voters, as community leaders, and as volunteers; they improve the quality of community institutions as time passes.
- If ever there was a time when citizens could be expected to muster the needed knowledge and to develop the reflective capabilities for good citizenship, that time has long since passed.
- To perform the service of citizenship education well, educational institutions will have to devote to it a quality of talent, time, and facilities comparable to those resources that are invested in developing the capabilities of adults as workers. (Canadian Commission for UNESCO, (1998: 24-25).

In 1997 the Fifth International Conference on Adult Education was held in Hamburg, Germany, where the first theme (of ten) was: "Adult learning and democracy: the challenge of the twenty-first century—Active citizenship, culture of peace, justice and equality, community participation, free will, intercultural dialogue, human rights" (Canadian Commission for UNESCO 1997, Fact Sheet 6). In 1996, the report of the International Commission on Education for the Twenty-first Century of UNESCO, in Part One (entitled "Outlooks"), identifies three perspectives: 1.) from the local community to the world society; 2.) from social cohesion to democratic participation; and 3.) from economic growth to human development. This report cited the Scandinavian model for adult education (UNESCO 1996, 104). Global support for liberal arts-learning-for-all as a source of power for human development is there, but who will act locally?

It is one challenge to look at present models and ideal concepts, to find the strands of history that lead back, but it is a more difficult challenge to identify strands and strategies that will lead forward. The "what" is always easier than the "how." How can we develop a strategy for the popularization of higher education and the reworking of citizenship education in the context of globalization?

CITIZENSHIP EDUCATION: LIBERAL ARTS LEARNING IN THE COMMUNITY

Just as the universities, homes to liberal arts learning, supported people in developing as national citizens through extension education, we now need these institutes of "higher education" to support us as we learn to be global citizens. We need this social change in our concepts, a change that could redress the imbalances wrought by economic change.

Within this global citizenship context, how might adult learners regain a place where non-formal higher education has a home in North America? How might IFWEA foster the popularization of liberal arts learning as part of an International Study Circle program on Globalization?

There are fragments in North America. In 1999 the WEA of Canada went back to another root in workers' education: co-operatives. The WEA undertook the development of what we called a learning cooperative, with ten individuals from the Metro Toronto community. Through the project activities, these individuals identified these shared values for the Educational Exchange:

- everyone has an equal right to education, personal enrichment and self-fulfillment;
- everyone has skills and talents to contribute;
- it is never too late to learn;
- every member has an equal vote in the decision making;
- every member has the opportunity to participate equally in determining the programs we offer ;
- every member will be encouraged to make a volunteer contribution;
- the lack of money is not an obstacle (WEA 1999: 1).

In 1997 the first Bard College Clemente course in the humanities was offered in New York as an experiment, bringing " the long-term poor out of poverty, and into a life of participation at the family, community and state level" (www.humanities.org\clemente.) Interestingly, Bard College had adopted a program in 1934 for undergraduates based on the Oxford tutorial system (www.bard.edu./about.) Oxford was the original university partner for the UK- WEA. I first read about the Clemente Course in an article by Earl Shorris in *Harper's* Magazine, September, 1997. Shorris first thought of the course in 1995, as he "understood that real civic participation would follow from the self-reflection naturally encouraged by reading and studying about the traditional humanities—literature, philosophy, history, art" (www.humanities.org\clemente.) Since that time the course has been offered in Massachusetts and Seattle. On the Massachusetts Foundation for the Humanities web site, I found these quotes from Clemente Course students:

- You can taste education, and it makes you want to do more;
- I have learned in this journey that even if the outcome does not change I must speak up and fight for what I feel is right or allow myself to be swallowed up by defeat (www.mfh.org.)

The WEA Educational Exchange reflects the democratic structure of WEA's, and the Clemente Course reflects the liberal arts content and dialogue methods of workers' education. Together they reflect the three characteristics of the WEA model: democratic governance, liberal arts learning and a dialogue between the learner's experience and the curriculum.

Shorris made one key observation about the Clemente course. The mentor must accept that the student may adopt a view other than his or her own. If the student develops critical inquiry skills and knowledge then they will have a choice, the small "p" politics of becoming learned. They may "use politics to get along in a society based on the game" or they may "choose to oppose the game itself" (Shorris 1995: 59). Social change advocates need to see these individual results not as a threat, but as part of the value in developing civic literacy, to remember that countries with high civic literacy are the most egalitarian (Milner 2002: 13).

CONCLUSION

As working people who are adult learners, working people—whether in the 1700's as documented by Mann, in the 1900's as documented by Rose, or in 2000 as documented by Shorris and Milner—seek to own their own education about life, and through this become more active citizens. Some countries have chosen to support this sector of adult education and as a result have a more vigorous, egalitarian democracy. Others like Canada and the USA could benefit from this as we move to global citizenship, and developing democracies need not only to develop children's education and adult training, but also adult education for citizenship development. IFWEA could foster these developments by adding a community model to their International Study Circles for Globalization, one that helps foster a global citizenship consciousness and national democracies by developing the thinking ability and knowledge of each individual as a citizen learner. The force of workers' minds and of their activism has been a source for social change, and can be source of social power within globalization.

If an activist in each university and community committed to join their knowledge in a liberal arts program for the public, we would have a powerful social force for global citizenship. To do this we would need to value cultural and integrating forms of workers' education, ones that enable adults to think through all perspectives on an issue that interests them. In North America we need to look back in history, prior to the 1960's, to see what community models for adult education existed to teach citizenship education, and we need to look to other countries that sustained this learning. We need to see where the fragments for redevelopment are in our local communities and to rethink curriculum in terms of global citizenship. Let's do it.

REFERENCES

Alford, Harold J. 1980. Editor, Power and Conflict in Continuing Education: Survival and Prosperity for all? *The Wadsworth Series in Continuing Education.* Belmont, California: Wadsworth Inc.

Baylis, John, Steve Smith. 2001. *The Globalization of World Politics, An introduction to international relations*, Second Edition. New York: Oxford University Press.

Bladt, Rita. 1990. "Worker Education in Western Europe" In *The Re-education of the American Working Class*, edited by Steven H. London et al. New York, Westport, Connecticut, London: Greenwood Press.

Blid, Henry. 1989. *Education by the people-study circles.* Sweden: ABF/Workers' Educational Association.

Cahn, Steven M. 1979. *Education and the Democratic Idea*, Chicago: Nelson-Hall.

Canadian Commission for UNESCO. 1998. *Report of the North American Preparatory Meeting For The1998 World Conference on Higher Education.* Ottawa, Canada: Canadian Commission for UNESCO.

Canadian Commission for UNESO. 1997. *Discussion Kit of the Fifth International Conference on Adult Education*, Hamburg. Ottawa, Canada: Canadian Commission for UNESCO.

Benner Cassara, Beverly. 1995. *Adult Education Through World Collaboration*, Malabar, Florida: Krieger Publishing Company.

Castles, Stephen and Alastair Davidson. 2000. *Citizenship and Migration, Globalization and the Politics of Belonging.* New York: Routledge.

Fox, Helen. 1994. *Listening to the World, Cultural Issues in Academic Writing.* Urbana, Illinois: National College of Teachers of English.

Hansome, Marius. 1968. *World Workers' Educational Movements, Their Social Significance.* New York: Ams Press.

Higgins, E. M. 1953. *David Stewart and the W.E.A.* Australia: Workers Educational Asociation of New South Wales.

Kelly, Thomas: 1970. *A History of Adult Education in Great Britain.* Liverpool University Press.

Kornbluh, Joyce. 1987 *A New Deal for Workers' Education, The Workers' Service Program 1933- 1942.* Urbana and Chicago. University of Illinois Press.

London, Steven H. Elvira R. Tarr. Joseph F. Wilson editors 1990. *The Re-education of the American Working Class.* New York, Westport, Connecticut, London: Greenwood Press.

Mann, Michael. 1986. *The Sources of Social Power, Volume 1, A history of power from the beginning to A.D. 1760.* London: Cambridge University Press.

Mann, Michael. 1993.*The Sources of Social Power, Volume 11, The rise of classes and nation states, 1760-1914.* London: Cambridge University Press.

Milner, Henry. 2002. *Civic Literacy: How Informed Citizens Make Democracy Work.* Hanover N.H.: University Press of New England.

Niemi, John. A. 1990. "Finland's Unique System of Adult Education" *Adult Learning.*

Nussbaum, Martha C. 1997. *Cultivating Humanity, a classical defense of reform in liberal education.* Cambridge Massachusetts: Harvard University Press.

Oliver, Leonard P. 1987. *Study Circles, Coming Together For Personal Growth and Social Change.* Washington DC: Seven Locks Press.

Radforth, Ian, Joan Sangster. 1987 "The Struggle for Autonomous Workers' Education: The Workers' Educational Association in Ontario, 1917-51 in *Knowledge for the People, The Struggle for Adult Learning in English-Speaking Canada, 1828-1973.* Edited by Michael Welton. Toronto: OISE Press.

Rose, Jonathan. 2001. *The Intellectual Life of the British Working Classes.* London: Yale University Press.

Shuker, Roy. 1984. *Educating the Workers? A History of the Workers' Educational Association of New Zealand.* Palmerston, North New Zealand: The Dunmore Press.

Stern Milton R. 1980. edited by Harold J. Alford "Universities in Continuing Education" in *Power and Conflict in Continuing Education Survival and Prosperity for all.* Belmont, California: The Wadsworth Series in Continuing Education. Wadsworth, Inc.

Schied, Fred M. 1995. *Learning in Social Context, Workers and Adult Education in Nineteenth Century* Chicago. DeKalb, Illinois: LEPs Press, Northeast Illinois University.

Shorris, Earl. 2000. *Riches for the Poor, The Clemente Course in the Humanities,* New York: W. W. Norton & Company.

Shorris, Earl. 1995. "In The Hands of the Restless Poor" *Harper's Magazine* (September 1997): 50-59.

Talbert, T. J. February, 1922. The Extension Workers' Code. *Extension Bulletin* No. 33. Kansas State Agriculture College Division of College Extension.

Taylor, Jeffery. 2001. *Union Learning, Canadian Labour Education in the Twentieth Century.* Toronto: Thompson Educational Publishing, Inc.

UNESCO. 1996. Learning: The Treasure Within, *Report to UNESCO of the International Commission on Education for the Twenty-first Century.* Paris: UNESCO.

Usher, Robin, Ian Bryant, Rennie Johnston. 1997. *Adult Education and the Post Modern Challenge: Learning Beyond the Limit.* London and New York: Routledge.

The Workers' Educational Association of Canada. 1986. *Challenge and Change,* Toronto: The WEA of Canada.

The Workers' Educational Association of Canada. August 1999. *The Education Exchange, Development Phase A Learning Cooperative Project.* Toronto: The WEA of Canada.

Web Sites

Bard College www.bard.edu/about
Clemente Course www.humanities.org\clemente
Massachusetts Foundation for the Humanities www.mfh.org
WEA U.K. www.wea.org.uk;
          www.ifwea.org

PART III: TRANSLATING FEMINIST, POST-COLONIAL AND POST-MODERN THOUGHT IN THE CONTEXT OF SOCIAL ACTIVISM

Chapter 5

ENHANCING PERSPECTIVE TRANSFORMATION THROUGH SERVICE-LEARNING STAFF

Sharon Murphy

ABSTRACT

This case study is an exploration of the enhancement of perspective transformation through a service-learning center, and more specifically, through the center's staff. Eyler and Giles describe *perspective transformation* as "seeing issues in a new way and a belief in the importance of using public policy to attain social justice" (1999, 171). The research questions examined in the study were: 1) Did *perspective transformation* play a role in the structuring of the service-learning center and its staff? 2) Are there organizational structures and training methods for staff to enhance students' perspective transformation? 3) What operating assumptions do service-learning staff follow for working with "the community"? As this study emerged from my polyvocality as researcher, activist, and employee of the center under study, I needed an approach that could support all of these vantage points. Thus, I attempted to blend some of the principles of hermeneutic participatory research and empowerment evaluation to construct methodological guidelines.

The findings of the study suggest opportunities for service-learning centers to further address the study's three research questions through increased planning and assessment. The study's recommendations challenge service-learning practitioners to enhance students' perspective transformation by identifying with them the barriers of oppression and injustice that negatively impact our communities. For those readers who believe that the transformation of oppressive perspectives and systems should be the goal of service-learning, it is my hope that this article will provide a framework and methodology that can be used to inspire and inform similar examinations.

INTRODUCTION

This case study is an exploration of the enhancement of perspective transformation through a service-learning center, and more specifically, through the center's staff. Eyler and

Giles describe *perspective transformation* as "seeing issues in a new way and a belief in the importance of using public policy to attain social justice" (1999, 171). The authors build upon Mezirow's theory of *transformational learning*, for "as educators our first commitment is to development of our students, and yet for many of us, social transformation is also central to our lives" (1999, 133). Such an emphasis for service-learning leaves behind feel-good measures whereby students visit local organizations simply to perform community service without critically reflecting on systemic injustices and how to transform them.

As the coordinator of a service-learning center, I embarked on this study because I wanted to inform our center's practices. I am deeply committed to seeking justice (social, economic, and environmental), and so I felt it was essential that we reflect upon and learn from our work with the community. I chose to question, along with the center's members, whether our efforts were focused on transforming oppressive perspectives and systems and to imagine what such efforts would look like.

FOSTERING A TRANSFORMATIVE LENS

I want to witness our and our students' development of transformative lenses: those ways of examining the world that keep us focused on transforming systems of injustice, rather than mere reforms within these systems. While there is no clear roadmap of how to proceed with such an undertaking, I provide the following synthesis of some authors' ideas in a way that gives us some guidelines.

A first step in fostering perspective transformation could be to have new experiences to shape new understandings. Hayes and Cuban (1997) borrow from Anzaldua's (1990) conceptualization of *borders* and *borderlands* and relate it to the process of service-learning. They explain that when their students serve in a community that is unfamiliar to them, the students develop new lenses. Hayes and Cuban state that service-learning helps students "see through both serpent and eagle eyes" (Anzaldua 1990, 378) through providing a wealth of opportunities for border crossings.

> These metaphors suggest how service-learning prompts students to understand their own culture in new ways, appreciate cultural differences, become more critically aware of social inequities and power relations, and envision a more democratic society (Hayes and Cuban 1997, 72).

However, I worry that if students "parachute" into unfamiliar territories with no guidance, they may not utilize their experience to form transformative lenses. For students to become effective agents of social transformation, Kissen (2001) suggests that students need help placing service-learning observations into theoretical contexts. In working with teacher education students, Kissen asked herself, "What tools can I give them to see the children in their service-learning placements as part of a system that disempowers women and children?" (2001, 17). While Kissen determined that her students ultimately did not attain the level of analysis for which she was hoping, she at least attempted to instill in students Manicom's assertion that "a feminist framework is a world view that takes as problematic the structural dependence of women on men" (Manicom 1984, 77). To help students build a framework for their service-learning observations, Kissen suggests starting with the students' experience as women.

> As Sandra Hollingsworth advises, mere exposure to feminist literature does not necessarily lead to action (1995). Like Hollingsworth, I must give my students more opportunity to examine their own history as women and more direct guidance in connecting feminist insights to their service learning placements. I want my students to look in the eyes of the children waiting in line for their evening meal at the soup kitchen and see themselves. But I also want them to ask why these children are hungry in a land and a city of plenty, and to think about what would need to happen in order to change that reality (Kissen 2001, 18).

What does need to happen in order for us to change the realities we witness? Hayes and Cuban (1997) seek social transformation through service-learning approaches which focus on the shifting of whole classes of people, rather than shifting individuals from one class to another.

> From one perspective, we might see our efforts to support college students in community service as a means of social change. However, from a more critical perspective (one that we share), traditional literacy programs do not really challenge the social structures that create and maintain societal inequities, but instead only enable a few of the already less marginalized population to make small advances within the existing system. Our students' stories suggest how they have disrupted power relationships within the literacy programs, albeit in minor ways. We hope that they will be able to do so in more significant ways in their future community work (1997, 79).

Similarly, Heaney (1996) describes his vision for education as a space to organize the shifting of whole classes, not merely as a place which provides individuals access to a higher socioeconomic status.

> Social change aims at a shift in the relative position of classes, not in the position of individuals within one or another class. Social change is not what happens when the offspring of a working class family joins the newly emerging professional classes. It is what occurs when workers, women, or other oppressed groups organize to overcome the hegemony of professional educators or bureaucrats and reclaim control over their own lives (1996, 44-5).

Working "With the Community"

What does it mean for faculty and students to work "with the community?" Are service-learners truly working *with* the community, or simply *in* it? Is their work transformative or a further reinforcement of existing power dynamics? While service-learning generally transpires in the surrounding communities of colleges and universities, such learning is not necessarily transformative. Hayes and Cuban (1997) describe some of the potentially problematic aspects of service-learning.

> Indeed, the concept and practice of service-learning has been criticized as a project that simply reinforces power relationships between those who 'help' and those who are

'helped.' But we ask ourselves if these clearly small challenges to the status quo are truly meaningful and impactful. Should we be engaging our students- and ourselves- in more radical action? What forms should such action take (1997, 79)?

Should practitioners define working with "the community" as working with a governmental or non-governmental organization, it seems that some community sectors may be marginalized. For instance, there are thousands, possibly millions of people who are not linked to any organization, church, school, or other institution (Arguelles 2000). Many of these people exist in *third spaces*, such as the homeless with no transitional housing program, the unemployed with no job training and placement program, the undocumented residents with no local advocacy organization. Additionally, even those organizations that serve traditionally marginalized groups may marginalize certain clients within the organization, typically along dominant forces related to race, class, gender, sexuality, ability, language acquisition, and others.

Another problem with defining working with *community* as working with an organization is that many organizations merely provide social services. While social services might sorely be needed in communities, as Darder (1991) observes, simply attempting to fulfill needs generally does not shift our society toward transforming the systemic injustices which damage our communities and their members. Therefore, while we will always need social services, critical analyses and voices expose the problems created by unjust institutions. Rather than simply seeking ways to help people in a broken, unjust society, service-learning practitioners and students also could focus attention on ways to transform systemic problems.

As the person who has been designated by some postsecondary institutions to guide their service-learning, I have faced many challenging questions regarding the geographical boundaries for working with the community. Can "the community" include regions outside of the university's community as well as on-campus groups? I have led or witnessed successful projects that have been conducted in partnership with on-campus groups and with organizations in other countries. What seems most important is the ultimate objective: are we doing this work to transform oppressive perspectives and systems, or to further reinforce them? Are we exonerating governments from their financial responsibility to serve the people, do our students displace local workers, or are we guilty of the involuntary servitude of our students? Does our work build the capacity of local groups or create dependent relationships? Do all the partners involved benefit? These are cautionary questions that I hope other practitioners consider when working with communities, however community is defined.

METHODOLOGICAL GUIDELINES

As the coordinator for a service-learning center of a private, liberal arts college in Southern California, I conducted a case study to examine the enhancement of perspective transformation through our service-learning center, and more specifically, through our service-learning staff. I designed a participatory evaluation of our Urban Fellowships. The Urban Fellows are staff members who are central to the center's operations. While the Faculty Director and I operate in supervisory roles, Urban Fellows work in the field as critical, direct links to a limited number of community projects and partnerships to guide and shape the college's service-learning. As graduates of the college, these Urban Fellows exemplify the outcomes of this college's education. One to two Urban Fellows are hired every six months for a year-long period.

The research questions examined in the study were: 1) Did *perspective transformation* play a role in the structuring of the service-learning center and its staff? 2) Are there organizational structures and training methods for staff to enhance students' perspective transformation? 3) What operating assumptions do service-learning staff follow for working with "the community"?

RESEARCH APPROACH

As this study emerged from my polyvocality as researcher, activist, and employee of the center under study, I needed an approach that could support all of these vantage points. Thus, I attempted to blend some of the principles of hermeneutic participatory research and empowerment evaluation to construct methodological guidelines. While I do not pretend to fulfill all of the tenets of these approaches, both proved useful in constructing a philosophical grounding for the study's research methodology.

Fetterman's (1996) explanation of *empowerment evaluation,* whereby the evaluation process is an empowering one, grounded my intent for the study to be an empowering process for the center's members. Such methodological guidelines alleviated concerns of objectivity and placed empowering concepts such as self-determination and understanding as the driving forces of the study. Similarly, in the tradition of *hermeneutic participatory research*, I designed an exploratory process whereby I developed a set of guidelines to provide focus for the study without being overly proscriptive. As suggested by Herda (1999) in her description of hermeneutic participatory research, I opened myself to the thoughts and stories of the research participants to consider new alternatives. I tried not to artificially impose a research tool or much structure to the interviews and focus group while we reflected together through dialogue. Through conducting the inquiry, I underwent a process of self-reflection which in turn led to the generation of recommendations.

While it may be difficult for practitioners of traditional research methods to accept findings resulting from such unorthodox methods, hermeneutic participatory research is subject to no more inappropriate biases than traditional methods. Hermeneutic participatory researchers attempt to be open and honest about their biases rather than attempting to control them, not acknowledging them, or being unaware of them altogether.

> The researcher who approaches a research problem within a critical hermeneutic tradition is no less immune to inappropriate biases and negative prejudices than the researcher who carries out more traditional kinds of research.... In critical hermeneutic research, our attempt is to bring biases out into the open, not to technically reduce or control them. The ahistorical and apolitical stance, which is assumed in the logical empirical and analytical traditions by virtue of the research mode, changes the nature of the data so that biases are hidden. However, all researchers come to the research field with much to place at risk and with a responsibility to be as clear as possible to see what they and others hold as true, right, and just (Herda 1999, 90-91).

PROCEDURE AND GUIDELINES

First, I conducted a thematic[1] analysis of all of the founding documents for the service-learning center to identify the founders' objectives for the Urban Fellowships. Once I created a list of objectives, I asked the center's founders to review the list and provide any revisions. As no revisions were submitted, the list of objectives remained unchanged and was formatted into a one-page prompt to be used in conducting a focus group and in collecting five narratives.

Second, I conducted a focus group with center staff, including three Urban Fellows and the Faculty Director. The Faculty Director was a White male psychology professor in his late forties. Two of the Urban Fellows were White females, one in her early forties who worked with our K-12 projects and one in her early twenties who worked with our youth and immigrant projects. The Urban Fellow in her twenties was the only staff member who was fluent in a second language (Spanish). One Urban Fellow was a Latino male in his late thirties who worked with our projects on homelessness.

Next, I collected narratives with five individuals who had worked with the staff and had been nominated to participate by the Urban Fellows. While none of the participants were asked to disclose his/her demographic information, I made the following presumptions of the participants. Two of the participants were White, female students, and a third was a Black, female student, all of whom were traditional age students who served a summer internship with the service-learning center. A fourth participant was a White, female Urban Fellow in her early forties who requested to further the discussion started in the focus group, and a fifth participant was a Black, community member who worked with one of our Urban Fellows and a few of our service-learning students. I provide these presumed identities to lend some context to the participants' comments, for in the United States, identities play a major role in the formation of perspectives and assumptions.

Figure 1 provides an overview of the research process followed in this study.

OVERVIEW: THE CENTER'S CONTEXT
FOR PERSPECTIVE TRANSFORMATION

While none of the center's founding documents used the term *perspective transformation*, the data suggested that certain aspects of the documents may have contributed to the creation of an environment where students' perspective transformation could be enhanced. The documents portrayed a perspective that the college had a long history of supporting "experiential learning," "field-based education" and "service-learning." The creation of a center was viewed as a natural extension of the college's existing commitment to "social responsibility" and a way to centralize what previously had been individual pursuits.

> Social responsibility, fused with interdisciplinary and intercultural learning, has come to be viewed as a distinguishing feature of a (the college) education. Faculty have been encouraged to experiment with service-learning courses and to develop projects that are

[1] To distinguish *thematic* from *content* analysis, I sought meaning in the text by considering a variety of ways to answer the research questions.

at the cutting edge in higher education (Report of the Social Responsibility Task Force 1998, 1-2).

(The college's) aim is to invigorate the study of the liberal arts, which have lost relevance for many students, by strengthening its relation to civic responsibility. (The college) has always related liberal arts education to responsible action in society (grant application 1998, 1).

The (service-learning center) is the structure through which (the college) will support these community-based research efforts, build new research out of our internship and field-based courses, provide the infrastructure that will sustain our innovative programs, and allow for assessment of these programs well into the next century (grant application 1998, 2).

The following list presents objectives for the Urban Fellowships that I identified from my analysis of the center's founding documents.

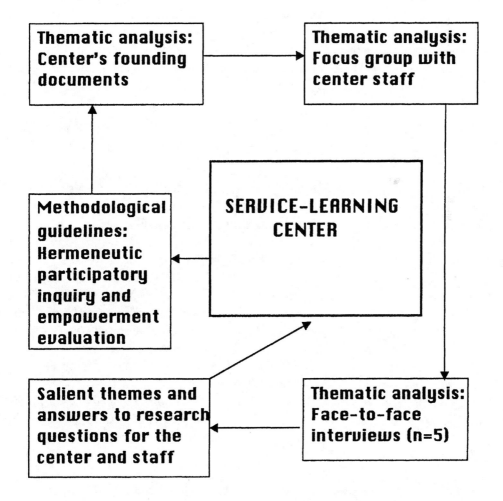

Figure 1. Process for examining perspective transformation through service-learning staff: The Urban Fellowships

The Objectives Identified for Urban Fellowships

1   To assist in the oversight and support of awardees, projects, and community partnerships
2   To assist with the administrative, clerical, and coordination duties related to the Center's activities, such as staff meetings, workshops, and events
3   To gather and disseminate longitudinal research data measuring the impact of community-based education on student learning and on our community
4   To continue to pursue (the college's) educational objectives
5   To provide a flexible structure both on and off campus to strengthen and support the College's social responsibility projects
6   To propose new projects for which the Urban Fellow would then be responsible for implementing
7   To provide assistance to faculty in dealing with liability release forms, contracts, insurance, and other technical matters for students' work with community groups
8   To assist in the recruitment of faculty and student award applicants
9   To work with the Faculty Director to form and maintain relationships with community organizations
10 To participate in workshops and conferences on behalf of the College and the Center
11 To build on the knowledge base of interested faculty in particular issues (e.g. homelessness).

STAFF NEEDS

After presenting participants with the objectives I identified from the Center's founding documents, recurring comments arose where participants articulated what staff needed to strengthen their performance. Much confusion surfaced as to staff's role and duties, and requests for better training and feedback regarding their role and performance were voiced. Older, White, female Urban Fellow: *I think what's apparent in everything we've said is that we as Urban Fellows need more training on our role and on the possibilities in how far we can go, where are our boundaries.... Something else that's related to training and jobs and roles is feedback. Where I come from in public education as a principal, I would try to give regular feedback informally to people I worked with, but and also there was built in regular feedback. I don't think we have these systems. I think in terms of personal growth for ourselves, it's a good idea to have that feedback.* Younger, White, female Urban Fellow: *I think I feel the same way too. I've kind of asked for that before, in relation to a lot of the problems I had during the summer. For someone coming right out of college where I don't have any managerial experience, they call me a 'micromanager'. I didn't know if I was doing it right, I think my personality really is the problem, or is it a real structural problem, or what, stuff like that. There is still a lot of emphasis on concrete problems, but not a lot of personal feedback.*

A student participant discussed the importance of examining the relevant ethical issues with staff while working on community projects. *White, female student: In general I think there should be a lot more focus on ethical issues. I don't know, like the students are very young and they don't always foresee the ethical concerns and then get caught up in them and don't know what to do about it. So I think, if the Urban Fellows, and not just waited for the students to come and bring like ethical issues to them and are in constant dialogue about what ethical concerns might come up. I think that that should be emphasized a lot more than it probably is because I think they really need students our age for people to talk about ethical concerns of working in the community.* This same student provided an example of the tension students may endure as mentor and friend to community members. Due to her service-learning experience at a juvenile detention facility, she believes many students would not know how to properly handle difficult situations without first teaching them how. *Maybe do some research on ethical concerns in general. First of all, give them like, you know, talk to them about it. And then maybe say if there were—say I was linked with your research what kind of concerns might come up. Like what if one of your kids tells you that they're going to AWOL. What do you do? Someone my age, the whole thing, couldn't figure out what to do. Maybe like, I mean, like on the one hand you're supposed to be like their mentor and friend and you want them to trust you. Here they are trusting you, coming in to tell you that they're going to AWOL. You don't want to betray their trust but you know it's a bad thing for them to AWOL so you feel like you should say something to their staff, so you know there's just— like what do you do? You know, I mean they should—maybe—I think a lot of times they don't go to others to talk about it. A lot of times they're just kind of always like, well, whatever, it will be okay, you know.*

There was also some discussion as to why certain staff members were successful. The race and experience of a staff member were identified by one participant as playing a particularly important role. Black, community member: *Of course you know, being a former homeless himself, he already has a sensitivity to the issue that most of the people that he's come across in the homelessness community have never been homeless. The advocates and activists provide the homeless community—most of those people, I would say 95% of them, 98% have never been homeless before. Whereas, he has—he has a deeper sensitivity; therefore, he soaks up the knowledge of it a lot quicker, and for poignancy significantly to those who have not been homeless, but have done it mainly from the textbook experience and across the desk at an office. To be a former cholo gangster and all that kind of stuff, obviously he's gone through a real life transforming...experience. What's double about this is that he is Latino, Mexican and Chicano—he's been through all of that and he's survived this and you don't get that. But being Latino, there's not many Latino leaders in the homeless movement....*

COMMUNITY

Little evidence emerged that the community played a role in assessing our service-learning. Explicit language was identified that service-learning staff members were to be "knowledgeable, community-based researchers who would inform educational practices" (grant application 1998, 2), but this did not appear to translate into any efforts to incorporate community voices to inform our service-learning. While the staff could have played a role in facilitating such assessment, data from the focus group and narratives suggested confusion over the staff's role.

What does the term *community* mean to members of the College? While I never asked the question directly nor did I hear any direct explanations, data clearly supported the notion that working with *the community* was considered equivalent to working with community organizations. Students and faculty identified a governmental or non-governmental organization with which they wanted to work, and they simply either served there or created a new project with the organization.

While it seems understandable that the service-learning center's members would want to connect with community organizations, we run the risk of ignoring those individuals existing in the *third spaces* that Arguelles (2000) describes. Unfortunately, when staff, faculty, and students equated working with "the community" to working with an organization, community members who were not part of an organization or who were otherwise marginalized might have been excluded from the college's service-learning. For example, there are those in our community that literally do not have a voice, such as animals and our ecological environment. Additionally, there were no organizations specifically for queer persons or Asian Americans in the local area of this study. With no discourse on what it means to work with *the community* other than *community* as equal to *community organizations*, what happens with those who reside and/or work near the College who are not community leaders, members of local organizations, or clients of social service providers? Most likely, these community voices went unheard.

RECOMMENDATIONS

For *perspective transformation* to play a forceful role in undergirding service-learning practice, center leadership should incorporate its principles into the selection criteria for staff, into their job descriptions, and into the preparation of staff. The Faculty Director and I assumed that with the Fellows' experience, they would be able to "hit the ground running," but in fact, with no concrete objectives available on which to evaluate them, the Urban Fellows were left to follow their own priorities for service-learning.

Taking care to select staff who can provide and guide students' "border crossing" experiences seems to be a particularly relevant criterion. Staff members who bring a diversity of identities and a wealth of experience in working with communities with which many students are not familiar could supplement instruction from lived feminist, critical, and postmodern perspectives. Staff could assist students with placing their service – learning experiences within theoretical contexts and with shaping students' transformative frameworks for working with communities.

Staff members also need a forum designed specifically for and by them, where they can reflect upon and inform each other's practice through readings and dialogue while periodically engaging in empowering evaluation of their work. While much attention has been placed on training and guiding our faculty and students, staff do not have a similar forum of their own. We did hold weekly staff meetings, but the participants' comments suggest that more time was needed to discuss complications and provide feedback. Together, staff could identify some of the salient themes from students' reflection papers as launching places for discussion of strategies and ethical concerns, hopefully advancing our own perspective transformations. Staff also could play a role in facilitating the community's assessment of service-learning. Staff could explore ways for a greater variety of community members to assess and inform service-learning, possibly conducting and facilitating *third space* research.

To clarify to staff the project goals and the nature and duration of commitment, I recommend that contracts are created for the student, faculty member, and community member which spell out what is to be accomplished over the course of the project. Such an agreement will allow the members of the contract to hold one another accountable and for staff to identify ways that they can support projects. Contracts also should contain a description of the nature of the community relationship and methods to assess the work of the project members. During the course of the project and most important, at its termination, the members of the contract should review the merits of the relationship and the work of the project. Contracts could serve as launching places for discussions of whether or not projects are posited within a framework for social justice to foster perspective transformation.

Further research is suggested to examine if simply working with social service organizations limits student perspective transformation. Service experiences, whereby students work with social service organizations without critically reflecting on systemic injustices and how to transform them, might not stimulate perspective transformation. Informing faculty, staff and students of the importance of transformative work and coordinating transformative service-learning opportunities is challenging but not impossible.

This study was intended as a mere first step in an examination of a service-learning center and its staff, their enhancement of perspective transformation, and their operating assumptions of what constitutes working with the community. The findings of the study suggest opportunities for service-learning centers to further address the study's three research questions through increased planning and assessment. The study's recommendations challenge service-learning practitioners to enhance students' perspective transformation by identifying with them the barriers of oppression and injustice that negatively impact our communities.

Unfortunately, as is too often the case in grant funded initiatives, the continuation of this particular examination process at the center under study could not be sustained. Undoubtedly, there were tensions raised by attempting to position the transformation of oppressive perspectives and systems as the focal point of the service-learning center. A few of the college's administrators did not agree with such an emphasis, as it challenged us to leave behind feel-good measures and raised uncomfortable questions as to how we and our institutions contribute to the oppression we say we are working against. However, the alternative is teaching students that feeling good about their work with communities is good enough. For those readers who believe that the transformation of oppressive perspectives and systems should be the goal of service-learning, it is my hope that this article will provide a framework and methodology that can be used to inspire and inform similar examinations.

REFERENCES

Anzaldua, Gloria. 1990. "La Conciencia de la Mestiza: Towards a New Consciousness." In *Making Face, Making Soul=Haciendo Caras: Creative and Critical Perspectives by Women of Color*, edited by Gloria Anzaldua. San Francisco: Aunt Lute Foundation Books.

Arguelles, Lourdes. 2000. "L.A. in Action." Panel presentation at the Conference on "The Power and Promise of Collaboration," The Executive and Extended Learning, Claremont Graduate University, Claremont, CA, March 20-21.

Darder, Antonia. 1991. *Culture and Power in the Classroom: A Critical Foundation for Bicultural Education*. Westport, CT: Bergin and Garvey.

Eyler, Janet and Dwight Giles. 1999. *Where's the Learning in Service-Learning?* San Francisco: Jossey-Bass Publishers.

Fetterman, David. 1996. "Empowerment Evaluation: An Introduction to Theory and Practice." In *Empowerment Evaluation: Knowledge and Tools for Self-Assessment & Accountability*, edited by David Fetterman, Shakeh Kaftarian, and Abraham Wandersman. Thousand Oaks, CA: Sage Publications.

Hayes, Elisabeth and Sondra Cuban. 1997. "Border pedagogy: A critical framework for service-learning." *Michigan Journal of Community Service Learning* (Fall): 72-80.

Heaney, Thomas. 1996. *Adult Education for Social Change: From Center Stage to the Wings and Back Again*. Washington, D.C.: Office of Educational Research and Improvement (ERIC Document Reproduction Service No. ED 396 190).

Herda, Ellen. 1999. *Research Conversations and Narrative: A Critical Hermeneutic Orientation in Participatory Inquiry*. Westport, CT: Praeger.

Kissen, Rita. 2001. "After the Soup: A Feminist Approach to Service Learning." Paper presented at the conference on "What We Know and How We Know It," American Educational Research Association, Seattle, WA, April 10-14.

Manicom, Ann. 1984. "Feminist Frameworks and Teacher Education." *Journal of Education* 166(1): 77-88.

Chapter 6

EDUCATION FOR SOCIAL CHANGE BETWEEN FEMINIST AND POST-COLONIAL THEORIES

Dawn M. Haney[*]

ABSTRACT

Is community development education a less oppressive way to educate people and conduct research? While many of us are drawn to community development education and research as a way to eliminate oppression, we risk ignoring the long and continuing history of oppression by characterizing our work as "truly" participatory. Particularly when white researchers and educators from the United States, Canada, Australia, or Western Europe decide to work in partnership with poor women of color in less developed nations in Latin America, Asia, and Africa, community development education, if left unexamined, risks repeating colonial relations. I use my experience in planning but choosing not to implement a participatory project with third world women to explore how easy it is to slip into colonial relations, even with the best of intentions. I draw on post-colonial feminist theorists to critique my work and develop a more cautious and complex version of community development education that constantly critiques itself to root out oppressive relationships between educators and participants.

INTRODUCTION

Community development education – does it always have the best interests of the community in mind? While others and I are drawn to community development education and participatory methods as being more ethical and less oppressive forms of research and education, some postcolonial feminist scholars are concerned that seeking "true partnerships" (as suggested in *Principles of Community Engagement*, CDC, 1997) may simply work to ignore the impact of past oppressive relationships. Particularly when white researchers and

[*] Corresponding Author: Dawn M. Haney, BS, Department of Health Promotion and Behavior, University of Georgia, 300 River Road, Athens, GA 30602. Office: 706-542-3313 Fax: 706-542-4956 Email: haneydaw@uga.edu

educators from the United States, Canada, Australia, or Western Europe decide to work in partnership with poor women of color in less developed nations in Latin America, Asia, and Africa, community development education, if left unexamined, risks repeating colonial relations. Many of my fellow white Western educators and researchers are seeking to break down colonial relationships, which is why we are drawn to community development education in the first place. While I salute our efforts, I believe that community development educators must not settle for "simple solutions" (like true partnership, improved communication, or balanced power) "to difficult problems" of working in postcolonial societies (Scott, 1988/2001, p. 257). More difficult solutions accept that "true" partnerships, "transparent" communication, or "equal" power relations will never be achieved, and to describe our projects in these terms 'white' washes a more complex reality. Rather than give up on community development education, postcolonial feminists seek a more cautious and complex version of community development education that constantly critiques itself to root out oppressive relationships between educators and participants.

Community-based and participatory methods of education and research have been promoted as "democratic and egalitarian" (Dickinson, 1999, p. 42), "reducing inequities" (Travers, 1997, p. 344), and "ensur[ing] that research and programs are relevant, meaningful, and culturally appropriate" (Sullivan et al., 2001, p. 131). These methods are action-oriented and participant-centered, particularly in comparison to traditional forms of research and education that are truth-oriented and centered on the ideas of expert researchers and educators (Reinharz, 1992; Travers, 1997; Wallerstein, 1999). Freire's (1970) literacy education, where illiterate adults in Brazil became empowered to enact social change through self-led learning groups focused on their issues of poverty and hunger, has been held up as an exemplar of community-based education (see Dickinson, 1999; Travers, 1997). The focus in community development research and education is often on community participation and relevance, empowerment, critical consciousness, and action to solve problems (Minkler & Wallerstein, 1997).

While participatory approaches to education and research do a much better job of including participants in the knowledge production process, these approaches are not a perfect solution. For instance, Sullivan and others (2001) report on the views of community participants and project staff in community-based research projects in Seattle, Washington. They comment that, "community-based research is often based on stereotypes of communities, may further stigmatize communities of color, and is often problem focused. Furthermore, people said that although institutions often purport to collaborate with the community, many power imbalances interfere with partnering on an equal basis" (Sullivan et al., 2001, p. 134). Although many projects are called "community-based" or "community development," even these projects often do not succeed in including participants in the knowledge production process.

Additionally, post-colonial theorists are suspicious of participatory approaches, particularly those brought into less developed areas by researchers and educators from more privileged areas such as the United States and other Western nations. Their primary concern is that labeling a strategy as "participatory" may simply mask unequal power relations between researchers and participants (Mohanty, 1991; Spivak, 1999). For instance, Spivak continues to be suspicious of the seemingly participatory microlending schemes (where people in developing countries obtain small, short-term loans to start small businesses), calling them "credit baiting" (Spivak, 1999, p. 223). Although she does not expand on her views on credit baiting, I see microlending as potentially problematic as it leaves unquestioned the capitalist framework and the benefits accrued by the first world if third world women buy into this system.

One benefit first world researchers and educators might gain from a community development project in the third world is feeling like they can be non-oppressive. Speaking of ethnographers, but applicable to community developers, the "celebration of collaboration as superior to the objectivity and 'speaking for' that prevailed in traditional accounts seems driven by a similar utopian dream of escaping exploitation" (Mascia-Lees & Sharpe, 2000, p. 50). Yet Mascia-Lees and Sharpe pessimistically (but in my opinion correctly) suggest that even the best anti-oppression intentions will not undo years of colonial exploitation. This strategy can allow community developers to feel like they are doing something about oppression, but leaves the continued impact of these postcolonial relationships unexamined.

Can participatory approaches appropriately be used in cross-cultural research and practice? They seem to be the most promising strategies for breaking down colonial relationships, yet they are not innocent approaches either. In this chapter, I focus on the potential problems with community development projects originating in first world contexts, aimed at third world women's development. I use the term third world women as a category within Western frameworks that describes the supposedly common experiences of women from less developed countries in Africa, Asia, and Latin America, while first world marks the supposedly common experiences of people in the United States, Canada, Australia, and Western Europe. Two assumptions are embedded in this distinction: 1) women from less developed countries in Africa, Asia, and Latin America have common experiences; and 2) these experiences are wholly different than the experiences of women in the United States, Canada, Australia, and Western Europe and different from men in their own countries. These terms are of course problematic as they lump together highly disparate experiences, usually ignoring the experiences of women of color and working classes in the first world and the experiences of privileged women in the third world. This third world/first world couplet also often assumes a hierarchy of development where first world is better than third world. Despite the problems with the assumptions necessary to name third world women as a category of people, I retain the term as a marker of how first world community developers often view these women.

Many of these approaches also could be useful in any project (not just cross-cultural ones) where it is important to break down power differentials between project members: teacher/students, researcher/researched, or community educator/ participants. However, the strategies noted here are guidance for the traditionally powerful person in the binary – the teacher, the researcher, the community educator, the first world. This is partly a reflection of me, the writer. As a White woman from the United States, my own concerns in my work inform the writing of this chapter. This chapter reflects my privileges (including time to write and academic rewards for publishing), as well as my attempts to deflect some of that privilege by publicly acknowledging and learning from some of my inadequacies. I continue to ask myself, and I invite you to critique: How might it look very different to have a "colonized" person rather than a colonizer write this chapter? Although I have drawn from theorists who identify with colonized people, their ideas are still filtered through my mind. Although I believe that I have something to say about first world women working with third world women, it is crucial to remember that my position in the world affects what can be written here. Acknowledging this bias is part of my process of breaking down colonial privileges.

THEORIZING WORK WITH THIRD WORLD WOMEN

How can first world people do community development work around the world in ways that do not reinscribe colonial relationships? When working with third world women, it seems that both post-colonial and feminist approaches should be utilized (Parpart, 1993). Feminist approaches bring an analysis of gender relations, but often focus too exclusively on the experiences of white women in first world. Post-colonial approaches analyze the continuing colonial relationships that continue to shape the lives of previously colonized countries. Yet these approaches focus on the political relationships that are primarily between men. Can we reconcile these theories to understand the experiences of third world women and produce meaningful education that is culturally relevant? I look at both feminist and post-colonial thought separately, and assess the use of postcolonial feminism in working with third world women.

Feminism

Feminist thought is varied; it is not possible to pin down one definition of feminist thought. Tong (1998) describes no less than eight different traditions of feminist thought, each with its own focus and contentions with other traditions. Basic definitions that most feminists would agree with might include feminism as "intellectual and political commitments to women" (Tong, 1998, p. 1) or the recognition that "women suffer discrimination because of their sex, that they have specific needs which remain negated and unsatisfied, and that the satisfaction of these needs would require a radical change" (Delmar, 1986/2001, p. 5). Feminists disagree broadly over what commitments to women should be made, how women suffer discrimination, and especially how radical change should come about.

Major movements of feminism in the United States include liberal, radical, and gender movements of feminism. These movements describe women's oppression as stemming from women's legal rights, women's biology, and women's social roles (Tong, 1998). They focus on women's sexuality and reproduction, bringing to the forefront issues such as abortion, mothering and child care, sexual assault, and birthing politics. These feminisms often posit gender as a primary oppression, with race, class, or sexuality being secondary, and have been critiqued by multicultural feminists in the United States for primarily focusing on the needs of white, middle class, heterosexual women (Collins, 1990).

Global feminism calls for feminists to make intellectual and political commitments to women worldwide, not just women within their local communities (Tong, 1998). This form of feminism has caused U.S. feminists to consider the oppression of women internationally, but especially within developing or third world countries, also called the Global South. In this view, exploitation of the South by the North for natural resources and cheap labor drives the oppression of women living in the South. Efforts to emancipate women must consider the effects of multi-national business and U.S. foreign policy on women's lives in the South. Global feminists have critiqued U.S. feminists from liberal, radical, and gender paradigms for seeing only sexual oppression (such as female genital mutilation or dowry abuse) and ignoring the United States' role in oppressing women in the South.

The very name "global feminism" is located within traditions of U.S. feminism. To a feminist from Uganda, Thailand, or Chile, this form of feminism is decidedly local. Other scholars have termed this form of feminism "Third World feminism" to locate the feminism in the particular places of Africa, Asia, Latin America, the Caribbean, and Oceania (Mohanty 1991). Others have used "post-colonial feminism" to name the colonizing relationships (both the past political relationships and current economic relationships) as the source of oppression (Rosser, 2000). This last form draws from the tradition of post-colonial thought, which I argue has some conflict with even global feminism situated within the United States.

Post-Colonialism

Like feminism, post-colonial thought is not all of one cloth. Even the seemingly simple question, "What is post-colonialism?" is critiqued for being too enmeshed in the Western humanist discourse that is more interested in meaning that function (Bové, 1990; Childs & Williams, 1997). Childs and Williams (1997) have privileged questions of when, where, and who over what in their *An introduction to post-colonial theory*. The word "post-colonial" may most simply be read as that which comes after the end of colonial relationships between European powers such as Britain and France, and Asian and African countries such as India and Nigeria.

Rather than reading the "post" in post-colonialism temporally, as after colonialism or after independence, many post-colonial thinkers view post-colonial as those relationships that continue between colonizers and colonized even after political colonization has ended (Ashcroft, Griffiths, & Tiffin, 1995). This focus on continued imperialistic relationships makes post-colonial scholars suspicious of any work developed in the first world to "help" the third world. Post-colonial scholars refuse to easily swallow the idea that some policies are offered as "pure assistance" when it is clear that so many policies are enacted to further entrench colonial relationships. They ask questions like "How does the U.S. (or other imperial power) benefit from the policy?" rather than be content with whatever assistance seems to be offered. Post-colonial studies developed out of literary and cultural studies, but provides a serious critique of community development education for the third world.

AN APPLICATION OF POST-COLONIAL FEMINISM

Global feminism and post-colonialism share some goals, but have conflicted over language and methods of how to reach those goals. Both feminism and post-colonialism want to "reinstate the marginalized in the face of the dominant" (Ashcroft, Griffiths, & Tiffin, 1995, p. 249). The politics of oppression operate within both fields, and an understanding of those politics is used in resistance. Rather than swapping the positions of the marginalized and the dominant, both feminism and post-colonialism are interested in questioning how oppression works and deconstructing the unearned position of the dominant (Ashcroft, Griffiths, & Tiffin, 1995). Drawing on experiences of oppression, feminism and post-colonialism share goals of dismantling systems of dominance.

Yet it can be dangerous to equate feminism and post-colonialism because they both map responses to oppression. They each privilege one way of knowing over others. Neither privileges the experiences of third world women. Like Black feminists have done in the United States (Collins, 2000), post-colonial feminist theory must start from the experiences of third world women. I have drawn primarily from third world and post-colonial feminists such as Gayatri Spivak (1994; 1999), Chandra Talpade Mohanty (1991), and Trinh Minh-Ha (1989) to explore concerns about first world educators working with third world women. They are concerned about authenticity of the subject, the role of voice, the role of power and the possibility for agency. I explore each of these concerns as I faced them in planning a collaborative research project on third world women's health, and end with suggestions for moving forward.

Project Introduction

With grant money from my College of Education's Multicultural Task Force, I began work to develop a web-based, multimedia curriculum for undergraduate health students to learn about women's health issues in developing countries. In the curriculum, I wanted students to think about how health is affected by economics, gender relations, and government policy, and that Western ideas may not always be appropriate for third world countries. To develop this curriculum, I planned to talk with matched pairs of participants: a health professional who worked in a developing country and one of their female clients. I wanted the health professional to describe the health problems they had worked on and possible solutions that took into account the context of the health problem. I also asked specifically for examples of how Western assumptions made their work more challenging.

I had also planned to talk to women dealing with health problems to get their first hand perspective on their health issues and the solutions that Western health professionals had brought. I wanted to audiotape these women, and include their stories in this web-based curriculum to let their voices be heard. I wanted to hear first-hand from women who had experienced genital mutilation, given birth with the help of a midwife, sought contraception information from health educators, and lived with HIV. These were women not usually discussed, much less allowed to be heard (through multimedia web audio) in a university health course in the United States. Their voices could offer a unique perspective that could not be covered by the health professionals alone. As explored through this chapter, I have come to see many of these goals as problematic, more likely to reinscribe colonial relationships than to dissolve them. As I worked through this process, my decision was to refrain from conducting the interviews with third world women, but this may not have been the best solution.

Naming the Subject/Inscribing the Subject

I began this project wanting to understand "third world women." By starting with third world women, I started with seemingly a set of individuals who share some commonalities, a common identity. I had given these multiple subjects a name: "third world women." This common name allowed me, as it has other feminists, to talk about experiences common to many women living in the third world but foreign to most women in the United States and throughout the first world. Feminists in the United States often focus on topics such as female genital mutilation/female circumcision, abortion, or sex trafficking (c.f. articles in *Ms Magazine* by Bakke, 2001; Galang, 2000; Otis, 2001; Rogers, 1999; and Rozen, 2001; as well as the film *Warrior Marks* by Walker & Pratibhua, 1993). In my project, I wanted to hear first-hand from women who had experienced genital mutilation, given birth with the help of a midwife, sought contraception information from health educators, and lived with HIV. Global feminists argue that feminists place too much focus on the sexual, ignoring the political and economic implications of global capitalism. Nawal el Saadawi noted, "Western women often go to countries such as the Sudan and 'see' only clitoridectomy, but never notice the role of multinational corporations and their exploited labor" (Gilliam, 1991, p. 218). Third world women's problems are not defined by third world women themselves, but are the product of first world feminists viewing the third world through their myopic lens of sexual difference.

Global feminists also question the use of the term "third world women" as being based in a false dichotomy that implies third world countries should aspire to be more like first world countries. Likewise terms like non-Western, non-industrialized, developing, and less developed define these countries entirely in terms of first world or Western expectations. The Two-Thirds World or Majority World turn the relationship around and assert the power of the majority of people who are labeled as third world. The Global South is a newer term created to geographically describe the countries often included as third world, using a term not based in economic comparisons. These terms are newly emerging, and have not yet become as widely used as third world or developing countries. I encourage readers unfamiliar with these terms to begin using them in their conversations about the "third world."

Although there is considerable criticism of the term "third world women," I retain the term for political reasons. Part of the purpose of this chapter is to draw readers (perhaps like you) who are comfortable thinking, "I work with third world women," and encouraging these readers to reflect on this practice. For those readers who are committed to using other terms that more accurately and less patronizingly describe the people included within the term "third world women," I support that practice but have chosen not to use it here. I continue to use the problematic term third world women as a marker for how (first world) feminists and people in the United States often think about poor women of color in Africa, Asia, and South America.

While global feminists maintain that naming this group of women as "third world" has powerful political implications, post-colonial feminists are still leery of even this move, resisting the naming at all regardless of the meaning attached. While global feminists see naming "third world women" as a strategy for mobilization, post-colonial feminists see naming as privileging their commonalities over their differences. As this group identity is used, people within this group are further entrenched in the colonial relationships they are trying to resist. By claiming the name of a marginal position, they further inscribe their position. One implication is that third world women are now constrained to speak *only* from the position of "third world woman." To speak at all, they must present themselves as "authentic" members of this group, meaning they must fit into the stereotypes expected of them by the first world listeners.

We begin to expect that third world women will act in certain ways that fit with our expectations of them (those expectations again that come from *our own first world needs*). We expect that the third world woman "leads an essentially truncated life based on her feminine gender (read: sexually constrained) and her being 'third world' (read: ignorant, poor, uneducated, tradition-bound, domestic, family-oriented, victimized, etc.)" (Mohanty, 1991, p.

56). We now want third world women to talk, but only about their difference: "We no longer wish to erase your difference. We demand, on the contrary, that you remember and assert it. At least, to a certain extent" (Trinh, 1989, p. 89). We allow difference to exist (perhaps even celebrate it), but still must control it: "You may keep your traditional law and tribal customs among yourselves, as long as you and your own kind are careful not to step beyond the assigned limits" (Trinh, 1989, p. 80). Although we (being those with the power to authorize speech) allow some differences, it is often only those differences that we are already comfortable with.

We question third world women's *authenticity* if they do not fit into our expectations. Third world scholars must aspire to fit into Western ideas of what the third world is in order to be heard. And they can only speak from their positionality, "as third world woman," never invited/allowed to speak on "other" topics that are not directly related to being a third world woman. When they do participate, they had better wear the mask of the authentic third world woman. "No uprooted person is invited to participate in this 'special' wo/man's issue unless s/he 'makes up' her/his mind and paints her/himself thick with authenticity" (Trinh, 1989, p. 88). They cannot be heard on their own merits, and they will not be included if they are not authentic (which again has nothing to do with being true to themselves, but being true to the Western images of the third world). Thus to be included, third world women must put on a mask and present themselves as others desire to see them.

Although I reported that I chose not to talk with third world women about their health issues, that is not entirely true but a whitewashing of a more complex reality. One of my health professional participants was an Egyptian woman who had practiced medicine in her country of origin and was now a public health student in the United States. She is both third world woman *and* a U.S.-based health professional. Where does she belong? Rather than speak to her about her experiences "as a third world woman" (which would have required her to be poor, uneducated and victimized), I spoke to her as a U.S.-based health professional. Rather than reflect on her complex identity (as done in Mohanty, 1990/2001) and how it impacted her insights on third world women's health, I forced her into one category, that of health professional. In part, this was required by the study design, where third world women were placed in contrast to (assumed first-world) U.S. health professionals. She better fit the stereotypes of a health professional than a third world woman, so I did not allow her to speak as a third world woman. My inability to critique this serious problem meant that I again erased the voice of third world women from my project, which was originally supposed to be about the voices of third world women.

Agency /Power

Community development education and research are interested in empowerment, and assume that people have agency, an ability to act on the world. Traditionally in feminism, at least in humanist or libratory versions of feminism: "All people have access to agency and can escape to freedom from oppression by exercising their innate wills" (St. Pierre, 2000, pp. 500-1). The unique skills and agency of the individual leads to emancipation. I thought I had planned a collaborative project, where women in third world countries would be able to speak directly about their experiences, rather than being filtered through others' thoughts.

Yet as my research project began, I had the project rightfully questioned by the Human Subjects Office at my university. They worried that this population was too vulnerable for me to work with under the conditions I had designed. I had planned to have the health professionals I was talking to recommend women for the study. I assumed that health professionals would not pressure women into participating. Even more naïvely, I assumed that these women would not feel any pressure to participate, even though people who may have power over their life were asking them. Despite my interest in empowerment and collaboration, I ignored the power relations between the health educator and participant.

Part of my ignorance stemmed from my tendency (a tendency of white Western feminism) to view power and empowerment as products that exist within someone or can be easily transferred between people: "Third world women *have the power* to speak about their experiences" or "The educator *will empower* colonized women." Power can be more usefully looked at as "relations of power" (Foucault, 1976/1990). Power does not reside in people, but moves between people. In fact, it is power relationships that define or construct the positions of individuals. For instance, power relationships are implicit in the terms colonized/colonizer or third world people/first world people; we cannot think about "third world women" without placing them within a hierarchy, lower than first world women or third world men. This power defines and constrains the type of relationship possible, and does not leave room for a "true" partnership to arise. There will always be excess baggage of colonialism in the way. The goal of community development education then shifts; it is not about removing power from the relationship, but working to make it flow more equitably between people. And recognizing that the work to make power flow is unending.

Voice

Seeking better communication, community development workers may attempt to give voice to the voiceless. This was a goal that I had at the beginning of an unimplemented project to bring the voices and experiences of third world women to undergraduate health promotion students. Like Christine Walley (1997), I sought the "'real' voices" of third world women, real meaning the authentic voices speaking the script of third world womanhood.

Spivak's look at feminism through post-coloniality made a strong argument against my Western notions of voice and individuality. She suggests that Western intellectuals resist the urge to "retrieve the voices silenced by imperialism" (Childs & Williams, 1997, p. 163). In my project, I wanted to retrieve those voices and hear them talk about their marginalized position as third world women. Spivak says that this is impossible: "The subject of exploitation cannot know and speak the text of female exploitation even if the absurdity of the nonrepresenting intellectual making space for her to speak is achieved" (Spivak, 1994, p. 84). Whatever they said, Spivak is sure that they could not speak of female exploitation in the way I wanted them to, in the way that would fit into my curriculum. Although I wanted to "give them voice," I still had expectations about what I would hear from "authentic" third world women who would speak about their multiple oppressions from colonialism and patriarchy. The first world audience uses its privilege to demand voices from the third world that are different: "Now i am not only given the permission to open up and talk, i am also encouraged to express my difference. My audience expects and demands it .... We came to listen to that voice of difference likely to bring us *what we can't have* and to divert us from the monotony of sameness" (Trinh, 1989, p. 88). In searching for "'real' voices" or authentic voices, we miss the fact that women's experiences of health are complex and often context dependent (Walley, 1997, p. 412). Even a focus on listening to voices risks noticing only those voices that are different or exotic in an "authentic" way.

Project Interrupted

I stopped pursuing this project as a result of my concerns with representation of voices, and my assumptions about agency, power, and inscribing individuals. My version of participatory feminist research completely ignored the power relations between me and the people I wanted to interview. I assumed some essentialized, authentic third world woman who had the agency to tell me her unique story and freedom to critique the work of the very health professionals who were healing her or her children. I was terribly naïve.

Yet I do not believe that I am alone in this naïvety. In retrospect I am surprised (and appalled) at how little resistance or questioning I faced through the development of this project. My advisors were behind it; my college gave me a small grant to conduct the project; my colleagues considered it an interesting and insightful project. Although my university program does not have an international focus where a better critique might be expected, my colleagues in health promotion and in education generally supported the project. True, the Institutional Review Board stepped in, concerned primarily about the relations of power between the health professionals and their clients. They were willing to work around this however, leaving much of the essentialist work based on agency, empowerment, and voice intact. Although I take the responsibility for my own naïvety – it still is my project after all – this chapter is an important addition to the field because the entire system is naïve. I know I am not the only one trying to do research in the third world with false and potentially damaging assumptions.

Since my limited budget and limited time limited my ability to work differently within these power relations, I chose not to pursue this part of the project. Yet, I continued to ask health professionals about their experiences, as if this were somehow safer and less complicated than talking with third world women. So instead of having a curriculum in which women were able to represent their own health problems, I ended up with a curriculum in which health professionals (presented as mostly Western) and I defined the "problem" of third world women's health. Even in these interviews, I still asked health professionals to describe the 'average third world woman' Mohanty (1991) describes. I did not ask third world women to participate because I was afraid of colonizing. Yet I went ahead and colonized anyway, perhaps even in a worse way because there was no possibility for an opportunity to not colonize.

Running away from the problem is yet another assertion of first world privilege. "At least the danger of speaking for the other has emerged into consciousness. But it is a very small step indeed, since it serves as an excuse for their complacent ignorance and their reluctance to involve themselves in the issue" (Trinh, 1989, p. 80). Recognizing danger and running from it reinforces the hierarchies between the first and third world. My project reinscribed first world health professionals' visions of third world women; the women themselves were never heard, for fear that I might not "capture" their voices correctly. How can we work with third world women, knowing that we enter a dangerous zone where every action feels to be a recolonization?

Cautious Movements

Part of my paralysis stems from a desire for mastery or authority – I wanted a "right" way to do work with third world women. Yet perhaps this search for mastery, for the perfect solution, is the very problem (Gallop, 1985). Gallop tries to write in a different relation to the Lacanian text she is struggling with, by exposing her confusions rather than repressing the contradictory and ambiguous portions of the text. I would like to think that this project is an attempt to expose my own confusions about working between feminism and post-colonialism.

While Gallop questions our pursuit of authority, she does not suggest that we simply give it up. As she comments, marginalized groups have spoken without authority for some time, with little effect. Instead of thoroughly refusing authority, Gallop states "One can effectively undo authority only from the position of authority, in a way that exposes the illusions of that position *without renouncing it*, so as to permeate the position itself with the connotations of its illusoriness, so as to show that *everyone*, including the 'subject presumed to know,' is castrated" or made ineffective through language (italics in original, Gallop, 1985, p. 21). This is a thin tightrope on which to walk – claiming and exposing the illusions of authority at the same time. Yet feminists like Mascia-Lees and Sharpe (2000) claim we must "take a stand" (p. 10) despite the pull of postmodern and post-colonial theory to critique rather than take action. Feminist theory as "an intellectual system that *knows* its politics" (Mascia-Lees & Sharpe, 2000, p. 19) requires action in solidarity with women, in this case, in solidarity with third world women.

GETTING CONCRETE: WHAT CAN WE DO?

So we understand that working with third world women is not easy – but we can't refuse to work with them either. So what do we do? Here are four mantras to remember, drawn from feminist and postcolonial researchers. Although not a cookbook, they can provide guidance as to what to watch out for.

1. Acknowledge that no participatory project is fully participatory

Every project, even those that work to be participatory, will fail at being fully participatory. For example, community members will likely disagree, sometimes vehemently about what course of action should be taken (Minkler et al., 2002). Any movement forward will not meet the interests of all participating. Also, any project will be limited by who chooses/has time to/is invited to participate. Rather than gloss over or cover up our inability to get it right, Judith Butler directs us "to interrogate what the theoretical move that establishes foundations *authorizes*, and what precisely it excludes or forecloses" (Butler, 1992, p. 7). Rather than try to establish a project that is "truly" participatory (and set ourselves up for failure), we instead must work to investigate the foundations we do lay, and ask what they authorize and exclude.

For example, in my project on third world women's health, my original foundation was to give voice to third world women. This feminist ideal authorized giving voice to third world women as an extremely important goal. Members of the Multicultural Task Force agreed that this goal was important by granting me money to complete this project. However, this foundation excluded me from examining the relations of power between health professionals and women seeking care. It also excluded me from seeing the relations of power between the researcher (me) and third world women, and my own use of third world women to construct the West and to construct myself as good, healthy, powerful, and intelligent.

Yet my decision not to interview third world women, but continue to interview first world health professionals also authorized and excluded certain actions. I used post-colonial theory to authorize my fears about working with third world women, my worries that I would never get it right. I used this authorization to continue to exclude third world women from producing knowledge about their own lives. This direct questioning of what is authorized and excluded forces us to be very specific about what our research does and does not do to break down colonial relationships. All decisions will authorize some actions and exclude others. Keep making decisions, but be clear about what impacts your decisions make.

2. Monitor and be open about what your project does and does not do

Careful monitoring of project decisions will help you be clear about what your decisions authorize and exclude. We must continuously ask how our work fits into colonizing patterns. Some of these questions are common to participatory work, while others extend participatory work towards becoming less colonial. Some questions you might ask about your work:

(a) Who decides which topics get worked on?

Which topics get the most attention? How are decisions made? What roles do participants and practitioners have in making decisions? These questions are commonly asked in participatory research environments, and fit well into feminist, post-colonial frameworks as well. When participants want to talk about something else than the topic you are interested in, Sylvester (1995/2001) reminds us to pay attention.

(b) How are the participants represented?

Are participants represented as knowers and doers within the project, or as passive recipients? Is participant knowledge discounted or does participant experience provide the basis for work? Are participants aligned with only the negative ends of binaries? What assets exist among participants? Although there is no "truly fair" representation of participants, seek multi-layered representations that present participants in more than one light.

(c) How is the researcher represented?

In participatory research and practice, we are often very concerned with the role of participants, but not always as clear about examining our roles as powerful practitioners (Wallerstein, 1999). Academic researchers must recognize that we often have inherent privileges in the relationship, including:

- I get paid to do my job, while my participants work for free or with token payments.
- I have the final authority on the use of any grant or project money.
- I have chosen this community, they usually have not chosen me.
- I can leave the community when I want.

These privileges (and others) give us unearned power in relation to our participants. These privileges must be recognized and resisted. We can do this by deferring our own power in these situations when possible. We can also question our classifications of practitioners as separate from participants. How can these roles be blended and blurred?

We must also ask how we are constructed as good and noble people within our work. We often focus on the great needs that third world people face, but do not ask what this focus on needs means to us. Trinh suggests, "The invention of needs always goes hand in hand with the compulsion to help the needy, a noble and self-gratifying task that also renders the helper's service indispensable" (Trinh, 1989, p. 89). Is our focus on needs just another way to construct the first world/third world binary within colonial relationships? How can we refrain from "inventing needs" by looking for self-identified needs or assets of our participants?

(d) Study the relationship between practitioners and participants

We can only ever study the relationship between the researcher and participant – we have no access to the participants' authentic experience (if there is even such an authentic experience to be had). Christine Sylvester (1995/2001) cautions against a sympathy that pathologizes others' problems, but leaves our own assumptions unexamined. We cannot identify with oppressed people everywhere, without subsuming their interests into our own, under the cover of sameness and thus obscuring the differences among oppressions (Grillo & Wildman, 1996). Sylvester (1995/2001) argues for an empathy that allows us to fit in relations to others, without appropriating their experiences as our own.

Yet even empathy is dangerous, as it allows easy comparisons based on similarity while obscuring differences (Grillo & Wildman, 1996). Rather than empathize, Spivak asks us to, "learn to speak to (rather than listen to or speak for) the historically muted subject of the subaltern woman" (Spivak, 1994, p. 91). We can only ever assess the dialogue between us, continually recognizing that our communication process is never perfect. Rather than trying to catch some authentic other, we should focus on the value of what Bhabha calls hybridity – the space between us (Childs & Williams, 1997). Instead of searching for the authentic (which is really only our own stereotypes about what the authentic looks like), recognize that by being in connection, we can only ever produce hybrid knowledge.

This sense of collaborative speaking differs from "giving voice" as it attempts to balance power while still critiquing how that knowledge is produced. Power should be moving between people *in both directions*, not just "transferred" from researchers to participants. The research relationship is inherently imbalanced, with most power flowing from the researcher to the researched. Extra care must be taken to give up some of the power, and allow power to flow in the other direction. One way to do this is to flow resources to political issues important to participants. Mbilinyi asks participatory researchers to be "willing to share power and resources with villagers, farm workers, urban slum dwellers, indeed with students and research assistants" and "to follow up on the political issues raised by participants, and remain involved when confrontations between 'the state' and 'the people' develop" (Mbilinyi, 1992, p. 63). We cannot only work on the issues that are important to us, but must support (in time and money) issues that are crucial to participants. Although a balance of power is not always simple to achieve in collaborative projects and must be continually negotiated, attempts at collaborative research better meet the goals of feminist and post-colonial research.

To monitor the flow of power, community developers must acknowledge their own subjectivity, how their own lives shape how they view the world. Within our research, we must reflect on our own position as researchers or practitioners – who are we? Why do we choose to study in this place, on this topic? What are our opinions on this topic, on this place, on these people? How does this subjectivity affect the research and practice that we do? We must "(re)search ourselves researching others" (Sylvester, 1995/2001, p. 517). Although this focus on the self should not devolve into studying only the self, our ideas and thoughts structure what happens within the relationship, and to ignore these subjectivities ignores the colonial relationship.

Part of our task is to see how we are implicated as Western intellectuals in the co-construction of the subaltern and the mighty West. It is not possible to get out of the colonizing trap, as the historical colonizing relationships are much larger than we could ever hope to dismantle alone. However, it is possible to study these relationships more intensely to understand how the West continues to construct the Other to construct itself. Examining how these relationships are constructed can be a useful teaching tool for undergraduates who are eager to focus on how different people from the Third World are, and how fortunate they are in comparison (Haney & McCormick, 2002). We all struggle with constructing ourselves as good, hard-working, well-meaning people. We must carefully scrutinize our own work, and invite scrutinization from others as to how our work aggrandizes ourselves while denigrating others.

(3) Nothing is safe – "everything is dangerous."

Give up the idea that there is one right way to work with third world women. There is no secret recipe book that has all the answers. The desire for a cookbook, a recipe book to tell us the "right" answers stems from our desire for mastery. Yet mastery is impossible, even undesirable. To gain mastery means to become a master – master of what, master of whom? There are no hard and fast rules to follow to safely ensure that our projects are not colonizing. We live and work within a matrix of colonialism – some of our movements will inevitably fall into colonial relationships. Yet not moving also places us in a colonial relationship where we are privileged to not have to think about these issues. So you might as well move, and have a chance to make some movements that are less colonizing than others. Or as Foucault says, "If everything is dangerous, then we always have something to do" (Foucault, 1983/1997, p. 256).

(4) Embrace uncertainty

If mastery is undesirable, perhaps we should embrace non-mastery and uncertainty. We must learn to say, "I don't know." We must learn to accept some practices without fully understanding them. We need to resist "leaping to solutions that collapse ambiguities" (Sylvester, 1995/2001, p. 516). This acceptance does not necessarily mean agreement, but a refusal to see others as "falsely conscious" of their lives. For example, Western feminists read female genital mutilation as sexual violence that must be ended (Walker & Pratibhua, 1993; Walley, 1997). Some African feminists have argued for more textured understandings of female circumcision that take culture and women's agency into account (Ajayi-Soyinka, 2000; Apena, 1996; Matias, 1996). Western feminists have labeled them "falsely conscious" – they just cannot see their own oppression. This claims that Western feminists see the situation better than African feminists (even if it is African feminists' own bodies that are being cut). Acceptance requires Western feminists to say, "In my viewpoint, female genital mutilation seems wrong, but I accept that I may not be understanding the whole picture." Acceptance privileges the meanings ascribed by those closest to the action, at least initially. It takes time to gain a better understanding of the complexities of culture; initial acceptance allows time for further exploration of the culture for later dialogue. Blind acceptance does not necessarily last forever, because as soon as we begin to interact we begin to change meanings. But it does take the time to say "I may not understand everything that is going on here" before naming others' oppression or victimhood.

While we are taking the time to build further understandings, María Lugones suggests that we should "learn to become unintrusive, unimportant, patient to the point of tears, while at the same time open to learning any possible lessons" (quoted in Alarcón, 1990, p. 363). Rather than asserting our own opinions incessantly, we need to be open to learning about others' opinions. We need to become "a bit quieter, a bit less determined to demonstrate assertiveness in encounters with those who may not agree" (Sylvester, 1995/2001, p. 516). Learning to live within uncertainty in unintrusive ways may be difficult. But we should appreciate the playful looseness, the surprise and irony that is possible when there is no one way to do things.

CONCLUSION

Community development education and research begin the process of working against patriarchal and colonial frameworks. Yet even participatory practices can never get it completely right. We must not become paralyzed looking for the one right way to work with third world women. We must not turn away from this work because it seems too hard or too complicated. Community based, participatory education begins to break down some of the barriers between the first and third world. Even with this work, we must constantly monitor the relationships between practitioners and participants, paying attention to power, representation, and voice.

A cautious, constant critique is necessary to continue to break down colonial relationships. Riessman says, "Feminists, for example, emphasize 'giving voice' to previously silenced groups of women by describing the diversity of their experiences. I share the goal but am more cautious. We cannot give voice, but we do hear voices that we record and interpret" (1993, p. 8). Mascia-Lees & Sharpe (2000) echo this note of caution: "even if as feminists we remain in opposition to men to construct ourselves, it does not mean that we must fear getting to know the non-Western 'other.' We may, however, be cautious in our desire to do so" (p. 30) as Strathern sees collaboration as "'a delusion, overlooking the crucial dimension of different social interests'" (qtd. in Mascia-Lees & Sharpe, 2000, p. 30). I like this title, "The Cautious Feminist." With this in mind, I can work on projects with a post-colonial feminist framework (like developing a curriculum about third world women's health), while at the same time I cautiously question what my work authorizes and what it excludes. As long as colonial relations exist, this constant critique will be necessary. We must never become complacent.

ACKNOWLEDGEMENT

This research was supported by a grant from the College of Education Multicultural Task Force, University of Georgia. I would like to thank the participants of this project, as well as Laura McCormick for her advisement. Torry Dickinson and two anonymous reviewers provided helpful comments on an earlier draft of this chapter, and Elizabeth St. Pierre and Mark Faust provided comments on the first draft of this paper inspired by their course on theoretical frameworks.

REFERENCES

Alarcón, N. (1990). The theoretical subject(s) of This Bridge Called My Back and Anglo-American feminism. In G. Anzaldúa (Ed.), *Making face, making soul = Haciendo caras: Creative and critical perspectices by feminists of color* (pp. 356-369). San Francisco: Aunt Lute Books.

Ajayi-Soyinka, O. (2000, March). *Who is afraid of agency? Theorizing African women out of the victim syndrome.* Paper presented at the conference African Women in Global Society: Issues & Perspectives, Athens, GA.

Apena, A. (1996). Female circumcision in Africa and the problem of cross-cultural perspectives. *Africa Update.* Retrieved May 21, 2000 from the World Wide Web: http://www2.h-net.msu.edu/~africa/sources/clitorodectomy.html

Ashcroft, B., Griffiths, G., & Tiffin, H. (1995). *The post-colonial studies reader.* London: Routledge.

Bakke, K. M. (2001). Kadra: FGM exposed. *Ms Magazine, 11,* 21.

Bové, P. A. (1990). Discourse. In F. Lentricchia (Ed.), *Critical terms for literary study* (pp. 50-65). Chicago: University of Chicago Press.

Butler, J. (1992). Contingent foundations: Feminism and the question of "postmodernism". In J.Butler & J. W. Scott (Eds.), *Feminists theorize the political* (pp. 3-21). New York: Routledge.

CDC/ATSDR Committee on Community Engagement. (1997). *Principles of community engagement.* Atlanta: Centers for Disease Control and Prevention.

Childs, P. & Williams, P. (1997). *An introduction to post-colonial theory.* London: Prentice Hall.

Collins, P. H. (1990). *Black feminist thought: Knowledge, consciousness and the politics of empowerment.* New York: Routledge.

Delmar, R. (2001). What is feminism? In A. C. Herrmann & A. J. Stewart (Eds.), *Theorizing feminism: Parallel trends in the humanities and social sciences* (2nd ed., pp. 5-28). Boulder, CO: Westview Press. (Reprinted from *What is feminism?,* pp. 8-33, in J. Mitchell & A. Oakley, Eds., 1986, New York: Pantheon.

Dickinson, T. D. (1999). Reunifying community and transforming society: Community development education and the university. *Research in Community Sociology, 9,* 41-63.

Foucault, M. (1990). *The history of sexuality: An introduction, Volume I.* (R. Hurley, Trans.) New York: Vintage Books. (Original work published 1976)

Foucault, M. (1997). On the genealogy of ethics: An overview of work in progress. In M. Foucault, *Ethics: Subjectivity and truth* (P. Rabinow, Ed.). New York: The New Press. (Interview conducted 1983)

Freire, Paulo. (1970). *Pedagogy of the oppressed* (M. B. Ramos, Trans.). New York: Herder and Herder.

Galang, M. E. (2000). Whatever Lolas want: Former "comfort" women in the Philippines build a house of justice and hope. *Ms.Magazine, 10,* 31.

Gallop, J. (1985). *Reading Lacan.* Ithaca, NY: Cornell University Press.

Gilliam, A. (1991). Women's equality and national liberation. In C. T. Mohanty, A. Russo, & L. Torres (Eds.), *Third World women and the politics of feminism* (pp. 215-236). Bloomington, IN: Indiana University Press.

Grillo, T. & Wildman, S. M. (1996). Obscuring the importance of race: The implications of making comparisons between racism and sexism (or other isms). In S. M. Wildman (Ed). *Privilege revealed: How invisible preference undermines America.* New York: New York University Press.

Haney, D. M. & McCormick, L. (2002). *Incorporating third world women's health into the undergraduate health curriculum.* Manuscript in preparation.

Mascia-Lees, F. E. & Sharpe, P. (2000). *Taking a stand in a postfeminist world: Toward an engaged cultural criticism.* Albany, NY: SUNY Press.

Matias, S. (1996). Female circumcision in Africa. *Africa Update.* Retrieved May 21, 2000 from the World Wide Web: http://www2.h-net.msu.edu/~africa /sources/clitorodectomy.html

Mbilinyi, M. (1992). Research methodologies in gender issues. In R. Meena (Ed.), *Gender in southern Africa: Conceptual and theoretical issues* (pp. 31-70). Harare, Zimbabwe: SAPES Books.

Minkler, M., Fadem, P., Perry, M., Blum, K., Moore, L., & Rogers, J. (2002). Ethical dilemmas in participatory action research: A case study from the disability community. *Health Education & Behavior, 29,* 14-29.

Minkler, M. & Wallerstein, N. (1997). Improving health through community organization and community building. In K. Glanz, F. M. Lewis, & B. K. Rimer (Eds.), *Health behavior and health education: Theory, research, and practice* (2nd ed., pp. 241-269). San Francisco: Jossey-Bass Publishers.

Mohanty, C. T. (2001). Defining genealogies: Feminist reflections on being South Asian in North America. In G. Kirk & M. Okazawa-Rey (Eds.), *Women's lives: Multicultural perspectives* (2nd ed., pp. 40-45). Mountain View, CA: Mayfield Publishing Company. (Reprinted from *Our feet walk the sky: Women of South Asian diaspora,* by Women of South Asian Descent Collective, 1990, Aunt Lute Books.

Mohanty, C. T. (1991). Under Western eyes: Feminist scholarship and colonial discourses. In C. T. Mohanty, A. Russo, & L. Torres (Eds.), *Third World women and the politics of feminism* (pp. 51-80). Bloomington, IN: Indiana University Press.

Otis, G. with Lerner, S. (2001). The global gag: Bush puts a chokehold on pro-choice activists while propping up anti-choice groups. *Ms Magazine, 11,* 17-20.

Parpart, J. L. (1993). Who is the 'Other'?: A postmodern feminist critique of women and development theory and practice. *Development and Change, 24,* 439-464.

Reinharz, S. (1992). *Feminist research methods.* New York: Oxford University Press.

Riessman, C. K. (1993). *Narrative analysis.* Newbury Park, CA: Sage Publications.

Rogers, B. (1999). Bitter harvest: Special report: How the sexual exploitation of girls has become big business in Thailand. *Ms.Magazine, 9,* 44-53, 96.

Rosser, S. V. (2000). *Women, science, and society.* New York: Teachers College Press.

Rozen, L. (2001). Hotel Macedonia: Women find new shelter from the sex industry. *Ms.Magazine, 11, 29-31.*

Scott, J. W. (2001). Deconstructing equality-versus-difference: Or, the uses of poststructuralist theory for feminism. Reprinted in A. C. Herrmann & A. J. Stewart (Eds.), *Theorizing feminism: Parallel trends in the humanities and social sciences* (2nd ed., pp. 254-270). Boulder, CO: Westview Press. (Reprinted from *Feminist Studies, 14*(1), pp. 33-50, 1988)

Spivak, G. C. (1994). Can the Subaltern Speak? In P. Williams & L. Chrisman (Eds.), *Colonial discourse and postcolonial theory: A reader* (pp. 66-111). New York: Columbia University Press.

Spivak, G. C. (1999). *A critique of postcolonial reason: Toward a hisotry of the vanishing present.* Cambridge, MA: Harvard University Press.

St. Pierre, E. A. (2000). Poststructural feminism in education: An overview. *Qualitative Studies in Education, 13,* 477-515.

Sullivan, M., Kone, A., Senturia, K. D., Chrisman, N. J., Ciske, S. J., & Krieger, J. W. (2001). Researcher and researched-community perspectives: Toward bridging the gap. *Health Education & Behavior, 28,* 130-149.

Sylvester, C. (2001). African and western feminisms: World-traveling the tendencies and possibilities. In A. C. Herrmann & A. J. Stewart (Eds.), *Theorizing feminism: Parallel trends in the humanities and social sciences* (pp. 501-530). Boulder, CO: Westview Press. (Reprinted from *Signs: Journal of Women in Culture and Society, 20*(4), pp. 941-969, 1995)

Tong, R. P. (1998). *Feminist thought: A more comprehensive introduction.* (2nd ed.) Boulder, CO: Westview Press.

Travers, K. D. (1997). Reducing inequities through participatory research and community empowerment. *Health Education and Behavior, 24,* 344-356.

Trihn, M. T. (1989). *Woman, native, other: Writing postcoloniality and feminism.* Bloomington, IN: Indiana University Press.

Wallerstein, N. (1999). Power between evaluator and community: Research relationships within New Mexico's healthier communities. *Social Science & Medicine, 49,* 39-53.

Walker, A. (Producer) and Pratibhua, P. (Producer and Director). (1993). *Warrior Marks* [Film]. (Available from Women Make Movies, 462 Broadway, 5th Floor, New York, NY 10013)

Walley, C. J. (1997). Searching for 'voices': Feminism, anthropology, and the global debate over female genital operations. *Cultural Anthropology, 12,* 405-438

Chapter 7

RESISTING 'TONGUE-TWISTER LANGUAGE': IN SEARCH OF A PRACTICAL FEMINISM

Tammy Findlay

ABSTRACT

This article explores strategies for strengthening ties between communities and universities, activism and academia. The article does this from the perspective of the language of feminist theory. It begins by arguing that a lot of the language of feminist theory is of the 'tongue-twister' variety, or is excessively complex, and therefore inaccessible, and provides examples to illustrate such tongue-twister language. The article then problematizes the ways in which feminist theorists, Judith Butler in particular, have tried to justify this language. It asserts that the use of tongue-twister language undermines democratic and participatory education in both the classroom and the community. It seeks to demonstrate that overly complicated works can be made clearer, and thus can better contribute to active education. The article concludes by pointing to a number of feminist theorists who have a strong commitment to practical language, and to the contributions they have made to practical feminism.

INTRODUCTION

Feminist theory is about women's experiences. Second wave feminist theory developed through consciousness-raising groups, where women began to link their experiences with wider relations of power and oppression. At its most basic level, it is a theory of social change. In the current context of neo-liberalism, globalization, militarism, and growing inequality, such theories are more important than ever. But since my first women's studies course as an undergraduate student, something about feminist theory has persistently bothered me. Struggling through feminist theorizing, not only as an undergraduate student but also as a graduate student, I have always wondered how this often dense and inaccessible body of work can live up to its radical promise. Although this issue has arisen for me repeatedly, at first I thought it too frivolous to write about. However, the more I thought about it, the more I came to see the urgency in outlining the need for practical language, because this 'tongue twister language' is both antithetical to equality—the fundamental premise of feminism—and is a serious obstacle to progressive social change.

This article, in three following sections, addresses language issues that relate to community development and education. It seeks to examine how academia and activism, theory and practice, might be brought together by attending to the language of feminist theory. The first section will define what 'tongue-twister language' is, and will briefly outline the main argument of the paper: that the political practicality of this jargon-filled language must be questioned. The paper will then move on to describe the ways in which this 'tongue-twister language' has been justified, particularly in the case of Judith Butler, a prominent feminist theorist. Finally, the paper will respond to these arguments, calling for a practical feminism that recognizes the relationship between accessible theory and social change.

TONGUE-TWISTER LANGUAGE IN THEORY

What exactly do I mean by 'tongue-twister language'? It is language - and here I am referring specifically to the language of feminist theory – that is unnecessarily wordy, and complicated. Alexandra Dobrowolosky has referred to it as "postmodernism's word play" (Dobrowolosky 2000, 3), and this seems like a choice description. A couple of examples should suffice.

It is widely known that Judith Butler's work is especially dense; thus she is probably the best- known tongue-twister theorist. I will quote Butler at some length to demonstrate what I am calling tongue-twister language. In her book *Gender Trouble*, she writes:

If the notion of an abiding substance is a fictive construction produced through the compulsory ordering of attributes into coherent gender sequences, then it seems that gender as substance, the viability of man and woman as nouns, is called into question by the dissonant play of attributes that fail to conform to sequential or causal models of intelligibility ... It is of course always possible to argue that dissonant adjectives work retroactively to redefine the substantive identities they are said to modify and, hence, to expand the substantive categories of gender to include possibilities that they previously excluded. But if these substances are nothing other than the coherences contingently created through the regulation of attributes, it would seem that the ontology of substances itself is not only an artificial effect, but essentially superfluous (Butler 1990, 24).

Later on, in the same book, she says:

As a genealogy of gender ontology, this inquiry seeks to understand the discursive production of the plausibility of that binary relation and to suggest that certain cultural configurations of gender take the place of 'the real' and consolidated and augment their hegemony through that felicitous self-naturalization (Butler 1990, 32).

Butler is not alone, however. Donna Haraway is another good example of the type of bewildering language I am discussing. The following passage appears in Haraway's *Simians, Cyborgs and Women*: "I prefer to call this generative doubt the opening of non-isomorphic subjects, agents, and territories of stories unimaginable from the vantage point of the cyclopian, self-satiated eye of the master subject" (Haraway 1991, 192). She also says that:

[t]he phallogocentric origin stories most crucial for feminist cyborgs are built into the literal technologies – technologies that write the world, biotechnology and microelectronics – that have recently textualized our bodies as code problems on the grid of C^3I. Feminist cyborg stories have the task of recoding communication and intelligence to subvert command and control (Haraway 1991, 175).

This language raises considerable problems of accessibility; this problem, it will be argued, is particularly inappropriate for feminist theory, which, at its root, seeks radical social change.

JUSTIFYING THE JARGON

This is of course not the first time the language of postmodern (and other feminist) theorizing has been highlighted. Butler actually received an 'award' for her obtuse form of communication when an academic journal, *Philosophy and Literature*, granted her a prize for "bad writing." It is important to note that, as Butler points out, "[t]he targets ... have been restricted to scholars on the left whose work focuses on topics like sexuality, race, nationalism and the workings of capitalism" (Butler 1999). Of course, the motives of this conservative journal must be questioned. Nevertheless, the criticism remains powerful, precisely because of the nature of the topics Butler identifies above. That these feminist writers are discussing marginalized groups, and entrenched societal inequalities, makes it all the more important that they present their work clearly. The problem is not simply "bad writing," but rather poor communication. What is at stake here is not merely the use of "good prose." It is the ability to effectively convey an agenda for social change.

Butler is well aware of the problem, acknowledging that "the whole exercise hints at a serious question about the relation of language and politics: why are some of the most trenchant social criticisms often expressed through difficult and demanding language?" (Butler 1999). She then tries to answer her own question. Her argument, simply put, is that such language is in opposition to male-defined communication. It acts to "de-stabilize" the established order. Language, for Butler can be used to challenge prevailing notions of "common sense" (Butler 1999). She argues that "[n]o doubt, scholars in the humanities should be able to clarify how their work informs and illuminates everyday life. Equally, however, such scholars are obliged to question common sense, interrogate its tacit presumptions and provoke new ways of looking at a familiar world" (Butler 1999, editorial). She goes on to assert that:

[i]f common sense sometimes preserves the social status quo, and that the status quo sometimes treats unjust social hierarchies as natural, it makes good sense on such occasions to find ways of challenging common sense. Language that takes up this challenge can help point the way to a more socially just world. The contemporary tradition of critical theory in the academy, derived in part from the Frankfurt School of German anti-fascist philosophers and social critics, has shown how language plays an important role in shaping and altering our common or 'natural' understanding of social and political realities (Butler 1999).

Butler even goes as far as to say that "plain speaking ... [is] a consumer expectation of intellectual life" (Butler 1999, xix).

In her book *Excitable Speech*, Butler claims that "[w]ith respect to the political discourse of modernity, it is possible to say that its basic terms are all tainted, and that to use such terms is to invoke the contexts of oppression in which they were previously used" (Butler 1997, 160). She maintains that because language is "performative," it can be "cited against its originary purposes" to create a "counter speech," or a "resigni-fication of speech" (Butler 1997, 14, 15, 41). In a similar vein, Diana Meyers uses the label "dissident speech" to describe language that is meant to challenge social norms and categories (Bar On and Ferguson 1998, xii).

This argument, however, ignores one of the most important lessons from postmodernism. Derrida argued that there is no discourse that exists outside of social relations. Lynne Segal also reminds us of "Foucault's warning that oppositional discourses are inevitably caught up in the relations of domination they resist" (Segal 1999, 32). Therefore, the utility of inventing a new (postmodern) feminist script is based on two problematic assumptions. First, it implies that some feminists are able to step outside of power relations, and create an emancipatory, de-gendered form of communication. Second, and assuming this first unlikely scenario is possible, it leaves the rest of us, who remain embedded in a variety of social relations, unable to participate in the dialogue.

One of my first-year social science students at York University, Jane Cao, made precisely this point in her reading journal, expressing her frustration at a lot of the writing that appeared in our course readings. She wrote the following passage in her reading journal:

> These articles are supposed to speak for women. However, I doubt women like my mom can understand them. They invent new foes, new causes and new languages. The special languages used are only for those really 'high' class and 'top' educated group but not for women like my mom or new female/visible immigrants. It is already a big social problem as women are lower educated than men. How could they ignore this and expect women … to understand that? … If they keep writing in this format, Women's Representation issue will be meaningless since it's not the way to protect or speak for women … So, please think about the audience and don't hurt them (Cao 2001).

It is telling that this was Jane's first journal entry, and then her first contribution to class discussion, and this is the issue she found to be the most pressing. It is also striking how similar Jane's observations are to the comments made by bell hooks in her recent book, *Feminism Is for Everybody*:

> While academic legitimation was crucial to the advancement of feminist thought, it created a new set of difficulties. Suddenly the feminist thinking that had emerged directly from theory and practice received less attention than theory that was metalinguistic, creating excessive jargon; it was written solely for an academic audience. It was as if a large body of feminist thinkers banded together to form an elite group writing theory that could be understood only by an 'in' crowd (hooks 2000, 22).

So even if this language is a form of resistance, as Butler claims, (and I am not convinced it is) it is a very elitist form of resistance, a privileged form, that excludes many – an unfortunate result from a body of theory concerned with the recognition of difference. Butler is certainly correct in saying that many "common sense" assumptions must be challenged. It remains highly doubtful, however, that language that alienates the very people it is meant to empower is the most effective strategy to employ. In this way, Meyer's 'dissident speech' does not even seem to apply since,

> [a]ccording to Meyers, dissident speech is emancipatory only insofar as it facilitates the recognition that satisfaction of the needs of sociopolitically excluded groups, is polyvocal, and does not homogenize such groups. At the same time, such speech must be integrated into a comprehensive struggle for a massive social, political, and economic reordering (Bar On and Ferguson 1998, xiii).

While Butler may meet the first criteria, a commitment to the second (i.e. excluded groups) is clearly lacking. Therefore, Butler's response is wholly unsatisfactory. Her defense of postmodern lingo demonstrates a lack of concern for feminist practicality as a tool for social change.

FEMINIST PRACTICALITY

Judy Rebick, former president of Canada's national umbrella women's organization, the National Action Committee on the Status of Women (NAC), recently described her disappointment over the type of language I am discussing here. She stressed the need for academics to resist the pressure and/or temptation to resort to jargon, and spoke of her conscious attempt to make her book *Imagine Democracy* readable to a wide audience. This is the basis for practical feminism.

Feminist practicality requires that one remain mindful of her/his audience. If an elite group of academics are the target audience, then Butler (et al.) has no need to worry. After all, some postmodernists insist that text itself is a political act. However, this does not do justice to Butler, who does have something significant to say. This is important to my argument. It is not that I cannot see any value in Butler's work; my concern is rather that her writing style makes this task much too difficult. My point is that her language is needlessly complex – that the same point could be made with less, and with simpler language, which would make Butler's work, more useful to community activists and educators. Here, I will focus on only one argument, although a central one, in Butler's work.

Let's consider the long passage I quoted earlier from Butler. What she is saying, is basically that gender, or the roles and identities that we associate with women and men, are not 'natural.' Instead, they are created through language and behaviour. This is something that many feminists have stressed, namely, that gender is socially determined, or constructed. That gender is rigidly constructed has ramifications far beyond academia. In concrete terms, this can mean a lot for women's organizing in their communities because Butler's point is not just that gender is not natural, it is that the women's movement, or in this case, the North American women's movement, depends on, and advances these strict notions of gender. She draws attention to the homophobia internal to the women's movement, and to the irony that although feminists have stressed that gender is constructed, many seem to forget this when it comes to the lesbian and gay community (Butler 1999, xxiv).

In Canada, a major debate that is dividing the women's movement is occurring around the issue of access to women's shelters by transsexual and transgendered women. A case occurred in Vancouver, in which a transsexual woman, named Kimberly Nixon, was prevented from joining a training group for volunteer peer councilors from the Vancouver

Rape Relief and Women's Shelter in 1995 "because she does not share the same life experiences as born and raised girls and women" (Jay 2002). Nixon filed a complaint with the British Columbia (BC) Human Rights Tribunal, and won the case in January 2002. Vancouver Rape Relief and Women's Shelter has since appealed to the BC Supreme Court, prompting controversy within the women's movement across Canada over not only the meaning of "women-only space," but of "woman" as well. Clearly Butler's challenge to our assumptions about what "gender" is, and who counts as a woman, or a man, is relevant to this debate in the community.

Judith Butler is certainly sympathetic to the goal of establishing closer connections between universities and other community organizations. She speaks of "crossing-over" from academia to the communities and the social movements in which she is active: "wondering if I could link the different sides of my life" (Butler 1999, xvii). It is unfortunate, therefore, that without a translator, Coles notes, or a Dictionary of Butler terminology, her work is unintelligible. (I have heard there is a "Butler for Dummies" edition, but I have yet to see it). Furthermore, when she cedes that, "of course, translations are sometimes crucial, especially when scholars teach," (Butler 1999), Butler is not only justifying the continued use of jargon, but is also accepting a sharp division between teacher/student, academic/activist.

As this book demonstrates, teaching is a political act. It can transfer radical ideas from the community to the classroom, and vice versa. I have found that in the classroom, excessively complicated language has been a significant obstacle to introducing feminism to my students. For many students, the university is the first place they are exposed to the ideas of feminism (which is itself a problem of accessibility). Learning new ideas, which challenge their basic understandings of the world, is intimidating enough for students, let alone trying to navigate through such difficult language. The frustration expressed earlier by Jane was common in the class, even by those students who were sympathetic to, or even excited to learn about, feminism. Here, the result was that complicated language was overwhelming, and often discouraging to students who had a genuine interest in feminism. Language becomes a convenient excuse to dismiss feminism entirely when students are already resistant, or hostile to the word 'feminism,' and especially to the prospect of learning about it.

The task is made even more difficult in a community setting. I recently taught in a program for labour unionists. Sentiment in the Canadian labour movement varies from strong support for feminism, to outright opposition. Introducing ideas about gender, race, and sexuality in this setting is very difficult. When one adds to this the wide divergence in ages, and educational backgrounds, a considerable challenge exists. I've tried to imagine assigning Judith Butler to these students, and I assume the response would be the same as if I gave it to my dad: "what's this 'mumbo-jumbo?'" And they would be right. The dictionary definition of 'mumbo-jumbo' is: "words or actions that are deliberately obscure in order to mystify or confuse people" (Hawkins et al. 1993, 452).

Feminism requires an entirely different understanding of the process of education. It is interesting to contrast Butler and Haraway with other feminist theorists such as Himani Bannerji, Patricia Hill Collins, or Lynne Segal. For them, theory and practice are intertwined, since theory grows out of experience. Bannerji calls for knowledge and education that is " 'active,' that is, oriented to radical social change," and sees feminism as potentially such a project (Bannerji 1991, 76). Active education begins with one's personal experiences as a method of analyzing social relations in a wider context. This "reflexive and relational social analysis" requires that race, gender and class be regarded as mutually dependent (Bannerji 1991, 94).

Women's experience also figures centrally in the work of Patricia Hill Collins. For her, theory is not reserved only for academics. She reminds us that "much of the Black women's intellectual tradition has been embedded in institutional locations other than the academy" (Hill Collins 1990, 15). For her, re-thinking who is an intellectual is a critical aspect of Black feminist thought (Hill Collins 1990, 15). Hill Collins recalls the speeches of "nineteenth century Black feminist activist Sojourner Truth [who] proved herself to be a formidable intellectual. And yet Truth was a former slave who never learned to read or write" (Hill Collins 1990, 14-15). She goes on to say that "[s]uch women are typically thought of as nonintellectual and nonscholarly, classifications that create a false dichotomy between scholarship and activism, between thinking and doing" (Hill Collins 1990, 15). Indeed, tongue-twister, jargonistic language also creates such dichotomies. It effectively prevents "the merger of action and theory" (Ibid., 29) that Hill Collins so poignantly emphasizes. We must take Hill Collins seriously when she says that "behavior is a statement of philosophy" (Ibid., 15-16), and we must question the philosophy behind inaccessible writing as a behavior.

Lynne Segal specifically engages with Butler (among others) in this regard. She takes issue with "a feminism which begins with the textual practice of re-theorizing signifiers of subjectivity [because it] is one which is incommensurate with, as well as distanced from, the perspectives and practices of Women's Liberation" (Segal 1999, 14). The Women's Liberation of the 1970s emphasize women's concrete experiences, and "[s]trategic priorities were usually paramount" (Segal 1999, 21). bell hooks adds that "[i]n its earliest inception, feminist theory had as its primary goal explaining to women and men how sexist thinking worked and how we could challenge and change it" (hooks 2000, 19).

Echoing both Bannerji and Hill-Collins, Segal "seek[s] to promote a combination of theoretical questioning and political engagements which enable more women to share in the self-questioning, the pleasures and, above all, the solidarities and egalitarian settlements that feminism, at its most generous, regards as the birthright of women everywhere" (Segal 1999, 6). Segal asserts that the focus on abstract theorizing is increasingly a problem among feminist academics, ignoring the history of feminism as "a theory and practice of social transformation" (Segal 1999, 15). Furthermore, feminist studies, which have traditionally been interdisciplinary, are more and more dominated by English and Cultural Studies departments, contributing to the reduction of feminism to metaphors, linguistic tricks, and word play (Segal 1999, 221). For Segal, "playful, transgressive emissaries of change or resistance" can only go so far in the absence of an analysis of social relations. Such a preoccupation with linguistic ingenuity also marks a growing elitism that a feminist practicality can begin to remedy.

There are feminists who take the need for practical language very seriously. Intelligible language is very important to bell hooks, for example. She laments that

> [i]t is sadly ironic that the contemporary discourse which talks the most about heterogeneity, the decentered subject, declaring breakthroughs that allow recognition of Otherness, still directs its critical voice primarily to a specialized audience that shares a common language rooted in the very master narratives it claims to challenge (hooks 1990, 25).

She reminds us that white male intellectuals dominate this (postmodern) discourse (hooks 1990, 24). Furthermore, hooks also points out the disturbing reality that "anti-feminist books tend to be written in an accessible language that appeals to a broad readership" (hooks, 2000, 115). Therefore, she imparts: "My goal as a feminist thinker and theorist is to take that abstraction and articulate it in a language that renders it accessible – not less complex or rigorous – but simply more accessible" (hooks, in Hill Collins 1990, 233).

In bell hooks' view, "feminism is for everybody." But currently, feminism, or at least a substantial part of it, is not for everybody. It is for a select few, so hooks addresses this problem throughout her book, and begins to outline what a feminism that actually is for everybody would look like. She describes her goal in writing her book as follows: "I want to be holding in my hand a concise, fairly easy to read and understand book; not a long book, not a book thick with hard to understand jargon and academic language, but a straightforward, clear book – easy to read without being simplistic" (hooks 2000, viii). She suggests that the feminist movement should produce pamphlets, written in simple language, should focus on educating children, youth and communities about feminism, and should move beyond writing to music, television, etc. as means of communication (hooks 2000, ix, 22, 23, 24, 112, 113). Also part of her project, a project that I consider to be characteristic of practical feminism, involves publishing "oppositional" works in popular magazines and newspapers such as *The Village Voice* and *Tricycle* (a Buddhist magazine) as a means of reaching a wider audience (hooks 2000, 9). This parallels the discussion earlier of Rebick's strategy with *Imagine Democracy*, which stressed the importance of writing an approachable book that can speak to a popular audience. Rebick also publishes a column in a popular Canadian magazine, *Elm Street*, and has started an on-line magazine called rabble.ca. Feminism should be, and can be, for everybody.

Feminist practicality prioritizes both accountability and accessibility. In this light, Audre Lorde emphasizes the importance of poetry. She argues that

> [o]f all the art forms, poetry is the most economical. It is the one that is the most secret, that requires the least physical labor, the least material, the one that can be done between shifts, in the hospital pantry, on the subway, and on scraps of surplus paper. Over the last few years, writing a novel on tight finances, I came to appreciate the enormous differences in the material demands between poetry and prose. As we reclaim our literature, poetry has been the major voice of poor, working-class, and colored women (Lorde, 375).

I understand there is some tension here, since poetry may not be the most accessible form of writing from the perspective of the reader. Lorde's point, however, is that it is accessible to the writer. This goes to Hill-Collins' insistence that all women, not simply academics, can share and/or write about their experiences, and therefore can contribute to feminist theory.

Lorde's sentiments were also reflected at the "Rebuilding the Left" conference in fall 2000 in Toronto, Canada. Rebuilding the Left is an initiative in several major cities in Canada aimed at building a 'structured movement' on the Left by bringing together various progressive parties and organizations in order to build concrete alternatives to neo-liberalism. At the conference, after a series of academics spoke, performer Faith Nolan wondered how to rebuild the left when most people are unable to understand what is being said. Canadian Auto Workers (CAW) trade unionist, Sam Gindin also emphasized the need for accessible, but not patronizing language. Faith Nolan, like Audrey Lorde, stressed the role of poetry and art as political activism, and as ways of reaching more people.

CONCLUSION

Alexandra Dobrowolsky refers to "the politics of pragmatism" (Dobrowolsky 2000) and Ann Ferguson calls for "feminist radical pragmatism" (Ferguson 1998, 205). Both seek a similar link between theory and practice as the 'practical feminism' that I have explored, although in my case, I have only discussed the linguistic aspect of what I see as impractical feminism. Practical feminism, of course, is not only about clear writing. As other essays in this collection demonstrate, practical feminism, or feminism that links academia and activism, theory and practice, exists in many forms and locations – in the classroom, in the household, in the workplace, and in communities. Although practical language is certainly not the only component of practical feminism, my argument here, is that it must be the starting point. Without a basic commitment to accessibility, any further development of feminist practicality is premature.

Rowland and Klein assert: "We have rejected theory which is too esoteric, too divorced from the reality of women's experiences, too inaccessible to the majority of women whom feminism is supposed to serve" (Rowland and Klein, 275). In other words, they are practical feminists. Practical feminism, as used here, is quite simple. It refers only to the idea that feminist theory should be written and presented in such a way it can be understood by a wide audience. Accessible language, then, is a political project, a project that aims to bring feminist theory to all women, and all women to feminist theory. It is a project that sees linking theories of social change to communities, as essential to transformations from a local to a global scale.

In many ways, the fact that such an argument even requires utterance points to the concerns raised by Lynne Segal and bell hooks about the direction that much of feminist theory is now taking. As such, the paper began by drawing attention to what I have called 'tongue-twister language', or feminist language that is needlessly complex. It then went on to comment on attempts (by Butler in particular) to rationalize this linguistic creativity. Finally, it argued that if feminism is to go beyond merely an academic exercise, and contribute in a significant way to social change, it must be accessible. Practicality must be central to a feminist theory that is linked to feminist practice, so I'll take the feminist theory, but hold the jargon, please.

REFERENCES

Bannerji, Himani. 1991. "But Who Speaks for Us? Experience and Agency in Conventional Feminist Paradigms." In *Unsettling Relations: The University as Site for Feminist Struggles*. Toronto: Toronto Women's Press.

Bar On, Bat-Ami and Anne Ferguson. 1998. "Introduction." In *Daring to be Good: Essays In Feminist Ethico-Politics*, edited by Bat-Ami Bar On and Ann Ferguson. New York: Routledge.

Butler, Judith. March 20, 1999. "A 'Bad Writer' Bites Back." *New York Times*. (Op-Ed).

—. 1999. *Gender Trouble: Feminism and the Subversion of Identity* (10th Anniversary Edition). New York: Routledge.

—. 1997. *Excitable Speech: A Politics of the Performative.* New York: Routledge.

—. 1990. *Gender Trouble: Feminism and the Subversion of Identity.* New York: Routledge.

Dobrowolsky, Alexandra. 2000. *The Politics of Pragmatism: Women, Representation, and Constitutionalism in Canada.* Don Mills: Oxford University Press.

Ferguson, Anne. 1998. "Prostitution as a Morally Risky Practice: From the Point of View Of Feminist Radical Pragmatism." In *Daring to be Good: Essays in Feminist Ethico-Politics,* edited by Bat-Ami Bar On and Ann Ferguson. New York: Routledge.

Haraway, Donna. 1991. *Simians, Cyborgs and Women: the Reinvention of Nature.* London: Free Association Books.

Hawkins, Joyce M. et al. 1993. *The Oxford Study Dictionary.* Toronto: Oxford University Press.

Hill-Collins, Patricia. 1990. *Black Feminist Thought: Knowledge, Consciousness, and the Politics of Empowerment.* Boston: Unwin Hyman.

hooks, bell. 2000. *Feminism is for Everybody: Passionate Politics.* Cambridge: South End Press.

—. 1990. *Yearning: Race, Gender, and Cultural Politics.* Boston: South End Press.

Jay, Suzanne. June 24, 2002. "Appeal to Protect Women-Only Space." *News Release.*

Lorde, Audre. 1997. "Age, Race, Class and Sex: Women Redefine Difference." In *Dangerous Liasons: Gender, Nations, and Postcolonial Perspectives*, edited by Anne McClintock, Amir Mufti, and Ella Shohat. Minneapolis: University of Minnesota Press.

Rowland, Robyn and Renate Klein. 1990. "Radical Feminism: Critique and Construct." In *Feminist Knowledge: Critique and Construct*, edited by Sneja Gunew. New York: Routledge.

Segal, Lynne. 1999. *Why Feminism?: Gender, Psychology, Politics.* New York: Columbia University Press.

PART IV: BROAD, CULTURAL CHANGE AND POPULAR EDUCATION

Chapter 8

HOSPITALITY IN A MOROCCAN VILLAGE: TRAVELS OF A FEMINIST ARTIST, AN ESSAY

Annalouise

Day begins at 3:30 for some, with the preparation of flour or cornmeal in readiness for bread baking. The women are dimly visible in the shady interior of the flour store, selecting the grain for corn bread and the larger round bread for all our meals. Hens scratch round the doorway; the one-winged goose stalks behind me, keeping a hoary eye on my legs. To my right, calling her mother to come and look, the kid stuck in a large water pipe is white and furry. Bleating in high excitement, hers is the only voice to be heard at this pre-dawn hour.

I got out of my warm wool covers, next to Mama's bed, so very early today. I'm wide-awake, but not before Mama. Already Mama is sitting, cross-legged, bowing from the waist in prayer. So fit at ninety, Mama amazes me; I try to emulate her, and fail. For a while, I sit in quiet meditation. Then, creeping silently past her, out into the cool inner courtyard, taking up my sketchbook, I creak out of the door. Watch out for that goose! It got me back for daring to boo at it, and it looked so 'armless!

Squatting over the mud oven is Fatirha. She grins up at me and waves me over. I pull up a breezeblock and watch. Fatirha is fanning the flames inside with one of the woven baskets that carried the bread dough. The oven is a large dome, two to three feet high and in diameter, a hole in front and a smaller one atop for the smoke, now covered by a metal lid, as the heat inside builds. Vines, cut down last summer, dried in heaps around the oven, are broken up for fuel. They burn with a fierce, steady heat. Cooling on top of the nearest heap of vine stems are several sweet-smelling hot round loaves, just out of the oven. The flames, circling hot inside, now brown the new bread, sat on the flat, long-handled pan, whilst sister Houria presses her fingers into the next flat dough, to make air holes.

Somewhere from inside the main house, Mama calls to the women, "make breakfast ready!" and tries to get me to leave off drawing and join her. I cannot. Not yet. But out of respect for her, I speed up - I've nearly caught it all! The scents, the smoke, the bright, clear blue morning skies, the hens, geese, dogs...now, who's that? Dust blows across from horses' hooves as a tall, red bay mare and her frisky colt canter in. Mohammed has the mother by a halter, he is not riding her. I go over to breathe softly into their shy noses. The mare breathes back, her colt bolts around to her far side - tethered by the foot, he cannot go far.

The other women are leading a small herd of Friesian cattle into the front of the farmhouse. They leave them tied to stakes in the hot sun and go about the next task. Memehda is already milking a mother with calf, in the shade of the cow-byre. The children are gathered around, hoping for a frothy cup-full.

There we are, caught in a time long-gone from English countryside scenes, where chicks are caught up into an apron, the hen held upside down, by her legs, and carried over to an earth dome, for her safety, and plopped into its shade with her chicks. Food and water have been placed inside. The goats and sheep are let out from their rough mud pens, and shepherded onto the far hillside by young lads with hapless dogs trotting behind. These dogs seem to do very little towards their keep, mostly kept at bay with well-aimed stones. They throw long shadows, which leap from their feet. A swirl of red dust sees them vanish over the horizon.

Such peace and such business; dry heat and cool shady interiors. From pre-dawn to dusk and beyond, the farming days stretch from horizon to infinity. Seven days a week, fifty-two weeks a year, hardly a sight of town, the women keep the machineless countryside farms alive and well. Yet, how do the women and the men respond when they think of the pleasure of tasting fresh corn bread? "Oh, this is how I remember my mother's used to be!" and "You cannot get such a taste in town!"

Yes, variety and freshness of flavour is what colours all the food, so vivid in tastes and spices: prunes, almonds and tender lamb, on a tangy saffron bed of couscous - oh! Then chicken, lemon and saffron potatoes on melting vermicelli and couscous, with cumin... the potatoes are brilliant orange yellow, and so firm and sweet - I'd never tasted such flavours. The food kept coming - and it slowly dawned on me to check... was this usual fare? "Oh no - it's in your honour, since you are now a family member, coming with our precious daughter, Yamina!" And, I realised, they'd cooked the last of their birds for me, given me much of the milk and most of the eggs for a week!

Now, it would have insulted them to have refused a morsel - yet how many travellers (in their noisy, gas-guzzling four-wheel drives, mountain bikes and surf-boards aplenty on top) take advantage and leave nothing but hunger in their wake? How much do we take for granted? Most of this 'wealth' comes from the heart of a people who are ignored and isolated in their own country.

The beauty and diversity of their land is suffering. Water is scarce, wood and trees limited, fuel is scraped together from last year's vine harvest, cowpats and dead trees. Water comes rarely through pipes, even at night. Then all the men folk rush out, even at two in the morning, to dig the ditches and direct the flow across the darkened fields. At their weary return. their women leap from their beds to bring water, food and coffee, at whatever hour. Then creep back to their beds in amongst their daughters and other women. The men sleep elsewhere, I haven't discovered why! Separate duties, separate eating times, men first. Women and children after.

But to come back to my point about leaving such fine work unappreciated. These people live lives of steady hard work, take no holidays, hardly ever visit town, have little knowledge of how others live. Many of them begged me to take them with me...one, Fatima, told me she is strong as an ox, and could happily lift a man, could she not hang onto my coat tails as I flew home? Yet they keep the land vibrantly healthy, thick with butterflies, beetles, insects and thousands of skylarks above fields free of chemicals... all could be lost.

The people who work this land deserve all praise and reverence, deserve to be helped and to be included in the country's wealth, and if possible, enabled to keep the land free of the damaging agro-chemical business which plagues our own. The same business which drove off our wild-life, poisoned our waterways and rivers, killed off the insects, pulled out hedgerows, tore out stands of woods could threaten this sacred land. This land needs trees to bring back the water level, needs water temporarily to sustain its precious harvest, and the people need our love and generosity. It will never match their own. But we can try.

Let us help their children, in their education programmes, to get planting and paying respect to the animal and insect life, to the soil and the farming heritage. — All of life is sacred in the Koran, yet the young often seem to stamp upon insects, especially the praying mantis!! All of life is there still, in these forgotten lands; let us not drop this precious gift in our rush to modernise. We made the mistakes — can we help others to avoid it and correct our own? I hope so.

The skills of a people come out of certain lack (financially) but no lack of ingenuity. Their sculpted homes are mud and straw - simple yet beautiful and cool, beneath their bamboo thatch. No need for all the trappings we have, and seem unable to exist without. But at what cost do we accomplish such luxury or clutter, I am asking myself now? Money is not everything. We have to leave it behind, and lose our health in the process sometimes. Lose our minds, too. Health and mental clarity seem high costs to pay for petrol fumes and big business, money-making schemes. To what end? Back to simplicity such as this land enjoys (some may say suffer) may not be desirable, yet I strongly feel we have gone too far.

EDITOR'S NOTE

In 2001, as she was visiting a small Moroccan village near the Algerian border, Annalouise took the photographs that appear in this book. She also wrote this essay, which shares her reflections about the direction in which we are headed, and the choices we can make.

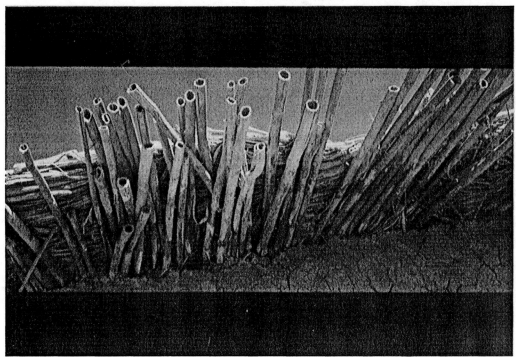

Photo by Annalouise, 2001

Photo by Annalouise, 2001

Photo by Annalouise, 2001

Photo by Annalouise, 2001

Photo by Annalouise, 2001

Chapter 9

EXPLORING THE WORLD
THROUGH ARTISTIC EXPRESSION

Teresa Schmidt

From the Pacific Northwest,
I am influenced by the light from the ocean,
and by movement of shadows on clouded mountains.
My work is about spirituality, spatial movement, light and transparency.
My subject matter attempts to connect human conditions
and emotion
to space and form.
I treat my images as characters on stage in an emotional uneasiness with
—as I see it—
this constant state of change and movement.
I love people and empathize with their feelings and conditions.
The visual variety possible within a single medium,
its gestures and exaggerations,
describe for me the extremes in life.
Rembrandt's light and animation,
Susan Rothenburg's violent gestures and surfaces,
and Alice Neel's naked humanism
all appeal
to my sense of truth in art and life.

"Agrarian Rhapsody," graphite, 17 X 14 inches, 2002

This drawing is an abstraction. Although my interpretation of the work, after finishing it, has helped me to decide on the title, my location in the farming land of Vermont and the beautiful black winter trees and hills inspired the image. The drawing forms part of a series entitled: Vermont Series. The image was drawn without a plan, spontaneously responding to my media and impulse in an effort to override my more predictable responses. I considered media, scale, and motion, and tried not to predict any planned outcome other than the elation of the location.

"Sharon's Convalescence," graphite, 14 X 17, 1998

"Sharon's Convalescence" represents a drawing of my friend, a portrait, while she was recovering from a serious operation. I was struck by her hands and face, and I was also interested in expressing her obvious suffering. I feel my job is to empathize.

"Timer," graphite, 52 X 45, 2002

"Timer," a very large drawing, was the result of a sketch made in ballpoint during a long faculty meeting. One of my colleagues, whom I admire greatly, was sketching and listening intently at the same time. His dislike of long, unnecessary meetings and his vocalization of this interested me. His neck and ears were as interesting; and, at the angle I looked at him, I almost felt as if I were looking at his face and eyes. Portraits of backs-of-heads are a challenge and provide interest for me. I think that the ordinary is often more profound and reflects the human condition best.

"Untitled," graphite, 14 X 17, 2000

This untitled drawing or sketch was one that I did of child field workers pushing rice bales for their harvest of the field. It's terribly hard work and by such young ones. My drawing was done to express the hardship and yet the resolve to endure the hardship. I love the people and their courage.

"Circle of Women," graphite, 14 X 17, 2000

"Circle of Women" represents my first evening at a residency with many other artists from around the world. The interest here was representing the meeting of so many different nationalities at once. And, although we were very different, we all had the same thing in common to draw us together: our work in art, poetry, and prose.

"Waiting for Time," graphite, 25 X 19, 1997

"Waiting for Time" is a much earlier drawing. It represents symbols of movement and, what I was attempting to suggest, as time passing: our ship coming in and our ship passing us by. Time seems to wait for no one, as they say. With my profession of teaching, and with a very busy schedule of activities, one barely has time to do one's real work: the art itself.

"Rushmore," etching, 16 X 13, 2002

This etching represents three views of my friend, her different moods and faces. They are actually studies for a placement on the page in different values, as well as images of the same person. My friend commented, "You made me look like Mt. Rushmore in one of the faces," so I titled it "Rushmore."

"Rain Forest Protestors," graphite, 17 X 14, 2000

"Rain Forest Protesters" represents the women joining together in an obviously hopeless attempt to stop the destruction of their forest and place of habitation and livelihood. These women have only their small, hopeless bodies to provide a barricade against the destruction. I was struck by this image and I tried to express the defiance and conviction expressed by the protesters.

For Isseis and Kibeis / Fr Niseis and Sanseis (35 X 64").
Oil, Barbed Wire; 1992.

Chapter 10

A GALLERY OF SOCIAL/POLITICAL ART: AN ESSAY

Yoshiro Sanbonmatsu

ABSTRACT

Boston's Gallery of Social/Political Art (GSPA) was started to encourage artists and non-artists to make and share social and political art in a public space. The Gallery, which has been located at the Community Church of Boston, engages an open board in the process of making democratic decisions about social and political art. The writer of this article, Yoshiro Sanbonmatsu, helped to start this gallery and has worked as an active board member since the beginning. Yoshiro Sanbonmatsu writes about how he started to paint political artwork at the end of the article and in the "Contributors" section at the end of the book. He provided a number of slides of his paintings, which appear in black and white prints.

INTRODUCTION

A call for artists declaring the founding of the Gallery of Social/Political Art (GSPA) was placed in periodicals and a few key locations in an area of Boston that was perceived to be highly energized and activist-oriented. The intent was to form a street level gallery open to all artists, and non-artists as well, who wished access to a public visual space for their social/political views. The gallery was to be founded on simple principles honestly applied. It believed in democracy, which meant access for all, and in equality, which meant respect for everyone's voice. It was not to be a showcase for individual artists; it was not to encourage individual aesthetics, ideas or goals as such; it was designed to be social/political in its scope and address current and socially relevant themes. It was to be a collective voice, ranging from radical to mainstream, urging eradication of social injustices.

The response was tepid and a meeting a year later of those interested signaled the problems the gallery would later face. Only thirteen artists and one non-artist attended and many were skeptical of the work and energy required to start and successfully operate a gallery. For them, time and money were a premium; free time went into their art and discretionary income into supplies. For some, a cooperative gallery with a thematic agenda ran counter their individual and artistic integrity. It seemed that most were primarily interested only in showing their works. The group decided against the formation of a gallery and opted to form an artists' support group, Artists for Social Justice (ASJ).

THE IDEA OF THE GALLERY

The idea of a gallery was kept alive by the enthusiasm of a few, which translated, with the help of a sponsor, into a show "Getting Together on Social Issues," so titled with the hope that it would harbinger additional ones. Fortunately, this first show attracted the eyes of two members of a radical church in Boston who suggested the show be moved to their assembly hall. Discussion ensued and the goals of the gallery and the radical vision of the church were found to be mutually supportive and a trial show was held. The reception was enthusiastic and the gallery, though remaining completely independent, joined them in residence. The arrangement was near ideal. Space for shows could be rented at a nominal rate; we had complete freedom to operate according to our tenets; and we were able to join an existing community that was actively current with a broad range of social issues and causes.

During the first season of operation, we over-scheduled and had to cut back because there was an insufficient number of volunteers, but there was sufficient interest to keep us encouraged. Most entries came from an ad placed in *ART New England*. We were not deluged but we got responses nation-wide, and in addition, comments as, "I never knew such a gallery existed." Alternative galleries abound but they are more than likely to be artist centered and not issue oriented. Our shows were thematically based: war and peace, sex and sexism, race and racism, and environmental justice. A catch-all show called individual concerns, not surprisingly, drew the largest group. Applicants were permitted to enter five slides of their work, of which at least one would be accepted as long the work reflected the theme of the show. Even non-artists were encouraged to show.

Though artists are inclined to feel that a work of art speaks for itself, we requested that each accepted piece be accompanied by an artist comment which would place the work, not in terms of the artistic merit or intent, but in the context of his social/political perspective. The show would then become a collective of social/political voices centered about a particular theme.

ORGANIZING THE GALLERY AND ART SHOWS

Operation of the gallery has never gone smoothly. We were plagued by the lack of volunteers and relied on the dedicated few, most whom lived outside of Boston. Though over a hundred artists had shown with us, most did not return. The reasons were many, ranging from single issue artists, dissatisfaction with the exposure the gallery received—political art is never a draw, and radicalism—though most were mainstream—associated with shows, to the more mundane reasons such as the lack of a professional staff and attendant courtesies and inconvenience of the location. Here too, a small core of returnees who believed in the gallery sustained its efforts. And surprisingly, new members always seemed to emerge.

In addition, there were recurring problems that conspired to make the gallery more artist-centered: more than a few argued to permit artists to include non-social/political pieces, permit small group shows, promote the sale of works and to apply for grants, arguing that supporting social/political artists supported social justice. Most artists seldom sold their works and, understandably, their first instinct is to survive, as art is their mainstay. The pressure to showcase artists for promotion and art sales was anticipated during the very beginnings of GSPA. The Artists for Social Justice, whose membership disappeared when no one came forward to take its helm, became an ad hoc organization. When it was suggested that those who wanted to showcase artists or allow nonpolitical pieces into shows use ASJ, no one was interested—they wanted a ready-made establishment.

The gallery as conceived stood against the art establishment's practice of awarding grants. Grants were dedicated to the improvement of the arts or the artists; the gallery was to be dedicated to social issues. Some felt that the gallery could be both a showcase and an instrument of social protest and tried to democratically work through the board, which comprised of any member who attended meetings, to modify the policy. Perhaps a grant could be found that would in no way compromise the gallery's tenets. Doubts were expressed: money would lead to upgrade, to improving the aesthetics of the gallery proper, to giving attention to appearance, to search for recognition, etc.

True, the showcasing of art and the artist would produce many more volunteers and create a lot of social energy for publicity and fund raising, all of which would feed the artists' hunger for attention and accomplishment. Artists could then say they were supporting, or was it marketing, social justice. They wanted the aesthetics and artistic success along with a marginalized kind of social activism. However, such a position would undermine the foundation of the gallery.

At times we faced our demise but moments of crisis always produced leadership and cohesion. There was always the danger that the art was just another show, but over time, the cohesion of the theme and the inspiration felt through the artist's comments proved uniquely satisfying for the public and for the participating artists.

ARTISTS AND THE POLITICS OF ART

Artists for most part are members of the establishment, formalized in their training and in their integrity and ambition. This formalism is habitualized, time-tested art history and is a part of the myths of our cultural legacy. Forgotten is the underlying reality of what transpired. Western civilization conquered the world and spread its dominant culture (male)—all is glorified in our history. But the truth is the light of enlightenment that was exported was essentially cultural imperialism (based on race) with its attendant genocide. Forgotten too is the cultural awe that the arts inspire to the detriment of our natural inclination to express ourselves. The most inhibiting is the use of the human voice in song. If everyone were able to, at anytime and anywhere, sing, solo or in groups, without formalized training, how much healthier would society be (though musicians might be up in arms). And similarly what percentage of the population feel inhibited because they've been numbed into "I can't draw."

The foundation of the art world remains the establishment with its board rooms, museums, trading houses, aspiring galleries and so on, all under-girded by treasures, i.e., money. It is not interested in freedom for those denied access; it is interested in genius and fame. The establishment assumes a preemptive philosophy that great art is an expression of freedom, a universality that ironically becomes unfreedom for the disenfranchised and marginalized. Artists are part of the establishment in this process. They are given a privileged position in society as the vanguard of free expression, but too often freedom means one's own and not the others.' This is not to say that artistic freedom should in any way be curtailed, but it should be realized that artists unwittingly curb the freedom of expression for others and, therefore, contribute to social injustice.

Traditional art operates on a transcendent principle that aesthetics leads beyond reality to higher truths. The core to this principal is the notion of self-expression and artistic integrity. There is art and there are artists but for a gallery of social/political art the bottom line is the question of social justice. It must be remembered that the history of art is implicated in the cultural genocide that accompanied the conquest of the world. "Memories of fire" lay buried and continue to smolder because of injustices done. Art needs to become honest —though not to necessarily espouse political/social views; it must encourage total freedom of expression, not only for those who make the so-called grade, but to provide access for the expression of injustices and demands of justice, immediate or in retrospect. Victims are the other who have been obliterated by historians of so-called great event and great men, just as cries for justice are shunted by the worship of works by the "great" artists.

CONCLUSIONS ABOUT THE GALLERY OF SOCIAL/POLITICAL ART

A social /political gallery is the other gallery. Traditional galleries for the most part are museum centered and aspire to showing 'great' works of art that meet certain criteria; the other gallery is street or reality centered and strives to give access to all and let the voice of the victims speak irrespective of aesthetics. It is victim centered and not artist centered— though it could be both. It is democracy at work in that it is participatory and provides access for all; it believes in equality because it fundamentally respects everyone and says one person's political statement is equal to another's, not deemed irrelevant and not worth bothering about. It thrives to speak out about the inequities and injustices of past, present and the likely future today, not posthumously in a mausoleum.

YOSHIRO SANBONMATSU'S AUTOBIOGRAPHICAL ART STATEMENT

I consider myself more social critic than painter and look at what happens today as an extension of a past that is buried by denial and covered by myths and lies. Unless we are honest and admit to what we've done and are doing, the problems of society will forever resurface. And to be honest we have to admit that history didn't or doesn't just happen— individuals, groups and institutions, especially those in position of power, govern the process.

The problem of ethnicity has more or less been the context of my life. Internally, however, I was brought up, like many Asians, to believe in social harmony and therefore be deferential to circumstances and the social order. With World War II and the civil rights and anti-war movements of the sixties my upbringing changed. The realities of American policy and politics, both domestic and foreign, obliterated that deference.

Michelangelo / Dorothea Lange (24 X 30"). Oil, 1994.

'76 (32 X 38"; 30 X 24"). Oil, 1991.

As Long As The Grass Grows (44 X 70"). Oil, 1993.

Mylai (30 X 24"). Oil, 1994.

Chapter 11

PRISON INTELLECTUALS AND
THE STRUGGLE FOR ABOLITION[*]

Mechthild Nagel

ABSTRACT

What happens when radical prisoners' writings are introduced into a college curriculum? I wish to offer the perspectives of "regular" college students and imprisoned college students. This article discusses the emergence of prisoners' neo-slave narratives and how radical education and prison experience have shaped the thinking of political prisoners. How can outside/inside organizing be strengthened and what might be the role of prison education in this process?

The prisons have made me what I am. The prisons have made me a revolutionary, the prisons have made me progressive and political, the prisons have made me a human being.

-Carl L. Harp

INTRODUCTION

On my recent trip to Mali to study prisons and penal abolition, a judge told me the following: "I used to be very tough on crime, sentencing every offender to long prison terms. One day my son was stopped on the street and told, 'Your father is a thief! He is stealing people.' Then I had a change of heart and am now rethinking punishment." He went to the International Conference on Penal Abolition (ICOPA IX) in Toronto in 2000[1] to learn from activists around the world how they have stopped prison expansion and are working towards

---

[*] For discussion and research assistance I am grateful to Tiyo Attallah Salah-El and Joy James. This paper has benefited from comments by Katie Williams and Torry Dickinson.
[1] The next ICOPA conference will be sponsored by the Prison Moratorium Project in New York City in 2004 (www.nomoreprisons.org). ICOPA X was held in Nigeria (2002).

penal reform and overhaul of the criminal justice system. Whether living in the global North or in the (post)colonial South, prisons are a preferred site for meting out punishment; in fact, prisons engulf us psychically in a way that Foucault identifies as "carceral society." It is difficult to imagine a society that would completely replace their Western penal code—replete with police, surveillance, and prison apparati—with traditional or transformative caring communities. From the new South Africa to the First Nations' sentencing circles, prison is part and parcel of the punishing codex. How do we create a movement that breaks that logic, the "race to incarcerate"[2] poor people, especially Latino/as and African Americans, on "the slave ship that doesn't move?"[3]

In this paper, I wish to address the ways that prison intellectuals have been instrumental in shaping our imagination vis-à-vis abolitionist strategies. In particular, I am interested in the way that Black political[4] prisoners write neo-slave narratives; writing as "slaves of the State" aka as 'Afrikans in Amerikkka' (e.g., Abu-Jamal 1995, Acoli 1998; N'Zinga 2000, NOBO 1995, Assata Shakur 1987, Forde/Mattis 2001, Abdul Shakur 1999). The imprisoned writer and social critic connects the radical movement against slavery of the nineteenth century with a concerted struggle against today's criminal injustice system. This critic and revolutionary also reflects on the challenges of border-crossings and on forging community ties which tear down the inside/outside walls of separation and isolation: Protest actions, such as "Millions march for Mumia" in Philadelphia, 1999; the Critical Resistance Conferences attended by thousands of young people; the Jericho Movement to free all U.S. political prisoners; the rallying cry of "Education, not Incarceration" of the organized youth of color in Brooklyn—these are examples of an emerging consensus against the criminalization of poor people and people of color; and these are just a few examples of actions coordinated by prisoners and ex-prisoners. In this article, I wish to reflect on 'outside' attitudes about prisoners and contrast them with 'inside' reflections by prisoners. But I worry about their iconic status, as heroes and martyrs; it's important to show that many of them struggle to become abolitionists and thus fight the system that physically and psychologically entombs them, often subjected to total segregation (cf. Elijah, 1995). The point I wish to make is that there is nothing self-evident about prisoners becoming involved in restorative justice and penal abolition causes, rather it is an evolving, protracted conscientization process.

TEACHING ABOUT PRISONS

For a number of years, I have introduced students to writings by Mumia Abu-Jamal and other political prisoners. I am a white, recent immigrant who teaches social philosophy at a public university in Central New York, which is surrounded by more men's prisons than colleges and universities. In my general education classes, we also read essays by noted Critical Race theorists who stress the white supremacist legal tradition. We discuss the contradictions embedded in the Thirteenth Amendment to the U.S. Constitution, which set

2 Cf. Marc Mauer's book *The Race to Incarcerate*.
3 Shaka N'Zinga, *A Disjointed Search for the Will to Live* (2000).
4 Political prisoner not only describes those who are imprisoned for their political associations and beliefs (such as Abu-Jamal, Leonard Peltier, Marilyn Buck, and the Puerto Rican *independentistas*) but also those who come to prisons because of certain social crimes and become political organizers, e.g., most famously, George Jackson whose assassination by prison guards sparked the Attica Rebellion in 1971.

slaves free at the same time that it re-enslaves them as convict-laborers when found guilty of a crime. The result of these discussions? White students tend to overlook de facto and de jure segregation, feeling temporarily sorry for Blacks and other people of color, but quickly recover their gut prejudices about who deserves to be uplifted and who ought to be demonized. A fairly typical response of students, who study Abu-Jamal's and other radical political prisoners analyses, notes the racism in the prison system but launches a vicious attack on prisoners who benefit from a free college education paid for by taxes (sic). The ideology of "pulling yourself up by your bootstraps" is very prevalent and under no circumstances should the condemned be given "special rights." One cannot expect any positive contribution from "them" and one should not waste any valuable resources on prisoners. Such passionate rejection of rehabilitative services is instructive for prison who swim against the tide of political sentiments of the white working and middle-class college student body and popular sentiments at-large. Perhaps such students would think differently, if they had attended a recent conference "What good can come out of prisons?" which highlighted college level education, art, parenting and restorative justice as viable alternative ways to the punitive 'correctional' (sic) model of justice.

What is the status of prisoners' rights? Is it true that "they have it given to them"? My civilian escort at a super-max prison in Central New York echoes this sentiment. She overheard guards complaining that prisoners had more rights than the C.O.'s (correctional officers). When I ask her to explain and give examples, she became silent. Civilians, who supervise college programs, and C.O.s alike resent the imposition of free college classes to a select group of men (15 out of 1200!) and often do everything in their power to sabotage liberatory education which address radical notions of freedom, equality, and social justice and which refuses to churn out well adjusted prisoners who accept their status as offenders and in turn repent their crimes. One of the veiled forms of sabotage is a sit-in by education program officials who are eager to learn about philosophy![5]

Recent laws are eerily reminiscent of the infamous Dred Scott Supreme Court decision, which declared that "the black man has no rights that a white man is bound to respect." The threshold for demonization continues to sink. In McCleskey v. Kemp (1987) the Supreme Court accepted the fact that racial prejudice in the allocation of the death penalty is the price to pay for upholding this barbaric practice. Not unlike my students, the majority of the high court is capable of evacuating logic and argue for a racist death penalty "as if there were no Civil War and no chattel slavery … [A]s if there were no Dred Scott decision, no Medgar Evers, Little Rock, nor 'Bombingham'" (Tibbs, quoted in Abu-Jamal 1995, 17).

Before they read *Live from Death Row* my students believed that prisoners, of course, ought to have no rights, and death row prisoners, particularly, ought to suffer for their crimes. After reading Abu-Jamal's works (and discussing the travesties of his own court case), most students shifted from a position of "no rights for prisoners!" to a reformist position that acknowledged that the criminal justice system is somewhat flawed and that prisoners deserve

---

[5]   Thanks to Olivia Armstrong for suggesting the term sabotage in this context. She participated in a college program in 1976 when she was imprisoned at Bedford Hills, New York. For a brief time the women were furloughed to attend Westchester Community College during the day, but the guards sabotaged the program by contaminating the women's urine. (The women could only participate if they were found clean of drugs.) The guards' act of sabotage was later quietly acknowledged by prison administrators to Ms. Armstrong who persevered and received a BSW on the outside and invited top-level officials to her graduation. (personal communication, October 2002)

some human rights protection. During one fall semester (in 1999), several students ended up writing to Mumia and his counsel. Some began to question the (racist, capitalist) ideology of criminal justice, and a few students have become abolitionists.

To dream of radical, community-based, approaches to transformative justice (Sullivan, Tifft 2001) is a rare feat—even in prisons. When I taught a political philosophy course in a medium security prison, I ended the course with a screening of *Battle of Algiers*, *Frantz Fanon*, *Black Skin White Masks* and Angela Davis' speech on penal abolition (at the ICOPA IX conference). We discussed colonialism, racism, and the ideological function of prisons. When we questioned how many people should be excarcerated from total institutions, at first, their answers didn't differ from the SUNY Cortland students, insofar as the prisoners accepted the fact that one deserved to be punished by long prison sentences for particular crimes. But one student thought about it and suggested that three percent of the total prison population should remain confined, which is about the percentage of people who never leave New York State prisons. (This is the same figure often cited in abolitionist circles, when it comes to the question of what to do with the difficult offenses, such as serial murders and sex crimes. The point is that most abolitionists would want to hold on to some form of total institution, rather than excarcerate all prisoners.)

What I learnt from that exchange is that there is nothing organic or natural about transforming into a radical critic of the carceral society. In this context I will turn to a discussion of slave and radical neo-slave narratives. I will highlight the work of two prominent writers who became incarcerated due to their political affiliations: Mumia Abu-Jamal and Assata Shakur. I wish to contrast their writings with prison letters and autobiographies of politicized prisoners, George Jackson and Tiyo Attallah Salah-El.

PRISON INTELLECTUALS

As John Wideman notes in his introduction to Abu-Jamal's book *Live from Death Row*, we need to differentiate between the ideological tenor of contemporary prison writers and 19th Century critics of slavery. In the ante bellum years, slave narratives distinguished between servitude (south) and freedom (north). Escape from slavery was the main goal to attain total political freedom. 19th Century abolitionists didn't necessarily have a class analysis (Garrison was anti-union); and, for complex reasons, the white labor movement was not involved in the abolitionist cause. Wideman notes that the equation of prison with slavery and the state of release with freedom dominates the genre of contemporary heroic (ex) prison stories and thus brings up parallels to slave narratives. By contrast, we see an emergence of radical neo-slave narratives that accomplish something quite different. 20th Century radical prison intellectuals have an acute awareness of imperialism, capitalism, racism, and sexism and have written how prisons and the death penalty are part of the logic of that web of oppression. They have a complex understanding of the notion of freedom and do not reduce it to liberty garnered by the individual heroic person who escapes slavery. As Wideman points out, even if Abu-Jamal is freed tomorrow, he does not enjoy positive freedom (right to housing, education, meaningful employment, etc.) in a capitalist, racist society (Abu-Jamal, xxxiv). However, Wideman does not point out that Abu-Jamal evolved into a fierce critic of the prison industrial complex. Abu-Jamal, a former Black Panther, acknowledges that only when his appeals were denied that his belief in the American justice system was shattered:

Perhaps I'm naïve, maybe I'm just stupid—but I thought the law would be followed in my case, and the conviction reversed ... Even in the face of the brutal Philadelphia MOVE massacre of May 13, 1985, that led to Ramona Africa's frame-up ..., my faith remained. Even in the face of this relentless wave of antiblack state terror, I thought my appeals would be successful. I still harbored a belief in U.S. law, and the realization that my appeal had been denied was a shocker (1995, xviii-xix).

Similarly, the Puerto Rican independentistas were at first incredulous when they faced obstacles in the court of law after their capture. Like Abu-Jamal, they understood the intersections of imperialism and racism, but underestimated the wrath of the system which declares them enemies to be neutralized:

We had incredibly naïve views about what the justice system was like. Even though one's against the system, the basic myth of democracy was still there. "'Ellos no pueden hacer eso!' [They can't do that!]" became a standing joke (Juan Segarra Palmer, cited in Jan Susler, 2000).

Several years ago, Abu-Jamal's essays were commissioned for NPR but due to pressure by the Fraternal Order of Police and candidate Bob Dole, NPR declined to air these essays which are now available on CD and in a new book *All Things Censored*. Abu-Jamal has faced several months of disciplinary custody for writing his books *Live from Death Row* and *Death Blossoms*. His death sentence has been vacated but he continues to be caged on death row, rather than in general population. Even though he could gain personal freedom for making certain political concessions, he refuses to do. He is relentless in his critique of Black churches in his recent book *Death Blossoms*. He resists the standard slave-narrative that stresses individual heroism—indeed he barely talks about his case, to the great surprise of my students. Angela Davis, too, finds this noteworthy. After meeting him in October 1999, she says that he "thinks collectively. He said that he always thinks about himself in relation to others, never about himself. Even if he is able to win his case it would not be a personal victory." Abu-Jamal also implored Davis to think about the parallels of their trials (i.e., the "Free Angela Davis!" campaign) and educate and mobilize people accordingly.[6]

As Abu-Jamal's experience shows, prison conditions for these political prisoners (even when they are cause célèbre) are particularly harsh. In a training session with a coordinator for volunteer services, i.e., a gatekeeper for prisoners' access to higher education and religious services, I was told about "unruly" inmates (sic). The coordinator mentioned that one person had to be restrained and disciplined for talking about slave-like conditions during lunch hour—"and that was like yelling 'fire' in a crowded theatre!" Over the years, criminologists and correctional personnel have analyzed the actions of six organizers who protested on Black Solidarity Day in SC Auburn in 1971 and subsequently were sent to SC Attica, where a mere six months later a prison rebellion erupted. They clearly were seen as masterminding the collective action. The Attica Rebellion was also sparked by the assassination of George Jackson, a Soledad Brother, whose prison letters were published a year earlier (and reissued by Jonathan Jackson, Jr., in 1994). In these letters, Jackson speaks of being a runaway slave, captured at age 18 (p. 4) and being a neo-slave (p. 111). His politicization is completed when he entered prison: "I met Marx, Lenin, Trotsky, Engels, and

---

[6] Peter Noel, "Mumia's Last Stand." in *The Village Voice*, Nov. 10, 1999, pp. 1-6 (online).

Mao. . . and they redeemed me" (p. 16). He fights the prison system but refuses the mantle of hero, writing repeatedly to Angela Davis that he is not a nice person. Echoing the sentiments of Carl Harp (the motto of this article) and Oscar Wilde's "Ballard of Gaol," he writes to his lawyer a year before his murder:

> This camp brings out the very best in brothers or destroys them entirely. But none are unaffected. None who leave here are normal. If I leave here alive, I'll leave nothing behind. They'll never count me among the broken men, but I can't say that I am normal either. I've been hungry too long. I've gotten angry too often. I've been lied to and insulted too many times. . . . I know that they will not be satisfied until they've pushed me out of this existence altogether. I've been the victim of so many racist attacks that I could never relax again. My reflexes will never be normal again. I'm like a dog that has gone through the K-9 process (1994, 27-28).

As Tiyo Attallah Salah-El writes in his unpublished autobiography, once the prison authorities learned that he was a prison abolitionist, all of his privileges were taken away. Among other personal items his typewriter was destroyed in a daily shakedown of his cell (cage is in fact his preferred word and does not have the charming connotations of monastic cell), because they was seen as a political threat to the establishment. Salah-El has coordinated for several years the Coalition for the Abolition of Prisons, Inc. and has overseen the quarterly journal, *Broken Chains* (past editions are available on noprisons.org). He writes explicitly about his journey towards prison abolitionism:

> I did not become an abolitionist over night. It took years of reading, studying, and asking lots of questions. Having teachers such as Monty Neill and Howard Zinn leading me into new fields of study was the key factor which in turn was indeed a blessing. Reading the works of Marx, Homer, Cervantes—looking at the powerful paintings of Picasso, Chico Mendes, African, Native American and Mexican art—listening to the powerful and beautiful music of Miles Davis, John Coltrane, ..., Bach, List ..., all played a part in my development. My imagination soared. I gained an international perspective regarding politics and prisons. I became a dialectical dreamer with my brain reeling with visions and dreams of a radically new society founded on a total transformation in human relationships and the abolition of prisons (139).

Salah-El's paper on abolition was read at the recent ICOPA X conference and was cited in a Nigerian newspaper that reported on the conference.

In *Eyes of the Rainbow*, by Cuban film maker Gloria Rolanda (1997), former Black Panther Party member Assata Shakur talks about her status as a 20th Century run-away slave—an apt self-description given the bounty for her issued by Governor Whitman; she recounts her jail term, at times spent in male prisons, where sharp shooters' guns were trained onto her cell 24 hours a day. Her case won international attention, when a petition was sent to the United Nations Commission on Human Rights in 1978. Shakur was broken out of prison by Marilyn Buck, Silvia Baraldini and Susan Rosenberg[7] in 1979 and now lives in exile in Cuba. In her autobiography Assata Shakur interweaves narratives of coming of age in the 1960s with accounts about the shootout on the New Jersey Turnpike, the several court trials

---

[7] As Joy James (1999) notes few people know about these women revolutionaries who are serving life sentences for their part in breaking out Assata (89). Baraldini and Rosenberg have since been released.

she was subjected to, and the disregard for the law by the authorities at every stage. She understood the repression, the torture, the interrogation, and the blatant illegalities due to her status as political detainee. At the time of her arrest, she was active in the Black Liberation Army, but it was not till her confinement that she learnt about the ideological function of imprisonment. Confronted by a guard who ordered her to work, Shakur disobeys, "You can't make me work." The guard's response was "No, you're wrong. Slavery was outlawed with the exception of prisons. Slavery is legal in prisons" (64). Shakur re-read the 13th Amendment and realized that racism is part and parcel of the capitalist system.

> That explained why jails and prisons all over the country are filled to the brim with Black and third world people, why so many Black people can't find a job on the streets … Once you're in prison, there are plenty of jobs, and, if you don't want to work, they beat you up and throw you in the hole. … Prisons are part of this government's genocidal war against Black and third World people (64-5).

Imprisonment radicalized her thinking about "aberrations" in the system. In a moving exchange with another prisoner, she shares her notion of "freedom":

> [I'd] rather be in a minimum security prison or on the streets than in the maximum security prison in here. The only difference between here and the streets is that one is maximum security and the other is minimum security. The police patrol our communities just like the guards patrol here. I don't have the faintest idea how it feels to be free (60).

Assata's autobiography, which chronicles her journey from childhood to being marooned in Cuba, is a very important example of a radical neo-slave narrative.

INSIDE/OUTSIDE ORGANIZING

We need to create different models of community. Instead of participating in the marginalization of prisoners, we need to work hard to expand our notion of activism, of coalition building to include prisoners, who do not have access to email, toll-free phone calls, and privacy. As Angela Davis points out we need to avoid patronizing prisoners, and instead listen to prison intellectuals and pay attention to prison activism. Prisons are rife with tensions and organized resistance. Prison visitors and program volunteers need to be mindful of their role to contribute to prison reform and be a watchful eye when state repression occurs. It was a political prisoner, Jalil Muntaquim, who organized the Jericho Movement a few years ago; in the meantime it has grown into an international organization and has been able to get release for some of the 150 political prisoners/ POWs in the United States. Muntaquim has just been denied parole (July 2002) after serving almost 30 years in prison for his participation in the Black Panther Party. He is caged in one of the oldest prisons in the US, in Auburn, NY, where he has started a Lifer's Committee.

In New York State, prisoners in all 70 state facilities prepared for a work stoppage for better working and parole conditions on January 1, 2000. Their organizing tool was the clandestine "Wake Up!!! Manifesto," first circulated at SC Sing Sing. In SC Greenhaven, prisoners held silent meals in defiance and preparation for January 1. Prison officials worked hard to preempt the non-violent action, issuing lock-downs, after finding 'suspicious' gun powder (which may have well been planted by guards) and shipping key organizers to Upstate prisons. Some officials speculated that it was Sing Sing and Greenhaven prison volunteers who incited the prisoners to organize—another assault by the system on the prisoners' intelligence! One of my students in an Upstate prison was punished to three months in the "box" (i.e., segregation) after he mentioned the "Wake Up!!! Manifesto" within earshot of a guard. The anonymous authors of the Manifesto charge:

> Why should we be the raw materials in the DOCS [Department of Correctional Services] prison industrial corporation which only serves the interests of politicians to be elected into office, and to provide jobs for rural Northern New Yorkers? Why should we work to maintain the prisons as porters, cooks, plumbers, masons, welders, tailors, roofers, painters . . . or in any capacity necessary to keep DOCS prison corporation functioning properly? (cited in Gonnerman, 1999).

Indeed, prisons could not be maintained without the slave labor as a recent work strike demonstrated. As I prepare to teach in a supermax prison, I learnt that in June 2002, a two-week non-violent stoppage occurred at that prison, and civilian staff members were called upon to put in an extra four hours to take over the prisoners' "job bids." What are some of the creative strategiess to contest a carceral society and PATRIOT acts?

- Foreign nationals, one of the fastest growing group of prisoners in the federal prisons, have alerted us to their plight, most recently, in Louisiana. Cuban immigrants took guards as hostage and demanded immediate freedom for being held illegally by the INS. These are prisoners, who have completed their sentences in federal or state prisons, only to find themselves detained in overcrowded county jails. Several family members of prisoners (of Cuban descent) staged a hunger strike and were able to get their sons released.[8]
- The fate of foreign nationals reminds us to create a global prison reform/abolitionist movement. ICOPA is such a model: The International Conference on Penal Abolition meets every two years and assesses global resistance movements inside prisons and out. This conference is unique insofar as it attracts pacifist activists, academics, journalists, ex-prisoners from all over the world to share analyses and strategies for change.
- We have to be creative on all fronts to fight for change. As abolitionist Salah-El (2000) points out we have seen an increase in jury defiance or hung juries, because they are unwilling to agree to stiff mandatory sentences. From families of prisoners to victims' groups, there is a growing movement for restorative justice that is more community-based and not as much state-run; however, in reality restorative justice advocates tend to rely on ethical and individual solutions and not develop macroscopic anti-capitalist analyses. Even though some of us are staunch supporters of abolitionism, we have to work in unlikely coalitions with the goal to raise consciousness about and resistance to the Omnibus Crime Bill, to the death penalty, to prison torture, etc. Sometimes this coalition work demands of us to take contradictory positions, e.g. to work with civil rights groups pushing for Hate Crime

---

[8]   Cf. Amy Goodman, Democracy Now, December 16, 1999.

legislation which increases penalties or work with battered women advocates demanding more police protection.

Yet, as abolitionist Fay Honey Knopp (1993) points out "[t]he issue of sexual abuse and how society responds to and punishes it is an abolitionist issue. ...The issues for people of color and feminist issues are inclusive not separate tracts" (53). She implores feminists not to give in to the "caging mentality" and to work on providing alternative programs for sex-offenders. Several case studies of successful programs in the Bay area are featured in the abolitionist handbook *Instead of Prisons*; however, more attention needs to be paid by feminist advocates to the intersections of race, gender, and citizenship. There is very scant discussion of these issues in restorative or abolitionist literature.

CONCLUSION

In the final section, I will return to the activist dimension of teaching, in particular, teaching in prisons. Prison narratives have a long philosophical tradition, but few professional philosophers would consider assigning both the Apology and Assata Shakur's autobiography in our introductory classes, even though both give a salient critique of the unexamined life, of justice, and of the existence of political prisoners. Both texts give us a tremendous opportunity to analyze the contrasting ideologies of statism and of revolutionary thinking.

Few of us consider the opportunity of teaching in prisons, even though rich philosophical discussions take place, and we have at least as much to learn from the men and women in prisons as they do from us "experts." One such text that probes this issue in a compassionate way is *The Soul Knows No Bars*. It brings up interesting social issues and importantly humanizes the students and questions the cruelty of incarcerating them for a lifetime. Leder even steps outside the teacher role and becomes a prisoners' rights advocate by seeking (and winning!) clemency for one of the students. Yet, the book is also fraught with problems; its author, a philosopher, is not in tune about "dishonest language"[9]: He refers to the students as "inmates" instead of as prisoners, a jargon that minimizes the effect of "caging" and foregrounds the "residential" aspect.

The different chapters, which center around a particular philosophical theme, highlight prison life, inner city Baltimore street life, violent offenses, remorse, etc., precisely, "alien" experiences to the author. Leder uses philosophy not unlike Socrates who uses to the trope of the midwife when he probes his interlocutors. He ponders, "How did the men first get involved in criminal activity?" (p. 9), and thus he seems insensitive to the claims of innocence made by at least one of the students. In this context of teaching in a total institution, this Socratic method seems paternalistic, the dialogues are overly confessional, and Leder exploits the self-revelatory aspects by providing photo and biographical snapshots of each man (all lifers) who agreed to participate in the making of the book. I particular am troubled by the condescending tone in which Leder conjures up a psychological profile ("But as I got to know him better, I realized here's a thoughtful man." Or "If he still steals, it's now mainly books for

---

[9] *Instead of Prisons* has a wonderful discussion of "The Power of Words" and "Nine Perspectives for Prison Abolitionists" which highlight the ideological dimensions of 'inmate' (i.e., prisoner), 'corrections' and 'correctional personnel', etc. (pp.10).

his shelf."). I doubt that he would have received approval for his "phenomenological method" from his Institutional Review Board if he had subjected his book project to academic and ethical standards.[10]

Leder's book certainly opens up new dimensions about prisoners and prison life to a white middle class audience that is untouched by persistent criminalization, and readers may find that these men are indeed compassionate, thoughtful, articulate, and not callous monsters. Yet, I worry about other academics who wish to follow Leder's footsteps, and who find themselves in a classroom full of stubborn men who prefer to talk about the article and not dwell on their own life experiences.

For "outsiders," prison education is certainly in many ways an opportunity for growth, for doing rewarding community service, for transgressing forbidden spaces and connecting with people who are truly forgotten and discarded. But this trespassing is fraught with problems, indeed for some of us compounded with a "white man's burden."[11] The challenge is to resist this ideology and learn from the exemplary work of political prisoners who shed light on injustices and encourage us to think of new forms of organizing to break down those walls, brick by brick.

REFERENCES

Abu-Jamal, Mumia. 1995. *Live from Death Row.* New York: Addison-Wesley.

_____. 1997. *Death Blossoms.* Farmington, PA: Plough Publishing.

_____. 2000. *All Things Censored.* New York: Seven Stories Press.

Acoli, Sundiata. 1998. *An Updated History of the New Afrikan Prison Struggle.* Harlem, NY: Sundiata Acoli Freedom Campaign.

Amnesty International. 1999. *Not Part of My Sentence: Violations of the Human Rights of Women in Custody.* New York, March.

Anonymous. 1999. '"WAKE UP!!!" Manifesto'. Cited in "Prisoners Plan a Work Stoppage To Protest Parole Cuts Strike Behind Bars," Jennifer Gonnerman, *Village Voice* December 22 - 28, 1999. online

Elijah, Soffiyah Jill. 1995. "Conditions of Confinement-Cruel and Unusual Punishment for Black Political Prisoners." In *Black Prison Movements USA. NOBO, Vol. II* (1). Trenton, NJ.: Africa World Press.

Forde, Anton/Trevor Mattis. 2001. *Contemplations of a Convict: Aphorisms for the Heart and Mind.* Haverford, PA: Infinity Press.

Jackson, George. 1970/1995. *Soledad Brother. The Prison Letters of George Jackson.* Foreword by Jonathan Jackson, Jr. Chicago: Lawrence Hill Books.

James, Joy. 1999. *Shadowboxing.* NY: St. Martin's Press.

Julien, Isaac. 1995. *Frantz Fanon: Black Skin, White Mask.* San Francisco, CA: California Newsreel.

---

[10] All universities and colleges are required to have IRB boards, which were instituted after the Tuskegee experimentation on poor Black men who suffered from syphillis were made public in the early 1970s. Prisoners are considered vulnerable populations and, therefore, particular guidelines have to be put into place in a research project to protect them from exploitation and other forms of abuse.

[11] Anton Forde/Trevor Mattis (2001) gives an interesting twist: "I wonder why most prison volunteers are older white women, when most of the prison population are young Black men?" (p. 11).

Knopp, Faye Honey. 1993. "On Radical Feminism and Abolition." In *We Who Would Take No Prisoners,* edited by B. MacLean and Hal Pepinsky. Vancouver: Collective Press.

Leder, Drew. 2000. *The Soul Knows No Bars. Inmates Reflect on Life, Death, and Hope.* Lanham, MD: Rowman and Littlefield.

Mauer, Marc. 1999. *The Race to Incarcerate.* New York: New Press.

Noel, Peter. 1999. "Mumia's Last Stand." *The Village Voice*, Nov. 10. online.

Prison Research Education Action Project (PREAP). 1976. *Instead of Prisons. A Handbook for Abolitionists.* Brooklyn, NY: Faculty Press.

Salah-El, Tiyo Attallah. (n.d.) *Autobiography of Tiyo Attallah Salah-El.* (Revolutionary Vagabond).

_____. 2000. "Jury Defiance." *The Coalition for the Abolition of Prisons, Inc.,* Vol.8, March.

Shakur, Abdul O. 1999. *Ghetto Criminology: A Brief Analysis of Amerikkka Criminalizing a Race.* Daly City, CA: Black Panther Press.

Shakur, Assata. 1987. *Assata. An Autobiography.* Chicago: Lawrence Hill Books.

Sullivan, Dennis, and Larry Tifft. 2001. *Restorative Justice. Healing the Foundations of Our Everyday Lives.* Monsey, NY: Willow Tree Press.

Suslar, Jan. 2000. "Puerto Rican Political Prisoners." *Radical Philosophy Review*, Vol.3(1): 28-40.

Chapter 12

THE ROAD LESS TRAVELED: RETHINKING PRISON EDUCATION

Rashad Shabazz

ABSTRACT

This article highlights the role prison education has had in developing radical political analysis in the post-Civil Rights movement, and advocates for both community activists and educators to support general education programs within prisons. In writing this piece, it is the author's hope to get both community activists and educators to think critically about the importance of general education programs in prisons, the role prison education plays in prison activism, and how the two are necessary in creating sustainable prison abolitionist movements. These movements dismantle state or private institutions of incarceration and the institutions that codify them: courts and policing. The concluding section provides some practical steps one can take to become involved in anti-prison activism.

INTRODUCTION

As indicated by a recent study by the Washington-Based Sentencing Project, 6.6 million Americans are under the jurisdiction of state and federal criminal justice agencies, which equals to 1 out of ever 32 people being on parole, probation, jail or prison—the majority of these people being poor and nonwhite (Salant, 2002). This means that a substantial amount of the current generation of young people will be socially and intellectually educated in penal facilities rather than high schools and universities. As is the case in many prisons, education is not mandatory. In many parts of the country, prison education programs are in fact being cut form state budgets. The shortsightedness of such policy decisions reinforces the current epidemic of state violence and racist repression through imprisonment by returning women and men back to their communities, which are often poor ones, without any educational or vocational training. Therefore, the state reneges on its professed commitment to rehabilitating the duly convicted and instead jumps on the bandwagon of dispensing both violent and psychological forms of punishment while guaranteeing high levels of recidivism.

IMPRISONMENT AND PRISON EDUCATION

The dramatic rise in the number of persons incarcerated over the past thirty years has lead to many scholars and activists to think critically about the position prisons occupy in society. Scholar activists like Angela Y. Davis ("From the Convict Lease System to Super Max Prison") and Ward Churchill (*Agents of Repression*), for example, have argued that prisons function to: (1) control social problems such as poverty and joblessness; (2) "neutralize" or diminish radical left-wing organizations—such as the Black Panther Party and the American Indian Movement—by criminalizing and subsequently incarcerating key persons; and (3) gather and dispense superfluous labor. In keeping with the tradition of radical thought around the function of prisons, literary critic and cultural theorist Barbara Harlow argues that prisons are not only institutions of punishment, but they are also alternative centers for radical intellectual training.

In *Barred: Women, Writing and Political Detention*, Harlow examines the role prison education serves in politically and intellectually educating prisoners. Says Harlow:

> Penal institutions, despite, if not because of, their function as part of the state's corrosive apparatus of physical detention and ideological containment, provide the critical space within which, indeed from out of which, alternative social and political practices of counter hegemonic insistence movements are schooled (Harlow, 1992:10).

In other words, Harlow holds that in spite of, if not because of, the attempted blunting of one's intellectual and political development, prisons also serve as "counter universities." In explicating this position, Harlow examines the literature of prison writers around the world. She finds that regardless of the schooling provided by prison officials (which in many cases is very little) prisoners organized and found alternative forms of education. In many cases this was done to better understand their own predicament. In the United States, for example, during the anti-prison movement in California in the late 60s and 70s, black prisoners formed "secret political study groups" in order to become well versed on the political and economic issues of the day. These study groups had members from organizations such as the Black Panther Party, Black Muslims, Symbionese Liberation Army, and the Black Guerrilla Family (the prison wing of the Black Panther Party). Those involved in the study groups played a critical role in organizing many of resistance movements within prisons during the early 1970s (Cummings, 1994: vii). Underground newspapers and newsletters from prisons were also seen as important educational tools. In an attempt to build a theoretical bridge between the contradictory functions of the prison as a university, activists and scholars alike have, of late, used the term prison intellectual to conceptualize prisoners as intellectuals and to understand their role in thinking about social change. Organically constructed, the prison intellectual is a by-product of: the repression and isolation of prison life, the establishment of the prison as the center of intellectual training; and to use George Jackson's words, the "attempted transformation of the black criminal mentality into a black revolutionary mentality" (Jackson, 1994:16).

To combat the growth of poverty and unemployment, which became rampant in the 1970s, states focused their attention on displacing what it saw as expendable and superfluous populations into prisons. According to historian Scott Christianson, by the early 1970's prison expansion began to take shape (Christianson, 1998:279-281). Picking up where President Johnson ended, Nixon's get tough policies on crime and the birth of mandatory minimum sentences were furthered by building more and more prisons. The increasing number of criminal justice employees (police officers, prison guards, etc.) set the stage for the massive swelling of incarceration rates. In 1960, African Americans were 39 percent of the prison population; by 1974, they were 47 percent of the population (Franklin, 1978:280). The number of Chicana/o prisoners also increased dramatically from the 1960s. Prisons were quickly becoming the new housing program for America's poor and non-white population.

Movements to combat the prison growth emerged. Mirroring the consciousness of existing movements—the growing insurgency of the struggles for black, Chicana/o, and Native American liberation; women's rights; and Third World solidarity movements—prisoners wrote and took action in solidarity. The Attica and San Quentin prison uprisings; the prisoner strikes in California, and the push for unionization of prison workers all reflected the growing consciousness of prisoners. "The Folsom Prison Manifesto and Demands and Anti-Oppression Platform," for example, made demands such as: better health care, an end to the punishment of politically active and politically conscious prisoners, better visiting conditions, and amnesty for political prisoners (Davis, 1971:57-61).

As a further reflection of the consciousness and activism of the movement era, many prisoners of color, especially black and Chicana/o prisoners, were increasingly seeing themselves as political prisoners. As a result, Black and Chicana/o prisoners began advancing the position that they were political prisoners because their incarceration largely stems from structural patterns of oppressive economic order. Angela Davis argues:

The vicious circle liking poverty, police, courts, and prison is an integral element of the ghetto existence. Unlike the masses of whites, the path which leads to jails and prisons is deeply rooted in the imposed pattern of black existence. For this very reason, an almost instinctive affinity binds the mass of black people to the political prisoner (Davis in James, ed., 1998:49-50).

Prison writer and revolutionary George Jackson, echoes Davis's statement:

These prisons have always born a certain resemblance to Dachau and Buchenwald, places for bad niggers, Mexicans, and poor whites. But the last ten years have brought an increased percentage of crimes that can clearly by traced to political-economic causes (Jackson, 1970:26).

The consciousness and activism of the post-Civil Rights prisoner was also reflected in print. As literary critic and historian H. Bruce Franklin observes, at the tail-end of the Civil Rights movement an explosion of literary works produced by black prisoners emerged. Politically sophisticated, revolutionary, provocative, and powerful, the writings of prisoners upended the notion of the dumb, ignorant criminal and culminated with the establishment of a prison intelligencia (Franklin, 1978:240-247).

Of the many prison writers during this era, none more epitomized the label of intellectual than George L. Jackson. When he entered prison in the 1960s, Jackson—who was given one year to life for stealing $70.00 from a gas station register—became politicized while in prison. As he says in his book *Soledad Brother*, "I met Marx, Trotsky, Engels and Mao when I entered prison and they redeemed me" (Jackson, 1970:16). By the end of Jackson's life—a life that was abruptly cut short by the bullet of a corrections officer—the man who did not finish high school had become an articulate political theorist and strategist; he was leading the prison wing of the Black Panther Party, while publishing two classic prison texts: *Blood in My Eye* and *Soledad Brother*. Speaking about the role of the prisoner in revolution, Jackson states: "You will find no category more aware, more embittered, desperate or dedicated, to the ultimate remedy—revolution" (Jackson, 1970:26).

Intellectual work by prisoners, although always politically conscious, began to reflect the political climate of the 60s and 70s as well as generate its own ideas to the growing insurgency. The birth of the Black Panther Party and the Black liberation Army was heavily influenced by Malcolm X's prison writings; as a result these organizations became critical of the state's use of penal facilities. Throughout the 70s, writings and books by prisoners were making their way into bookstores. The prison writings of Black Panthers Eldridge Cleaver and George Jackson, for instance, showed that these disparate voices were not a passing fad. As a response to the public's interest in prison writings, presses were born to give voice to prison literature. However, by the early 1980s, the conservative rhetoric of the Reagan administration clipped the wings of prison writing, causing many of these presses to be shut down. It seemed that the growing anti-prison insurgency, including, for example, the San Quentin (August 21, 1971) and Attica rebellions (September 13, 1971), as well as street activism by anti-prison and anti-racist organizers, began to frustrate state officials. Subsequently, these activities helped bring about a wave of repression onto the shoulders of prisoners. According to prison analyst H. Bruce Franklin, "By 1984, every literary journal devoted to publishing stories and poems by prisoners was wiped out" (Franklin, 1998; page 14). Legislation like the "Son of Sam" law was put into place to restrict prison writing, related laws kept prisoners from making profits on writings. It was said that these laws were put into place to "protect the victim." Furthermore, at San Quentin and Soledad prisons, cell searches increased. Franklin argues that, instead of looking for weapons, these cell searches focused on finding "manuscripts" (Franklin, 1998: 11-12).

To make matters worse, penal institutions were also being used as ways to stimulate markets. Criminologist Nils Christie argues that "crime control" (policing, prisons, etc.) began to further its own cause by transforming itself into a lucrative industry; the new control exercised by police and prison officials posed as an entity of public service, but, in reality, it became more concerned with making profits (Christie, 1994).

Though alternative forms of education in prisons have been important in developing prison intellectuals and radical activism, I do not want to make the case that alternative prison-education can or should replace general education programs. It is necessary that states live up to their promise of rehabilitation by instituting general educational programs, which will complement their alternative education. This can help to offer some stability to the lives of those who leave correctional facilities. The marriage of alternative and general education is not only important for the health and well being of prisons, but it is also critical in developing sustainable prison abolition movements. Why? Because without general education programs inside prisons—reading, writing, grammar, mathematics, geography, and history—some of the more radical political analysis developed by prison intellectuals will be difficult to teach to other prisoners if they are illiterate or have no general education background. Furthermore, the observations and analyses of prisons by prisoners are and have been critical to the success of prison abolitionist movements (the writing of George and many of the Attica prisoners were indispensable to the development of the anti-prison movements in the early 1970s). This is simply because it is their voices that informs and shapes the movement, mostly through the literature that prisoners produce; and their ability to do so is directly influenced by their ability to read and write. Thus, without some form of general education within prisons, abolitionist organizations are left without a voice.

As states cut prison vocational and education programs while advocating for the building of more prisons (as is currently happening in Delano, California), schooling increasingly becomes more extinct both inside and outside of prisons. It is evident, through the current chain of events, that the state is not interested in instituting rehabilitation or attacking high recidivism rates. For example, a recent study by the Sentencing Project found that 67.5% of those released from prison were rearrested within three years (Salant, 2002). It is unconscionable that such egregious rates of recidivism exist even though studies show that in-prison programs—vocational, educational, and substance abuse—help reduce recidivism. The conclusion we are left with is that, rather than instituting the necessary programs to slow high recidivism rates and prison population growth, states, instead, have committed themselves to practicing punishment and ensuring high that the number of people in prisons remains high.

CONCLUSION

We are at a critical impasse. Now more than ever, teachers, activists, organizers, and educators are needed to fill the void the state has left. Both the activist and education communities have a role to play in addressing this situation, by becoming involved in direct community action. We can respond to this growing crisis in several ways. Some of these include: teaching classes; helping to supply prisoners with educational materials (i.e., Books Through Bars organizations); putting on a prison workshop; helping prisoners to become familiar with local and national colleges that have correspondence or online courses; teaching GED courses; working with prison newspapers or journals; attending local prison board meetings and advocating for more prison education programs; asking local high schools, churches, and universities to donate money and or resources to prison education programs; and contacting local prison activists' organizations and donating your time, energy, and resources. It is only through an organized effort by both the community activists and educators that prison education can indeed become a reality. For, without it, there is every indication that recidivism will not slow; that communities, which have been devastated by imprisonment, will continue to be victimized; and that the abolitionist community, which seeks to dismantle the prison apparatus, will loose one of its most important voices.

REFERENCES

Christie, Nils. 1994. *Crime Control as Industry: Towards Gulags Western Style.* New York: Routledge.

Christianson, Scott. 1998. *With Liberty For Some: 500 Years of Imprisonment in America.* Boston: Northeastern University Press.

Churchhill, Ward. 1988. *Agents of Repression.* Boston: South End Press

Cummings, Eric. 1994. *The Rise and Fall of California's Radical Prison Movement.* Stanford: Stanford University Press.

Davis, Angela Y. 1971. *If They Come in the Morning.* San Francisco, United Committee to Free Angela Davis.

Harlow, Barbara. 1972. *Barred: Women, Writing and Political Detention.* Hanover: Wesleyan University Press.

Franklin, H. Bruce. 1998. *Prison writing in 20th century America.* New York: Penguin.

Jackson, George. 1994. *Soledad Brother: The Prison Letters of George Jackson.* New York: Lawrence-Hill Books.

Jackson, George. 1990. *Blood in My Eyes.* Baltimore: Black Classic Press.

James, Joy, ed. 1998. *The Angela Davis Reader.* New York: Blackwell.

Salant, Jonathan D. 2002. "Record-setting 6.6 million Americans behind bars or on parole." *San Francisco Chronicle*, 26 August, final edition.

Shabazz, Rashad, "State University of the Ghetto: Prison Intellectuals and Black Liberation in the Post-Civil Rights Era." Masters thesis, Arizona State University, 2002, n.d.

Chapter 13

Making Music: Popular Education on Cultural Change

An Interview with Rick Allen

Abstract

When Rick Allen, singer and guitar player, agreed to perform for a nonviolence rally at Kansas State University (KSU) in fall 2002, participants of the University Campaign for Nonviolence had an opportunity to talk with him about music, politics, and inclusive visions of culture. This interview with Rick Allen was conducted by Torry Dickinson, as steering committee member for Kansas State University's Campaign for Nonviolence.

Here Rick Allen discusses what music has taught him about the connections among people. Through his work as a disc jockey, writer, composer, and musician, Rick Allen has explored the ways that music tells the different, yet connected life experiences of generational groups, social classes, ethnic groups, and women and men. An avid reader and follower of international politics, Rick Allen talks about how racism in the United States and in South Africa compelled him to compose a song about apartheid during the time that Nelson Mandela was still imprisoned. In this interview, the host of "The Rick Allen (Radio) Show," calls out for people to reach out to each other with mutual respect, and to participate in the making of open cultures.

Introduction

Rick Allen calls for alternative, democratic cultures to become the center of social life.

Like other radio personalities, musicians, and artists, Rick Allen has promoted the valuing of democracy and social equality through performance and radio. Radio shows often serve as centers of popular education. Likewise, popular education and cultural change are carried out in various ways, including through public libraries, university libraries and courses, secondary and elementary schools, museums, archives, oral history projects, community centers, television programs, newspapers, books, internet sites, and music groups.

INTERVIEW WITH A MUSIC MAKER

Q: You already know that I'm interested in how society is changing. What are the most interesting kinds of music that are developing today and what do they tell us?

A: I see young Black women taking a singer/songwriter approach. I see more young Black women playing the guitar and singing songs that are introspective yet broadly relatable. In the past most Black female artists were relegated to a performing role only (Aretha Franklin being a major exception); and they usually had to, or were under the impression that they had to, present a glamorous or sexy image. This is not to say that this was a substitute for talent. To the contrary, I think that there are overwhelmingly more non-Black artists who make it using image over talent. But I think that even the most talented Black female artists had to play the glamour game; even Bessie Smith had to wear evening gowns.

Artists like Tracy Chapman, Macy Grey and Alicia Keys, although sometimes playing it both ways, have broken out of the restraints of having to don wigs and spangles in order to reach an audience. Chapman, Toshi Reagon and others who compose and perform with guitar or piano are capable of presenting their music without the backing of a band. Like Rap, this makes their listeners more able to visualize making their own music. Like Rap, it opens possibilities for those who want to make music but feel daunted at the prospect of highly orchestrated and choreographed shows. It puts music making back into their hands. Maybe everyone's music shouldn't be heard, but everyone has the right to, and should be able to, make music for her/himself, if they wish.

Q: What else is going on that is new, and what's important about this?

A: The blending of Rock and Roll music with Rap is another important development. Kid Rock, Bloodhound Gang, Everlast are among those who incorporate Rap into a musical format (or vice versa). This brings Rock and Roll music right back to the grass roots level. It also makes older listeners more inclined to pay attention to new music without the automatic rejection they give to more hardcore forms of Rap. In addition, because older music is often sampled, these artists help younger, newer listeners become acquainted with older music that they too might have rejected out of hand. I don't think we will ever completely overcome the attitudes that cause people to think that all music made after they reached maturity is worthless, and that all music that came before they started actively listening is irrelevant and useless. But we are coming closer.

Q: Can we step back a moment? Let's say that you find yourself talking to someone ("old" or "young," or somewhere in between) who has no idea how to appreciate the social/political messages in musical pieces that have been written by composers from other generations or social groups. What would you tell this person to look for?

A: The first thing to consider regarding music is whether or not it appeals to your ears. There are artists whose political and social attitudes are compatible with mine (Holly Near and Phil Collins, for example), but I find it impossible to listen to their music. There are other artists whose politics I might disagree with, but whose work I find irresistible. Many Country and Western artists and Rhythm and Blues artists fall into this category. James Brown endorsed Ronald Reagan and God only knows what Hank Williams' politics were, but I consider them to be among history's most important and greatest musicians. I would say that it's very important not to judge by label or genre.

It's very important for those outside of Rap's cultural/generational core group to pay attention to the lyrics of a particular piece, as well as to keep in mind that Rap is the realization of the democratic and egalitarian principles behind good rock and roll music. For Rap music, an artist doesn't need a band or even to know how to sing. The only tools necessary are a tape recorder and an ability to express oneself in rhythm and rhyme. Outsiders (let's call them "adults") often deride this aspect of Rap, but I think it is the best part of it; Rap is open territory. Certainly some aspects of Rap can be off-putting, and it may not attract a lot of folks outside of its target audience, but it shouldn't be dismissed out of hand.

One of the best things about music is the endless archive that exists and the endless work that is to come. There is always more to enjoy and there always will be.

It is important to tap into the universal "vibration" musically. Open yourself up to new sounds, realize what we, as a human race, share and then your ability to enjoy different types of music will expand.

Q: Do radio listeners respond in positive ways to overt social messages in music?

A: Sometimes a social/political statement can be made even when the lyrics of a song don't directly deal with these issues. Listen to the blues, not modern or even electric-style Chicago blues, but the Delta blues of Muddy Waters, or the rural blues of Skip James, or Robert Johnson, and you can be politicized merely by the empathy it evokes. The same is true with the bluegrass music of Ralph Stanley, the women's blues in the form of Tammy Wynette and especially Loretta Lynn, and the working man's music of Hank Williams. When you really 'hear' what they are saying, whatever ethnic/social/racial differences you may have with the singer/writer, these differences become irrelevant. Hank Williams sings about every day men and women who hurt from heartbreak, who get up and go to work every day because they have to, and go out on Saturday night just to dance or drink or fistfight the pain away.

Q: Can you tell me more about how you make sense of social and political themes in rock or other genres?

A: When seen together, songs tell a more complete story of working women's and men's daily lives. Tammy Wynette in "Stand by Your Man" (a sorely misunderstood song) sings, "Sometimes it's hard to be a woman, giving all your love to just one man. You'll have sad times. He'll have good times, doing things that you don't understand. But if you love him, be proud of him. After all, he's just a man." She's singing about the man in Hank William's "Setting the Woods on Fire." "I'll gas up my hot rod Ford. We'll be hotter than a poker. You'll be broke, but I'll be broker. Tonight we're setting the woods on fire." And this man is merely the Country equivalent of the guy who is: "Sitting on the dock of the bay watching the tide roll away, thinking "Looks like nothing is going to change." All this guy can hope for is a partner like the one in Tammy's song with whom he can go out and soothe his soul like the guy does in Hank's song. Tammy's song is the day right after the kids and husband are out of the door, Hank's is payday night, and Otis's "Dock of the Bay" is the morning after.

What person who has ever grown to adulthood could fail to relate to Ralph Stanley singing: "I wandered again to my home in the mountains. Where is youth's early dawn I was restless and free. I looked for my friends but I never did find them. I found they were all Rank Strangers to me."

In "It Is a Man's World" (another wrongly maligned song), James Brown says, "This is a man's world, but it wouldn't be nothing without a woman or a girl." Does one have to be poor or black or American or even a James Brown fan to "get" that? It *is* a man's world. That's one of the things that is *wrong* with it. It would even be a sorrier place without women in it.

Q: That's a really different way of looking at songs. You've brought a lot together. And you've almost reversed the way feminists typically see Tammy Wynette and James Brown; I've listened to "It's a Man's World" so many times-"Man makes money, and man makes toys," and it's always seemed like the most sexist song I've heard. I'll go back and consider how James may be pointing out how men also lose out from male rule.

A: James is not necessarily making a conscious feminist or anti-sexist statement. The point is that he is almost certainly not making a sexist one. Men do control the economy and men have traditionally made many, if not most, of the technical advances. This is not because men are smarter but because women have been prevented not only from achieving in these areas, but from education (specific and general) as well. For every Marie Curie or Georgia O'Keefe there are generations of Artemisia Gentelleschis who were not only denied opportunity, but also the education that would enlighten women as to their potential. Even those who overcame this obstacle were often dismissed out of hand because of their sex.

The first thing denied to enslaved people is education. Keep them ignorant and teach them to "know their place," and you can keep them down, *for a while*. Imagine if American slaves had been allowed to learn to read and write. Manumission papers, passes off the plantation, bills of sale forged by slaves would have helped bring the "peculiar institution" down long before the Civil War. Add the intimidation and indoctrination used to convince them that they are incapable of self-determination and you have an even more effective system of oppression. The lingering effects of these tools are still evident in women who confine themselves to "traditional" gender roles or minority children who think that excelling in school or speaking good English is negative, and "acting White".

Q: Can you summarize your advice about learning to listen to music?

A: In the end, the best piece of advice I can give anyone about pop music comes down to two things: 1) Listen to Bob Dylan as much and as often as you can. Almost every style of popular music is represented in his work-Rock and Roll, Rhythm and Blues, Country and Western, Bluegrass, Gershwin-style pop, Blues, Jug Band music, Folk-and he addresses most of the vital social and political issues of this century, and of the last century: Racism, the Middle East, hypocrisy and, of course, love, romance, and family. And 2) remember the words of George Clinton: "Free your mind and your ass will follow."

Q: What formative events have shaped your perspective on music and society?

A: My life, somewhat selfishly, has always revolved around music. I would say that, while I may have been more oriented toward music due to growing up with music-loving parents, if there is any genetic influence, then my grandfather—a violinist, Bassist, Sousaphone player, singer (and one of the few Black opera singers at his time)—certainly is a main source.

As a consequence of living in the world of music, most of my social attitudes either relate to the music I listened to or grow out of my experience making music. The concepts of racism and overblown racial pride most often seem ridiculous to me. It is difficult for musicians in general, I think, to concern themselves with a person's race or religion (and lately, sex and sexuality). This is because we all share the need to make music and to make ourselves feel less alone, though still unique, by socializing and making music with others like ourselves. 'Can the cat play?' is usually the first and most important issue for us.

I think that that type of attitude may have a lot to do with my looking to make my life in music. The world of music is, to some degree, a safe haven from the harsh realities of the outside world. Not only am I judged more on my ability (or on the lack of it), but I am also given a greater chance to display that ability. A good player/singer always has to value someone, somewhere. A musician can always find someone to listen to her/him. Unfortunately, Black lawyers, politicians, CPAs, etc., rarely get to show what they can do. They may get interviewed and not hired. They may get hired, and then not be challenged or have their input taken seriously.

Q: So, for most jobs, there's a myth that meritocracy exists, but in the music world it's real?

A: I would say that's probably true.

Q: Can you tell us how your parents shaped you and helped you become a critical thinker?

A: Many of my social views were probably formed as I observed my parents. While they may have had views that I might disagree with, they never influenced me negatively when it came to my attitudes toward race or religion. They always encouraged my friendships with different types of people and they made sure that my family traveled. We saw a great deal of the United States before I was even in high school. My father, especially, made me feel that nothing was beyond my capabilities, and that my desires and dreams were worthwhile and legitimate.

Q: Can you talk about any particular cultural events in your childhood in Detroit that changed you, and helped make you become the person you are? What made you understand that people should help shape social life, culture and history?

A: When I think of certain musical "events" that had an affect on my life, several pop automatically into my mind. I remember seeing Little Richard on "American Bandstand" when I was five and thinking "I don't know what that is that he is doing, but I want it in my life forever." And I also know that seeing the Beatles on the Ed Sullivan Show and hearing them on the radio were very important events in my life. I had always loved music, but had given up playing the piano. I played the trumpet for a while, but I never liked the music that I was forced to play (and I never got that good at it either). But the Beatles empowered me. They didn't have to dance like James Brown or Elvis (but they didn't just stand there either); and I cannot now, nor could I ever, dance. The Beatles blended the sweetness and soul of Smokey Robinson with the wildness of Little Richard. They played guitar like my earlier heroes, the Everly Brothers, and they were just so damn cool. I didn't have a description for how I felt until a year or two later when I heard the Who's "I Can't Explain." That title explains it all. And I still can't.

Q: What historical events shaped your early thinking?

A: I'll never forget being home with just my mother, watching the news about the Bay of Pigs and the Cuban Missile Crisis, and asking her if there was going to be a war. Hearing my mother say that she didn't know what was going to happen at that point was the most frightening thing I had ever heard. The fear of nuclear war was already strong in me and I used to worry about it during every air raid drill at school. To hear a parent say that they didn't have an answer, and therefore no control over our safety, was terrifying. As much as anything that followed, this made me seriously opposed to war in any circumstance.

Q: When did you start questioning society and seeing that something was wrong with the world?

A: When I was 10 or 11 years old I went with my friend Michael Stewart and his parents to a fishing cabin in a town called Pinckney in Western Michigan. Mike and I decided to walk through town. His mother made us put on our best clothes as it was a Sunday. As we walked down what was the main street of Pinckney, we passed several clusters of kids who began pointing at us and laughing. They shouted, "Hey, Nigger. Hey, Nigger." I really don't recall ever hearing that word out loud before, certainly not in anger and derision.

I remember that we looked around for the adults we knew would protect us. No one came to our aid. None of the adults even chided the kids for their rudeness. Brought up by our conservative parents, we found this to be maybe the strangest aspect of the situation. I felt like I was trapped in an episode of "The Twilight Zone"; it seemed as though all of their faces were reflected in a funhouse mirror and that the gauntlet of obscenity, which we had to walk through, would never end.

I also remember walking from the baseball diamond to our elementary school and seeing boys tease a Black Latino classmate because he was Jewish; I argued perhaps ineffectively, with them but ended up making the only gesture I could think of at the time which was to leave them and walk back to school with the kid.

In the forty years that have followed, I have always found that logic is still useless in the face of bigotry.

Q: Do you have any answers?

A: Music has always been where I have turned for refuge from the meanness I encounter. I would rather be in a subculture that shares similar ideals than to be an important member of "real" society. The fact that more of my songs don't speak of social change is as much due to my frustration with trying to get people to look at things sensibly as it is to my limitations as a writer.

I don't have an "answer." Maybe because it has never made sense why bigotry exists. How can a person's color or age or sex or sexual orientation count for more than her/her character? It doesn't, and it can't unless people let it.

Q: Can you talk about, and maybe even sing, one of your own songs that comments on society?

A: One of my favorite compositions is "The Line." I composed the music and lyrics, and I sing it in solo performances and with my band. This song has a 1991 copyright, but the meaning isn't lost today, as different apartheids continue to develop. Here, I'll sing "The Line" for you.

Johnny Johnny he disappear from under the moonglow
Solid rock would break into tears if it knew what the moon knows

You'd better get acquainted with me
I'm not a secret I'm a mystery
Mark you a mark right here
That's where the line goes

The Jackal jumps and struts on two legs through the streets of Soweto
The serpent slithers up the side of the house and he slips in the window
Well it's like walking in the track of the cat
You know what I'm told it happens just like that
Mark you a mark right here
That's where the line goes

Johnny come on like Tommy Joad half a world from the dustbowl
Looking more and more like heroes of old
As the word of his deed grows
Well Mama hurts but she never cries
She knows her Johnny will be standing by
Mark you a mark right here
That's where the line goes.

I wrote this song before Nelson Mandela was released from prison. Though the song was written with South African apartheid in mind, there are certain elements in it that reflect my own attitudes as a Black American in the United States, most especially the line: "I'm not a secret. I'm a mystery." Take the time to find out who I am, and who we are.

Q: This song of yours is one of my favorites. But I never understood parts of it. Could you tell me more about its meaning, and what you were thinking about when you wrote the lyrics?

A: "The Line" grew out of a desire to speak out against one of the most utterly immoral political situations in modern history, and it grew out of my desire to spell out my feelings about it. I learned about apartheid when I was in elementary school; I have felt from my first knowledge of it that, if any cause was worth fighting for, the destruction of that evil system certainly was. I used to fantasize about becoming a Lafayette for a revolution I considered completely and utterly justified.

Apartheid was not only evil, but it was pompous and self-righteous. The South African government and most of that nation's white people subscribed to an antiquated philosophy of manifest destiny and racial superiority, seemingly without feeling the tiniest bit of rationalization or the nagging guilt that pestered American slaveholders or "Injun fighters." It was a philosophy that was looked upon by most of the rest of the world as, at the very least, particularly smarmy and distasteful and backward. I think even the zenophobes who hated and feared immigrants in their own industrialized countries would not allow for the injustice of an invader perpetrating the de facto enslavement of an indigenous majority.

When I composed "The Line," my writing was influenced by the time I turned on the television and caught the last half of a news feature on South Africa. A kindly looking and pleasant-spoken woman was being interviewed inside of a Johannesburg soup kitchen, which she ran almost single-handed. She talked about her 'Christian duty' to help the less fortunate and she touched me with her genuine, goodhearted concern. As she spoke and pointed out more of the restaurant, the camera pulled back, showing the exterior of the building and stopping at the view of the front window. Below the sign welcoming the needy was another one. It said, "Whites Only."

Nelson Mandela is someone I have always had the utmost respect for. Imprisoned in the prime of life, with no indication that he would ever leave alive, he maintained his faith and dignity, and personified the nobility of his cause. If anyone can be said to have a right to revenge, even to the point of outright, mad destruction, then who more than Mandela? Instead, when he did finally leave prison, he preached and legislated reconciliation, tolerance, and even forgiveness.

Q: Who does Johnny represent in "The Line"?

A: When I began writing this song, Nelson Mandela was still in prison, and none of those peaceful virtues were in my mind, with regard to South Africa. This song was written after I read that the practice of snatching anti-apartheid activists (real or imagined) from their beds was called "disappearing" them.

Johnny, in my song, was disappeared by the apartheid's state agents. Even though he has been disappeared, Johnny still walks the night, taking guerrilla revenge and inspiring hope. Johnny rescues children and feeds and protects the hungry and downtrodden, even while planning his next strike against the oppressor.

Johnny, the quintessential male rock and roll name, is part Robin Hood, part Golem, part Johnny Too-Bad. Johnny is an outlaw, but he is not a criminal. Like Tom Joad, he is forced into his situation by a system that just doesn't give a damn about him and his kind; in fact, the system is openly and proudly hostile. Whatever Johnny has to do to survive and to help his people is justified by the injustices done them, and by, what appears to be, the hopelessness of their plight. "The Line" is also a companion to Tom Joad's speech at the end of the *Grapes of Wrath*; wherever you find injustice, Johnny will be there to fight it.

I still subscribe to the theory that understanding (and reconciliation) comes when one puts oneself in the shoes of another. "The Line" contains what I think may be the best line that I ever put into a song, one that I think expresses the frustration of any oppressed person or people when trying to get "The Man" to understand their pain and/or outrage: "I'm not a secret; I'm a mystery."

Q: When radio advertising started to be based on computer-tracked sales, you were one of the last major FM deejays who was allowed to run his/her own list of songs, and to make your own commentary. How did the transition from more freely programmed radio shows to market-based radio shows affect what we hear and how we relate to music?

A: Radio is programmed from information gleaned from focus groups. They are convened usually during the day on weekdays and made up mostly of people who have nothing else to do at that time on those days. Focus group participants are played songs or parts of songs; then they are asked if they like, somewhat like, somewhat dislike, or dislike the songs, or if they are unfamiliar with the songs. This results in an artificially skewed result for a number of reasons. For example, many types of people (like the employed) are excluded from these focus groups. The memories of those who are included are not always accurate. Radio airplay is not based on musical taste or quality and play-lists are heavily influenced by racial prejudices and targeting.

Q: What kinds of transitions do you make between different kinds of songs?

A: Now my talk-sets are pretty minimal. I toss in facts relevant to the band, such as where they are playing or when their new albums are going to be released, along with personnel changes, etc.

Q: WYSP 94 FM in Philadelphia is known as a classical rock station, but during the time you controlled the play-list, you played songs from different genres, right? What kind of introductory remarks did you make before you played something new, like Rap?

A: I would let one song generally determine the next song. Sometimes that would be determined by lyrical theme or musical flow. Sometimes I would concentrate on a particular artist and then I would try to highlight what I thought were his/her best or most deserving pieces.

Q: What did you say before you played something that most Rock and Roll listeners would consider "corny" or out their realm, like Country and Western?

A: I never apologized for what I was about to play. I tried to treat what I thought was the best music by the best artists with an equal hand. I tried to show that there was not *that* big a leap from, say, Bob Dylan to Hank Williams or even Muddy Waters. Sometimes I could show that by playing different versions of the same song or by showing how a Rolling Stones or Led Zeppelin song was "borrowed" from an earlier Blues or Country song. I think that people who don't "get" Country and Western have not understood the origins of Rock and Roll, and they are basically snobs.

Q: What kinds of feedback did you get from your listeners? How did this affect the way you educated them about music and encouraged them to explore music and culture?

A: I tried not to lecture or sound like I was running a seminar. I would usually just explain the history or origins of a song or a type of song.

The best feedback was from a 14 year-old who asked me to play some "Buddy Walters."

"Buddy Walters"? I told him I wasn't sure what he was talking about.

He said, "Buddy Walters. You play him all the time. You know that song: "I'm A Man".

That's when I knew he was talking about "Mannish Boy" by Muddy Waters. That really pleased me. Here was this kid staying up till the middle of the night to hear something that he couldn't even identify. That wasn't something that his contemporaries or the press told him was "cool". It moved and touched him, even though he didn't know what it was. That was extremely gratifying.

Q: Given the high level on commercialization in radio and other forms of media, can you think of ways to prepare other d.j.s and station managers, and owners to become involved in popular education on the air, which might help lead to change?

A: This will never happen as long as it's not profitable.

There is nothing wrong with popular music. There is nothing wrong with having hit records. Plenty of brilliant artists have sold a lot of records: The Beatles. Dylan, Joni Mitchell, Aretha Franklin, Stevie Wonder, even Miles Davis. Sometimes being popular means that you are just that good. Sometimes it means that you appeal to the lowest common denominator. Sometimes both.

Radio programmers are not in the least interested in educating their audience; they are interested in profit.

The audience has their share of the blame, too. Many of my pre-teen (and even younger) nieces and nephews are crazy about the Beatles, as are the young children of many of my friends. One of my nieces has been nuts for Jerry Lee Lewis since she was about seven years old. I have a nephew who has been a Little Richard-fan since an even younger age. If kids hear a lot of this music, they will like it. They may also like 'NSync or the Backstreet Boys, too. Well, we had our versions of those types of acts when I was a kid, too.

The reason that people don't hear enough Van Morrison or B.B. King, etc., on the radio is that they don't buy their records. If they did, things would be different. If every time adults buy their kids a Backstreet Boys or Britney Spears record, they would also buy them a Beatle or Smokey Robinson album, then we would all eventually hear the difference on the kids' cd players and on the radio.

PART V: HISTORICAL PERSPECTIVES ON SCHOLARLY ACTIVISM

Chapter 14

DEVELOPING A NEW CONSCIOUSNESS AND SOCIETY: AN ESSAY ON RACISM AND RACE

Shomarka O. Y. Keita

ABSTRACT

Despite some progress made, social and natural scientists still have much work to do in creating an intellectual foundation to help in the fight against racism and to address the consequences of racism. By racism the author means that form of systemized bias, oppression and structured inequality that is directed against those different in physical traits, such as skin color, or those *deemed* different in a biological sense. Drawing on his background as a physical anthropologist, physician, educator, interest in Africa and the African diaspora, and interest in jazz, the writer examines racism from a global perspective and explores different, cultural ways that groups have begun to eliminate it. The essay that follows is not intended to be a formal scientific treatise, but instead an informal commentary; it takes as a point of departure racism in 'New World' societies.

While other forms of oppression, along with other bases such as culture or religion, have sometimes had just as severe results, this social scientist and scientist argues that that racism, specifically anti-"black," and anti-"red," have been the worst forms of oppression seen in human history. This is because of the ongoing legacy of past acts rooted in these ideologies. This legacy can be identified in all of the so-called multi-racial societies of the "New World." Australia and New Zealand can be included because of the way the word 'black' or 'blackfellow' was used in the past (and sometimes even now). The cultural impacts of racism are explored in relationship to forms of cultural resistance.

INTRODUCTION

The specific results of past racism include the general problem of structured inequality and the wasted lives over the generations for which it is responsible. An incalculable benefit to humanity was denied because of stolen opportunities. The ability for communities to fully succeed as communities was destroyed. (The few individuals who somehow overcame racism pale in importance from an internal perspective.) By 'succeed' I refer to true self-determination.

Another legacy is a system of values that denigrates the lives of the oppressed in everyday life. Hence some people get offered less sophisticated medical care, even when money is not an issue. The life chances of those called "black," are decreased. This is exacerbated by those whose skin color and physiognomies are most different from the European norm. In North America, where discrimination is based on categories, and where black was being defined differently in various states—but still on a genealogical basis—lighter skinned individuals with traits regarded as "European" seem to be becoming more favored in the public space, in contrast to the past where belonging to the category was the target of oppression. This practice of favoring "nearness to physical whiteness" was perhaps always the practice in Latin America, including Brazil, where merely having tropical African *ancestors* was not as much of a "problem" as looking "black" or more "black" (see below); and of course this is equally racist and encoded in beliefs about "improving the race" which meant having offspring as phenotypically European as possible. Carried to its logical extreme in practice it is easy to see where this would lead. Racism has affected the values of the oppressed themselves, and of other "minorities," such that there is an internal problem of valuation. This is not a new observation. It is true that in other parts of the world the valuation of lighter skin has little to do in origin with European domination, but that hegemony has nevertheless reinforced indigenous prejudices and perhaps given them new meanings. This deserves careful study.

NAMING RACISM IN GLOBAL, HISTORICAL SOCIETY

As noted in South America one finds the same legacies of racism. However, there is a difference. Discrimination was/is not based on a genealogical fact (African or Indian ancestry) but on the actual appearance of an individual or community. To some degree, wealth may mitigate this system, which is just as racist as its U.S. counterpart, only different.

In fact, it has been said that such a social value is placed on lighter skin (as close to white) that it is conceivable than some women would view their children's chances as being better if they were "illegitimate" but more European in appearance, than the products of a marriage and stable family, but less European (and especially "African"). If true this should provoke disgust and a lot more.

One of the most heinous effects of racism is inculcate hatred of physical traits themselves, declaring them to be intrinsically ugly. The damage to the psyche of Afro-South and North Americans and Indians has been and continues to be tremendous.

The devaluation of people with certain traits is an ideology that should be overturned with a diversification of values, not the effort to make certain traits disappear, either by assimilation via intermarriage or by lessening the chances of some to reproduce. Of course, on some Caribbean islands the Africans were worked until they died; it was more cost effective to replace them with new enslaved folk than to let them be more human: that is, to let them have families and live more complete lives.

RACISM IS IN CULTURE/NOT NATURE

For some the conflict between folks with different external characteristics is deemed "natural," in spite of numerous examples of cooperation and various exchanges on initial contact, between those who "look different." Some scientists have seriously raised the question of whether or not people from different ethnic groups see each other as species, and react with boundary formation in the same manner. No doubt one could learn to see people as this different but this is not to be confused with its instinctual counterpart among other animals, when this is the case.

It is true that some people here recoiled at the sight of others who were very physically different from themselves; for example, a century ago a famous zoologist of European birth from Harvard reacted very negatively to seeing West African New World descendants.

Another reaction was noted by the late jazz pianist Horace Tapscott, while serving in the U.S. military in western states (but not California). In his autobiography *Song of the Unsung* Tapscott notes how Euro-American ("white") children thought his dark-skinned infant daughter was "so pretty" and wanted to touch her skin. Perhaps children have to learn what is aesthetically correct, and what is supposed to be pleasing or attractive. Perhaps "blondes have more fun" is as much an ideological as aesthetic statement. I will not explore its origins here, or the earlier version ("gentlemen prefer blondes").

Of course there is research now that has explored what anatomical traits across cultures seem to have in common in the assessment of attractiveness. Such studies only address facial morphological architecture, and not traits like hair and skin color, and hence do not aid in the historical understanding of the focus on where the received aesthetic values come from in the general Western society. Although 'brown is beautiful' and 'black is beautiful' were uttered, we see a racist hegemony of aesthetic values insinuating itself again and even into minorities. This past "civil rights" phenomenon is not post-modernism, but an example of hegemonic racism, in a phase of reassertion. Many are concerned about genital mutilation, but what of the biological and mental mutilation related to the world of hair straightening products, skin bleachers, etc.?

Racism has had many cultural consequences. One area of interest is popular music classification and treatment of performers. It is a curious thing that there is a hall of fame for "Rock" music, but none for rhythm and blues—the major parent of "rock-and –roll,"—a name, which, if memory serves, actually comes from a rhythm-and-blues song. This is ironic. It is strange that rhythm and blues would have a section in the rock hall of fame and not the reverse, but an analysis of power and hegemony perhaps explains why. Music is also frequently labeled by the "racial" identity of the performer and not the style of music (except, of course, in opera, and maybe jazz, although in the latter case there is much problematic placement of non-jazz music into the jazz category).

On another level, most of the money made on African-American music is not made by Afro-Americans, and does not benefit the community. This is true when the issue is either the products of Afro-American performers, or the products of those whose style is Afro-American (via the eyes shut test). What irony! And exploitation.

This is also true of college sports. Why are there no "historically black" colleges that benefit from Afro-American talent in the same manner as other schools? The Afro-North

American *community* does not benefit in any serious way from its own cultural/entertainment production!

Another important example of the results and legacy of racism relates to social security payments at retirement, as well as Medicare. I note that these begin in one's mid-sixties, and there is talk of pushing up the age of retirement. Now if the men and women of a particular community have a median age of death or an average lifespan that is lower than the mid-sixties, there is a gross injustice. These folk never receive the benefits for which they paid during their working lives. In other words, there has been a transfer of money from colored and poor white folks to the more elite who tend to have longer life spans. This is a different way to understand "Driving Miss Daisy."

Now there is talk of social security being "broke," but it would have been broken a long time ago if the society had been just, if there had been no health disparities (and racialized and engendered work disparities?).

Is the nightmare over, or has it just begun? The terrorism of fundamental health inequality is not to be dismissed.

EXPOSING BIOLOGICAL ASSUMPTIONS IN RACIST
IDEOLOGY AND IN OUR RACIST GLOBAL SOCIETY

Racism: *Natural* rhythm. *Natural* propensity to be impoverished. *Natural* propensity to have an illness. *Natural* propensity for sports (except for waterskiing, etc.). *Natural* tendency to have a family breakdown. In the racist and sometimes racial paradigm, differences are said to be "natural" and therefore unchangeable or unfixable, immutable. Historical roots and causes are ignored, so is ongoing oppression. Even after "diversity" training, people walk away saying that they will be "sensitive"; but they still think, at a deep level, that other groups are fundamentally "different" in some profound sense (which means biologically different). Therefore, I think that it is important for me to address the issue of biological race, the basis of the social notion, although obscured, and therefore neglected by some cultural theorists.

Races were/are defined as units of humankind that are based on anatomical traits. The individuals in these units by definition are more alike each other than to any individual in another group for any measurable traits/parameters. This is a conceptual view held by many people, and sometimes it is operationalized even in "scientific studies." But everyone knows that at *some level* this notion of group differences is incorrect, yet they cling to the groups. The reason for this is not always clear.

Let me state this again. The "racial" groups are defined by sets of anatomical traits that distinguish them from other groups. (Remember all definitions are tautologies.) The boundaries created by the anatomical distinctions are assumed to exist for all other biological systems. So racial classification is about boundaries based on one set of traits, which are assumed to extend to others. What theoretically follows from this is that individuals should place in the same "racial" groups, no matter what other biological systems are used for classification purposes.

However, as stated, everyone knows that there are problems with the idea that "races" and the individuals comprising them are this distinct from other such units. For example, one's own blood brother, or one who has one's "racial traits" may not have the right blood type to save one's life via transfusion. Surely this is important, and compromises the validity of these units in a common sense way to most folks. One does not accept a rendom blood transfusion from one's so-called race.

There is more. Scientists who used to create units (varieties or sub-species) within species of non-human animals discovered that their classification schemes would frequently not hold up whenever traits not in the definition were added to their studies. Units defined by coat color and eye shape *within* a species did not hold up if other anatomical traits were considered. This is called non-concordance.

Scientists also found that traits would vary gradually across the geographical range of species, making it hard to distinguish breaks. This is called clinal variation. Scientists also sometimes found far-flung, geographically separated groups of the same species that resembled each other in terms of the same external traits of another group; this is known as polytopicity. The zoological taxonomists also had to admit that there was an arbitrariness of the criteria that they used to generate their subspecies (races). Of course there is complex geographical variation for most animal groups, and the question is (for a species) when do differences rise to a level of consistency to officially recognize a level of distinction.

Researchers studying humans, and "races," also discovered problems with the idea that human variation was structured into units consisting of uniform individuals. They found that once they looked at individuals within these units in terms of *numerous genetic systems*, that there was more difference between the individuals within the "races" than between the average values for the "races." This means that the boundaries implied by the anatomical definitions are false at the level of the whole person.

Scientists also found that many of the external traits for humans are clinal, as the zoologists noted for other species. So, for example, skin color is darker in general as one approaches the equator, and there are usually no sharp boundaries.

The existence of lines of descent traceable through males and females also shows the lack of boundaries. Y chromosomes are only transmitted to males. Mitochondria, the power plants of cells, have DNA. Mitochondrial DNA is only passed through females. So men get their mitochondrial DNA from their mothers. When studies on individuals from around the world are carried out, it is found that individuals will often group like a family tree, into subfamilies with others not having their external physical traits. Hence it is false to have the idea that races consist of individuals who have the exact same ancestral lines back into the beginning of *Homo sapiens*.

Of course, in more recent times we know that there are other individuals who have stereotypical European skin color and facial architecture, and who also have a mitochondrial lineage from recent tropical Africa. (In this case, I refer to people whose great-grandmother was jet black and whose other ancestors were "white"). So we know from our current experiences that having an ancestor with particular physical traits does not mean that a descendant will have them. Y chromosome or mitochondrial DNA, do not dictate the anatomical traits that scholars have used to make classification schemes. This is another way of pointing out that this unique sex lineage DNA is not primarily responsible for facial and skin characteristics in a major way. At another level we also know that full siblings can sometimes vary so much that people will classify them into different "races" –the implications of this are obvious when considered in the deep time of human evolution and microlution.

The term race in the sphere of human social interaction does not refer to true natural units within our species. There are no natural instinctual boundaries between the groups based on anatomical or molecular traits. The boundaries are taught cultural and socio-historical and political products, which were invented by a socio-political system. The "scientific" products of the eighteenth century, meaning the racial schema based at core on external traits, were by law converted into categories of social interaction. Hence Yoruba, Wolof, Akan etc. speakers in the U.S.A. and Latin America were reduced to a monolithic, faceless mass of "NEGROES," "BLACKS," "NIGGERS," all the while being worked to death and set up for trans-generational destruction. Yet their descendants in various forms used their communal *culture* and resourcefulness to survive and almost prosper, and most certainly be creative, even make contributions to arts, science, polar and space exploration, although not nearly in the numbers which they would have had things been different. These folk managed to create musical and religious forms that have impacted the world, and generate a great civil/human rights struggle which has influenced many, and made the US an easier place to live for all non-Anglo immigrants although they rarely acknowledge this reality. *The price has been paid with blood, and yet the struggle to gain equivalent life experiences, a human right, has not been realized.* Much work remains for all.

The units of the racial classifications, the products of a scientific exercise in grouping, were converted into social units by politics and myth. The "natural" units of social life, rooted in the social and linguistic histories of various regions, were destroyed in the main, as the process of creating a different social world took place. This "new", post-1450 world consisted of units that forced folk to see each other in terms of groups based on external, anatomical traits—the basis of racial definitions—hence the concept of a racialized social system, in my view.

Some folk would extend the notion of racialization to any group *conceived* as being genetically or biologically different, but this would be historically inaccurate. Racialization continues when the system tries to convert Afro-Latinos/as, Nigerian-Americans, etc., into generic, mono-dimensional "blacks." These folk must insist on the primacy of their cultural identity. The system racializes in another sense when it declares the nationals of some countries to automatically belong to this or that "race", which actually makes for some interesting mental contortions. Fight racialization, racists and racism; acknowledge deep cultural ties and create humane political solidarity.

REFLECTIONS ON LIBERATION'S COMPLEXITY

This commentary raises various issues for thought. Some activists and/or serious scholars must understand the tremendous damage that racial thinking has done, and does. In some cases, there is little damage, but there may be perpetuation of inappropriate models of interpretation. For example, some conflicts in ancient history have been interpreted as being "racial." This implies that the people fought *because* of their differences in height or skin color.

To give more specific examples, some have interpreted the conflict between the Malian government and ethnic Tuaregs as a "racial" ("black"/ "white") conflict. (Some Tuareg are in the Malian government.) Or they have seen slavery/hereditary caste in the Sahara as "racial" in inspiration. Historical data suggests more plausible explanations, even if now some of these folk have incorporated a "racial" perspective in their own interpretations, a well-known phenomenon that is also a part of globalization.

Scholars must begin to exorcise racial thinking from their own work. Racism has to be acknowledged in all of its subtle modern and post-modern manifestations, and dealt a blow with the hammer of fine critique, and a spirit of liberation; action must be taken at all levels, so that we can avoid the need for Malcolm's dictum: "By any means necessary."

CONCLUDING THOUGHTS ON ENDING THE NIGHTMARE OF RACISM

The new biological data coupled with historical knowledge and social awareness render the myth of race transparent. From a science perspective there are breeding populations, bioethnic communities of descent; there is geographical variation in biological traits. There may be bio-population differences in disease frequency which have a genetic basis; but genetic differences between geographical units, or even real breeding populations does not rise to the level of differentiation deserving the taxonomic category of "race." The social inequalities of entities called races in the social landscape of various societies are not natural. The inequalities result from racism ultimately. The society at large and those who have been oppressed are both responsible for liberating us from the historical nightmare whose consequences are so visible. Let us end this terrorism.

This project is not un-patriotic. Many frequently say that America mistreated the enslaved Africans and/or their descendants. But this may be incorrect. What is America? Is it the abstract ideas? The American ideal, the idea of America, did not mistreat these folk. It was Euro-America who oppressed them. The American ideal—at least partially— is what helped to liberate them to the degree that this has happened—their own humanity with its sources provided the major inspiration. It was white supremacist ideology that oppressed, distressed and suppressed black folk, not the American ideal, the philosophy.

Indeed, Afro-North Americans furthered the American Revolution, heroically. Afro-North American institutions, like Howard University Law School, the Southern Christian Leadership Conference, and numerous others held up the ideals of human freedom, while Euro-American culture and society somehow fooled itself into thinking that it had maintained some moral high ground. The Kerner report, commissioned by the government, frankly and truthfully stated that white racism was the cause of the 1960s rebellions/riots, or whatever one would call them. The road to Damascus is long. The idea of America did not oppress blacks, white folk did. However, perhaps the idea of America as oppressor of Native Americans *is* a topic worth exploring.

Chapter 15

THE LIFE OF THE PEOPLE: THE LEGACY OF N.F.S. GRUNDTVIG AND NONVIOLENT SOCIAL CHANGE THROUGH POPULAR EDUCATION IN DENMARK

Marilyn Jackson

ABSTRACT

When the movie *Gandhi* came out in 1982, the author was involved in peace and anti-nuclear organizing. From that vantage point, she observed that many people were moved by the movie to do nonviolent actions and demonstrations as a tactic to impact public opinion to create social change. The process of education is a step that happens before public demonstrations, which Gandhi must have been part of, and which is often overlooked as a tool for nonviolent struggle. The very processes of dialogue and community building are elements that shape a society toward nonviolent change. Popular education is a phrase used to describe the process of educating people from all walks of life, though particularly the poor and disenfranchised, in a democratic process oriented toward empowering them to make social change for the better in their lives (Hurst 1995, 1). Besides disseminating knowledge, popular education can provide a forum for individuals to develop skills to dialogue, to discuss and work out with one another the very issues they are facing and out of this to plan actions appropriate for each situation. Social-change movements take shape when individuals put their heads and hearts together to forge the social interactions needed to build society. Celebrating the uniqueness of each culture and community is another way to bring people together to create a common language and cultural fabric with a story of the past and a vision for the future for society.

INTRODUCTION

Myles Horton, co-founder of the Highlander Folk School in Tennessee, differed from well-known organizer Saul Alinsky on whether education or organizing came first. Horton felt that if you educate people, they will become organized. Alinsky saw it the other way around (Bell 1990, 115-117). However, Civil rights activist Rosa Parks, when asked by talk show host, Studs Terkel, what Highlander had to do with the fact that she chose not to move to the back of the bus in Montgomery, Alabama in early December 1955, she replied, "Everything" (Hurst 1990, 1).

There is a less known story to be told about popular education in Denmark. Nicolai Frederik Severin (N.F.S.) Grundtvig inspired the folk school movement, which played a beneficial role in the transformation of Denmark from a rural society to a modern industrial society, in a relatively peaceful manner, compared to other European countries. N.F.S. Grundtvig (1773-1882) emphasized the importance of nonformal education and cultural expression for the common people in a developing society. He started the folk school movement in Denmark which spread throughout Scandinavia and beyond and influenced popular education theory used today.

EDUCATION AND PROGRESS IN DENMARK

Author Steven Borish made an extensive study of Denmark and its popular education or folk school movement in his book, *The Land of the Living: The Danish Folk High Schools and Denmark's Non-Violent Path to Modernization*. He first stumbled upon this quest while living in a Kibbutz in Israel, where he found that Danes were the life of any party (Borish, 1991, 49-50).

He later learned how they had protected and saved most of the Jews living in Denmark during World War II (1991, 93-100). Borish set out to discover how this tiny country came to be so rich in civic sanity and values. Denmark was rated at the top of the Index of Social Progress (ISP) Scores for World Social Leaders, conducted by Richard Estes of the University of Pennsylvania School of Social Work in 1984. The study rated countries by their achievements in social welfare and "social provisioning" for citizens in times of difficulty. The United States was rated near Mexico, El Salvador and Tunisia in 1980. The study questions the assumption that people in the United States on average are better off than those in less developed countries, implying that "more" and "bigger" don't necessarily mean "better" (1991, 67-70).

Denmark was once an empire but lost its colonies and fell on tough times. Though small and with limited natural resources, they were able to respond by turning inward and develop the resources they had. Education and political negotiation, rather than violence, were tools used to dig out of hard times (Borish 1991, 67-70). Denmark's losses in the Napoleonic Wars were catastrophic, but in the aftermath, in the early 1800's, village schools became havens for self-improvement and solidarity. Out of these schools came a class of peasant farmers who increasingly agitated for a say in the affairs of the nation. Later, "When a second wave of revolts swept over Europe in the 1830's and 40's, these common folk, having learned from their history," again "turned to education rather than to violence to improve their condition. It was then that N.F.S. Grundtvig's ideas found fertile ground" (Willette 1998).

During Grundtvig's lifetime, major land reforms brought the conditions for many tenant farmers, held back since feudal times, to eventually acquire their own farms (Borish 1991, 115-124). The leaders of these reforms also included landowners and political leaders, who were not always in agreement, but by struggling with and negotiating the issues, finally allowed changes to come. A practical reason was that the "removal of inefficient feudal constraints on the tenant farmers and their agricultural production could benefit not only the farmers but the Danish economy as a whole (including, of course, the estate-owner class)" (Borish 1991, 145). Idealism was involved too:

> The European literature of the Enlightenment, with its mixture of philosophy, careful social debate and practical instructions about agricultural techniques could be read by the educated upper class, as well as a priest here and there. It was decisive that enlightened and reform-minded men came to power at a point in time where a comparatively large number of the powerful and landholding class could gradually come to see that there were advantages in introducing certain changes. It has often been maintained, that these changes happened here in Denmark in a peaceful way, just before they were the cause of bloody revolution in other places (Borish 1991).

Later, the bourgeois middle class again gave leadership to a movement for a constitutional government and basic civil rights, with support from new self-owning farmers. "They pressed their demands for overthrow of the absolute monarchy and on 21 March 1848, yet another peaceful revolution took place in the streets of Copenhagen." The king acceded peacefully; on June 5, the following year, the new Constitution was signed (Borish, 1991, 179).

The first folk high school opened "at the time of the start of the municipal self-government movement and of the ratification of a free constitution which superseded two hundred years of absolute monarchy." Grundtvig wrote that "unless the school is reformed so that from being a tomb and a grave for children it may develop into a plant nursery for life, the death struggles of the revolution will sweep across all nations and eradicate both educated and uneducated alike" (Willette 1998).

N.F.S. GRUNDTVIG

As a child, Grundtvig was tutored by his mother and was an avid learner. His father was a Lutheran minister and he learned from the heated debates of contemporary events that took place among the parish's guests. A paralytic woman, Malene Jensdatter, kept an eye on the children while being confined to a chair (Royal Danish Embassy 1998, 3), and recounted songs, stories, myths and legends from his native Sjaelland. This may have had something to do with his love of the Danish language and Grundtvig's love of the common people (Borish 1991, 159).

Though he became a minister like his father, Grundtvig was also a thinker, writer, politician and author of books, poetry, hymns and popular songs. He advocated retaining Danish and "Nordic" culture, along with his theory to create schools where people gather to learn about our mutual civic and social lives. He called them "folk high schools," "folk" meaning "the people" and "high" meaning beyond grammar school. The first schools created were aimed towards youth and young adults. Today, people of all ages attend folk schools in Denmark as well as in other Scandinavian countries and beyond.

Intensely Danish and Lutheran, Grundtvig was influenced by the philosophical and political currents of the eighteenth and nineteenth centuries. He began as a young adult, with a dull academic career of theology. Then he discovered world literature and the new philosophies of the early 1800's. He immersed himself in poetic and historical study with a

strongly nationalistic interest in history and mythology and spent years subsidized by
scholarships and engaged in historical research and translating ancient Nordic documents.

RELIGION AND FOLK LIFE

Grundtvig developed a perspective on the relationship between religion and secular
society which made room for both. He believed that our "folk-life is a necessary prerequisite
for living Christianity." During the Dark Ages of Western Europe, secular studies were put
aside and the study of Christianity had center stage (Sanford 1962, 906). Secular learning was
eventually brought back to educational institutions. By the time Grundtvig lived, upper class
schools taught about culture, but this usually meant the study of Greek and Roman cultures.
On a secular level, there was a realization of the value of knowledge of the arts and other
forms of culture, but the value of developing popular local culture for the masses of people
who were poorer and less educated was overlooked and de-legitimized by upper class
standards.

Grundtvig is known to have said, "man (human) first and then Christian" (Knudsen 1976,
5). He believed people should know about their own cultural heritage, the history of their
people (folk) first, and basic knowledge about what it means to be a human being. Christian
teachings, he felt, enhance and build upon the human experience. Christianity that leaves out
humanity is hollow and underdeveloped or stunted.

GRUNDTVIG'S TRIPS TO ENGLAND

Early in his career, Grundtvig laid down his priest's robe for a while to study philosophy
and to publish a magazine. In his early years as a theologian, Grundtvig did not filter his
controversial opinions well and rocked the boat from time to time. He was censored for ten
years, from 1826 to 1837. Several times, he received grants from a rather benevolent king, to
support his translation of ancient Nordic and Anglo-Saxon literature, including old sagas as
well as Beowulf (Royal Danish Embassy 1998, 6). After being censored he went to the king
again to ask for funding to continue his study of ancient texts in England. He told the king,
"They are an important source of information about Denmark's ancient history, but have been
completely neglected in their place of origin" (Borish 1991, 164).

Grundtvig made three trips to study at Oxford and Cambridge in England. Feeling outcast
when he was censored, these trips rejuvenated his soul and his studies. He gained strong
impressions of civil and literary life and studied Shakespeare in English. He was impressed
by the active civil life in Britain, which he saw as having its origin in the personal freedom of
British society.

This "greatly influenced his public and political activity in the decades to come" (Royal
Danish Embassy 1998, 9). He gained "a dramatic insight into the crisis of English society"
and saw the impact of industrialization on the common people, developing concern for the
future of how this would impact Denmark. "Even those Englishmen who give themselves
time to do anything but to make money, look with hidden horror on every new invention and
colossal use of the mechanical forces, which in time will make all the old craftsmen and

artisans obsolete and turn them into dumb tools in the hands of the master of the machine, into thoughtless slaves in the hall of the factory-owner" (Reich 2000, 4).

One evening Grundtvig had a long dialogue with a woman who influenced him. Their meeting, seen from the outside may appear trivial, "but spiritually and intellectually" it was an "inner revolution." At a dinner party, June 24th, 1830, Grundtvig met Clara Bolton, "the charming young wife of a doctor." The revolutionary incident was simply the conversation that passed between the two of them. "That entire evening [they] sat engrossed in discussion about human existence, continuing long after the rest of the company had left for the bridge tables in the neighboring rooms. When it was past midnight their host, somewhat concerned, came in to ask what kept them so long; to which Clara Bolton, looking up at him with her pretty brown eyes, replied, There is nothing in the world that Mr. Grundtvig and I could not talk about!" (Royal Danish Embassy 1997, 3-4).

After that night, Grundtvig began his well-known distinction between humanity and Christianity referred to earlier (Drejergaard 2000, 1). They apparently never met again, but years later he would still refer to his meeting with the "lady of Greece." Clara Bolton's ideal was not the "ascetic saint with his eyes set firmly on eternal salvation, but rather the ancient Greeks, proudly shouldering their destiny and openly accepting life with all the joys and pain it entails" (2000, 4). Another source explains, "From that conversation he was suddenly resolved to oust gloom and infuse Christian living with the sun-drenched spirit of classical Greece. Like Francis of Assisi 600 years earlier, Rev. Grundtvig now saw this world as radiating the glory of God. People should taste and revel in the beauties and sorrows of this life for its sake" (Killough 1998, 2). A direct link has been suggested between this encounter and Grundtvig's "solitary and ridiculed stance twenty years later in support of the first Danish radical women's liberation-fighter, Mathilde Fibiger" (Reich 2000, 5).

During his third trip, Grundtvig studied at Trinity College in Cambridge. There he was struck by the "collegial atmosphere" between teaching staff and students. "They lived as a community even outside classes and lectures, dining together, meeting on the playing fields and debating with one another over afternoon tea." It didn't surprise him that students had a natural respect for their tutors, but that there was a "similar respect clearly shown by the teaching staff for their students," which "contrasted sharply with his experience of the Danish educational system" (Royal Danish Embassy 1997) following the "rigid German university model then dominating in Scandinavia." There was an "easy camaraderie among teachers and students and professional equality, comrade to comrade" (Killough 1998, 3).

In England, Grundtvig experienced the British type of university education and "was removed from the parochial atmosphere of a small country whose economic life had been stagnant for two decades." Seeing "the hustle of the industrial revolution in its British beginnings," he "began to think in terms of that active participation in public life which characterized the next two decades, even leading him into parliament after the granting of a new constitution in 1849. He began to see the need for a confrontation of social and cultural factors with basic Christianity, and out of this confrontation came the call for a 'civic and noble academy'" (Knudsen 1976, 4).

About this time he developed the concept of "folkelighed," which translates to "folk life" or "life of the people." Folk life required a balance between education, politics and religion (Christianity). Grundtvig felt that neither of the first two can function if not supported by a "free spiritual life and free discussions of the human condition and of faith," supported by the church. He returned to Denmark opposing the authoritarian state-church system in England

and was inspired to speak up for more spiritual freedom as well as renewal of the Danish church (Reich 2000, 8).

During his studies in England, Grundtvig confirmed his understanding of the importance of the cultural history of the Danish and other Nordic peoples. He felt Danish should at least be as important to study as foreign and "dead," or no longer used, languages and cultures offered in classical studies. He said Danes and other Nordic people should know about the Danish and Nordic mythological history and not be forced to just study about Greek and Roman culture. He wrote about the need for a Nordic university and felt this alternative kind of learning could exist alongside formal education already in existence.

Grundtvig went to England as a romantic, old-fashioned spirit and returned as a romantic, liberal spirit of a special kind. In 1830, King Charles in France was deposed and "revolutions sprang up in Belgium, Poland and Northern Italy." In England the old Tory regime was replaced with parliamentary reform. At first, "Grundtvig did not sympathize with the revolutionary and democratic forces. He feared that revolutions would spread to Denmark and England and that a new democratic system without a responsible public would bring about chaos" (Reich 2000, 6). On the other hand, "he feared that the leaders would gain far too much power unless the people were given access to such a degree of democratic education on social affairs that the people's voice might speak freely and strongly." Accordingly, he suggested the idea of a democratic "high" school, at which all would be eligible to study, using the Danish language and Danish history as the reference point from which to study social affairs, with a view to participating in the democratic constitution that would come (Royal Danish Embassy 1998, 11).

Grundtvig used the term "high school" in the sense of university and equal in status to schools based on Latin languages, but without required examinations. He had been developing a folk school plan for twenty years, which was almost complete, when Christian VIII, the last of the absolutist kings, died before he was able to establish such a school (Royal Danish Embassy 1998). Though his concept for a folk school was not carried out exactly the way he planned, others were inspired by his fundamental writings on education, for schools for the people, which fostered the Danish folk school movement.

Grundtvig was opposed to domination in a way that was different from the European emancipation tradition, with its emphasis on liberal individualism. "He was on guard against the idea that the way to obtain freedom is to dissolve the power structure." What you get may be worse than what has been replaced. He wanted to substitute for violent revolution, a "peaceful transformation of all elements in society based on a mutual recognition that all had the right to exist." He believed that each institution and "individual could both teach and learn in a dialogue predicated on mutual respect" (Borish 1991, 169).

Grundtvig came to support the movement for democracy in Denmark. He began to write legislative reforms for greater freedom in school and church. He developed a political program in which the key words were "freedom" and "folkelighed," which could be called "popular democracy," advocating extensive, almost unlimited freedom in every intellectual and spiritual field as well as in economic matters, quite similar to British liberalism. He emphasized that the new democracy should be in fullest agreement with the people themselves and the culture and outlook that characterized them. He was elected to the constituent assembly and sat as a member of the Parliament in his later years. "Grundtvig laid great store by live debate," and "emphasized the importance of the opposition and public opinion in keeping the Government on the right course" (Royal Danish Embassy 1998, 11-12).

CULTURE AND EDUCATION

On the relation between culture and education, Grundtvig wrote that "learning is one matter, but culture and competence for living as human beings and citizens is another. Both can be combined, although hardly by the masses... . They must be separate in order not to seek to suppress, confuse, or corrupt one another. Culture and competence must always be relevant to the momentary life of the people; learning must be relevant to the total life of mankind. When learning is genuine, it encompasses culture and competence, but the latter can only encompass learning in an intuitive sort of way. Learning will be misleading, particularly among educators, if it is not juxtaposed by the culture of a people, which compels learning to recognize the life here and now; the culture of a people will become superficial if is not kept alive by learning... . Wise educational institutions must therefore be gauged to progressive enlightenment and culture" (Knudsen 1976, 25-26).

This philosophy had a political edge which bolstered those from the peasant class who challenged the cultural elite with the concept that the culture of "the people" (or folk) was just as if not more valid than learning gained elsewhere, as it was most relevant to most people's every day lives. Erica Simon writes that "the protest of folk-enlightenment against elite culture is the background for what in Denmark is spoken of as the Culture War" (Simon 1984).

MOTHER TONGUE, FATHER TONGUE

Grundtvig wrote about the importance of knowing one's "mother tongue," which is "a living expression of the unique character of a people," in which all the originality of even a genius has its root. When intellectuals do not master their own language:

- the cost involved is the very life of the people, when the mother tongue is scorned, suppressed, and downgraded so
- that it is used only in practical, everyday matters, used only in academies to introduce foreign and dead languages, as
- is the case with us, and constantly ridiculed because it expresses foreign niceties in a crude manner (Knudsen 1976, 163).

Grundtvig feared that if academic institutions in Denmark didn't feature the Danish language, it would become extinct, along with many aspects of the Danish culture. He called the mother tongue "the soul of the people"(1976, 163). He wanted the "Danish ballads, proverbs and maxims, with all their Danish imagery, their wisdom and innocent jest"... to be "revived, dusted off, launched and promoted." He warned against too much reliance on books in creating an environment of cultural education, but admitted that he himself had his nose in a book from early to late (1976, 164).

Mother tongue is the language a mother (or father) speaks to a child. Language expresses the creativity and uniqueness of each culture. While learning our mother's (and father's) culture and language, we also learn the basic lessons and stories which guide our human development and sense of identity.

Grundtvig felt that "in the folk-high-schools, not only should the mother tongue be emphasized but also oral ability - speech instead of writing." He "often used the expression 'the living word,' and though he wrote more than any other Dane, he maintained that the spoken word was the most important means for active communication between people." He [Grundtvig] asks:

> Why do religion and art not achieve the same for us as for the Greeks? It is because we lack the living words, which can only be inefficiently replaced by dead letters. We are alphabet-bound people, we read and write, so that our hands become paralyzed and our eyes blind, while living words spoken to average people about essential matters are seldom or never heard.... We have of course seen children born with tongues and ears, but not with books under their arms or pencils in their hands.....When human communication occurs orally, people are more on the same footing than when written material dominates, because everyone can speak, while writing is a ruler's tool (Christensen 1987, 6).

A parallel concept (from a time where the roles of the sexes fell along traditional lines) was "fatherland." Grundtvig wrote that "The history of the fatherland... is neither more nor less than the 'recollection of our fathers.' It is the living narrative from mouth to mouth, from generation to generation, about the remarkable things that have happened in the country and to the country. The depth of love that a people has for its country can be measured by the living flow of this narrative with its high and low tides... "(Knudsen 1976, 164). Just as the invisible world becomes alive and strong only on the mother tongue, our living relation to our past and our future depends on our sense of continuity with our ancestors and our descendants (1976, 43).

THE ROLE OF SINGING IN FOLK
LIFE AND POPULAR EDUCATION

Grundtvig's positive humanistic and religious view toward life inspired him to write hundreds of hymns, songs and poems (1976, 119). The lyrics contained much positive imagery, referring to the nordic people and God's work in the world and through nature. He believed in the uniting effect of people singing together.

Singing together became a tradition in the folk schools as a result of Grundtvig's inspiration. Singing uplifted people who lived together in learning communities, and helped foster the positive development of personal relationships, which are the building blocks of any social and cultural movement. Folk School teacher, Frederik Christensen, wrote how singing is a way to bond and to get to know one another. Teaching in our schools only becomes dynamic and exciting if we insist on the "experiences of the heart." That is why the teacher must meet his pupil by saying, "Tell me what you are fond of, then I shall tell you what I am fond of - and we shall then find our way together....If you will sing your song for me, then I shall sing my song for you." The hope then is that we have a song to sing, and that we know what to answer when asked: "What are you fond of?" (Christensen 1987, 7).

THE HIGHLANDER CONNECTION

Singing was an important part of the Civil rights movement in the United States' South during the 1950's and '60s. Myles Horton, who started the Highlander School in Tennessee, knew the importance of song for education from visiting and studying the folk schools of Denmark before starting the Highlander School. Highlander played a supportive role during the Civil Rights movement, as well as through other decades of social struggle before and since then. Myles Horton wrote about Grundtvig's philosophy on the importance of singing together and how this fit into the folk school movement:

> [Grundtvig] believed that people found their identity not within themselves, but in relationship with others. He believed that through songs and poetry, students could grasp truths that might otherwise escape them, and that singing in unison was an effective way of inspiring people and bringing them closer together.... His many poems and songs carried messages of hope and joy and expressed confidence that the Danish people, once enlivened and enlightened, would act to shape the emerging democratic society.... His willingness to break with traditional and conventional wisdom was illustrated by the shockingly unconventional imagery in his hymns and poems which were, contrary to the traditions of the times, written in language the people could understand and enjoy....(Horton 1988, 6-7).

Horton realized how folk schools provided a way for the people of Denmark to deal with the changing times in the early 1800's as industry and other modern forms of commerce were taking hold. Folk schools, supported by the government, continue to provide a way for a democratic society to deal with modernity. Horton wrote:

> It became obvious that the early schools could only be understood in their historic setting, marked by the end of absolute monarchy and beginning of constitutional government. Social movements of farmers and laborers and the culture movement of folk songs and ballads, all were part of the national revival. I learned that the Folk High Schools were shaped by and helped shape these movements (Horton 1983, 28).

During the early Civil Rights struggles, the Highlander School may well have been the only place where whites and blacks in the Southern United States could come together and learn to get along as well as to educate and organize with each other. Pete Seeger and Woody Guthrie spent time at Highlander singing folk songs. Folk songs come out of every culture, and at Highlander singing was especially encouraged as part of the process of educating for social change. Myles Horton's first wife, Zilphia, had a gift for using music, drama and dance to advance labor union concerns and civil rights. By collecting songs and encouraging Highlander students to collect and sing them, she involved communities around Highlander, helping heal wounds, lessen suspicion, and foster cultural pride (Parker, 1993, 22).

Zilphia also helped give "We Shall Overcome" national and international renown. Originally an Afro-American folk song, "We Will Overcome" became a Baptist hymn and was sung by union members to maintain picket line morale at a Charleston, S.C. strike. Two women members from that union sang it at Highlander in 1946. Zilphia recognized its emotional appeal, slowed the tempo, added verses and sang it at meetings. Pete Seeger...learned it from Zilphia in 1947, altered its title to "We Shall Overcome," added verses and sang it at 1950s folk song concerts around the country. Folk singer Guy Carawan., who with his wife Candie worked at Highlander, further refined it, and added the verse, "We Shall Not Be Moved," during a police raid on Highlander in 1959. It was sung at Highlander workshops, at civil rights gatherings from the 1960s and became the freedom song heard round the world (1993).

DANISH FOLK SCHOOLS TODAY

There are around 100 folk schools in Denmark today. They are mainly residential; most students and teachers live at the school. About two per cent of Denmark's adult-population attend every year. They do not teach professional subjects of traditional universities, nor do they issue diplomas. Learning is largely through dialogue, more than lecture. Physical exercise is non-competitive. "Schools educate for life, for responsible citizenship and for just learning how to cope. Their faith is that the best learning is not solitary but interactive, and not just between students and masters but among students themselves" (Killough 1998, 2).

There are over 400 folk schools across the Nordic countries, including Sweden, Norway, Finland, Iceland, Greenland and the Faeroe Islands (Royal Danish Embassy 1997). Other European countries, including England, Germany, the Netherlands and Poland, have some folk schools patterned after the Danish model. Other European countries have similar popular educational movements as well, though not necessarily claiming a direct connection with the Danish model (1997).

SCANDINAVIAN AMERICANS AND OTHERS INFLUENCED BY THE FOLK SCHOOL MOVEMENT

The folk school tradition did not cross the ocean with the Danish immigrants and plant as firmly in the United States with its unique political environment and flourish as well as it did in Denmark and the rest of Scandinavia. Many Danish Americans and those interested in the folk school legacy have tried to create this experience in the United States. Folk schools have similarities to the popular American tradition of camps and retreat centers where people live, eat, sing and socialize while learning together. One difference is that folk schools in Scandinavia are mostly if not completely, government sponsored. Young people originally spent several weeks at a time at a folk school. Many European countries have longer annual vacations for working people which make it more possible for them to attend. A few institutions, patterned after Danish folk schools, developed in the United States and lived on, such as at Highlander.

Other movements must have been influenced by Grundtvig's ideas, and by the folk school movement, such as the strong Scandinavian folk cultural movement, which influenced my identity as a Swedish American. The Concordia Language School in Bemidgi, Minnesota, sponsored by Concordia, a Norwegian Lutheran College, has a program to teach children different languages so that they can become ambassadors for peace around the world; expressing a similar cultural educational philosophy.

I must admit, I have never been to a folk school in Denmark, but I have attended a few American offshoots. In the 1980's I attended a meeting of the Folk Education Association of

American, for a long weekend in Amherst, Massachusetts. We met at the offices of Scandinavian Seminar, an organization that arranges for college students to study at folk schools in Scandinavia, for elder hostels and travel programs in Europe for people of all ages. They claim roots in the Scandinavian folk school tradition. The gathering was informal and we learned about folk schools in the U.S. and other places in the world. As people introduced themselves, they were apologetic if they were not Danish or even Scandinavian.

There was a representative from the Study Circles Resource Center in Topsfield, Massachusetts, which fosters study circles around the U.S. One man was working with folk schools in Holland. A young woman who taught at a Danish folk school described their program that featured sports but also included other socially relevant subjects. I was impressed how meals were handled inexpensively and simply. We were on our own for breakfast, shared chores in preparing lunches and formed small groups to go out for dinner in lovely Amherst.

Growing up Swedish Lutheran American, I heard the term, "Happy Dane" and "Sad Dane," but didn't understand their meaning until studying Grundtvig and the folk schools. "Glad" or "Happy" Danes were Danish Lutherans who followed Grundtvig's teachings and enjoyed their folk culture as well. "Sad," or "Holy Danes," frowned on this type of behavior.

I attended two Danish American conferences organized by "Happy Danes," with my parents in the 1990's: the Fall Meeting, at the Danebod folk school in Tyler, Minnesota and the Conference on Life and Learning in Solvang, California. Most participants were elderly, though at Tyler they have a "family camp" as well. My family was asked a few times why we were there, since we weren't Danish. It is sometimes hard to shake this idea that the folk school is just a Danish thing or even a Scandinavian thing. The United States is home to so many people whose mother tongue and father land were originally elsewhere, doing a multicultural folk school perhaps would be a new twist. Myles Horton at the Highlander School applied the folk school philosophy to a specific region in Tennessee, though most people who went there probably never heard about Grundtvig and the folks schools in Denmark.

The Danish American gatherings had several singalongs each day, up to 45 minutes in length.

Hymns and folk songs were sung, one after another, sometimes in Danish, sometimes in English, with fervor and familiarity. The program format was usually in the conventional lecture style but there was a wide range of subjects, from religion, social-political and global issues, to psychology. They were always followed by discussion with the participants. In Tyler there was storytelling time and both culminated with a Saturday evening concert or cultural program. At the end of each day many got together for circle folk dancing. Meals and frequent snack times were highly social events, so dialoguing continued. Meals included announcements, singing and prayers and everyone was expected to sign up to help clean up or set up.

DANISH VALUES

Steven Borish devotes an extensive portion of his book to Danish values, which he suggests may well have been shaped at least in part by the folk schools' effect on the Danish populace. These include Democracy, Egalitarianism, equality of Gender Roles, Balance and

Moderation. One chapter on the Danish values of Balance and Moderation talks about qualities of modesty and humility, saying Danes don't believe in boasting too much and guard against thinking that one person is too much more important than another. One of Grundtvig's hymns expresses this balance and modesty, among other values:

> Much higher mountains so wide on earth are found
> than here where mountains only are hills
> But the Dane has his home where the beech trees grow
> near the coast with its fair sweet memory
> and most wonderful we find, in cradle and grave,
> the flowering field in the flowing sea.

It concludes,

> Much more precious ore so white and so red
> have others received in mountains or trade,
> Among Danes the daily bread is yet not smaller in the poor man's hut;
> And thus have we gone far in wealth when few have too much, and fewer too little
> (Borish 1991, 245).

Other values include Skepticism, Caution, and Independence. There is apparently much participation and discussion regarding political matters, indicating a healthy democratic climate and tolerance for different points of view. Even though Denmark joined NATO, it chooses from time to time not to go along with their majority opinion. Even though it joined the European Union, the same trend exists, and initially they have held back from adopting the Euro. Another value Borish noticed is a tendency to bend the rules. I feel this must be a nice counterbalance for a socialistic country with a potential for a lot of bureaucratic rules (1991, 260).

Borish devotes an entire chapter to "Hygge and the Art of Celebration." Hygge (hee-geh) is a Danish social value, meaning celebration, or partying—having a good time, being festive. It is not as simple as it sounds, however. Certain elements are present to create spontaneous and genuine fun. One factor is to take the time to prepare a pleasant setting. Although one can have a "hyggeligt" time alone, with more than one, it works better when everyone participates in creating the experience and in turn, when together, that everyone is made to feel included and not ignored (1991, 264-280).

Other values include Welfare, Social Responsibility and Social Conscience, with a dislike for militarism and violence (1991, 310). Steven Borish added to this the Grundtvigian concept of folkelighed, or folk life, which he experienced to mean having the proper ethic of social cooperation and an attitude of "enlightened, responsible and tolerant participation in the exercise of power" (1991, 306).

FOUR DANISH FOLK HIGH SCHOOLS

Borish spent a year studying at three Danish folk high schools. Students shared quarters and food preparation, and sometimes other work projects. There were regular periods for group singing. The first folk school he attended was started comparatively recently and devoted to environmental education. He was still working on his competence in the Danish language and had mixed experiences with the classes. He didn't feel that one teacher was that great, and struggled to get along among some of the students in building a windmill, but by the end, somehow everyone could enjoy a good party together.

The second school was more formally tied to the Danish Lutheran church (1991, 371). The core curriculum included literature, social studies/history and Christianity, with electives in leadership subjects, creative arts, athletic subjects, self-sufficiency and outdoor life (1991, 378). The classes were a mixture of lecture and dialogue. He had difficulty liking the food, but again, there was "hygge." One teacher complained that classes felt like a prop students needed to get through so they could go and have a good party afterwards (1991, 382). It's not that Danes just like to have a good time; the ability for positive socialization is an important factor to hold together the masses of people who must be able to organize and work together in good times and bad in a democracy.

At the third school, one of the teachers was non-responsive to students, so they took to skipping class and meeting elsewhere on several occasions. Another teacher, however, was excellent and really engaged them in learning and dialogue (1991, 400-403). Borish felt that the noncompetitive atmosphere of the folk schools with a supportive peer and staff make it a place where people are very often willing to reach out and help others to have a positive experience (1991, 398).

The Tomkins Institute, of Cape Breton College in Nova Scotia, published a book about the International People's College, which goes beyond Danish culture and promotes international understanding by inviting people from around the world. English is the main language spoken, so it is one of the few folk schools to attend if you don't know Danish. They have 26 hours of traditional, creative and innovative course work each week as well as assignments such as washing dishes, cleaning and office work. Outside of class, students can be involved in art or social and consciousness-raising projects, as well as athletics and recreation. Cultural sharing is expected to thrive formally as well as informally and students are encouraged to present their view of their country during special programs (Warren 1987, 15).

GRUNDTVIG'S IDEAS APPLIED TO MULTICULTURALISM

Grundtvig wasn't chauvinistic because of his commitment to all things Danish. However,

his lifelong work as a universal historian which culminated in an immense three-volume treatise on the history of mankind, "was not written from the point of view of a narrow nationalism." He was convinced that each people, each tribe, each nation on earth had a valuable role to play in the unfolding of world history. This unfolding was taking place in its own time and its own way in accordance with God's plan of creation (Borish 1991, 167-168).

While expressing his love for Denmark, Grundtvig didn't look down on any cultures, or feel superior to them. However, he didn't assume that all grass roots movements were necessarily for the good or right (1991, 168-169).

That having been said, many who may have been indirectly inspired by Grundtvig's heralding of the mother tongue, did not always have his correct understanding. The Sami [pronounced "saw me"] (also called Lapp), a people indigenous to Scandinavia but in the minority, were forced to forget their Sami language and to learn the language of the Scandinavian country that moved into their traditional territory. Although there probably are some folk schools today that help the Sami learn and retain their language, there is much history to the contrary. Johannes Marainen, a Sami Teacher and Researcher in Sweden, grew up in an intact Sami environment. When he went to school, they were taught the "mother tongue," which was Swedish and were not allowed to speak their native language. Outside school he tried to hide his ethnicity but was called "Sámi devil" everyday (Marainen 1998).

It is common for less dominant cultures to have to struggle to compete for livelihood and to preserve their culture. As in Denmark "culture wars" are waged around the world today. Latin American writer Carlos Fuentes shares a similar experience. "We [Latin Americans] have to know the cultures of the West even better than a Frenchman or an Englishman, and at the same time we have to know our own cultures. This sometimes means going back to the Indian cultures, whereas the Europeans feel they don't have to know our cultures at all. We have to know Quetzalcoatl and Descartes. They think Descartes is enough" (Mura 1988, 144).

Fuentes grew up living in both the United States and Mexico and learned that while Mexico had a history of crushing defeats, the United States would celebrate victories, one after another. Sometimes the names of Mexico's defeats and humiliations were the same as victories in the U.S. "To the south, sad songs, sweet nostalgia, impossible desires. To the north, self-confidence, faith in progress, boundless optimism" (Fuentes 1988, 85).

The ethnic studies programs at colleges in the U.S. have faced a similar battle against cultures, including the fringe Scandinavian studies, taught on campuses. Where I am a student, at the Western Institute for Social Research (WISR, pronounced "wiser"), we have "Multicultural is WISR" Tshirts. Often, cultural diversity depends on economic equity, not just lack of prejudice. Though we are still in a very capitalistic system, WISR promotes social democratic economic values by making academic study more affordable for a wider spectrum of learners. We have neither grades nor tests, like the folk schools, however there are requirements to complete. Many have found this less competitive atmosphere a more satisfying way to learn.

INFLUENCES OF THE DANISH
MODEL ON OTHER MOVEMENTS

The American community-college movement, according to the Royal Danish Embassy (1997), was inspired by the Danish folkehøjskole movement. Two progressive educators in the early 20th century, Joseph Hart and Eduard Lindeman, were influenced by the folk high school (Stack 2001, 1). E.C. Lindeman was the first person who used the term "andragogy" in North American literature. Andragogy refers to adult education that respects the humanity of the adult as learner, vs. pedagogy, which refers to the teaching of children in an authoritarian manner (Hiemstra 1990, 1). The term, "pedagogy," has also been used universally to mean method of teaching, regardless of age, even in Denmark, and alternative "pedagogies" have been developed that are not based on an authoritarian model.

Though all Danes aren't conscious of the rich history of N.F.S. Grundtvig, it is often said that when you enter Denmark, you meet him at the border (Borish 1991, 158-159). On the overall influence of folk schools in changing the type of society in Denmark and in summation, one author claims:

> Today, the folk high school is given credit for stimulating the Danish cooperative movement and the eventual formation of the Social Democratic Party in 1870. This view of cooperative community, nurtured in the Danish Folk High School, formed the ideological framework for the Danish welfare state and Denmark's global perspective of world community (Stack 2001, 1).

In other Scandinavian countries, where folk schools took hold, social welfare is also strong. In the book *Sweden, The Middle Way On Trial*, a student of social policy is quoted to say that the Swedish Social Democrats "were the first socialist party in the world to be able to increase gradually the power of the state in economic life without revolution or large-scale nationalization" (Childs 1980, 18). Perhaps it is too great an assumption to name one single movement as cause for a large-scale trend, but it seems obvious that popular education is an important step for citizens to learn to work together democratically to address social issues.

Though it is difficult to transfer institutions across cultures, Steven Borish suggests that this model can be useful for developing third world cultures today that struggle with a mostly rural economy as Denmark did in the early 1800's (Borish 1991, 414). Though it may be hard to transplant institutions, we can be inspired by them, as N.F.S. Grundtvig was inspired by his visits to Cambridge and Oxford to bring seeds of fresh educational ideas to plant in Denmark, and as Myles Horton brought the folk school vision to start the Highlander Center in Tennessee. The story of Denmark, who lost its empire, dealt creatively with that loss and learned to stand up to the superpowers of Europe while learning to take care of its own citizens, can offer a model of hope for others facing the superpowers of the modern world.

COMPARISONS TO GANDHI

Grundtvig's life work, similar to Mahatma Gandhi and Myles Horton, was to help liberate the common people who are usually taken advantage of by the upper rungs of society. Like Grundtvig, Gandhi also emphasized the importance of language and felt that one of the first requirements of a free man was "the ability to express himself well in the language of his childhood" (Erickson 1969, 259). Another similarity was that, like Grundtvig's promotion of indigenous culture, Gandhi promoted native crafts for national identity as well as local economics (1969, 260). Grundtvig was born during and was influenced by Europe's Age of Enlightenment and wrote in his diary in 1804 of "his desire to dedicate himself to the enlightenment of the peasants." (Jayakumar 2000, 1). Similarly, Gandhi studied in England and was influenced, though a century later, by the legacy of Enlightenment thought (Lal 1997, 1) which questioned established beliefs (Morris 1975, 434). A Danish missionary to India organized a school for Indian girls, modeled after Danish folk schools but rooted in the Indian nationalist movement. Mahatma Gandhi laid the foundation stone (Larsen 2000, 2).

CONCLUSION

Taking a critical look at what really effected development in Denmark, Steven Borish writes that,

> from the last half of the nineteenth century, the Danes began a sustained movement down their own alternative pathway to modernization. Some of its major themes have been (1) the predominantly peaceful surrender and sharing of absolute power by established social elites; (2) the abandonment of external military conquest and interference in the internal affairs of other countries as ways of solving the nation's problems; and (3) the flourishing of people-oriented, cooperative solutions facilitated both by a complex of grass roots social movements and a generally benevolent and permissive state (Borish 1991, 422).

The movement for rural modernization, "based on these trends, allowed Denmark to develop into one of the world's most productive systems of agriculture. Although not rich in natural resources, they became at the same time one of the most prosperous and genuinely democratic nations the world has ever known" (1991.)

Borish summed up some universal principles from Danish history that speak to problems of human development in modernizing and postmodern societies. First, the folk high schools were built on a deep faith in people and in their ability to intelligently alter and improve their situation as a result of their education. Equally important, they were not schools where a set of correct data was taught which people were instructed to memorize for examination. Second, they taught an alternative to nationalism, to respect that other cultures have an equal role to play in history. Third, folk high schools kept a connection with people through their whole lives through the social networks that developed as well as by welcoming people of all ages to learn. Fourth, though teachers and taught may not have been of the same class, they were connected not only by national identity, but by a common concern for revitalization and self-improvement. Teachers did not patronize; the goal of early schools was the improvement of the life of the farmer. Education was not imposed from above as a development strategy, but developed in a grass roots and local, decentralized way (1991, 414-416). Today, rather than land reform, a different age brings different goals, but Borish noticed students with university backgrounds attending the same school along with those who never finished seventh grade (1991, 412).

Borish reiterates that, crucial as folk schools have been, a fundamental feature of the Danish path to modernization is illustrated by two key events of transformation, the Danish Land Reforms (1784-97) and the peaceful surrender of absolute royal authority (1848-49). In both cases, the surrender of authority was made by "representatives of a social elite to members of social classes over which they had long exercised virtual absolute rule." Leaders of the Land Reforms had the "ardent desire both to correct social injustice" and to increase general prosperity. This model does not mean that dominant elites must give up all power, but that the "possession of unreasonable social and economic power must be non-violently replaced by a more limited set of privileges." What is "unreasonable," he notes, goes right to the heart of the matter. However, "the net effect of reform must be a greater sharing of available resources during an era of crisis-driven social change." Without these kinds of dynamics, Borish notes, developing countries fail at modernization and remain stuck and embroiled in war and poverty (416-419).

A main concern of Danes and other Scandinavians today is whether "these older progressive strategies can work in today's relentlessly competitive global economy." I recently heard Anita Gradin, a former Swedish European Union (EU) Commissioner and a Swedish Democratic Socialist, speaking at the University of California at Berkeley, state that the member countries of the EU generally agree on the need to form compromises between social welfare and the competitive forces of the market economy, though the latter is becoming an ever greater force.

Popular education is usually promoted as a tool of liberation for the underclass. However, as we see in the history of Denmark, well-meaning people in the upper and middle classes need to join in to create a more fair and just society. They need to let go of some power as lower classes become empowered, but both need to work together. A spirit of celebration, and common goals, help lift us out of the disparity of greediness vs. neediness. Society needs structures to develop the verbal skills to dialogue as well as respectful and functioning relationships committed to follow through. The crises in the world today are more critical than ever, with the threat of nuclear war and environmental devastation. People worry about Wall Street trading, but what about the despair of people who would bomb the center for stock market trading and kill themselves at the same time? The people, the folk, must include all of us, working together, for life to continue.

REFERENCES

Books & Articles

Bell, Brenda, John Gaventa & John Peters. 1990. *We Make the Road by Walking*, Philadelphia, PA: Temple University Press.

Borish, Steven M. 1991. *The Land of the Living, The Danish Folk High Schools and Denmark's Non-Violent Path to Modernization*, Grass Valley, CA: Blue Dolphin Press.

Childs, Marchis. 1980. *Sweden: The Middle Way On Trial*, New Haven, CT: Yale Univ. Press.

Christensen, Frederik. 1983. "Nikolai Frederik Severin Grundtvig," November, Black Mountain, N.C; 1987. *Option, Journal of the Folk School Association of America*, Vol. 11, No. 3-4, Fall.

Drejergaard, Bishop of Funen, "Humanity and Christianity," *Report from the thirteen Anglo-Scandinavian Pastoral Conference in Odense and Copenhagen 2000*, http://fyns.mellemkirkelige.stiftsudvalg.dk/rapport3.html.

Erickson, Erik. 1969. *Gandhi's Truth*, New York, NY: W.W. Norton & Co.

Fuentes, Carlos. 1988. "How I Started to Write," *The Graywolf Annual Five: Mutli-Cultural Literacy*, Rick Simonson & Scott Walker, eds., St. Paul, MN: Graywolf Press.

Hiemstra, Roger & Burt Sisco, "Moving from Pedagogy to Andragogy," *Individualizing Instruction*, San Francisco, CA: Jossey-Bass, 1990, http://home.twcyny.rr.com/hiemstra/pedtoand.html.

Horton, Myles. 1983. "Influences on Highlander Research and Education Center, New Market, Tennessee, USA," *Grundtvig's Ideas in North America: Influences & Parallels. Workshop Sponsored by Scandinavian Seminar College*, Copenhagen, Denmark: Det Danske Selskab.

Hurst, John. 1995. "Popular Education," *Education and Social Change*, Spring, Volume 9, Number 1, Berkeley, University of California, http://www-*gse.berkeley.edu/Admin/ExtRel/educator/spring95texts/popular.educ.html*.

Jayakumar, Daniel, "Glimpses From the Life of NFS Grundtvig," Danish Indian History & Research Society -DIHRS, ESTB 2000, *http://www.dihrs.dk/DihrsEn1.htm*.

Killough, Patrick, "A Danish Folk School in North Carolina," www.patrick killough.com/education/danish.html, 6/7/98.

Knudsen, Johannes. 1976. *Selected Writings: N.F.S. Grundtvig*, Philadelphia, PA: Fortress Press.

Lal, Vinay, "Mahatma Gandhi," Website: *http://www.sscnet.ucla.edu/southasia/History/Gandhi/gandhi.html,* 1997.

Larsen, Elisabeth, "The Life and Work of the Danish Missionary Anne Marie Petersen," Danish Indian History & Research Society -DIHRS, ESTB 2000, *http://www.dihrs.dk/DihrsEn1.htm*.

Marainen, Johannes, "Indigenous and Minority Peoples' Views of Language," Hancock, MI,: Terralingua, 1998, http://cougar.ucdavis.edu/nas/terralin/ip&lgs.hml.

Morris, William. 1975. *The American Heritage Dictionary of the English Language*, New York: American Heritage Publishing Co.

Mura, David. 1988. "Strangers in the Village," *The Graywolf Annual Five: Multi-Cultural Literacy*, Rick Simonson & Scott Walker, eds., St. Paul, MN: Graywolf Press.

Parker, Franklin & Betty J. Parker. 1993. "Myles Horton (1905-90) of Highlander, Adult Educator and Southern Activist," *Pioneers and Heroes, Part II from the Americas*, Black Mountain, NC: Option, Journal of the Folk Education Association of America, Vol. 17, No. 2, Fall.

Reich, Ebbe Kløvedal, "Grundtvig in England," A Public lecture delivered in the University of York to Open the International Consultation on N.F.S. Grundtvig, 24-27 August 2000, www.grundtviginengland.org.uk/_/library/confprocedngs/reich/paper.htm.

Royal Danish Embassy, "The Danish 'Folkehøjskole:' N.F.S. Grundtvig, Scandinavia, USA, Europe," Washington, D.C., www.denmarkemb.org/hojsk93.htm, 9/23/97.

Royal Danish Embassy, "N.F.S. Grundtvig," Washington, D.C., www.denmarkemb.org/grundt.html, 6/22/98.

Sanford, Nevitt, ed., 1962. *The American College, A Psychological and Social Interpretation of the Higher Learning*, New York, NY: John Wiley & Sons, Inc.

Simon, Erica. 1984. "Grundtvigian Folkelighed and The Culture War," Black Mountain, NC: Option, Journal of the Folk Education Association of America, Vol. 8, #3-4, Summer/Fall.

Stack, Samuel & Gwendolyn Jones, "The Danish Folk High School in Appalachia," Lock Haven University of Pennsylvania, www.lhup.edu/library/InternationalReview/danish.htm, 2001.

Warren, Clay. 1987. *Grundtvig's Philosophy of Lifelong Education Through the Living Word*, Tompkins Institute for Human Values and Technology, Occasional Paper No. 3, Sydney, Nova Scotia, Canada: University College of Cape Breton Press.

Willette, Rusty. "Grundtvig and Danish Educational Practice," *Best Practices in Education*, Copenhagen, Denmark, March 5, 1996, Webmaster@bestpraceduc.org, 1998.

Institutional Resources

Augustana College, Rock Island, IL.

Concordia Language Village, Bemidgi, Minnesota, http://www.cord.edu/dept/clv/aboutus/index.html.

Farstrup-Mortensen Memorial Lectures, Bethania Evangelical Lutheran Church, Solvang, CA.

Highlander Research and Education Center, New Market, TN (called Highlander School before 1960).

Scandinavia Seminar, Amherst, MA, www.scandinavianseminar.com.

Study Circles Resource Center, Pomfret, CT.

Western Institute for Social Research, Berkeley, California.

Chapter 16

Situating the Contemporary Grassroots Cooperatives: Intellectual and Political Origins

Joyce Rothschild

Abstract

Grassroots collectives and cooperatives are spreading, both in the developed countries and in the less developed countries. After providing numerous illustrations, this article looks to the 19th century example of the Rochdale Pioneers and the debate between Marx and Bakunin for the intellectual and political origins of the modern day cooperatives. Briefly, it argues that with Marx's ascendancy at the First International in 1872 came the ascendancy of the belief in a strong, central state, albeit a provisional one, to direct economic development. This silenced, or at least eclipsed, the opposing preference for de-centralized development, with direct worker control of work organizations and citizen control of community institutions. The modern day grassroots cooperators owe much to the latter "anarchist" ideas from which they sprang. A deeper understanding of the 19th century debates can inform current choices facing the worldwide co-operative movements.

Introduction

It seems that they are springing up everywhere: these grassroots collectives and cooperatives. Emerging first in the most developed regions of the most developed countries, collectivists were evident, as I found, by the mid-1970s in California. This told me even then of their rejection of private ownership and hierarchal organizational forms and of their desire to build "alternative" enterprises that in themselves would constitute functioning models of how work could be organized cooperatively and democratically in a future society (Rothschild and Whitt, 1986). By the mid-1980s, the locally grown collectives had spread by the hundreds or thousands across the middle of the United States and Europe, but by then, many appeared to flow from concerns of the women's movement. Many of these 1980s collectives were populated mostly by women and oriented to providing products or services particularly for women such as the battered women's shelters, the rape crisis centers, and the feminist health clinics. During the latter part of the 1990s and up to the present, many of the new collectives and co-operatives seem to be developing in economically distressed parts of the U.S. and of the world. For reasons that Dickinson has pointed out elsewhere, non-wage women in the peripheral countries are often at the center of these efforts to create alternative and cooperative forms of work organization that are outside of capitalist and state control (2001: 252-257).

To be sure, there are differences between these distinct waves of collectivist development, but what is most striking to observe is the *resonance* between the themes on the websites of the women's co-operatives today in India and the themes I heard voiced by the counter-cultural collectivists I interviewed in California in the 1970s. BOTH are about collectivities of people coming together to earn a livelihood. Both are about earning that livelihood without recourse to the state bureaucracy or the capitalist class. Both figure that they can manage themselves and make decisions democratically concerning the product (or service) they will provide, its design, it pricing, it's marketing and so forth without the help of bosses. Both set out to work in a cooperative (non-competitive) fashion and on an egalitarian footing. Both are looking to do something that has an inherent social utility, but yet will earn them a livelihood and where they can control their own time and work process.

The themes sounded by the modern day cooperators, from the young adults producing an alternative newspaper in California to the women sewing quilts in India, sound so modern, so cutting-edge, that it would be easy to think of them as new. Their concerns do arise, of course, out of the particular way that capitalism has developed in the world, the particular ways that it uses or expels certain classes of persons. And accordingly, there are some specialized aspects of their critiques and their methods of organization. However, the idea that workers or direct producers could (and should) come together on an equal footing and produce goods and services, without reliance on the capitalist, is definitely *not* new.

HISTORICAL ROOTS OF U.S. COOPERATIVES
AND THE ROCHDALE PRINCIPLES

In the United States, for example, workers' cooperatives have a history dating back to the revolutionary period. The historical record from 1790 to 1940 identifies more than 700 producers' cooperatives. These cooperatives appeared in four distinct waves—the 1840s, the 1860s, the 1880s and the 1920s-1930s (Aldrich and Stern, 1978). As each of these previous waves of workers' cooperatives were not randomly occurring in time, but rather, came on the heels of other major movements for social change, the historical pattern suggests that cooperative formation may be the outgrowth, the living organizational legacy so to speak, of broad movements and aspirations for profound societal change.

We know that producers' cooperatives, as they were called in the 19th century, represented efforts by workers to retain highly skilled craft production in the face of increasing mechanization and standardization in industry. In addition, the early producer co-operatives attempted to put into practice the ideals of democracy, equality and community, turning direct control over the means and the product of production to the producers (Shirom, 1972). That the workers' cooperatives were really a social invention of the 19th century, a product of the particular economic displacement and of the degradation of work that went hand in hand with the industrialization process, is implied in the Rochdale Principles: These written principles, created by a group of workers, mostly weavers, who had formed the Rochdale Society of Equitable Pioneers in 1844, are taken, even today, as definition and guide in the development of co-operatives all over the world.

Succinctly, the Rochdale Pioneers distilled their practices into seven key principles of co-operation: First, membership in the cooperative must be open and voluntary, without discrimination by race, gender, color, religion, political party or anything else. Second, a co-operative must be democratically controlled by its members on a one member-one vote basis. The third principle related to surplus is also critical. Any surplus the co-operative obtains should be used to develop the co-operative enterprise further (i.e., reinvested in the co-op) or it should be returned to its members, in proportion to their transactions in the co-op (this applies especially to consumer co-ops). Fourth, each co-operative should strive to retain its autonomy. If it does enter into agreements with government agencies or with outside banks, it should do so in a way that allows the member-owners to retain democratic control and cooperative autonomy. Fifth, the co-operative should strive to educate and train its members (and their children) so that they can wisely and democratically manage the co-op, now and in the future. Sixth, where possible and mutually beneficial, the co-operative should cooperate with other cooperative endeavors. And seventh, the co-operative should be involved and concerned for the welfare of the community in which they operate, working however possible for its sustainable development. (See, Mercer, 1931; the International Cooperative Alliance, 1995; and http://www.1strochdalenyc.net/aboutcoops.htm for somewhat different takes on this list of principles).

Today, over 150 years later, the Rochdale Principles continue to guide co-operatives the world over. The co-operatives that have developed since the 1840s are basically of three types: Consumers co-ops have been created by and for their member-owners mainly for the purpose of obtaining a needed product or service of the quality and type wanted and at a better value. For example, contemporary consumer co-ops have been formed to provide their members with electric utility service, health care service, food, clothing, housing, hardware and so forth. Credit co-ops are really a special type of consumer co-op, as they exist to provide credit (i.e., capital) at more attractive rates or to persons who might not otherwise have access to needed capital. By pooling their resources, donating their time and cutting out the capitalist requirement of profit, the consumer co-op is able to provide these goods at higher quality and/or lower cost to their members. A second type of co-operative is the farmer co-op. These co-ops, of which there are so many in the U.S., join together many smaller farm producers for the purpose mainly of helping them to process and market their goods. Here the co-op may also provide needed credit, equipment and supplies to their member-owners (the farmers). The farmer co-ops are actually a sub-type of a third type of co-op, often called a worker cooperative (or collective). This is a broad term for a co-operative that brings together, as the farmer co-ops do, the direct producers of a product (or providers of a service) in such a way that they must work on the creation of their work product, from beginning to end, together. In other words, where the farmer co-ops bring together direct producers *after* they have already produced their food, for the remaining purpose of processing and marketing their product, the broader worker co-ops bring together the direct producers at an earlier stage in the work process where they must create every aspect of their product or service together. Here the workers may be journalists, bicycle repair people, taxi cab drivers, hammock makers, health care providers or counselors, to choose only a few real life examples that come to mind. The *key* to identifying all of these types of enterprises as co-operatives and/or collectives is that they have a collectivist-democratic organizational structure wherein their owner-members, operating in an egalitarian and democratic fashion, manage their own organizational affairs. (See, Rothschild, 1979 for eight key organizational features that characterize the collectivist-democratic organization).

Their purpose is to provide a livelihood (in the case of the worker co-ops) or to provide certain consumer goods or services (in the case of the consumer co-ops) to their member-owners, and in so doing, to help their communities and young people develop. As will be seen later in my discussion of the Mondragon system, some co-operative *systems* try to link numerous worker co-ops with credit and other consumer co-ops and with community institutions such as co-operative schools. Each supports the other in necessary ways, enabling the whole system to grow exponentially.

All seven of the Rochdale Principles distinguish cooperatives from capitalist enterprises, just as all eight of my previously stated principles of the collectivist-democratic organization distinguish co-operatives from bureaucratic enterprises (Rothschild, 1979). *The purpose of the collectivist or cooperative organization is not profit maximization, just as it is not to keep a hierarchy of command or status (or privilege) intact.* If I had to choose just one of the Rochdale Principles, for me, it would be the Democracy Principle that is most essential to the definition of a co-operative: the shared commitment to democratic member-owner control of the co-op on an equal footing. However, the ICA (the International Cooperative Alliance) which represents thousands of consumer co-ops today considers the first three of the Rochdale Principles essential in the very definition and functioning of a co-op, and Professor Mercer, an early advocate of co-operation in this century writes eloquently in 1931 of the essential intertwining of all seven of the Rochdale Principles in the definition and vitality of the worldwide cooperative movement (Mercer, 1931).

Today, after a fifty year hiatus, we are in the midst of a fifth wave of cooperative formation which began, as I see it, in the mid-1970s in the U.S. with thousands of small-scale collectives on the two coasts, subsequently morphed itself at least twice (in association with both the women's movement and the environmental movement) and is now reaching around the globe. The current wave is larger than any of the previous four, and it has seen the emergence of more cooperatives (by a multiple) than the rest of American history combined. It is noteworthy, and not coincidental I think, that the 1970s—80s wave of collectives and cooperatives in the U.S. and Europe emerged on the heels or in tandem with some of the most vigorous social movements in U.S. history: the civil rights, the antiwar, the environmental and the women's movements, just as the cooperatives in the less developed countries are emerging today in tandem with the anti-globalization movements.

Rather than stress their differences, as the cooperative form changes to meet differing circumstances, I would like in this paper to point to the common *roots* these modern day cooperatives all have in the ideas, political debates and social movements of the 19th century, for it is in that 19th century context that well-defined efforts to create workers' cooperatives took shape. I believe that the key debates and choices facing the modern day co-operators come into bolder relief once their 19th century origins are better understood. I will start by indicating some magnitudes, where possible, and drawing some examples from the current crop of cooperative work organizations. I then turn to the main burden of this paper which is to draw out the intellectual and political origins of the co-operative idea because it is only in situating the contemporary cooperatives in the original ideas and movements from which they grew that I think it becomes clear what these various worker cooperatives over time and place have in common and what their fundamental shared purpose may be.

SOME EXAMPLES OF WORKER COOPERATIVES

In many nations of the third world, private voluntary organizations (PVO's), non-governmental organizations (NGO's) and work cooperatives, comprise a huge element of the institutional developmental sector. Though distinctions are made in scholarly literature between PVOS and cooperatives, in reality, it may be difficult to distinguish one from the other. By and large, the social service NGOs, which function locally at the grassroots level generally do aim and adopt a participatory, cooperative form of organization, the NGO may not explicitly label itself as a cooperative. The cooperative examples in the third world can also be broadly categorized either as institutional or indigenous (Young, Sherman, and Rose 1991). Young et al (1991) classify institutional forms of cooperatives as those which rely upon external organizations, and indigenous cooperatives, as those that are the manifestations of the local social system and are thus embedded in its local cultural forms.

Among the biggest success stories in the third world women's cooperative movement is the Self-Employed Women's Association (SEWA) started in 1972 in Gujarath, India. As discussed in Part I of this volume, SEWA grew out of the Textile Labour Association (TLA), India's oldest and largest union of textile workers founded in 1920 by a woman, Anasuya Sarabhai (www.sewa.org). Ela Bhatt, founder of SEWA, recognizing the need that poor non-wage women have economic organization not welfare, formally registered SEWA as a trade union for self employed women in 1972. Since 94% of the female labor force in India are in the unorganized sector, and hence remain as an invisible group, this is an extremely large group that the "government doesn't plan for" in the words of Ela Bhatt ("Made in India," SEWA film, Plattner 1998). SEWA was founded to give these women a voice and a means of achieving full 'emploreliance' (www.sewa.org). Currently, SEWA has a membership of over 300,000 women spread over 6 states in India, with nearly two thirds of the women belonging to the rural sector (www.sewa.org).

Based on occupational skills and functional needs, SEWA organizes its members into numerous cooperatives. SEWA women provide the share capital for the cooperatives and obtain employment from them. A woman may be a member of one or more cooperatives. A democratically elected executive committee of workers runs each cooperative. The largest cooperative is SEWA Bank with 125,000 members (www.sewa.org). The final authority is the executive committee. SEWA makes sure that the executive committee is predominantly filled with working class women and not the middle class support staff. Bhatt says that the current ratio of 86% working class women on the executive committee ensures that the middle class women do not dominate the decisions in the group meetings. In fact, in the video documentary on SEWA, Bhatt gives an insightful analysis of the meeting process and remarks that the middle class urban women by their very presence can subconsciously dominate meetings, since the poor, rural women, will tend to show a reluctance to voice themselves in the presence of the 'educated' middle class women ("Made in India," SEWA film, Plattner 1998). Clearly, some real thought by the participants is going into the development of their internal democratic processes of decision-making at SEWA.

Moreover, SEWA's rural credit arm has had a substantial impact in helping women break their cycle of indebtedness (Sebstad 1982). Leslie Calman in her study of women's movements in India reports that SEWA has not only helped to bring material opportunities and benefits for women, but has also helped in increasing the self esteem and confidence level of the women, inculcating in them valuable leadership and teamwork skills (Calman 1992).

Kutch Mahila Vikas Sangathan (KMVS) is another women's cooperative that has earned a reputation for successfully organizing women in the rural areas (Ramachandran and Saihjee 2000; Patel 2000). Like SEWA, KMVS also uses rural credit programs to provide a means for women workers to negotiate and earn a livelihood from the market place. Importantly, both KMVS and SEWA are engaged too in the political consciousness of the women by actively creating and using various media outlets and forms of communication. Here again, the middle class women involved in the organization seem to be sensitive to the democratic and participatory norms of the cooperative and strive not to let themselves dominate the internal decision processes (Ramachandran and Saihjee 2000).

While the above two cooperatives are primarily operated as NGOs, there are plenty of cooperatives in the third world which function under the auspices of a government institution or as a state agency by itself (Young et al., 1982). These government-associated co-ops in the rural areas, how they operate internally and the gender relations within them, require considerably more research attention.

The Grameen Bank and the Center for Agricultural and Rural Development Program (CARD) in Bangladesh provide two other examples of women's' cooperatives that have received much attention in South Asia (Gow 2000). Christine Eber's (1999) study of the bakery and weaving cooperatives run by the indigenous women in Chiapas, who are linked to the Zapatista democratic movement provides many examples of a third world women's cooperatives that have received academic attention.

Other notable women's cooperative networks and organizations include: the Angora knitting yarn women's spinning cooperative in Chile (http://www.angoraknittingyarn.com/hand-spinning.htm), the Cherokee native women's cooperative in Oklahoma (http://www.ruraldevelopment.org/nwcp.html), the Santa Ana handicrafts cooperative in Guatemala (http://www.xelapages.com/santa_ana/), the Argan oil cooperative in Morocco, (http://www.idrc.ca/reports/read_article_english.cfm?article_num=883), and the Artcamp rural women's cooperative in Mexico (http://www.artcamp.com.mx/pages/info1.html).

While daily survival needs may appear uniquely pressing in the poorest parts of the world, the desire for opportunities to earn a livelihood with dignified, locally controlled work stretches around the world. There wasn't much economic activity or opportunity in the Basque region of Spain near the town of Mondragon in the 1940s when a new priest in town and his students started to gather in study circles to discuss how economic self reliance could be built in the region with a system of self-managed worker cooperatives. As a footnote to history, it was only when the priest's five students realized that they had no future with a private enterprise in the area, and that there was no future in a state-sponsored program, that they "gave up hope of reforming capitalist firms" and created a cooperative enterprise in 1956 (Whyte and Whyte, 1988:33). Since then, the Mondragon system of cooperatives has come to include over 150,000 members employed in over a hundred enterprises. Today, they are a large maker of refrigerators and stoves, the largest tool-and-die maker in Spain, provide dozens of other products and services in their network of co-ops, run their own training center, provide their own social security system, provide start-up funds for new co-ops through their own bank, and teach the skills of democratic management along with regular and technical subjects in their own schools, from kindergarten to a Master's Degree! Their remarkable story has had effect on the development of worker cooperatives even in the U.S., particularly in stimulating trade union interest in industrial co-ops here (Whyte and Whyte, 1988: 266-272), Their relative success in retaining their democratic forms, even in the face of capitalist market pressures, are detailed in Cheyney (2000). That the Mondragon cooperative movement developed without the encouragement of the state is an understatement: When they started, the Basque region was occupied by Franco's forces, and many of the local opposition leaders had been jailed or killed or had gone underground (Whyte and Whyte, 1988:225-237). That was the context.

In contrast, in Yugoslavia the entire economy was organized under President Tito around principles of worker self-management, with state sanction and encouragement. In Eastern European countries like Poland, thousands of worker cooperatives were formed after World War II, and estimates in the early 1980s placed 800,000 Polish workers or 6.7 percent of the workforce in the co-ops (Kowalak 1981).

During the Cultural Revolution, China too embarked on a program to develop the cooperative sector, and by the early 1980s, millions of people were estimated to be working in the cooperatives, although in China the worker cooperatives are not autonomous from the state, and official definitions of the cooperatives are blurred (Lockett 1981). It is hard to get information in the mainstream media as to how the cooperative network is doing in China today (http://www.nzchinasociety.org.nz/gungho.html).

The West European nations have substantial numbers of industrial cooperatives that emerged during the 1980s out of industrial plants, which otherwise would have been shut down. During the 1990s Germany especially and the other Western European nations as well saw the rapid proliferation of thousands of collectivist-democratic social movement groups growing mostly out of the peace movement, the anti-nuke movement and the Green movement (Leach, 2002). Within these collectives, participants have put consensus-based decision-making into practice on a massive scale with direct actions involving up to 10,000 people. In some cases they have established co-operative cultural/political projects where they can work artistically and freely, without interference from the state or from private capital; and activists have developed practical skills and methods for deepening their practice of democracy and for preventing the emergence of any kind of hierarchy in their groups (Leach, forthcoming).

Out of some of these grassroots collectivist organizations, some rather large-scale social movement networks are forming. For example, the "Women in Black" network brings together numerous women's peace groups and other direct action groups in conferences and websites where they can share information about methods and happenings. Similarly, the Independent Media Center (see, www.indymedia.org) brings together some 80 independent media centers worldwide, each of which is run in a collectivist-democratic fashion, and each of which grew out of the anti-globalization expression and action in Seattle in 1999. In this way, the ability to communicate on the internet seems to be greatly increasing the federative activity among and between the grassroots collectives and co-operatives, and the shared information appears to be inspiring growth in collectivist organizations of all kinds.

In the United States, as I have stressed in other work, literally thousands of grassroots collectives and cooperatives had developed in the 1970s through the 1990s, particularly if you count all the alternative service providers, like the rape crisis centers and battered women's shelters, along with all the co-operative restaurants, retail stores and producers of various goods. In the United States, we also have a number of holdovers from the last great wave of cooperative formation in the 1920s and 30s—the garbage collection cooperatives started in San Francisco by groups of Italian immigrants (Perry 1978) and the plywood production cooperatives of the Pacific Northwest (Berman 1967). And we even have a number of communal communities still standing from the 19th century (Kanter 1972).

Women's co-operatives are also developing today in some of the poorer regions of the United States such as in Appalachia where, for example, sixty home-based workers (mostly women) have created a cooperative, not-for-profit micro enterprise called Appalachian By Design which provides training and allows them to produce knitwear from their homes for regional and national markets. By connecting the knitters to markets through their sales to retailers, Appalachian By Design creates essentially a cooperative network of rural home-based workers, and in so doing, it offers a viable and self-managed livelihood to poor women in an economically distressed region (Oberhauser 2002). Micro-credit co-operatives are also developing in distressed regions of the U.S., allowing third party (bank) loans to be given to poor people who, by forming co-operatives to pool their collateral, are able to get access to capital to start micro enterprises. These co-op members may meet monthly to help each other to pay back the loan so that the capital can then be made available (i.e., rotated) to the next co-op member (Anthony, 2002).

INTELLECTUAL AND POLITICAL ORIGINS

In the 19th century, two great social and political doctrines confronted each other in the development of the first workers' cooperatives, and in a sense, they continue to confront each other in many modern day co-ops. To understand the debates taking place in the co-ops today, the choices before them and the choices they make, we must turn to their intellectual and political roots.

The Marxian Heritage: A Cautious Embrace

In my firsthand observations of the contemporary grassroots collectives in the United States (Rothschild and Whitt 1986) I found many of their members give credit to Karl Marx for the idea of worker's cooperation. In point of fact, however, Marx had only a little to say about cooperatives in his otherwise voluminous writings. What he does say indicates that he saw potential for workers' liberation in these organizations. Surveying the workers' co-operative movement in the mid-nineteenth century, Marx observed:

> The value of these great social experiments [cooperative factories] cannot be over rated. By deed, instead of by argument, they have shown that production on a large scale, and in accord with the behest of modern science, may be carried on without the existence of a class of masters employing a class of hands; that to bear fruit, the means of labor need not be monopolized as a means of dominion over, and of extortion against, the laboring man

himself; and that, like slave labor, like serf labor, hired labor is but a transitory and inferior form, destined to disappear before associated labor plying its toil with a willing hand, a ready mind, and a joyous heart [quoted in Avineri 1969, pp. 179 801).

Although Marx surely viewed the co-operative form as a step toward the emancipation of workers and the coming of socialism, his embrace of the cooperatives was not wholehearted. To Marx, co-operatives, as individual units, would necessarily be limited in what they would be able to accomplish within the context of the surrounding capitalist society. In themselves these individual cooperative units could not bring revolutionary change in the larger society. Nevertheless, co-operative factories are revolutionary for Marx in that they "represent within the old form [of property] the first beginning of the new" (Marx 1909, p. 521). However, he immediately goes on to note in Volume III of *Capital* that "they naturally reproduce, and must reproduce, everywhere in their actual organization all the shortcomings of the prevailing system. The "antagonism between capital and labor is overcome within them" but only at the cost of converting the laborers into capitalists— albeit collective ones.

The Marxian Heritage: Cooperatives as a Transient Form on the Road to Socialism

Marx saw this new form of collective property and associated workers as a necessary but transient phase in the progression to true socialism at the national level. Cooperatives "show the way, in which a new mode of production may naturally grow out of an old one, when the development of the material forces of production and of the corresponding forms of social production has reached a certain stage. As capitalism had grown on the basis of the rise of the factory system, so too would the factory system (and the system of credit) provide the foundation for the gradual extension of cooperative enterprises on a more or less national scale" (Marx 1967, p. 440). However, the growth of the co-ops alone would not be enough to transform society. Centralized authority would be needed. In his famous *Inaugural Address* Marx says:

> The experience of the period from 1848 to 1864 has proved beyond doubt that, however excellent in principle, and however useful in practice, co-operative labour, if kept within the narrow circle of the casual efforts of private workmen, will never be able to arrest the growth in geometrical progression of monopoly, to free the masses, nor even to perceptibly lighten the burden of their miseries. . . To save the industrious masses, cooperative labours ought to be developed to national dimensions, and consequently, to be fostered by national means [quoted in Avineri 1969, p. 180).

This idea of the need for centralized state authority is the key to understanding Marx's attitude toward cooperatives. It is also a controversial idea that has been the basis for divisions among socialists particularly between libertarian socialists, or anarchists, and more traditional Marxists for more than a century. It is an idea too that has played a crucial role in the development of actual co-operatives: Some, reflecting their Marxian heritage, have sought state sponsorship for their co-operatives; others, reflecting their anarchistic instincts, have sought to remain autonomous and grassroots.

The ideas of Marx nevertheless have had a great deal of influence in spurring the development of worker co-ops and in determining some of the specific forms they have taken. In detailed interviews with grassroots co-op members in the United States, I found that many of the people who created these organizations embrace Marx's critique of private property, his analysis of capitalism as increasingly irrational and riddled with contradictions, his concepts of alienation and exploitation, and his vision of a future society that is classless and just, where direct producers control the means of production. For example, a cooperatively run health clinic that I studied states as part of its formal statement of goals, "all people working in health care should receive adequate but not excessive compensation. No one should gain profit from the sickness, death or misery of others. There should be an end to profit making in health care." At a collectively owned newspaper I studied, a member described their purposes this way:

> What I see that we are doing is trying to create soviets. We're creating organizations of people's power.... Capitalism is getting more and more into crisis everyday and in defense of themselves people are organizing . . . creating institutions that fulfill people's needs. The more crises, the more organization will occur. By the time the final crisis arrives, the [alternatives] will be everything. The new society will kind of just grow up through the roots and the old society will just be brushed aside.

Almost by definition, the very act of creating a co-operative workplace implies a rejection of conventional wage labor. *The contemporary co-operators and collectivists see themselves in opposition to mainstream capitalist institutions, both in terms of the types of products or services they are trying to provide,* for example, free and preventive health care, alternative news coverage, legal services for the dispossessed, *and in terms of the nonhierarchical, democratic processes by which they are trying to run their organizations.* This is as true among the contemporary German collectivists as it is of the collectivists in the United States (leach 2002; Rothschild and Whitt 1986).

Marx has not been the only influence upon co-operatives. Many co-operatives, particularly those in the United States and Europe where they are largely independent of the state sector, owe at least as much to the intellectual legacy of the collective anarchists (who opposed Marx) as to Marx. Other co-ops developed under state coordination or sponsorship, as in China and, for example, in the former Yugoslavia, may be more Marxian in their inspiration and functioning. In this respect, co-operatives are particularly important as theoretical objects of study and as concrete models in that they may be the only existing institutions that bridge the gap between Marxian and anarchist thought by bringing together and synthesizing principles from both traditions.

The Anarchist Heritage: Organization without Hierarchy

The Greek word *anarchos*, the root of anarchism, means literally "without a ruler." It signifies the existence of organization without external authority or a ruler, implying that social order can be achieved solely by internal discipline. In the mass media, however, the term anarchism and, more frequently, anarchy, are unfortunately associated with the idea of chaos and disorder, and with nihilism and terrorism. Although this is a popular misunderstanding of anarchist thought, a sympathetic historian admits "few [doctrines] have presented in their own variety of approach and action so much excuse for confusion" (Woodcock 1962, p. 9). Because of the general lack of knowledge about anarchism and because anarchist principles play a large role in co ops, we wish to clarify these ideas, and in so doing, to resolve the seeming paradox of an anarchist organization.

One caveat should be borne in mind: anarchism does not contain a systematic and determinate social theory. Its libertarian attitude admits a variety of viewpoints and actions. This is one reason why anarchist contributions to democratic organization tend to remain obscure.

In spite of the range of anarchist thinking and its resistance to codification, all forms of anarchism do share common features. The first premise of anarchist organization is what Colin Ward (1966, p. 389) calls the "theory of spontaneous order": "that, given a common need, a collection of people will, by trial and error, by improvisation and experiment, evolve order out of chaos—this order being more durable and more closely related to their needs than any kind of externally imposed order." This belief in a naturally evolving cooperative order can be traced to Kropotkin's proposal (1902) for an extensive network of mutual aid institutions. With external authority abolished, Kropotkin believed that people's "natural" tendency toward "mutual aid" would express itself in the evolution of countless local associations granting mutual support to each other.

Mutualism, collectivism and anarcho-syndicalism are all closely linked in the history of anarchist thought. Proudhon, who in the 1840s was the first writer to adopt willingly the pejorative term 'anarchist,' developed the idea of mutualism. By that he described a future society of federated communes and worker's co-operatives, with individuals and small groups controlling (not owning) their means of production, and bound by contracts of mutual credit and exchange to ensure all individuals the product of their own labor. Mutualists established the first French sections of the International in 1865. Collectivists, following the Russian revolutionist Mikhail Bakunin in the 1860s, continued to stress the need for federalism and workers associations but tried to adapt these ideas to industrialization by arguing that larger voluntary organizations of workers might control the means of production. Bakunin himself believed in the need for a violent revolution, a revolution that he felt would come not from the industrial workers of Marx's vision, but rather would come from the Russian peasants (Feuer 1983, p. 552). A fierce struggle developed between the followers of Marx and those of Bakunin at the Congress of the First International at The Hague in 1872, with both factions intense in their battle to control the International. Marx charged Bakunin with being an unscrupulous Russian agent, saying, "I do not trust any Russian" (Feuer 1983, p. 551), and accused him too of fraud. Both charges were later found to be false (Morris, 1993). Although it was true that Bakunin had organized a caucus in political opposition to Marx, Marx cannot exactly be seen as tolerant of dissent in his vituperate response. In turn, Bakunin called Marx "an authoritarian and centralizing communist" and suggested that Marx's concept of the 'dictatorship of the proletariat' would turn out to be "a vile and terrible lie." The struggle ended not only with Marx winning the leadership of the International, but less well known, with the victorious Marxists **expelling** Bakunin and his followers from the International and shocking the delegates by transferring the General Congress from London to New York, where it languished and died (Feuer 1983, p. 552). This decisive split at the First International was a watershed event that is much too little known, even among left scholars and activists. It is an event that had far reaching implications for the subsequent development of socialist movements in the world.

It was the opening shot in a general split in the history of socialist movements between those who support a central management model of socialism and those who support a decentralized popular control model. The outcome of the battle at the International ensured the ascendancy of the former.

The main substantive split between the Marxists and the anarchists in the nineteenth century was over the use of state authority. Engels, of course, had argued bluntly for the impossibility of eliminating authority relations in work and industry (1959, pp.481-85). The Marxists were unwilling to relinquish the state bureaucracy as an instrument of power and wished to use it to implement socialist authority, while Bakunin and the anarchists were unwilling to accept hierarchical authority, proletarian or otherwise. Hierarchical authority relationships were anathema to the 19th century anarchists because they violated their first principle of individual liberty. Further, the anarchists were not disposed to believing Marxian claims of the eventual "withering away of the state." For the anarchists, a revolution would require dissolving not only capitalist property relations but also the structure of authority of the state, which they viewed as inherently coercive, and not in merely switching who controls that structure. For Bakunin and his collective anarchists, "the only way to successfully abolish both Capital and the State is to abolish both *at the same time* and to reconstruct society from the bottom-up. This is the only way to political and economic justice" (Leach, 1998).

Following Bakunin came Kropotkin and his fellow anarcho-communists in the 1870s, and, based in the French trade unions, the anarcho-syndicalists in the 1880s. The latter stressed the trade union as an organ of struggle (for example, the general strike) and as a basis for future social organization.

While differing in emphasis, all of these strains of anarchist thought have much in common. All think in terms of two basic types of social institutions providing the organizational structure for a future free society: (1) the "commune" or "soviet" and (2) the "syndicate" or "workers' council." Both are seen as relatively small, collectively controlled, local units that would federate with each other for the sorts of larger social and economic affairs that benefit from mutual aid and exchange. The communes or soviets would federate territorially; the syndicates or workers' councils would federate industrially. Today, clear examples of a commune structure are found in the kibbutz community assemblies in Israel (Rosner 1983) and examples of syndicates or workers' councils existed throughout the former Yugoslavia and, in less pure form, in parts of Western Europe. Collectives in the United States are in the main anarchistic forms of organization. In their commitment to decentralized, small, voluntary associations, they are anarchistic. To the extent that individual alternative organizations support the development of full blown "alternative communities" within their own locales and support regional federations or networks of similar cooperative organizations, they subscribe to the anarchist federative principle. Their goal of creating functional work organizations that provides a product or service without recourse to hierarchical authority is anarchistic, as is their dual emphasis on community control over community life and workers' control over workplace decisions. The Israeli Kibbutzim communities (which have now sustained themselves over 50 years or longer) and some of the 19th century communes in the U. S. are some of the best examples of this integration of community control of the community assembly and workers' control of the workplace assembly.

The Anarchist Heritage: The Means are the Ends

The features mentioned so far relate to anarchist goals. Cooperative organizations also utilize many of the methods and tactics of anarchism. A key feature of anarchist strategy is the insistence upon a unity of means and ends: "Anarchism doesn't want different people on top; it wants to destroy the pyramid. In its place it advocates an extended network of individuals and groups, making their own decisions, controlling their own destiny" (Ward 1972, p. 289). *Anarchist strategies thus stress a congruence of means and ends*. Anarchists would not propose a mandatory organization to re-educate people for a free society. They would not advocate violent means to achieve a peaceful society, nor would they choose centralized means of attaining a decentralized society. They would not accept authoritarian rule or even a charismatic personality animating a democratic community.

In some of the contemporary German collectives, for example, the "autonomen" often use pseudonyms in their public writings and they may even wear masks when speaking in public in large measure because they are so keenly aware of the dangers of charismatic leadership and the cult of personality. With their masks and their pseudonyms, they are insisting that people pay attention to the message, not the messenger (Leach, 2002).

From a congruence of means and ends flows the concept of "direct action." Direct actions are directly relevant to the ends sought and are based on individual decisions as to whether to participate in the proposed action. They offer a way to put ideals into practice today, not generally by asking the state to intervene, but rather by taking action individually and collectively to improve things in the desired direction. Examples of direct actions include the general strike, resistance to the draft, consumer boycotts, the creation of food co-operatives, credit unions, tenants' unions, squatting in unoccupied dwellings to provide housing, and setting up worker-run workplaces.

Members of collectivist organizations see themselves as providing working models for a future society. If they succeed, they engage in what Buber (1960, pp. 44-45) called "pre revolutionary structure making. "As Buber observed, people's behaviors and ways of thinking change gradually and they only do on the basis of new experiences. Thus, an event called a "revolution" from the heads of radical theorists. The essential task for participants is to create the cannot come about merely *empirical basis* for a new society—alternative organizations that demonstrate practical but collectivist ways to get tasks done and through which people can learn and change. That this is the political meaning members ascribe to their cooperative organizations is implied in the words of a person at a collectively owned newspaper I studied:

> When we're talking about collectives, we're talking about an embryonic creation of a new society. Collectives are growing at a phenomenal rate all over this country, and the thing to understand about collectivism is that it is an attempt to supplant old structures of society with new and better structures. What makes ours superior is that the basis of authority is radically different.

The co-operators also see their worker-controlled workplaces as closely tied to efforts to assert community control over community resources. For instance, free health clinic operators, in their statement of goals said, "Health care workers, patients and community members should determine the priorities of health institutions and of the entire health care system . . . Health services should be neighborhood based and easily accessible in every community." Similarly, leaders of the food co-op spearheaded a campaign to establish rent control and greater tenants' rights in the community where most of their membership lived.

My main point is that the decision of co-operators to build and work in organizations in the present that embody what they want to create on a societal level in the future is essentially a political strategy in the anarchist mode, whether self-conscious or not. Put another way, it is a "prefigurative politics", a unity of means and ends. It is an attempt to create an organizational arena in the here and now that will offer greater voice and control to those who do the work of producing goods or providing services and that can therefore offer more egalitarian relationships among people.

STATE SPONSORSHIP VS. GRASSROOTS DEMOCRATIZED CONTROL: THE KEY POINT OF DEPARTURE BETWEEN MARX AND BAKUNIN

As we have noted, Marx was ambivalent toward the workers' cooperatives that were spreading in his day. Avineri (1969, pp. 179- 80) shows that Marx saw co-ops as representing revolutionary new forms of property— social property— that would prefigure the coming of socialism. But Marx also believed that co-operatives would have to be developed on a national scale, under public sponsorship, if they were to improve working conditions significantly for the masses or arrest the spread of monopoly in the economy. Most members of contemporary co-ops are probably not aware of Marx's specific ideas about cooperatives, but if they were, they would likely prefer grassroots development to the centralized, government sponsorship of co-ops urged by Marx.

The point at which Bakunin departed from Marx is the point where the contemporary co-operators tend to depart from Marx: on the seizure of state power versus the dismantling of it. The Marxists felt that without the state apparatus at its disposal, the proletariat would not be able to assert its will or to suppress its capitalist adversaries who might attempt a counterrevolution. Thus state power had to be in invoked, if only temporarily. In opposition to this idea, Bakunin spoke of the dangers of a "red bureaucracy" that would prove to be "the most vile and terrible lie that our century has created." He warned that state socialism would produce an overwhelming centralization of property and power, and ultimately a bureaucratic despotism.

This is really a dispute over political means, not ends, but it has serious repercussions for the ends attained. Where Marxian theory naturally leads to the support of state socialist parties and the nationalized control of industry, anarchist theory urges direct means of appropriating capital, namely, local and autonomous workers' co-operatives federated in support of each other. While many of the contemporary co-operators are more likely to have heard of Marx than of Bakunin and though they may tend to attribute more of their intellectual debt to the ideas of Marx than to the ideas of anarchist theory, *I conclude, however, that in their everyday practices they owe as much or more to the ideas of anarchism.*

I do not wish to overemphasize the historical differences between anarchists and traditional Marxists. The two were in essential agreement in their critiques of private property and in their view of wage labor as essentially alienating and exploitative. *They both saw the need for fundamental social transformation. Their main disagreement was, as we have pointed out, over the proper role of the state in bringing about that transformation.*

Marx saw, of course, that ever greater levels of inequality were essentially built into the capitalist system, and Bakunin did not disagree, but Bakunin went further than Marx in insisting that the State would always and inevitably represent capital, that it was coercive by its very nature, and that even a "proletarian" state would prove coercive. In butting heads with Marx, Bakunin was arguing that *both* liberty and equality were essential. Indeed, he argued that liberty is possible only in an egalitarian society: "Liberty without socialism is privilege, injustice...Socialism without liberty is slavery and brutality" (quoted in Morris, 1993: 110).

Empirically, the contemporary collectives and co-ops in the United States have tended to follow the anarchist strategy of local development, but then, in the United States context, they may have had little choice in the matter. In the U.S., the state has tended to be indifferent to workers' cooperatives, and even when, under "liberal" Democratic presidents, it has been open to sponsoring co-operatives, it has supported farmer, marketing or consumer co-ops, not worker based co-ops. Thus, the farmer co-ops and the Bank for Co-operatives that grew up in the 1930s, in the context of the New Deal, were designed primarily to store and market farm products in a more efficient manner. The position of individual farmer businessmen was kept intact, and for the most part, processing, transport, and retail trade remained in private hands. Over time emphasis was placed on integration into larger units that could better control price and markets, so that the farmer "co-ops" today are entities such as Sunkist, Ocean Spray, and Land O'Lakes. Similarly, the Carter administration did create the National Consumer Co-operative Bank, but it was explicitly intended to support consumer cooperatives, not worker cooperatives. Indeed, its original statute required that it loan at least 90 percent of its funds to consumer co-ops such as food or housing co-ops, with a maximum of 10 percent set aside for worker co-ops. Even within this limitation, the Co-op Bank ended up giving less than 10 percent of its loan capital to fledgling worker co-operatives. Thus, again we see that where there has been national public sponsorship of co-ops in the United States it has been directed at workers as consumers, not as producers. This is in contradiction to the classical Marxian *and* anarchist conception of workers, and above all, as producers.

The primary goal of the collectives and co-operatives I studied was to build workplaces that bring more egalitarian relations to the division of labor and that establish collective control over the labor process. Naturally they were also concerned about the quality of the products or services that they provided which is the consumer's point of view. Can we expect the capitalist state to sponsor true worker co-ops, which, by definition, redefine the relationship of workers to the means of production? This is one of the key questions facing the contemporary cooperative movements. *Should the co-operators choose local, autonomous development of their enterprises, sometimes federating with other like-minded co-ops in their region or locale, or should they apply for the sort of state support that could spur their own development?*

COOPERATIVES AS PRECURSORS OF THE NEW SOCIETY

In sum, the anarchist roots of workers' co-operatives are not as well exposed as the Marxian ones. I believe that five major factors have contributed to the eclipse of anarchism: First, the Marxists won the political battle at the First International at the Hague, resulting in subsequent greater visibility and organizational support for Marxian perspectives. Second, anarchist thought is so non-doctrinaire, even vehemently anti-doctrinaire, that it has not and probably could not exhibit a unitary approach to organizational or political issues. As a result, their view is probably harder than the Marxian view is to summarize and to teach. Although it does promote a consistent core of ideas, **liberty with equality and a unity of means and ends,** they are harder to summarize because they are, in a way, more diverse and complex. Third, and partly because of the two preceding reasons, much less has been written about anarchism than about Marxism and far fewer historical movements have taken place in the name of anarchism, which further reduces the prominence of anarchist principles and ideas. Thus the heritage of anarchism has been muted. Fourth, and related to the above, Bakunin wrote in six different languages, and a good English translation of his work was not available until the mid-1970s (Morris, 1993). Thus, ironically, it was left to Marx and Engels to render what Bakunin was arguing, and given the bitter antagonism between them, this may not have been the fairest source (Leach, 2002). Fifth, and most importantly, because the anarchists from the start viewed state power as corrupting, potentially coercive and as inevitably captured by the capitalist class, and because their whole philosophy is one of building an alternative economy and society from the ground up based entirely on the efforts and will of the member-owner-workers at the local level, it was never in the interest of those who would control the state apparatus to be drawn to anarchist principles. Where Marx (partly) provided a rationale for Communist Party control of the state in the Communist nations, and Adam Smith and those who believe that the "market" is efficient provide a rationale for control of the capitalist state by the capitalist class, why would those in power in either of those systems, or those who aspire to power anywhere, ever advocate anarchism? The anarchists are suspicious of power structures: they seek to abolish hierarchical structures, leaving more room for democratic decision-making at the workplace and community levels. As Weber teaches us, material interests and ideological belief sets go hand in hand. As I see it, it is simply not in the interest of those who aspire to being at the top of any hierarchical structure, whether Capitalist or Socialist, to subscribe to a set of beliefs that would abolish, or discredit the value of that structure of power, privilege and status.

The co-operatives themselves have often arisen from dire circumstances. In the 1840s, Rochdale, Lancastershire, England was a town whose economy was dominated by the textile industry. They were noted for their fine flannels. But, with the mechanization of production, many workers lived in poverty, averaging 26 cents a day. "From all around came reports of weavers clothed in rags, who had sold all their furniture, who worked 16 hours a day yet lived on a diet of oatmeal, potatoes, onion porridge and treacle" (E.P. Thompson in Birchall, 1994: 34). The women in the area were reported "to give birth standing up, their arms around two other women, because they had no change of bed clothing; the very people who had spent their lives weaving clothes and blankets for the world had come down to this, rags on their backs and no blankets on their beds" (Birchall, 1994:35-37). Yes, the circumstances were dire when a group of weavers, skilled tradesmen of their day, came together to try to pool their resources and survive economically. They had already tried pleading with the capitalists, striking, petitioning Parliament, none of this had produced anything useful. So, they decided to try forming a co-operative. After several **failed** attempts to muster the necessary resources, the Rochdale Society of Equitable Pioneers was born on August the 15th of 1844 with 28 member-owners, each purchasing one share for one pound. While most of the original members were weavers, there was also a shoemaker, a clogger, a tailor, a joiner and a cabinetmaker in the group (Birchall, 1994:42). Four months later, they finally opened their tiny shop on Toad Lane, selling butter, sugar, flour, candles and a few other items. The provisions were so scanty that passersby made fun of them (Birchall, 1994:13). However, because they became known for providing "pure quality, good weight and honest measure" at a time when adulteration of products and fraudulent weight were common among retailers, sales grew, and by 1850, they had 600 owner-members. They were not men prone to abstractions. They were just trying to figure out a decent, common sense way to run a business, equally and jointly. As Mercer puts it, they were "philosophers of action". It was 1860 before they decided to try to distill the methods and practices they had evolved into a set of principles of co-operation. Their example inspired many thousands of co-ops (particularly consumer co-ops) to develop along similar lines (ICA, 1995), but their story is also indicative of why and how co-operatives develop today. Today, as then, in the economically distressed regions and countries, where ordinary people have been displaced or degraded in their work, where they are down and where they have lost hope that the capitalists or the state will "save" them, these are the circumstances that have given rise often to the co-operative, democratic alternative.

From where did the Rochdale Pioneers derive their 'common sense' preference for an egalitarian and cooperatively run workplace? It is hard to say. They were caught in that transition from an agricultural economy to an industrial economy. Dickinson and Schaeffer write that during the pre-capitalist era, workers often farmed communally or in collectives. As the world economy expanded, farmland was increasingly privatized and working people were denied customary access, thereby reducing in-kind income and increasing market dependency. Farmers today, particularly in the periphery, are often turning to land reclamation and urging the creation of new collectively or cooperatively owned and run farms (Dickinson and Schaeffer, 2001).

This could be another source of cooperative spirit, one that pre-dates the Rochdale experiment, and indeed, that may have affected the 'common sense' of the Rochdale Pioneers as they set out to create co-operative work, although in their case, in the retail trade.

In many ways, the workers' cooperatives today go much farther than the Rochdale Pioneers in their understanding and methods of democracy. For example, the Rochdale members managed by periodic election of members to offices, where today's collectivist members have been practicing and extending their methods for open discussion and consensus-based decision making (Rothschild and Whitt, 1986; Iannello, 1992; Leach, 2002). However, the philosophical and practical lineage is there: from the workers' cooperatives of the 1840s to the women's cooperatives of the new millennium. Five waves of co-operation later, co-operatives still represent a functioning synthesis of Marxian and collectivist/anarchistic ideals. *They provide a means for dissolving the antithesis between capital and labor at least within a limited arena, bridging the gulf between "mental" and "manual" work within their boundaries. They return to those who do the work of the organization the collective management of their work process and the ownership of their work product, and in this way, they serve as a utopian organizational model for a future society.*

Where Marx had stressed that power derives from ownership of the means of production, Bakunin and his fellow anarchists stressed the necessity for control over the means of production. The modern day co-operators insist on both, although in my observation, of the two, they are more emphatic about democratic control over the workplace, however the ownership is arranged, and in many cases, they avoid or overlook the incorporation laws altogether, at least when they are small, allowing them to gloss over the legal issue of ownership. In contrast, they are generally studied and insistent on the ways of democratic management, i.e., on the ways of affording voice and control to all.

The collectives that I studied in the U.S., like those that are presently developing in Germany, plainly wanted to keep their distance from the state (Leach, 2002; Rothschild and Whitt, 1986). They are instinctively anarchistic. However, one would not expect the United States government to support some sort of grassroots, radically democratic control of economic assets. In the early 1980s, the U.S. Congress did give bi-partisan support and pass into law several statutes that aided the capital formation of Employee Stock Ownership Plans (ESOPs) by giving the ESOPs a special exemption under ERISA law and by giving them special tax advantages. The story of how this ESOP legislation came to pass is a long one (Rothschild 1984), but even where the U.S. government has passed legislation that would seem to support worker ownership, as in this case, the overwhelming majority of the resulting employee-owned firms (and there are thousands of such firms, involving millions of workers in the U.S. today) have only a little to do with democratic worker self-management of the work process (Rothschild 1984; Melman 2001).

Nevertheless, we still need to remain open minded in our consideration of the likely benefits and costs of cooperatives' affiliation with the state, especially in the less developed countries. In the former Yugoslavia, for example, Tito was widely credited with transforming many state controlled industries into healthy worker self-managed cooperatives. For many years, the worker self-managed enterprises in Yugoslavia were raised as the shining example of economic productivity and workers' cooperation in the world. Of course, they could not have seen this level of development without state support. However, with the balkanization of Yugoslavia, research needs to be done on what happened to these self-managed workplaces and to the ideas that sustained them and made them popular.

Another example of a successful workers' co-operative that has benefited from state support is the Kerala Dinesh Beedi Worker's Cooperative in the state of Kerala, India. In this cooperative, more than 33,000 worker-owner-members have joined hands to build their future through democratically run and linked enterprises. In this case, the Communist government of the state of Kerala provided leadership in the formation stage of the co-ops, and they were responsible for the initial financing of the co-ops (Issac, Franke and Raghavan 1998). Issac et al. (1998) argues that the state was absolutely instrumental in setting the conditions for this cooperative system's development and success.

While the co-operative principle permits some variety in style, method and form in various parts of the world, the modern co-operative movements may find that the most crucial contemporary questions return them to the political debate first heard in the 19th century at The Hague between the Marxists and the anarchists. In their critique of private property, the contemporary co-operators may be understood in the context of their Marxian heritage, but in their form and function, they must be situated in the anarchist tradition of 'direct action': Their fundamental commitment is to establishing producers' democratic control over their processes of production, shared ownership of the fruits of their work and egalitarian relations of work. *In the here and now, they seek to establish functioning models of how one might wish to work and relate to others in a utopian society. They are precursors of a new society.*

REFERENCES

Aldrich, Howard and Robert Stern. "Social Structure and the Creation of Producers' Co-operatives". Paper presented at the Ninth World Congress of Sociology. Uppsala, Sweden, 1978.

Anthony, Denise. "Micro-Lending Institutions: Using Social Networks to Create Productive Capabilities". *International Journal of Sociology and Social Policy* (special issue on Economic Sociology) 17 (7/8, 1997): 156-178.

Avineri, Sholom. *The Social and Political Thought of Karl Marx.* Cambridge: Cambridge University Press, 1969.

Babb, Florence. "After the Revolution: Neoliberal Policy and Gender in Nicaragua." *Latin American Perspectives* 23: 27-48, 1996.

Birchall, Johnston. *Co-op: The People's Business.* Manchester, UK: Manchester University Press, 1994.

Buber, Martin. *Paths in Utopia.* Boston: Beacon Press, 1960.

Calman, Leslie. *Toward Empowerment: Women and Movement politics in India.* Boulder: Westview Press, 1992.

Cheyney, George. *Values at Work: Employee Participation Meets Market Pressure at Mondragon.* Ithaca: Cornell University Press, 2000.

Dickinson, Torry and Robert Schaeffer. *Fast Forward: Work, Gender and Protest in a Changing World.* Lanham, Maryland: Rowman & Littlefield, 2001.

Eber, Christine. 1999. "Seeking Our Own Food: Indigenous Women's Power and Autonomy in San Pedro Chenalho, Chiapas (1980-1998)." *Latin American Perspectives* 26: 6-36.

Engels, Friedrich. "On Authority." In Lewis Feuer, ed., *Marx and Engels: Basic Writings on Politics and Philosophy.* Garden City, N.Y.: Anchor Books, 1959.

Feuer, Lewis. "Marx, Karl." *Encyclopedia Britannica,* 15th edition, 1983.

Gow, Kathleen. "Banking on Women: Achieving healthy economies through Microfinance." *WE International* 48-49:11-13, 2000.

Iannello, Kathleen. *Decisions without Hierarchy: Feminist Interventions in Organizational Theory and Practice.* New York: Routledge, 1992.

Issac, Thomas, Richard Franke and Pyarelal Raghavan. *Democracy at Work In An Indian Industrial Cooperative: The Story of Kerala Dinesh Beedi.* Ithaca: Cornell University Press, 1998.

Kowalak, Tadeusz. "Work Co-operatives in Poland." Paper presented at the First International Conference on Producer Cooperatives, June 1981, Copenhagen.

Kropotkin, Peter. *Mutual Aid: A Factor in Evolution.* London, 1902.

Leach, Darcy. "Bakunin's Critique of Marx: Seeds of a Reconstructed Socialism?" Unpublished paper, the University of Michigan, 1998.

Leach, Darcy. *No Power For Anyone: Collectivist Democracy in German New Social Movements.* Dissertation in progress, The University of Michigan, 2002.

Lockett, Martin. "Producer Cooperatives in China: 1919-1981." Paper presented at the First International Conference on Producer Cooperatives, June 1981, Copenhagen.

Marx, Karl. *Capital.* Vol. 3. New York: International, 1967.

———. *Capital.* Vol. 3. Chicago: Charles H. Kerr. 1909.

Melman, Seymour. *After Capitalism: From Managerialism to Workplace Democracy*. New York: Alfred Knopf, 2001.

Mercer, Thomas William. "Foundations of Co-operation: Rochdale Principles and Methods". *Review of International Co-operation* No. 9, September 1931.

Morris, Brian. *Bakunin: The Philosophy of Freedom*. New York: Black Rose Books, 1993.

Oberhauser, Ann. "Relocating Gender and Rural Economic Strategies". Working Paper, Department of Geography, University of West Virginia, 2002.

Patel, Seema. "KMVS, Working Towards Environmental Justice for Rural Women in India." *WE International* 48-49: 36-37, 2000.

Plattner, Patricia.. "Made in India" Video documentary on SEWA. Women Make Movies: New York, 1998.

Rosner, Menachem. "Participatory Political and Organizational Democracy and the Experience of the Israeli Kibbutz.". In C. Crouch and F. Heller, eds., *International Yearbook of Organizational Democracy*, pp. 455-84. New York: Wiley & Sons, 1983.

Rothschild–Whitt, Joyce. "The Collectivist Organization: An Alternative to Rational Bureaucratic Models." *American Sociological Review* 44 (August 1979), 509-27.

Rothschild, Joyce and J. Allen Whitt. *The Cooperative Workplace: Conditions and Dilemmas of Organizational Democracy and Participation*. Cambridge: Cambridge University Press, 1986.

Rothschild, Joyce. "Worker Ownership: Collective Response to an Elite-generated Crisis". *Research in Social Movements, Conflict and Change*, Vol. 6 (1984): 167-194.

Saihjee, Aarti and Vimala Ramachandran. 2000. "Flying with the Crane: Recapturing KMVS's ten-year journey." Unpublished research work, courtesy, KMVS.

Sebstad, Jennifer 1982. " Struggle and Development Among Self Employed Women: A Report on the Self employed Women's Association, Ahmedabad, India." Washington D.C.: AID.

Shirom, Arie. "The Industrial Relations System of Industrial Cooperatives in the U.S., 1880-1935." *Labor History* 13 (1972): 533-551.

Ward, Colin. "The Organization of Anarchy." In Leonard Krimmerman and Lewis Perry, eds., *Patterns of Anarchy* pp. 386-96. Garden City, N.Y.: Anchor Books, 1966.

Ward. Colin. "The Anarchist Contribution." In C. George Benello, ed., *The Case for Participatory Democracy*, pp. 283-94. New York: Viking Press, 1972.

Whyte, William Foote and Kathleen Whyte. *Making Mondragon*. Ithaca: ILR Press, 1988.

Woodcock, George. *Anarchism: A History of Libertarian Ideas and Movements*. New York: World, 1962.

Young, Crawford, Neal Sherman and Tim Rose. *Cooperatives and Development: Agricultural politics in Ghana and Uganda*. Wisconsin: University of Wisconsin Press, 1991.

Young, Gay. "Gender inequality and industrial development: the household connection." *Journal of Comparative Family Studies* 24 (1993): 1-20.

PART VI: USING THE POWER OF SCHOLARLY ACTIVISM TO DEVELOP INNOVATIVE PROJECTS

PEDAGOGICAL FARMING: ONE EXPERIENCE COMBINING HORTICULTURAL RESEARCH, EXTENSION EDUCATION, AND ORGANIC FARMING

Rhonda R. Janke

ABSTRACT

In agriculture, is there anything new under the sun? In this chapter, I tell my story, as both a researcher, and as a farmer. I will also discuss some of the advantages, and novel aspects of pedagogical farming as a tool for learning, teaching, and engaging in extension research and education. As a new working model, this system will be contrasted to other teaching/extension models used in agriculture. The context for both my farming and my extension work is sustainable agriculture, and under this broad umbrella; specifically organic production practices (see Box 1). Within agriculture in general, these are still considered novel approaches, and a brief history of this movement will be included in this chapter as background. Thus, I am attempting to implement a new model or paradigm for agricultural research and extension (by farming) within a new area of agricultural practice and research (organic and sustainable agriculture).

INTRODUCTION: MODELS FOR EXTENSION AND RESEARCH

The model for traditional research and extension work, now over 100 years old in the U.S., is for research to be conducted by researchers, on research plots, and the results are "extended" or taught to farmer audiences throughout the state (Call, 1961). Variations on this theme have been introduced over the years, and include university demonstration plots that might be the result of farmer suggestions, but exist as non-replicated "example" plots. In the 1970's, this university-centered model was challenged by researchers, mainly at international research centers, who found that farmers often would not or could not use the results from research stations, and thus created a model for "on-farm research." This model involves farmers in the research process, conducting many of the research studies on farms with assistance from researchers primarily for data analysis. Universities now encourage the use of this method (see Miller et al. for example) and assist farmers individually and as part of research networks. Farmers have actually been conducting their own research for years, in primarily un-replicated plots, to try out new ideas and products. These are usually called on-farm demonstration, and may be for farm families' personal use, or may be featured at field days, where the information is shared with other farmers and with researchers.

Box 1. Definition of Sustainable Agriculture from the 1990 Farm Bill, which is the basis of the USDA/SARE funding program for sustainable agriculture research and education.

"The term sustainable agriculture means an integrated system of plant and animal production practices having a site-specific application that over the long term will:

- Satisfy human food and fiber needs.
- Enhance environmental quality and the natural resource base upon which the agricultural economy depends.
- Make the most efficient use of nonrenewable resources and on-farm resources and integrate, where appropriate, natural biological cycles and controls.
- Sustain the economic viability of farm operations.
- Enhance the quality of life for farmers and society as a whole."

Note: the word "organic" has a very specific meaning, as defined by the National Organic Standards Board, within the USDA. To use the word organic in selling products, producers, processors, and retailers must follow the guidelines, which can be found at www.ams.usda.gov/NOP/. They must also apply for, and be certified by an accredited certifying agency, unless they qualify for an exemption. For example, farmers who sell less than $5000 of organic sales per year are exempt from certification, but still must follow the guidelines to use the word "organic" on labels or sales literature.

Other techniques from the international agricultural research arena have also found their way into the North American context, see for example Robotham and McArthur, (2001), and also Conway and McCraken (1990). These researchers often propose something called "agro-ecosystem analysis," which dissects a farm into its components for purpose of analysis, which then suggests new approaches to researchers unfamiliar with the farming system under scrutiny, but rarely involves the farmer as anything more than an informant. The farm, and its component parts, can also be compared using various measures of sustainability with this technique (Lightfoot and Noble, 2001).

Fairly recently in the U.S., this technique of analysis has been found useful in teaching and extension work as the "case study" approach. In this model, a single farm is used, and the physical layout, the farming practices, and the approach of the farm operator/operators are described in a narrative, supplemented by tables, photographs, and charts. More than one case study can be compiled, and accumulated examples of farms are used as teaching tools for particular methods, such as the adoption of sustainable agriculture practices like crop rotation and cover crops. Real working farms are featured in these case studies, but university students and faculty often write up these case studies, abbreviating critical information acquired by farm families (see Mallory et al. 2000, for example). Another fairly recent model that combines university and farmer knowledge is the development of university demonstration farms. These are sometimes intended to be similar to commercial farms in a particular region or climate, and sometimes designed simply to contain fields with crops common to an area. Farmers are often asked to serve on advisory panels, but the land, labor, funds, and many of the ideas come from university, its staff, and students. Examples exist from coast to coast (for example references see Washington State University's Robin Hill Farm, and the University of Maine Roger's Farm).

There is no one "right" or "wrong" way to conduct agricultural research and outreach, and all of the methods described so far have been shown to be useful historically, and nearly all are still used in one form or another today. Various methods can be combined, and are complementary. Table 1 summarizes and contrasts some of the methods/models discussed. I personally have used and/or participated in all of the techniques described, and have found them all useful to a point. However, still missing from the equation is the concept of "whole farm research." In sustainable agriculture, the whole farm is the unit of interest, not one particular crop, or animal production system. Even in the case study approach, the focus is often on the adoption or use of a particular product (e.g. a new variety of rice) or a new practice (e.g. reduced tillage), and why the farmer does or does not use the product or practice on their farm. Demonstration farms also tend to lack the unity implied by "whole farm planning," as staff and students turnover, and competing ideas and agendas come and go over a short period of time.

This field of study was completely missing from my formal training. I attempted to fill this gap through academic studies at Kansas State University (KSU) (Janke and Freyenberger, 1997), by reviewing any and all literature I could find on the topic, and by looking for tools, courses, computer software and books that referred to the concept of "whole farm planning." I also began to fill the void by becoming a "researcher who farms," rather than just working with "farmers who conduct research." In addition to filling an intellectual void, I also use the farm as a source of inspiration, not unlike the way some artists, such as Monet, and Renoir have done (Fell 1991). I'm not the only researcher who farms; I have several colleagues at KSU who work in research or extension and farm with family members, some who "farm" as absentee land-owners, and others who have an active, working farm. However, I'm not aware of any others who have written about their experiences and how farming has informed their university work.

What an eye-opening experience! Having a farm, vs. only talking about farming, are two totally different ways of doing things. Instead of just spending my time talking to rooms full of farmers, with their arms crossed, scowling, about the benefits of including alfalfa in their crop rotation to improve soil health, I also have the opportunity to invite 9-year old Hannah and her mother to my farm, to participate in raising my chickens. I invite my neighbor over with her nephews, ages 3 and 5, and, for their first ever, handpicked strawberries. We teach them how to find the ripe berries, and pull the stem out before they eat them. I sell my produce at the local farmers' markets, and answer questions from customers, ranging from "do potatoes really grow under the ground?" (yes!) and "did you make that honey?" (No, my bees made that honey). I also get to explain what "organic" is all about, and hear grateful comments such as "I'm so glad you are here," and "I just loved those eggs I bought from you last week!"

Table 1. Various Models for University and On-farm Agricultural Research

Relative age of idea or concept?	Model	Researcher Involvement?	Farmer Involvement?	Res. x Farmer Interaction?	Roles
old	University research plots	XXX		L	Researcher has complete control from design of experiment through execution and interpretation.
	University demonstration plots	XXX	X	ML	Researchers may test ideas from farmers on university land in un-replicated, demonstration plots.
	On-farm demonstrations	X	XXX	M	Farmers test own ideas, or ideas and/or products suggested by the university on their own farm. Farmer interprets results.
	On-farm research	XX	XX	MH	Farmers test own or researcher ideas on replicated plots on their farm. Researchers may assist with data analysis, both involved in data interpretation.
	University demonstration farms	XX	XX	M	University sets up a working "farm" on their own land, often managed by an employee or students, farmers might serve on advisory panels and suggest ideas.
	Rapid Rural Assessment/Agro-Ecosystems Analysis, and Case study farms	X	XXX	MH	Real working farms are written up as case studies by students or researchers as a snap-shot of information about certain practices, within a whole farm context.
new	The researcher as farmer	XXX	XXX	same person!	Researcher is also the farmer on his/her own piece of land. Economic realities are no longer abstractions. Dilemmas and trade-offs become immediately obvious.

I also find the challenges of actually putting together a sustainable agriculture farm almost daunting. You would think, that with a Ph.D. in crops and soils, and eight years of experience at one of the first organic research centers in the U.S, the Rodale Institute. I would be well equipped to handle this. I also had the good fortune to have grown up on a working dairy/crop farm. And after reading all those publications on whole farm planning too?! A piece of cake, right?

WHAT IS SUSTAINABLE AGRICULTURE?

A brief history of the sustainable agriculture movement is necessary to lay the groundwork for understanding the revolution that is taking place, quietly, in the countryside around you right now. Anthropologists believe that agriculture, or the planting and harvesting of crops, began roughly 10,000 years ago (Goodman 1988). Prior to that, the human species survived by "hunting and gathering" their food. As the population density increased in certain parts of the world, it became more convenient, and provided a more stable food supply if crops, originally grains, fruits, and vegetables, were planted and cared for. There is some debate however, whether grain was originally domesticated for use in bread, or for beer! Animals, such as cattle, sheep, and horses were also domesticated, or kept and cared for. The net result was the beginning of systems of crop and livestock management by humans.

Agriculture can be disruptive of natural ecosystems in many ways, though what proponents of organic agriculture tend to criticize most in modern agriculture is the chemicals used. Tillage systems, over grazing by animals, and monoculture (planting the same crop year after year, and on large tracts of land) also disturb nature, reduce bio-diversity, and limit habitat for endangered species. The chemical era of farming is largely thought to have begun after World War II, or in the late 1940's. However, research on fertilizer products began in England at the Rothamstead Experiment Station in the mid 1800's, and toxic poisons such as arsenic were widely used in fruit orchards by the late 1800's (well documented by Whorton, 1975).

By the mid-1930's, J.I. Rodale brought a new word to the U.S., "organic," originally used in England to refer to a new method of farming that relied more on adding more organic matter to the soil, such as compost, and reducing other disruptive impacts of agriculture. J.I. Rodale began to research these methods on his farm in Pennsylvania, and published the first magazine describing these methods beginning in 1942 called "Organic Gardening and Farming." The 1930's were clearly a wake-up call in U.S. agriculture, with the well-documented "dust bowl" era, caused by over-tillage, a drought, and lack of attention to good farming practices.

The post WWII era clearly brought more chemical tools to farmers, including nitrogen fertilizers, originally used as explosives during the war, and many pesticides, also a by product of war-industry research. As time went on, more farmers adopted these practices, and eventually, research was conducted that found that some of these chemicals were not good for humans, wildlife, or the soil. The publishing of *Silent Spring* in 1962 by Rachel Carson was clearly a turning point in public opinion. In this book, Carson documented the effect of a widely used insecticide, DDT, on wild birds, and got both the attention of the reading public, and of the scientific community.

I was only four years old when *Silent Spring* was published, but I remember hearing about the "ecology movement," as I was growing up. Sustainable agriculture as a term was not in use yet. I was interested in both nature and in farming, and went on to study agriculture, first getting my undergraduate degree in Kansas, and then studying agronomy (crops and soils) and plant ecology at Cornell in graduate school. In the late 1970's and early 1980's, the phrase "alternative agriculture" began to be used, but suffered from misconceptions, and was constantly questioned as "alternative to what?" While I was pursuing my education, others were starting to farm using these alternative methods.

Organic farms were sprouting up around the country, and the first USDA study to document these farms, and their success was published in 1980 (USDA 1980). The author, a young agricultural economist, was promptly dismissed, since his report was cautiously optimistic about the future of organic farming. This finding went against the grain of the dominant agricultural paradigm at that time, and thus began the battle, that is still on-going, in agricultural institutions around the world. "What do you mean, you can farm without chemicals? That's impossible!" they would exclaim. Those who subscribed to the dominant agricultural production model at that time tended to take the use of chemicals in production as unquestionable. Perhaps this is not surprising, given that many of the researchers and policy makers began their careers in the post WWII era, amid slogans like "atoms for peace," "better living through chemistry," and the advent of "miracle drugs."

At Cornell, I began to "wake up" to the political realities of the world, and chose a research topic that would allow me to look at alternatives to chemical farming; non-chemical weed control in alfalfa. I began to learn from my fellow students, from my professors, from seminar speakers that came to campus, and from my travels that there are many ways to farm in the world, and that organic farming was not only possible; it was almost inevitable, in the large scheme of things. After all, only sustainable agriculture will ultimately survive, since by definition, non-sustainable agriculture is, well, non-sustainable, right?

My first job after graduate school was as a researcher at the Rodale Institute, founded by Bob Rodale, after J.I. Rodale's death. We conducted dozens of replicated research studies with field crops, vegetables, and apples, including several long term experiments, that validated the USDA report's findings, that organic agriculture was not only possible, but that it was also productive, and economically profitable. In this position I also had many opportunities to travel, and I was fortunate to be able to see first hand organic farms on several continents; in Japan, India, Senegal, Nigeria, Honduras, Germany, England, Holland, and several states within the U.S. From these travels I learned the age-old lesson that the more we are different, the more we are the same. Sustainable agriculture on all continents seems to include cover crops, paying attention to soil quality, increasing crop and non-crop (even weed!) diversity, and attentive, skilled managers. We were regularly asked to testify to congressional committees in Washington, to describe our research studies and results, and to ask for congressional appropriations for more tax supported research on organic farming.

As a result of these efforts, and also lobbying by many other organizations, the 1985 farm bill for the first time included a definition of sustainable agriculture, and authorization for funding for research on this topic (Norman et al. 1997). The first funding was appropriated in 1987, beginning what is now known as the "USDA/SARE" funding, or "United States Department of Agriculture, Sustainable Agriculture Research and Education Program." Despite this success, even now, less than 1% of tax dollars going into agricultural research fund projects specifically on organic production (Sooby 2001). The 1990 Farm Bill authorized a panel, the National Organic Standards Board, to develop national organic standards for organic farmer certification. It took 11 years for them to complete their task, with the national standards approved in February of 2001, taking effect in 2002.

MY STORY

I moved to back to Kansas in 1994, to accept a position at Kansas State University as the "Sustainable Cropping Systems Research and Extension Specialist," the first person in Kansas to have this position. In other states, similar positions, and centers have been created over the past decade. However, as you might guess, the topic is still controversial. My job as a faculty member at a mid-western Land Grant University is to conduct research, and provide research-based information to farmers in the state of Kansas. When I got to Kansas, I purchased a ten-acre "farm" that included an historic (1870 construction) stone house. I then began to explore a new way to do my research and extension work.

So why take on a weekend job, as a farmer? It is how I stay sane (I think) in what feels like an increasingly insane world around me. It is how I keep balance in my life. It is also about "walking the walk" and not just "talking the talk." This is also how I contribute to my community.

I immediately began to convert the farm to organic production, and certified the farm as "organic" after the three-year transition period. I named the farm "Parideaza," in yet another spelling of the ancient Persian word for walled garden, not because I wanted a wall to keep the world out, but more because I wanted a personal, protected retreat space, both physical, for plants, animals and humans, and also a mental retreat space. (For more information about the farm, see Box 2). I am doing this for both personal and political reasons.

Personal reasons? I like to eat things that I grow. I love to pick fresh peas off the vine as snacks, while weeding the young tomatoes. I love working outside in the sun, even in the hot, windy, Kansas summers. Fresh strawberries for dessert? Yes! Eggs from the store? Never. My eggs have bright yellow yolks, lots of flavor, and I know that the hens have an entire orchard to roam, and I know exactly what they've been fed, since I feed them.

How can this much fun be political? Everything that we do is political. Each purchase we make, or don't make, is a statement. Each act that we do is an example to others of what we believe in, what we stand for, a statement of our value system.

Many people who have recently discovered sustainable agriculture become excited when they find out that food doesn't have to be grown using the now common factory model (described in lurid detail in the recently published *Fast Food Nation,* Schlosser 2001). They quickly want to go out and tell the world about their discovery, and "convert them," in a way similar to that used by some religious zealots. Personally, I find this approach demeaning, and too similar to sales persons trying to sell me "widgets" or advertisements on television trying to get me to buy a new car or the latest brand of clothing. My personal path to this way of agriculture has been slow and gradual, and I have learned by watching others, reading, and thinking. One of my goals with the farm is to provide a learning environment, for myself, and for others, who also find this path, through experiences in their own lives.

Box 2: A brief description of Parideaza farm

"Pairidaeza: the Persian word for walled garden, became the Roman 'paradisus,' and the English word - and image - of 'paradise.'" (Morgan and Richards, 1993). One of the early words describing an enclosed garden of fruit trees and gardens watered by canals and designed as much for beauty as gastronomic pleasure.

Total Acres: 10

Vegetable garden - about 1/2 acre, with only 1/10th acre (about 4300 square feet) planted to vegetables each year. The remainder is grass alleyways, cover crops, fence, and shelter belt trees. Crops include lettuce, other greens (kale, chard etc), asparagus, broccoli, onions, garlic, leeks, cucumbers, tomatoes, potatoes, peppers (hot and sweet), carrots, parsley, fava beans, snap beans, edible flowers,......

Flower garden - mostly for pleasure, but extra lilies were planted for sale at the farmers' market.

Orchard - about 1/3 acre, with 50 trees, including apples, pears, peaches, apricots, persimmons, and cherries. Fruit has not come into full production yet, so has been primarily for home use. Four grape vines are also planted within the vegetable and flower gardens. A raspberry patch has also been established, and one vegetable garden bed is devoted to strawberries.

Bees - 2 hives, with a total yield of 50 lb of honey.

Chickens - laying flock of 25 hens and one rooster (with the goal of raising an additional 25 or so roosters each year as broilers, for meat). Grain for the chickens is purchased off farm from an organic producer. Manure is used in the compost. I get about a dozen eggs a day in the summer, and a half dozen a day in the winter.

Sheep - breeding flock of 11 ewes and 1 ram produces 14 to 17 lambs per year. These are sold as breeding stock, and for meat. The wool and pelts are sold to local hand spinners, quilters, and as value added products such as yarn and felt slippers. Soap is made from the sheep lard. About 5 acres are fenced in the "main" pasture, and another 2 acres in the "back" pasture. Rotational grazing is in the plan, but not in place yet. Hay and grain are purchased off farm.

Woodlot - used to gather firewood, and to establish some herb crops.

Medicinal Herb production - is in the plan, but not in place yet due to the lack of equipment, e.g. drying racks, storage space, and a root washer and grinder.

Shitake mushrooms- oak logs were inoculated this spring, with production scheduled to begin this coming fall.

Grain? - also in the plan, on a small scale, but details such as harvesting, grain cleaning, and storage need to be worked out. Both perennials (wheat grass, dock, plantain) and annuals (rye, wheat, oats) will be grown.

The only **equipment** used is a rototiller and lawn mower. Occasionally a tractor is rented to mow and/or seed the pasture. Horses were used one spring to plow three of the garden beds. The rest is all hand labor, with hand tools. Lots of hay mulch, mostly purchased, is used for weed control.

Companion animals - one dog and three cats. These help with mouse control in the house and garage, and the dog keeps chicken predators at bay (for the most part).

Annual production - I recorded approximately one ton (2000 lb) of product sold, as vegetables, eggs, and meat during the course of a year. This number should go up as the orchard comes into production, but I don't expect to increase the size of any of the other enterprises any time soon.

Labor supply - up until now, just me, with occasional help from family and friends.

LESSONS LEARNED

Some of the most interesting things about having a farm are all the surprises. In the eight years that I have been combining research, extension, and farming, these are a few of things that I have learned, which I would not have discovered otherwise:

Reading and talking about whole farm planning, and actually doing it are two very different things. One advantage of having a farm, even a small farm, is that I can actually try out the tools for myself, and see which ones work, and which ones take a lot of time, but do not yield results. I had originally underestimated the importance of business planning in all of this, since my background and interest was in the natural sciences, or "how to grow things." I found that taking a course on how to write a business plan extremely helpful, and have also learned that very few farmers now have a business plan, or any other plan, for that matter. A business plan, in this context, means more than "guess I'll sell my wheat to the co-op again this year." It entails extensive soul searching (what do I really want to do?), market research (who else is doing this, and what do they charge for similar products?), writing, and financial projection (five-year cash flow, return on investment, etc.). And by taking this course WITH other farmers, I got to see the "guts" of their farm, as we all shared our trials and tribulations. I would not have leaned all of this if I had been an instructor, rather than a participant.

One of the principles of sustainable agriculture is diversification, but in the real world, on my farm, this is easy to say, but hard to do. For example, each new enterprise (in this case, an "enterprise" refers to a part of the farm, profit center, or sub-farm, rather than the whole farm) requires a new set of skills, and the learning curve, and the time required to acquire these skills should not be underestimated, even when the information is readily available, and local experts offer their advice and time as a mentor. Each enterprise also has its' own professional association, meetings, newsletters, and organizational commitments that take time if one decides to get involved. For example, even for my small farm, organizations available to me in central Kansas include the Kansas Sheep Producers, the Kansas Honey Producers, the Fruit Growers, the Vegetable Growers, the local Farmers' Market Association, Organic crop Improvement Association, Kansas Organic Producers, etc. One can spend a lot of money on dues, and a lot of time at meetings if they aren't careful. Meeting others who are trying to do the same thing you are is more valuable than reading a book about it however, so most of the time is well spent.

In addition to diversification, integration of enterprises is highly valued as one of the principles of sustainable agriculture. For example, the manure from the chickens is used to make compost, which provides the fertilizer for the vegetable crops. Chickens can also be raised within the orchard, to help reduce the insect pressure on the apples and other fruits. However, using sheep to graze the grass in the orchard is a disaster! Sheep prefer to eat the trees first, and the grass last, so if you want to save your trees, the sheep stay out. Also, the concept of "free-range chickens" is nice, but within limits. If chickens are allowed in the vegetable garden, they scratch up each newly seeded bed, innocently looking for insects, but destroying the next crop. They also create a food safety concern, since manure from the chickens could harbor diseases such as Salmonella and Listeria, which could be passed on to consumers on fresh picked vegetables. In farm magazines, these enterprise combination disasters are rarely if ever mentioned, or are glossed over, and the details are obscured by naive enthusiasm for the new enterprise.

Most advice provided to me by well-meaning individuals who have read about these enterprises, but not actually done them, is not particularly useful. Each time I give a farm tour, whether to novices, or "experts," I am given suggestions. Some are worth considering, but most are ideas I have already tried and rejected for various reasons, or ideas I have thought about, but am unable to implement due to lack of time, money, or other resources. As someone who is asked to give advice to others in my extension work at the university, this has been a humbling, and sensitizing experience. I have come to the conclusion that most Midwest farmers were raised to be extremely polite, and simply do not say anything when they have been given advice that they cannot use. Thus, many researchers may not realize that they are on the wrong track for many years, until a rural sociologist conducts a study of "adoption of practices," and finds that many barriers exist. It might be quicker for the researcher to try the practice first themselves, or ask someone directly what they REALLY think. Also, the saying, "the devil is in the details," is absolutely correct. For example, recommending a tillage operation for weed control may be a correct statement in general, but the practitioner, or farmer needs to know exactly WHEN to cultivate, HOW DEEP to set the cultivator, how WIDE the spacing between the sweeps on the cultivator should be set, and at WHAT ANGLE. Only someone who has performed these operations in the field can know these details. It is also going to differ between soil types (sandy or clay), soil moisture conditions, and the type of crop being cultivated.

The economic aspect, or potential for profitability for a new enterprise, should not be underestimated as a factor that is considered carefully before adoption. I do not really want to try a new crop if I am going to work hard all summer, and then only break even on costs when it comes time to sell the crop. Where is the sustainability in that? Providing accurate cost-benefit scenarios prior to recommending a new practice, and then keeping careful records as the new practice is adopted, is the only way to find out if the crop or practice is truly profitable.

A key part of profitability is marketing, and many sustainable agriculture writings recommend direct marketing, or selling directly to the consumer, as a way to obtain a better, retail price, than selling at the lower wholesale price. However, I have found that direct marketing TAKES TIME. To sell vegetables at the local farmers' market, I not only need to pick the produce, but I must wash it so that it is presentable, package it in units my customers will buy, create attractive signs and labels, load the truck, and then be present at the market for several hours. This is in contrast to picking the produce into boxes, dropping it off at a single location, and then getting my check in the mail.

Marketing as part of a group, co-op, or community is also promoted in sustainable agriculture, but this also takes time. I've participated in a marketing co-op called the "Blue Earth Organic Growers," and have found the experience overall to be quite rewarding. However, even to coordinate the production and marketing among six people takes monthly meetings throughout the year, numerous phone calls, and additional record keeping, to track our products through the market. The labor sharing and camaraderie among peers is priceless however, and it is still one of my favorite ways to market. We have also attempted on a trial basis the concept of "subscription" marketing, also called "community supported agriculture." In this system, subscribers agree to purchase a bag of produce each week, which will vary from week to week, depending on what is being harvested. For example, in the spring, peas, lettuce and onions are ready, and later in the summer potatoes, garlic, and tomatoes are in abundance. There are frustrations to this form of marketing however, when one customer comments that her kids will not eat broccoli, and another customer prefers more of "x" and less of "y." We can accommodate these preferences for 5 customers, but not if we were to grow to 50! The CSA's with more than five customers have learned to handle these little wrinkles, either by having the customers fill their own bags, from a table of items from which to select, or by encouraging customers to either give away or trade items they do not want.

I have also learned that each community market has its own atmosphere, and political dynamics. In the city of Manhattan, the farmers' market is well established, and some of the larger, long term growers can dominate the political decision making process. I have had the opportunity this spring to help the town of Wamego, much smaller than Manhattan, start their first ever community market. We made a conscious decision to include artists in the market as well as food vendors, and bring in music each week to attract new customers, and create an atmosphere where people can "hang out," as well as just shop. So far this has been a very pleasant experience, and the vendors are cooperating, not competing, since we need more vendors to attract more customers. Ask me in 20 years if this is still working out! Test marketing new products at the market can also be a fun experience. I have found that by providing educational materials about the nutritional value of weeds, attractive packaging, and by picking only the most succulent, nice looking weeds, I can sell them in the market, for the same price I sell lettuce! However, chard and kale, two other nutritious greens that I like to grow, are not selling, and I often bring them home and eat them myself, or give them away to friends.

As a female, in not one, but two "non-traditional" occupations for women, do I have a feminist analysis to present? Not really. I'm a horticulturalist, not a sociologist, but I have three observations to offer. If one looks at farming from an historical perspective, or even looks to traditional farming systems in other countries, farming is probably more of a common denominator for women than it is for white men. I can identify with an African farmer, planting her crops by day, and cooking and cleaning her home by night! Many of the mid-western roles traditionally taken on by farm women, such as growing the vegetables, caring for the animals, apply to what I do, and so for me, the idea projected by the farm media of the farmer as "he" has never quite fit into my brain (for further discussion see Sachs 1996, for example). As an agricultural researcher however, I'm continually depressed by the statistics, that only about 5% of agricultural researchers, extension workers, soil conservation employees, etc. are women. Completing college in 1980 as one of many women undergraduates I assumed that in 20 years I would be in a work environment that was about 50:50. The reasons for this stalemate have been explained for me by Virginia Valian's recent work (1998), but the way out of this dilemma is not at all clear to me. The third observation is that when I go to sustainable agriculture meetings, and look at the leadership in the grassroots farm organizations that support sustainable agriculture and organic farmers, the proportion of women is a lot closer to 50% than the 5% I see at conventional farm meetings, and in the hallways of my university. I'm not sure how to explain this, and one can quickly get into a "chicken and the egg" discussion. One of the fundamental goals of sustainable agriculture includes healthy communities, quality of life, which includes balance. Perhaps gender balance is being practiced, not just discussed, by the proponents of sustainable agriculture.

In conclusion, one of the biggest rewards of having my own farm, and direct marketing my products, is the feeling that I am giving my value system a physical reality that it did not have before. I think that organic food is healthy, and that eating locally grown, fresh food is a direction that our society needs to go. Now, I am not only growing food for myself, but for others nearby, and they are getting to put a little bit of what I've grown with my own hands into their mouths, and bodies. Communication can take many forms besides words, such as music, art, and in my case, food. I can use the booth at the farmers' market for direct education, such as fact sheets on conversion to organic, but the indirect communication of simply how good food can really taste should not be underestimated. Visits to my farm can convince even the casual observer that chickens do not have to be raised in factories, and that sheep can be raised on grass, and not in feedlots.

These rewards are not without costs, since I give up my Friday nights from May through October to marketing, and spend time throughout the week in the evenings on farm tasks. You will not often find me out on the lake in a sailboat. A part of my social life revolves around farm activities, and meeting some new farmers while hauling lambs, canning tomatoes, or exhibiting grand champion onions at the county fair.

CONCLUSION: THE FUTURE

Sometimes I look at the future of U.S. agriculture, and it seems very bleak. Family sized farms are still disappearing at an alarming rate, a trend that began at the turn of the century, and is still accelerating. Clearly dangerous chemicals such as arsenic and DDT have been taken off the market, while others are still out there. The book *Our Stolen Future* by Colborn et al. (1997) is probably the most recent version of *Silent Spring*, documenting the effects of several classes of chemicals that act as endocrine disrupters on a global scale, damaging the developmental and hormonal systems of widely dispersed species including alligators, birds, frogs, polar bears, and humans.

One dreary winter, I read both this book and also *The Coming Age of Scarcity: Preventing Mass Death and Genocide in the Twenty-First Century* by Dobkowski and Wallimann (1998). In this book the authors point out several natural resources that are predicted to become more scarce on a global, not just a local level, in the next 50 years or so. These include water and fossil fuel, both important inputs used for the production of food. They also point out that our current socio-political systems are poorly equipped to deal with these coming scarcities. This age of scarcity is possible, and even likely, in my lifetime. I may live to see the day when this global experiment, human civilization, either passes or fails this major test. Some Native American prophecies also point to this coming bottleneck, or decision point (see Mails, 1997, for example).

Isidor Wallimann, one of the authors, happened to be in Manhattan in the spring, and agreed to lead a discussion about his book. His outlook was surprisingly optimistic, and he pointed us to another book, *Short Circuit: Strengthening Local Economies for Security in an Unstable World* (Douthwaite 1996). This book is filled with case studies, of communities, creating their own local food systems, local currencies (printed "bartering" coupons), and local energy sources. Some communities will survive the coming age of scarcity.

I had a chance to see some of this in action during a visit to Argentina this past winter. As the national economy crumbles around them, and banks refuse to release people's life savings to them, some communities have developed these bartering systems, and active research is taking place on micro-hydro electric generators as alternatives to dams, ram pumps deliver water uphill at nominal cost, and windmills capture the power of the wind. An active network of sustainable agriculture schools is teaching a new generation of farmers to grow food from locally made compost, not purchased fertilizer, and farmers' markets are thriving. The total organic production of Argentina exceeds that of the U.S., (though most of it is exported to Europe, and not consumed within Argentina).

Can this happen in the U.S.? Can it happen in Kansas? I find myself interested in not only providing "research based information to Kansas farmers" through my work at KSU, but also in helping Wamego be one of those communities that survive. Even if the coming age of scarcity never comes, our quality of life will be enhanced, and our community will become stronger, through these efforts. Maybe my friend Hannah will decide to raise chickens in her own backyard next summer? Maybe she will begin to sell eggs to her neighbors?

Sometimes people ask me if I ever get discouraged that it is taking so long for sustainable agriculture to become more mainstream. First of all, for something to be solid, it needs to take a long time to develop. Secondly, if we look at history, many major changes took a long time. For example, from the signing of the "Declaration of Sentiments" at the first Women's Rights Convention in Seneca Falls, NY in 1848, the beginning of the movement for women to get the right to vote, until 1929, when the goal was achieved, took 81 years, and several generations of both women and men in the effort (DuBois 1992). The struggle to get equal pay is still not over. To get arsenic off the market, and not only out of agricultural use, but also out of household products like paint and medicine, took over 50 years! (Whorton 1975). Everett Rogers, in his literature review titled *The Diffusion of Innovations* (1962) documents that it takes between 14 and 50 years for new ideas to be adopted. And most of the cases reviewed in his book were examples of the adoption of a particular product, not a general practice, such as sustainable agriculture. I am prepared to be a part of this work for the long haul.

There were pioneers before me, including J.I. Rodale, who first raised the flag for organic agriculture in the U.S., and the Nearings, who have inspired several generations with their books, *Living the Good Life* (Nearing 1970) and *Continuing the Good Life* (Nearing and Nearing 1979), in which they describe in detail how they put their personal and political values into action by growing their own food, living frugally, and using their time, not for wage labor, but for speaking, writing, and thinking. They began their journey in the 1920's, and also had a sense that the rest of the world was going down the wrong path. I hope that others, in the future, will find space in their lives to slow down, read, think, and consider their own path into the future. Maybe that path will include growing their own food, buying food directly from farmers, and not from the store. I also hope that they will support their communities' artists, trades workers, as well as farmers, and think about a new model of bio-regional networks, and not succumb to the globalized, "same-ness" that seems to dominate our lives now.

REFERENCES

Call, Leland E. 1961. *Agricultural Research at Kansas State Agricultural College (KSU) Before Enactment of the Hatch Act (1887).* Bulletin 441. Agricultural Experiment Station, Kansas State University of Agriculture and Applied Science, Manhattan, KS.

Carson, Rachael. 1962. *Silent Spring.* Houghton Mifflin, Boston.

Colborn, Theo, Dianne Dumanoski, and John Peterson Myers. 1997. *Our Stolen Future.* Penguin Books. NY.

Conway, G.R., and J.A. McCracken. 1990. *Rapid Rural Appraisal and Agroecosystem Analysis. in Agroecology and Small Farm Development,* M.A. Alteieri and S.B. Hecht, Eds, CRC Press Inc., Florida.

Dobkowski, Michael N. and Isidor Wallimann. 1998. *The Coming Age of Scarcity: Preventing Mass Death and Genocide in the Twenty-first Century.* Syracuse University Press. Syracuse, NY.

DuBois, Ellen Carol, 1992. *The Elizabeth Cady Stanton-Susan B. Anthony Reader.* Northeastern University Press. Boston.

Douthwaite, Richard. 1996. *Short Circuit: Strengthening Local Economies for Security in an Unstable World.* The Lilliput Press LTD, Dublin, Ireland.

Fell, Derek, 1991. *Renoir's Garden.* Simon and Schuster, NY.

Goodman, Felicitas D., 1988. *Ecstasy, Ritual, and Alternate Reality; Religion in a Pluralistic World.* Indiana University Press, Bloomington, IN.

Janke, Rhonda and Stan Freyenberger. 1997. *Indicators of Sustainability in Whole Farm Planning: Planning Tools.* Kansas Sustainable Agriculture Series, No. 3. Kansas State University, Manhattan, KS.

Lightfoot, C. and R. Noble. 2001. "Tracking the ecological soundness of farming systems: Instruments and indicators." *Journal of Sustainable Agriculture.* 19:9-29.

Mails, Thomas E. 1997. *The Hopi Survival Kit.* Penguin Putnam Inc. N.Y.

Mallory, Ellen B., Tim Fiez, Roger J. Veseth, R. Dennis Roe, O.M. Camara, D.L. Young, H.R. Hinman, and Donald J. Wysocki, 2000. *Thomas Farm Case Study.* PNW 523, A Pacific Northwest Extension Publication, Washington State University (available at http://caheinfo.wsu.edu).

Miller, B., E. Adams, P. Peterson, and R. Karow. (no date) *On-Farm Testing: A Grower's Guide.* EB 1706. Cooperative Extension, Washington State University, Pullman, WA.

Morgan, Joan and Alison Richards. 1993. *The Book of Apples.* Ebury Press, London.

Nearing, Helen. 1970. *Living the Good Life.* Schocken Books, Inc. N.Y.

Nearing, Helen and Scott Nearing. 1979. *Continuing the Good Life.* Schocken Books. N.Y.

Norman, David, Rhonda Janke, Stan Freyenberger, Bryan Schurle, and Hans Kok. 1997. *Defining and Implementing Sustainable Agriculture.* Kansas Sustainable Agriculture Series, No. 1, Kansas State University, Manhattan, KS.

Robotham, M.P. and H.J. McArthur, Jr. 2001. Addressing the needs of small-scale farmers in the United States: Suggestions from FSR/E. *Journal of Sustainable Agriculture* 19:47-64.

Rogers, Everett M. 1962. *Diffusion of Innovations.* The Free Press. NY.

Sachs, Carolyn. 1996. *Gendered Fields. Rural Women, Agriculture, and Environment.* Westview Press, Boulder, CO.

Schlosser, Eric. 2001. *Fast Food Nation: The Dark Side of the All-American Meal.* Houghton Mifflin Company. Boston, MA.

Sooby, Jane. 2001. *State of the States: Organic Farming Systems Research at Land Grant Institutions 2000-2001.* Research report. Organic Farming Research Foundation, Santa Cruz, CA.

U.S. Department of Agriculture. 1980. *Report and Recommendations on Organic Farming.* A special report prepared for the Secretary of Agriculture. U.S. Government Printing Office, Washington, DC. 154 pp.

University of Maine, *Rogers Farm.* (no date), Stillwater, Maine. http://www.umanine.edu/mafes/farms/rogers.htm.

Valian, Virginia. 1998. *Why So Slow? The Advancement of Women.* The MIT Press, Cambridge, MA.

Washington State University, *Robin Hill Park Demonstration Farm.* (no date). Cooperative Extension in Clallam County, http://clallam.wsu.edu/robinhillfarm.htm.

Whorton, James C. 1975. *Before Silent Spring; Pesticides and Public Health in Pre-DDT America.* Princeton University Press. Princeton, N.J.

Chapter 18

Organic Balance as a Conceptual Framework for Social Change Movements

Susan L. Allen

"Think of the tennis player waiting to receive a service, the Tai Chi expert ready to move in any direction, the caring human being ready to sense the signals from another person or group, the health professional alert to the least sign of change in a patient near a life and death crisis. These people are in balance."

Robert Theobald, The Rapids of Change

INTRODUCTION

Going up and down on a teeter totter was my introduction to balance. Of course, I was aware of the old-fashioned scales used to weigh out flour and justice; and at some point I wondered why gyroscopes and healthy diets also maintained balance but of such a different sort. But it was when I spent time in a hospital observing patients, as one bodily system and then another became "out of balance" — juxtaposed with trying to write a "balanced" journalism story about it — that I noticed the difference between organic and mechanistic notions of balance. Life wasn't a machine that switched "on" or "off"! However, and importantly, it was this either-or model that seemed to frame our thinking about it.

The teeter-totter worldview that fills our language and lives with extremes like *either* sick *or* well, up or down, win or lose, us or them — came to worry me so much I began to study entropy and redundancy — and learned everything in the world adjusts and readjusts to sustain dynamic equilibrium within the systems which compose our universe, from aquariums to bodies to the biosphere.

Eventually, I wrote a book aimed at improving the either-or, "reductionistic," reporting style that is taught to journalists. I suggested that by "adding a W" for the whole system to the original who-what-when-where-why questioning framework of journalism we systematically could build into each story a more holistic perspective and, thereby, begin to make a more contextual, whole-system framework for decision-making accessible to global citizens.

Instead of simply countering one extreme point of view with another extreme view, we could learn to ask: "where does this seemingly disconnected story or idea fit within larger contexts through time and space?" Rather than reducing balance to two opposing views within a story or stories, the organic model places each point of view within its environment - more like one element within a mobile.

I came to think the accepted wisdom of gaining knowledge only by breaking things down into the smallest components without considering context was a critical lapse in Western thinking because, as a conceptual tool, it is so limiting. The mechanistic model leads our minds, laws, values and our whole culture toward fragmentation, extremes, fanaticism, and crisis-oriented reactions: Either "fight or flight," "rich or poor," "right or wrong."

In a fast-changing world teeming with information and possibility — where mass destruction is well within human capability — the absence of an encompassing conceptual tool for analyzing the world and our place in it is dangerous. It also is unnecessary.

"Unnecessary" because everything in life exists within a context. We are not machines. By applying a framework which reveals this, perhaps we can begin to view what we thought were disconnected details from a perspective that allows us to see some connections. Fortunately, for the first time in history, a global "circulatory system" also exists — in the form of cheap air travel, the internet, satellite TV and e-mail, among others — that can make insights about context and perspectives accessible, quickly, to global citizens.

It is hard to grasp this new way to see reality, however, because discoveries making a more holistic worldview possible have existed only within our own lifetime!

The point I hope to make here is that applying a dynamic, organic, ecological model of "balance within a continuum" to all incoming information is a more pragmatic way to understand the world than the old mechanistic, either-or model because it provides a lens through which we can see connections within a diverse but inclusive whole. It gives us a "tree to climb" from which we can see more of the forest.

Where might topics and issues that appear in this volume — fair trade, equal rights, participatory democracy, public education, nonviolence, feminism, ecological concerns, and the other progressive social concepts — "fit" within the global and cultural system? What common ground do they share? What role do they play, singly and together, in system sustainability?

Thirty years ago the importance of grasping a "bigger picture" was part of the public dialogue. Maybe this is because the new technological, communication and transportation innovations that made it possible were brand new and we saw the "threat and promise" of interconnectedness and interdependence (from photos of the earth in space to the discovery of acid rain) for the first time. A truly global perspective was high contrast to the isolated and myopic worldviews of our youth.

However, I work with students now and have begun to realize most young people do not think about the role they play with respect to balance within the whole system. Many want to be socially active but too often they work from extreme perspectives with no conceptual framework that links their work to anything larger or moderates their own tendencies to react and become extreme. I am hopeful that revisiting these ideas about balance will remind all of us to ask questions that are critical to sustainability and, perhaps, give us a calmer language to generate awareness and public dialogue about these abstract ideas and ideals: To what extent is Western civilization built on an unquestioning acceptance of a mechanistic worldview? Can we nurture a healthier, transformed civilization without gaining a more holistic perspective?

How can socially progressive groups work together on behalf of mutual concerns? Can we find common ground — not only among "us" but also with the many "thems"?

Imbalance occurs naturally and unceasingly in the world, of course, and when in control it keeps life flowing. The urgency today is that, for the first time in the history of the world, human beings have evolved to the extent that extreme imbalance is stressing personal, social and global systems beyond their natural capacity to recover. Like patients attached to life supports, we Earthlings need to generate a second opinion about our predicament and decide if we want a worldview that leads to extremism or one that trusts organic balance to frame our collective future.

PART ONE: BEYOND TEETER-TOTTERS

Linking a Universal Patterns to Global and Personal Change

Dynamic, asymmetrical balance is vital to the survival of all systems. This is so because the world as we know it appears to be a single system composed of ever-smaller interdependent systems. With his famous $E=MC^2$, Albert Einstein even told us that when all of the bits and pieces of the universe move fast enough (the speed of light squared), everything is composed of the same "stuff" — energy. All of the seemingly separate parts of any system — diverse species, varied cultures, kinds of work, kinds of energy, categories of traits ascribed to males and females by our social system — all play a role in sustaining the system, just as the seemingly separate parts of a body are necessary for sustaining physical and mental health.

What I am suggesting is that, even beyond biology and the natural environment, dynamic, asymmetrical, organic balance also is necessary to sustain healthy human cultures.

Extrapolating from physical to social patterns is risky business; however, it is painfully obvious that when imbalance occurs within the body, within the environment, or within the mind (although it will not find perfect balance because that would mean stasis and death), unless the system constantly re-adjusts toward better balance, it risks disaster.

I suggest:

1   when social systems get out of balance in the extreme, like a gyroscope tilting precariously to one side, they also risk disaster;

2   over generations, Western civilization (and in various ways other world cultures) has in fact tilted increasingly out of balance;

3   subsequent imbalance now is harming individuals, societies, and the environment; and,

4   all of us who are fortunate enough to be alive today have the opportunity to participate in a massive social re-balancing movement that must occur if our civilization is to survive.

Borrowing from a pattern that occurs throughout nature, I'll try to illustrate what I mean by "dynamic, organic balance" — as opposed to dualistic, teeter-totter balance.

Why Use this Model

Not surprisingly, the natural world has provided us with the perfect conceptual model for learning we live within an interconnected, interdependent system that is not ultimately divisible into isolated parts. The relatively newly discerned DNA molecule illustrates the pattern in a double helix structure that repeats itself throughout nature (Watson, 1968). All organisms in the universe (and even mathematical simulations of star formation!) are represented by spiraling arms that never fully separate (Discover, 1989).

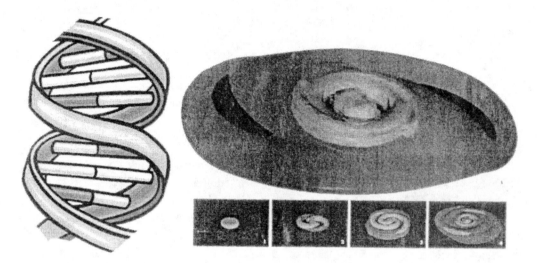

From the double helix structure in human DNA to the simulation of star formation, a pattern revealing wholeness appears (Discover Magazine, 12/89)

The basic construct that appears in DNA also appears in the ancient yin (moon) yang (sun) concept. What we think of as the "yin yang symbol" originally was the result of early-day Chinese scholars' observations of the sun, and their measuring and charting the length of daily shadows in an annual cycle of the sun, as in the following illustration (Capra, 1975).

Just as mystics and observers the world over have intuited in various ways, Taoist sages deduced from their observations that, although human perceptions are limited, the natural world is an indivisible whole. Within the whole system there are discernable patterns; within patterns perpetual adjustment assures system sustainability and the whole system must maintain dynamic balance to survive; and, like everything else, human beings are a part of this moving web of life.

One can observe patterned movement within the whole by watching a mountain throughout the course of one day. First one side is in shadow and then the other side. As one aspect reaches its zenith it leads into the other just as moments that compose the continuum of a day flow seamlessly along. There is not *either* dark *or* light; both dark and light are aspects of *one* whole, moving continuum. It is we who name and perceive a separation.

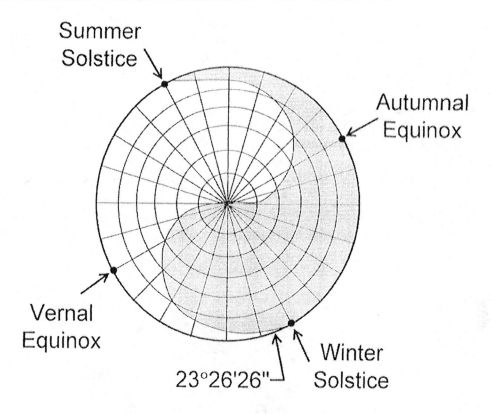

The continuous, organic design also is illustrated by a Mobius strip, named for German astronomer and mathematician August Ferdinand Mobius. Like the yin yang model, the Mobius strip continues to amaze mathematicians, artists and scientists with the simple way it illustrates the inseparable wholeness of the universe (www.scidiv.bcc.edu/math).

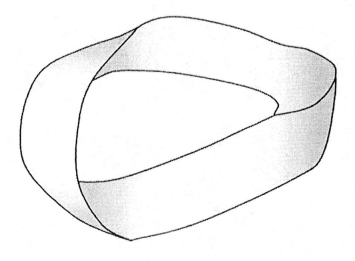

Mobius Strip

A simple Mobius strip can be made by cutting a flat strip of paper about an inch wide and 8-10 inches long. The flat piece of paper symbolizes our traditional Flat Earth "myth-conception" that the world consists of opposites — like top and bottom. The more accurate Mobius model is formed by giving the paper a half-twist on one end and joining it to the other end, to match the pattern of the DNA molecule, the yin yang symbol, and many other examples of continuum from nature. The beauty of this concrete representation is that we can see for ourselves the seamless continuum where opposites seeming never fully separate.

Artist M.C. Esher's 'Parade of Ants' can walk completely around the one-sided, one-edged structure without falling off!

Limited, "flat-earth" perceptions and the social-cultural constructs they foster are what have divided the world into so-called parts and opposites. For thousands of years humans have been limited by an inability to acquire perspectives necessary for revealing wholeness. We simply did not have the intellectual or technological tools to grow beyond the teeter-totter worldview.

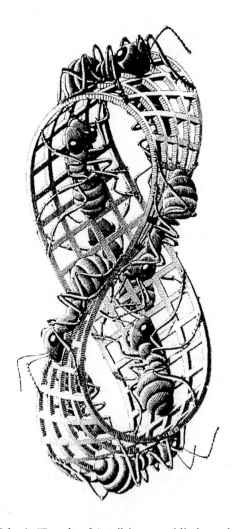

M.C. Esher's "Parade of Ants" (www.scidiv.bcc.edu/math)

It wasn't until 1965 that the electron microscope was first put to practical use; and it was four days before Christmas, 1968, when we saw planet Earth from space for the first time! Although science and technology now have given us tools to acquire holistic perspectives — on both outer space and inner space — human thinking and culture have not kept up.

Within the confines of humanity's "given," myopic notion of time and space, we do in fact see what can be called top or bottom, active or passive, black or white, "male" traits and "female" traits; but we ignore the vast continuum within which the polarities reside. Reductions like this are like blinders on a horse, however; they reveal our own lack of context and perspective, not reality. And although we have been told the opposite is true for centuries, the point of life actually is not to subjugate some parts of the whole and proclaim one part "winner" (as some still want us to do). In the long run, for any of us to survive the whole system needs to "win."

All systems contain both active (yang) and passive (yin) elements within a whole continuum and never only one or the other. There is no such thing as day without night, change without sameness, male without female (even within an individual), even life without death. As the double helix illustrates, there is a vast continuum between any two extremes that flows one into the other and "never fully separate." What is necessary is balance.

The Organic Balance Organizational Model For Social Movements

To illustrate how even the social world seems drawn to conform to this universal pattern, I'll use the yin yang model, again, because like DNA and even the mobile, as opposed to the teeter totter, it better illustrates complex, life-like dynamics. Through the symbol we can plainly see the extremes and also that there is a whole continuum in-between; the black and the white but also the entire color wheel.

The aim of the pictures which follow is to suggest that Western societies (and in various ways all world cultures) have grown increasingly 'out of balance' for generations. Our lives became out of balance, in short, because "yang" (action side) aspects had more survival value when our ancestors were slaying dragons and settling the West. However, like time and Esher's ants, human needs march on.

Our human ability to change directions mid-history and re-orient (some would say co-create) our own social evolution may be the universe's most ingenious fail-safe mechanism. Just in the nick of time it seems, humans appear to be noticing that survival now depends on re-valuing the yin, realizing the continuum, and re-balancing the whole.

As most of us typically visualize balance, it looks like **Figure 1**. The image is of one whole cut into two equal parts.

Figure 1: Traditional teeter totter worldview

Based on **Figure 1**, a balanced system would look like **Figure 2**, with the so-called halves put together.

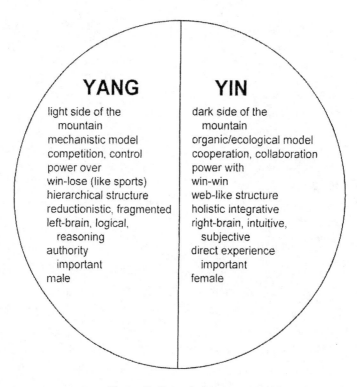

Figure 2: One whole system

Of course these illustrations are static while life itself is in constant, asymmetrical but patterned, motion — as the 5,000 year old yin yang model in **Figure 3** illustrates.

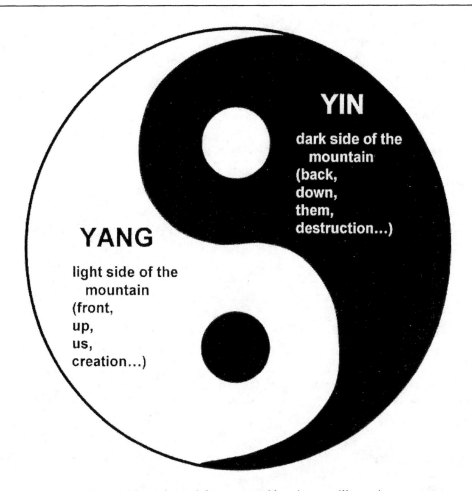

Figure 3: Organic model represented by yin yang illustration

As mentioned, we in the West have been taught to think of the world in dualities like the ones listed within the two halves of the illustrated whole; and, in fact, our linear, Western vision of the world has led to many remarkable insights - like notions of freedom, individual worth and the scientific method! However, we generally assume even our most admirable thoughts exist apart from an inclusive continuum: *either* free *or* not free, individual or community, for example, when actually there are endless combinations in-between.

In every part of our lives, from perceptions to ethics to laws, we have come to associate one half of the world with yang side traits and the other half of the world with yin side traits - as though they could exist in isolation. And, at this point in human social development, we have evolved languages that practically force us into extremist assumptions based on this teeter-totter conceptual model.

For example, brain research tells us the left lobe of the brain (controlling the right half of the body) is associated with linear, sequential thinking; it is more analytical, rational, logical... The right lobe of the brain (controlling the left half of our body) is more intuitive, holistic, simultaneous, visual, creative... But we tend to overlook that they exist within one brain. It is easy to see how the value assigned to yin and yang traits transfers into our social world when we realize how strongly formal education (as well as all informal, culture learning) has emphasized the yang aspects and devalued the yin aspects. Children used to be punished for using the yin-side, left hand; we shake hands with the right; the groom stands on the right, etc.

The language of a hot academic topic, "leadership styles" illustrates this very well. The yang side is linked with action:

> aggressive, independent, unemotional, objective, dominant, competitive, logical/rational, adventurousness, self-confident, ambitious, worldly, act as a leader, assertive, analytical, decisive — as well as with masculinity and males.

On the other hand (no doubt the left), the yin side is associated with passivity:

> emotional, sensitive, expressive, tactful, security-oriented, nurturing, tender, cooperative, intuitive, independent, sympathetic, warm, the opposite of all of the yang characteristics listed above — and with femininity and with women. (Park, 1996). (Park argues for more androgynous, balanced styles, by the way.)

Among all assorted delineations of yin and yang by various disciplines and professions, yin identifies the "dark side of the mountain," an ecological worldview, cooperation and collaboration, power "with" others, win/win problem solving, right brain(left side), integration, female — and lesser.

In all of them, yang identifies the "light side of the mountain," a mechanistic worldview, a hierarchical, win/lose model of interaction, power "over" others, left brain (right side), authorities, male — and superior.

Physicists and philosophers refer to this division as "old paradigm" (Isaac Newton, Rene Descartes, a mechanistic explanation for the world) and "new paradigm" (Albert Einstein, the new physicists, an organic view of the world), wherein the old over-emphasizes yang and the new seeks greater balance.

The point is, the "old" idea — that the world is split into two halves with yang as the superior half — has been around a long, long time in human terms. It is built into our thinking and society at every level and in every instance we have failed to attend to the fact that all of the parts live within one interdependent, interconnected whole that needs constant re-balancing to survive (see Capra, 1984).

My conviction is that our individual and collective mission for the next few decades must be to consciously choose to improve the balance within our individual personalities, our power structure, our cultures, and our environment. Although all manner of creativity and "extremes" also exist within the continuum and are necessary in moderation, we need to evolve beyond an either-or worldview that tells us in every instance competition is better than collaboration, male is better than female, rational thinking is better than intuition, "we" are better than "them."

The dangerous truth is that because of generations of over-emphasis on and over-valuing of yang-side attributes — our world has come to look something like **Figure 4**. If the world were a gyroscope we would be headed for spin out!

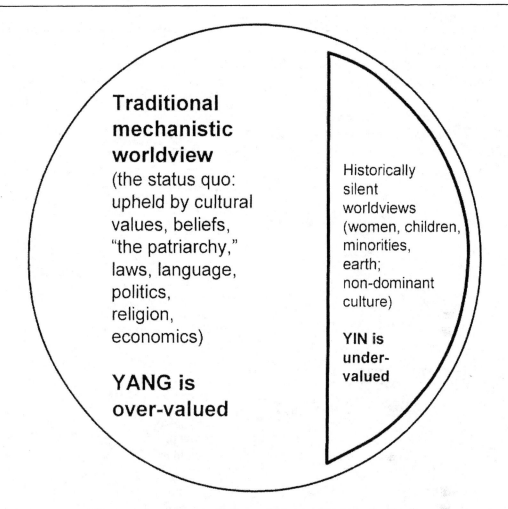

Figure 4: A world out of balance ('koyaanisqatsi,' to the Hopi)

It is because of an historical imbalance of power on the yang side that our heavily yang-oriented opinion leaders have been able to overlook problems caused by extreme de-valuing of yin-side attributes. In fact, traits that define the yang side *at the expense* of the yin side define success and characterize the status quo in our world today whether exhibited by males or females. And those who obtained power over others by applying yang traits think it would be best if they just kept it. The result, however, is a world that has become dangerously out of kilter — for example, in the direction of exclusivity instead of integration, individual over community, and so forth.

The everyday significance of appreciating that life is an all-inclusive whole that needs to fluctuate between yin and yang is enormous. Instead of striving for and rewarding only or mostly yang-associated traits we need to acknowledge that human beings contain within ourselves and our societies both active and passive attributes and all variations in-between — and learn to value more of our options. Going back to the human body-universe analogy, for example: how is ignoring a gangrenous wound on our little finger different from ignoring poverty and injustice in Afghanistan or Appalachia? How is over-valuing the competitive drive when an athlete cheats by using steroids different from tilting toward insider trading and other extreme win-lose tactics on Wall Street? And, in fact, how might over-valuing our heart or lungs at the expense of our lymph system be different from over-valuing American culture at the expense of Tibetan culture?

The eventual result of imbalance will be system failure every time.

Serendipitously, at the same historical moment when this imbalance has begun destroying individual mental health, devastating the environment, causing continual violence and war — any one of which will lead inevitably to personal and global system failure — curiously but, in fact, as the organic, yin-yang model would predict, various counterbalancing forces have begun to be heard.

Figure 5 illustrates this (although, within the context of the drawing, movement actually would come from re-adjustment of the small circle of yin within the yang and visa versa).

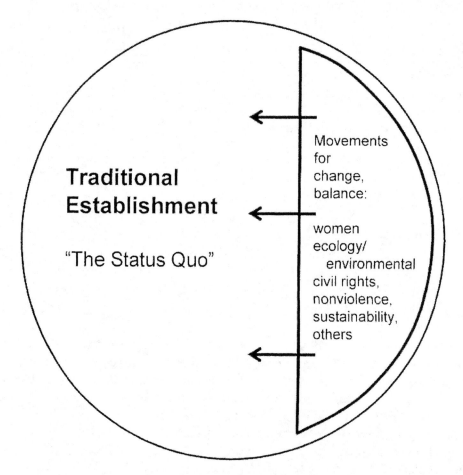

Figure 5: Social movement toward better balance in the system

How this movement toward rebalancing began is a mystery. Is it a miracle or is it a fail-safe process built into the human brain? Perhaps when a critical mass of individuals became healthy enough within themselves to recognize the need for balance, they began pushing society to become better balanced, as well. Like blackbirds gathering into that identifiable pattern as they go south for winter and like specific thoughts forming within our brains, groups of seemingly independent people and ideas have coalesced into a series of social "movements." When the small groups began to grow they became visible to all of us.

"Healing the Split"

Ideas presented here are not new, but I am bringing them up once again for several reasons. One, as Andre Gide once said, " Everything that needs to be said has already been said. But since no one was listening, everything must be said again." (Gaylin, 1978) Two, I have noticed that many of these movements have gained so much strength in such a short time that people born in the last 30 years may not even realize they are living in the midst of a massive re-education project that will have as great a consequence as the agricultural and industrial revolutions! And, three, individuals and groups may be strengthened by realizing they stand on common ground with others in a comprehensive framework. At present, even many people working within social change movements behave as though they live in an either-or world; and too many of them are as vulnerable to fragmented and extremist thinking as are the traditionalists and conservatives who resist them.

I would like to make the case that the women's movement, ecology movement, civil rights movement, nonviolence movement, and other social change movements can be seen as parts of this largely unconscious force pushing us to bring greater balance to our world by re-valuing the so-called yin elements in our lives and world. All of these movements can be examined within the context of the yin yang re-balancing concept. Choosing several examples at random:

- Since over half of the world's population is female, it makes sense that feminism would be the first major social force in history that emerged to demand re-examination of humanity's blind acceptance of a world biased toward (male-associated) yang traits. Through any lens male dominance just wasn't fair. However, the "women's movement" is much more than a call for women's equality. Feminists who understand balance do not want to trade extremist yin for extremist yang or eliminate the genders. Feminists who understand balance value both yang and yin — within ourselves, our societies and our world. Ultimately, the women's movement insists on the survival necessity of bringing better balance to the system.

- The ecologist's admonition, "you can't do just one thing" is an axiom for the interconnectedness and interdependence of the whole global system. The organic balance-based ecology organizations and environmental movement are working desperately to bring public attention to the fact that humanity needs to collaborate with the natural environment (a yin trait which would serve to integrate) rather than always putting perceived human needs above it (a yang trait based on hierarchy and either-or). We don't need to go "back" to the agrarian societies of yesteryear or dismiss technological or other advances for balance to be gained. The point of organic balance within a continuum is to recognize and act on the enormous range of options between extremes.

- Fair trade, living wage, worker cooperative movements and similar economic movements function at an even more subtle level to bring better balance to the world by emphasizing the survival necessity of diversity — among peoples, among types of food we eat, among types of labor we pay for or energy we use — and, also, by "bringing up the bottom rung" of the human economic spectrum so that more members of the population continuum may participate in a full life. Public education and participatory democracy movements are working to re-balance the world by attempting to "wire more and more people into the system" through more (yin-like horizontal rather than *only* yang-like hierarchical) power sharing.

- A new argument about alternative energy going on in my windy state illustrates the confusion caused by innovations and individuals that appear progressive but still are working from the either-or paradigm. Most ecologically-astute Kansans realize alternative power is important, and they want to use the locally-sustainable, renewable wind as an energy source. When "wind farm" companies approached them at first they were delighted. It became apparent, however, that the companies continue to apply yang-exclusive corporate methodologies, that are both unecological and under the control of a few wealthy owners even as they suggest changes that appear on the surface to be examples of the ecological, rebalancing movement.

  By looking at this dilemma through the lens of the organizing principle I suggest in this article, we know to ask for more alternatives! The real choice is not between *either* corporate wind factories *or* no wind power at all. Similarly, we don't have to choose between either corporate hogs or no bacon; or, indeed, between either corporate capitalism or no capitalism. There is a range of possibilities within both time (this works now but it might not work tomorrow) and through space (wind might be locally sustainable but water power would work better in other areas).

- "Be a man!" or "Be more lady-like!" are culturally-enforced admonitions many people receive at some point and cringe because it makes us feel lesser. It is supposed to! These are blatant expressions of dualistic thinking on a personal level. They parallel subtle and insidious messages everywhere in our world that remind us to maintain the status quo. Since "yang" traits are rewarded in these systems that "yang" built; and since "yin" traits are ascribed to women, nontraditional masculine males, children, the earth and "others," guess who gets to retain power-over everyone when the directive is observed? Our lives are filled with stereotypes which function to keep individuals (all of whom contain both yang and yin within) from finding better personal balance and, thus, being less likely to question the status quo, including the socio-economic system.

  The new "redefining masculinity" movement and the women's movement among others focus on issues of intrapersonal imbalance and the social, cultural, policy inequities that maintain it. Extreme and extremist opposition to women in sports, stay-at-home fathers, gay rights, and even androgyny, for example, are fighting the tide of change from dysfunctional dualistic people to much more healthy holistic humans.

- The growing nonviolence movement participates in re-balancing at the personal, community and global levels. Resolution of life's conflicts actually is not limited to *only* "fight *or* flight," and we do not have to reconcile all discord with only win or lose, as we've been taught. There are multiple personal and social behaviors in-between extremes that can help us manage inevitable human conflict and other natural disorder.

When a "critical mass" of yin begins to re-balance the system — through trial and error and the asymmetrical dynamics and short- and long-term cycles of the seemingly separate pieces — then our world will be a much healthier place. Particular traits and whole movements will disappear into acceptability — and inevitably there will be fluctuation between yin and yang throughout the spectrum of possibilities, forever.

Somewhere in the collective being of the universal system there must be a force like gravity, that pulls us to "heal the split" between different parts of ourselves, between person and person, between the conscious and the unconscious, between spirit and substance, and on and on (Morris, 1989). Whatever the force, it shows us over and over that within any system, "If one suffers we all suffer together and if we survive it will only be if we do it together."

So, how can we reach a "critical mass" of people who could help re-balance the system and insure our survival? That has been the guiding question of my career.

PART TWO: OVERLAYING THE ORGANIC MODEL ON A CAREER

Most readers will know the story of the "Hundredth Monkey." While feeding sweet potatoes to monkeys on a Japanese island, researchers discovered an amazing thing about the adoption of new ideas. They taught some monkeys how to prepare the potatoes in a new way and, at some point, all of a sudden, *all* of the monkeys in the tribe began exhibiting the behavior — without being taught (Keyes, 1984).

The Hundredth Monkey thesis is that when an idea reaches some certain level of awareness and acceptance, it spreads seemingly by itself. We call it "reaching critical mass," and think of it as "an idea whose time has come."

In the complex world of people, where we are members of one global "tribe," whether we like it or not, (regardless of what one thinks about the original story), I would argue that the 'hundredth monkey' phenomena applies. As individuals, what we do impacts the whole system because, for one thing, we never know when we might be the "hundredth monkey." However, and importantly, as conscious human beings living in community with the rest of the planet, we also have the opportunity and responsibility to decide which ideas we want to adopt and thus how we want to guide our social evolution.

Further, the people who live in democracies and want an idea turned into policy must be presented with the idea in a large enough number that they, in turn, can elect representatives who share their views.

The question that has motivated my own career for the past 30 years (and my challenge to other progressive thinkers and social activists) has been a version of the slogan, "what if they had a war and nobody came?" It is, how can we create a sustainable, peaceful and just world if nobody has the conceptual tools to envision it?

In other words, who among us is working to expose the organizing principle based on holism, interdependence and balance to the tide-turning other "99," a critical mass which actually translates into millions of global citizens?

Most people have bet their lives on the status quo and may not believe it is in their best interest to acquire a more holistic perspective. Yet, a critical mass of global citizens will have to adopt a more holistic and organically balanced — as opposed to a fragmented and dualistic — worldview if we are to build a framework for safer decision making. I sometimes think of this work as "applied poetry," because of the way it can change one's customary ways of seeing and open new areas of individual awareness - if we can get people to listen!

At some time in the late 1960s, after seeing first photos of the Earth in space and experiencing the sobering reality of nuclear drift and lessons in holism and connectedness from that famous Butterfly's Wing (which flaps in Brazil and causes a breeze in my backyard), *it dawned on many of us that we seem to have been cursed and blessed to be alive* at a time in the history of the universe when a global, cultural transformation is taking place all around us.

As mentioned, the emerging ideas (which have ancient roots) describe our evolution from a mechanistic to a holistic worldview and are loosely referred to as the "new paradigm." The underlying aim of the newer model is to fit the world with something like trifocal 3-D eyeglasses so a majority of us can begin to see a little farther and stop tripping over our feet all of the time. The essential perspective is that the Earth, along with its inhabitants, will not be safe until we learn to view it in all its glorious diversity as an interconnected and interdependent whole.

My career has been guided by the notion that at least some of us who want these ideas to reach critical mass need to help make them accessible. It seemed to me that the information-education needs in today's world demanded an approach befitting a global information age but that none of our established institutions, including schools, churches, family or media (even the new electronic technologies), seem to have noticed there is a new job to do.

Thinking Globally: Media Anthropology

From some combination of reasons not entirely clear to me, I began developing a "way" to reach people — a discipline, a profession — which came to be called "media anthropology." Its general purpose is to "inform global citizens" about the potential of this holistic, "anthropological perspective."

At first, I studied anthropology because I love the patterns it reveals and the connections it enables us to see. Anthropology showed me the necessity both for our uniqueness and our common humanity. I was liberated by the alternative ways of seeing and being in the world that it brought to light. It was the only subject matter I could find that seemed (at that point in my life) to have no dogmatic boundaries. Problem was, I wanted to apply what I was learning out in the real world, and anthropologists (with few exceptions) not only had no interest in public education, too many anthropologists were and still are caught up in the old worldview, like everyone else. So I took up journalism and mass communication.

Journalism, I reasoned, at least had an ethic of informing and educating the "general public," and had developed the channels and methodologies to do it. Once again, however, journalists (again, with a few exceptions) had no notion of the value of whole system context and analysis. So, during this period, I tried to find a language to talk to journalists about holism and balance and came up with the idea, of "adding a W for the whole" to the "who-what-when-where-why" questioning framework of journalism (Allen, Journalism Educator, 1987). The strategy was to systematize a way of making more context and perspective available to the general public (i.e. to all of us). I chose journalism because journalism supplies the information which gives most of us the only news and views we ever get about ourselves and our place in the world and, although it doesn't tell us "what to think," it does set our intellectual and political agendas and boundaries. "We're bombarded with information," I argued to reluctant professors. "What we need is a framework on which to hang the seemingly disconnected details."

In the early 70s, as a few academics in my neck of the woods began realizing the necessity for "interdisciplinary" perspectives, I was able to combine ideas from anthropology, journalism, public education, and even from futurism, new physics and the mystical traditions (although I didn't tell them that part) into a doctorate (Allen, 1980).

Some of my academic research was designed to discover whether readers would have an interest in media content which had the potential to share anthropological perspectives. (Allen, Journalism Quarterly, 1975). This ambition flew in the face of the journalism profession's insistence at that time that "no one cares about international or intercultural news" or any of those "holistic points of view, whatever they are, thank you very much."

It is chilling, following September 11, 2001, to remember that the pejorative journalistic label for this presumed lack of public interest in the rest of the globe was "Afghanistanism."

I became fascinated by the structure of imperialism and abuses of power which kept intact the polarizing either-or (us vs. them, yin vs. yang) world when I conducted media anthropological research on international/intercultural news flow in the Pacific Islands. There I realized that what islanders were told about the world and visa versa still followed colonial trade routes. Later, I would learn about the direct parallels between power imbalances on the international level and power imbalances in all other interactions, including interpersonal relationships. "Oppression is oppression" and, in the same way, "abuse of power is abuse of power," whether perpetrated by a nation, boss, corporation, one's own "alter ego," or an abusive husband.

In the early years of the Information Age, it seemed to me that mass communication and the new electronic media including the internet would make alternative choices and perspectives so wide spread and accessible that the domination and withholding of power by the few would become as outdated as gold bullion. Although that potential still exists, as we know, powerful people just keep finding new ways to salvage the extremist worldview that maintains the status quo.

I tried applying some of the ideas that would replace polarizing notions with more contextual ones by writing what I hoped were "perspective building" newspaper columns, by editing a small multicultural newspaper, by being a student of culture and social change. I worked in Washington for a U.S. Senator for a time, imagining that a large political "megaphone" for these ideas would expedite the work. I quickly gave up on that idea, for myself; however I continue to believe some of us have to work within the established political arena — along side our grassroots-level colleagues, media and other allies we can find.

One fundamental ingredient of a better balanced human world has to be more widespread participation in decision making. Following that, if the voting public is going to be well enough informed and educated to make wise choices about our shared futures in the crucial years ahead, we need a much better informed and educated general public.

As futurist Alvin Toffler said, we need to "wire more people into the system" (Toffler, 1975). And, as forefather Thomas Jefferson said, "I know of no safe depository of the ultimate powers of the society but the people themselves; and if we think them not enlightened enough to exercise their control with some discretion, the remedy is not to take it from them but to inform their discretion" (Fulbright, 1979).

One result of my media anthropology focus was the book, *Media Anthropology: Informing Global Citizens* (Allen, ed., 1994.). It includes a foreword by Mary Catherine

Bateson (daughter of two of anthropology's most well-known public-interest and holistic-thinking anthropologists, Margaret Mead and Gregory Bateson), which was nice symmetry. In this book, I and some like-minded anthropologists presented ideas about how we might create a subdiscipline for both anthropology and the communications professions designed to reach the general public with a more holistic way of seeing the world.

I want to stress: 1) by media anthropology, I mean sharing holistic perspectives that are available from anthropology with the broadest possible, 'media,' audience, not teaching the content of anthropology, *per se,* or "preaching" a limited or limiting dogma "through" the media; 2) creativity and "extremes" (even ones we may not like) also exist on the continuum within any whole; 3) organic balance is in constant fluctuation — never a static state. The goal is to make people aware of the organic organizing principle so — one at a time, as we are ready — we can use it to help us make better sense of all the other information coming our way. I thought and still do think that providing access to this kind of whole-system perspective (and "method of analysis") is *sine qua non* to motivating global citizens to make peaceful, just and sustainable choices about our futures.

Acting Locally, Acting Now: A Campaign for Nonviolence

Professionally, I have earned my living as director of a university Women's Center for the past several years. The traditional role for such women's offices has been to "clean up the mess" of violence against women, after the fact; attend to victim safety and health care; provide therapy and legal options for (mostly) women in crisis from abuse. At some point, it began to dawn on me that my work actually reflected someone's definition of insanity, by "doing the same thing over and over again and expecting different results." By agreeing to confine ourselves to prescribed, traditional responses to violence — i.e. the therapy model for victims and the legal model for the violators — and only to attend to violence after the fact — we were never going to "get ahead" of the violence or change the system that generates it.

On this small scale, we once again were ignoring holistic context, falling into the reductionist conceptual trap by individualizing a community problem, and ignoring the continuum of problems and solutions.

We needed *both* to help the sufferer *and* to attend to the suffering at its complex source. We needed to attend to cultural imbalances; to challenge norms surrounding violence; to use the force of "people power" (as we have little else) to demand resistance to institutional and individual abuses of power that exist within the status quo; and to begin the step by step, ongoing activity of finding better balance in the system. In this case, that meant resisting injustice by cultivating active nonviolence on our campus.

When I realized the first 10 years of the new millennium had been named the "Decade for a Culture of Peace and Nonviolence" by the U.N. it was an epiphany! I realized global "peace and justice" language readily translated into the local language of "safety and equity," and that talking about local violence issues in the vocabulary of nonviolence gave us some advantages: a gender-neutral, non-threatening language that could help us to deal with perpetrators as well as attract male allies; a whole world of tactics and tools from the nonviolence movement that teach us ways to practice nonviolence and "get ahead" of violence; a way to confront system-wide imbalances of power (injustice) that are precursors to violence and which many of us believe is the only real way to end violence; and a holistic instead of either-or organizing framework for thinking about the whole state of affairs.

At first working at a Women's Center in a small town seemed a far cry from practicing anthropology. However, my concrete, real-world problem — to address violence against women on our campus— suddenly looked like a microcosm for the whole issue of rebalancing power and culture. (Allen, Association of Feminist Anthropology, 2001.) If my need to solve campus violence was the "mother of invention" that led me to look at nonviolence as a methodology, then "oppression" was the grandmother. There is a direct parallel between "if you want peace, work for justice" at the global level and "if you want safety, work for equality and fairness" at the local level. "Justice and equality" are not static end-states; they are attainable only through the asymmetrical ebb and flow of organic balance.

"Don't Agonize, Organize"

After years of noticing that crime on campus did not lessen despite the best efforts of women trying to help other women be more safe, by thinking holistically, we are beginning to ask better questions. We are reframing our thinking about violence. One question we hope to answer is: Can we begin to address the whole continuum of violence on our campus (withholding information, subtle and blatant discrimination, harassment, bullying, economic disparity, lack of political voice, assault and rape) by applying the concepts, tactics and tools of the nonviolence movement?

I see the Campaign for Nonviolence, or CNV as it has come to be called on my campus, as a local experiment in how to inform people and invite them to look at a serious public health problem within this "whole," if small, system — from the ground up, by building community and creating new expectations; by attending to personal, interpersonal and community factors; by making our work sustainable.

The motto of the CNV is "Nonviolence begins with You/Me," the wording of which was a beginning strategy for introducing people to interconnectedness and interdependence within the system. We are asking people to look at violence in the context of culture; to go beyond only "fight or flight" responses to violence and to consider the continuum of violent acts and to be open to a range of ways to counter them.

We are trying to move people's concept of violence beyond the accepted notion that violence is the victim's personal problem — an individual anomaly in an otherwise peaceful community — and move toward understanding violence as a system-wide public health problem that can be addressed by applying many methodologies. We are asking the whole community to assume its responseability for violence by practicing and expecting nonviolence throughout the system.

Connecting the CNV to Other Progressive Work

Our small campaign for nonviolence connects to the organic rebalancing movement by reflecting the evolution in our thinking from the reductionist, extremist, dualistic view (fight or flight, individual or community) to the dynamically-balanced, holistic view. We are learning to acknowledge all of the personal and cultural interconnections that actually are involved when a coed is raped by her date, a gay man is assaulted on the street, a staff person is discriminated against, an employee is harassed — or any other act on the continuum of violence and abuse of power that occurs on college campuses.

We are working to expose violence as an issue of power; and we are working toward a better balance of power in this community: more horizontal and less hierarchical. We are working to *underlay* a web-like network of "people" power beneath the established institutional hierarchy so we can assume some control and responsibility for our own environment. We are learning to look to one another to be part of the solution to the endemic problems and to empower individuals-together with the ability to respond.

We will know when we are making a difference in this local re-balancing act in ways beyond a lower crime rate (which will take awhile). We will see less winking and turning a blind eye to the precursors to violence; less denial that date rape occurs; less willed naiveté about who is perpetuating most of the violence; more authority figures and opinion leaders speaking out against abuse of power and for nonviolent "community principles" by standing with us and declaring that "nonviolence begins with me;" more nonviolence (and peace studies) content integrated into the curriculum; more non-traditional people hired in more well-paying and powerful positions; more economic parity; compliance with re-balancing policies like affirmative action and Title IX; and, eventually, we will hear fewer harassment and discrimination complaints, see lower crime statistics; and find more people wanting to work and study in our "safe and fair" community.

CONCLUSION

Using organic balance as an organizing principle creates common ground and a shared language among progressive social movements as they attempt to redress imbalances in our selves, our society and our world in multiple ways. Some groups work on the power imbalance between the rich and the poor, some between men and women, some between the earth and the humans. It may help us to think of this work in the context of "healing the split" between polarities and honoring the whole continuum of possibilities in our world.

CONTRIBUTORS

Rick Allen is a music critic and writer, songwriter, individual performer and leader of his band, Rick Allen and the Upsetters. In addition, as a full-time disc jockey for WYSP, 94 FM, Philadelphia, Rick Allen has formed an important center of the urban intellectual movement to redefine political culture through rock, folk, blues, soul, country and western, and other musical forms. Because of his extensive knowledge of music, literature, and politics, Rick Allen was one of the last disc jockeys with a major FM station in the U.S. who was allowed to choose his own songs for his radio show; in the last decade, songs played on major radio stations have been determined by advertisement dollars and are listed in terms of commercial importance by computer-programmed selections. As a music critic and writer, singer and guitar player, composer, and disc jockey, Rick Allen has served as a popular educator who has explored cultural alternatives for the U.S. and other places around the world. His major influences are Roy Rogers, Jack Kerouac, Muhammed Ali, Susan Sontag, Bob Dylan, Little Richard and Suetonius.

Susan L. Allen is an applied anthropologist who currently works as director of the Women's Center at Kansas State University. As director of the Women's Center, she is helping build a grassroots "campaign for nonviolence" and is hopeful, for the first time in years, that by adapting the tools and tactics of the global nonviolence movement we can help create safer and more equitable local environments. She has worked since 1968 to develop a sub-discipline and profession combining anthropology, journalism and public education for the purpose of helping people evolve more "anthropological," holistic perspectives. Working through the East-West Center in Honolulu, and applying her doctoral knowledge from the University of Kansas (where she completed her Ph.D.), she did fieldwork in the Pacific Islands and Japan, but she didn't truly experience culture shock until she worked for the U.S. Senate. Susan Allen has a long interest in appropriate development and undevelopment, and was involved for many years with the Manhattan, Kansas-Nindiri, Nicaragua Friendship Cities program.

Annalouise was born in 1948, Aquarian, in an England that had never known teenagers before. She first rode a motorbike behind a leather-jacketed, long hair from the Ricky Tick Club, in Windsor. A member of the first group of squatters and home rehabilitators in the Finsbury Park area, Annalouise later became a central organizer of her local LETS initiative in London, a local exchange trading scheme that coordinated the bartering of services between people; LETS bartering networks became widespread throughout England, allowing, for example, day care providers to exchange services with computer technicians, and all outside of the cash economy.

Annalouise has always loved exchange of ideas, singing, dance, drum-rhythms, musicians, painting, cartooning, photography and illustrating children's books. Exposed to trauma at a tender age, she found herself working as facilitator on Creative Arts camps, taking her two children with her, and learnt the healing arts that she later turned into therapy.

These skills followed on from three children's books, and illustration/cartooning for alternative energy publications, to become a truly innovative Creative Arts Therapy for those in danger of exclusion from school and society. The work brings together all nationalities, and helps build bridges of appreciation across a divided education system, helping parents and teachers to cope and comprehend and adapt the straight jacket of our education as it is.

When Annalouise returns from eight months' traveling in 2002-3 (collecting her daughter on her way through Australia), she hopes to bring her many talented friends (clowns, counselors of teen sexuality, etc.) together to form a place of play, where, linked to a farm and putting their hands in the dirt, people can learn respect and love, and be allowed to get angry, make mistakes safely! Annalouise, a photographer and multi-media artist, traveled to Morocco in 2001, photographing many family, community, and natural scenes; two of these photographs appear on the book cover, and others appear with her essay.

John A. Bilorusky received his B.A. *cum laude* in Physics and *cum laude* in General Studies, University of Colorado, 1967; his M.A. in the Sociology of Education, University of California at Berkeley, 1968; and his Ph.D. in Higher Education, University of California at Berkeley, 1972. John was a co-founder of WISR in 1975. Before that, he taught social sciences at the University of California at Berkeley and community services at the University of Cincinnati, and was Director of Graduate Studies at University Without Walls-Berkeley. He is the author of many published articles and papers on higher education and social change, adult learning, and practical, community-based research methods. He has served as a consultant evaluating liberal arts colleges and educational innovations, conducting public policy research, and helping others to create community-based colleges.

In John's one-on-one work with learners, he strives to bring their skills, insights and experiences to the surface so that they can then use and further develop their knowledge in the course of ongoing community and professional activities. Through this process, John reminds the learners that they, he and others are collaboratively engaged in a kind of serious knowledge-building that can be empowering. As President of WISR, John has a variety of administrative responsibilities ranging from everyday functions to those more commonly associated with a CEO. But first and foremost, John spends most of his time collaborating with students and faculty at WISR to preserve and advance the qualities that have made WISR so special.

Torry Dickinson, who grew up in different parts of the United States, seized the opportunities to explore the innovative projects that interested her, and she learned to value organizing her own learning, education, and work. She would like to bring together different groups of open-minded, applied intellectuals to initiate global development patterns that will benefit the world's large majority. And, in the near future, she would like to bring this book's writers together in this kind of working meeting. Torry is dedicated to enhancing egalitarian public education at all levels, and she thanks her former public-school teachers and classmates for giving her the social and academic knowledge that relates to her everyday work.

As she completed graduate work in sociology at SUNY-Binghamton and taught college, Torry pursued her interest in opening up and applying community- and global-change processes to multidisciplinary, research-based projects in diverse learning environments. Torry Dickinson now works as an Associate Professor of Women's Studies at Kansas State University in Manhattan. Co-written with ecologist and ethnic-conflict researcher Robert Schaeffer, Torry Dickinson's most recent book is *Fast Forward: Work, Gender and Protest in a Changing World*. As she conducts her research on feminist-informed social change projects, Torry Dickinson thinks about how we can work together in open, equal, and creative ways to create affirmative social relationships.

Tammy Findlay is a Ph.D. candidate in political science at York University in Toronto, Canada. Her work and research are related to issues of gender and Canadian politics, gender and public policy, and gender and democracy. Her publications include "Democracy on the Line: Reflections on Gender and the CUPE Strike," *Problematique*, 7 No. 1 (2002), with Sabine Hikel, and, "Why a 'Two-Nations' Women's Movement: Feminism in 'English Canada' and Quebec," in *The Politics of Nationalism: Essays on Canadian Nationalism, Citizenship, and National Identity*, Andrew Nurse and Raymond Blake, eds., Toronto: Harcourt and Brace, forthcoming. Her work history combines factory work, research, and a variety of academic and community teaching. She is involved in feminist activism in her university, union, and community.

William H. Friedland is Research Professor and Professor Emeritus after having been Professor of Community Studies and Sociology for 22 years at the University of California, Santa Cruz, his place of retirement in 1991. He was the founding chair of the Community Studies Department. Prior to his coming to UCSC, he was on the faculty of Cornell University from 1961 to 1969.

After working as an assemblyline worker in Detroit (1942-1949), he became Assistant Education Director of the Michigan CIO Council and worked as an engineering representative of the United Automobile Workers union.

Bill Friedland completed his B.A. and M.A. degrees at Wayne State University, Detroit; he received his Ph.D. in Sociology from the University of California, Berkeley. His early research involved the analysis of working class movements, unions, and socialism in Africa. While at Cornell, Bill Friedland began to research migrant agricultural workers and developed the Cornell Migrant Labor Project in which he trained undergraduates for field study as migrants. His research at Cornell focused on agricultural labor.

After joining UCSC to start Community Studies, Bill Friedland's research concentrated on the sociology/political economy of agriculture, working with rural sociologists and an international cluster of researchers with whom he has been active since 1978. As author, co-author, and co-editor, he has written numerous publications on agriculture, including: *Migrant Agricultural Workers in America's Northeast*; *Manufacturing Green Gold: Capital, Labor and Technology in the Lettuce Industry*; *Destalking the Wily Tomato: A Case Study in Social Consequences in California Agricultural Research*; *Towards a New Political Economy of Agriculture*; as well as non-agricultural publications, including: *African Socialism*; *The*

Knowledge Factory; *Student Power and Academic Politics in America*; and *Revolutionary Theory*. Bill Friedland is currently completing a book on California wine and grapes.

Dawn Haney is a doctoral student in the Department of Health Promotion and Behavior and a teaching assistant in the Women's Studies Program at the University of Georgia in Athens, Georgia. She also is pursuing graduate certificates in Women's Studies and Qualitative Research as part of her program of study. She is interested in understanding and improving the relationships between health educators and program participants, particularly when those interactions are cross-cultural. As a master's project, she developed, implemented, and evaluated a web-based curriculum on third world women's health with a goal of introducing undergraduates to cross-cultural interactions in health promotion. This project's development formed the impetus for the chapter in this volume; a paper summarizing the evaluation results is currently in preparation.

Dawn first became interested in community-based health promotion as an undergraduate at Michigan State University, where she was a member of a student organization focused on changing the college environment that supported risky drinking. Students took the lead on changing drinking norms by planning highly successful alcohol-free activities such as alcohol-free tailgates before home football games and parties for holidays like Halloween and St. Patrick's Day. While working collaboratively with staff members at the university, she and fellow students were collectively empowered to identify key problems that faced students and to become change agents on their campus. Comparing this experience with more typical health promotion programs has encouraged her to attempt to understand community development and empowerment, particularly how staff members can facilitate or derail these processes.

Dawn Haney has recently accepted a fellowship position at the Centers for Disease Control and Prevention (CDC) in Atlanta, Georgia to work with WISEWOMAN, Well-Integrated Screening and Evaluation for Women Across the Nation, which provides cardiovascular disease screening, intervention, and medical referral for low-income, uninsured women aged 40-64. She will be assisting with program evaluation and transferring lessons learned to new settings. Dawn can be reached via email at haneydaw@uga.edu.

Mal Rooks Hoover is a graphic designer who was born in Manhattan, Kansas. As a college student, she learned that she could draw, and sometimes she drew horses and riders, a main interest of hers. Always interested in science, Mal Rooks Hoover received her B.S. from Kansas State University (KSU) in 1978. She currently is the medical illustrator for the College of Veterinary Medicine at Kansas State University, a position that she has held since 1980. On her own, she creates pen and ink drawings, and pencil/graphite illustrations for pleasure. Mal Rooks Hoover served on the University's Commission for the Status of Women, and now she is an active member of the University's Campaign for Nonviolence. Recently one of her drawings of a thoroughbred racing horse appeared on the cover of the *AVMA Journal* (July 15, 2002). Using two Moroccan photographs taken by London artist Annalouise, Mal Rooks Hoover designed the book cover for *Community and the World*.

Marilyn Jackson first experienced popular education through forums in the Lutheran church while living in Northern Illinois as a teenager during the Vietnam War era. She attended summer camps as a child and worked at church camps as a young adult. Still active in Swedish cultural activities, she has served as cultural leader for several years in a Berkeley, California chapter of Vasa, an international Swedish fraternal order.

Marilyn Jackson worked as a lay minister at a church in Minneapolis, where she became involved in peace and justice movements in the early 1980s. She has continued working in peace and justice education and in organizing with the Ecumenical Peace Institute in Berkeley since the mid-1980s. In addition, she has helped organize numerous public events to raise consciousness about Native Americans in Illinois and California, including with the Indigenous Peoples Day Committee in Berkeley.

Marilyn Jackson currently weaves together her social-change, education, and writing interests through full-time graduate work and work. Marilyn is completing her Ph.D. in Higher Education and Social Change at the Western Institute for Social Research (WISR) in Berkeley, where she also works on a part-time basis; WISR is an alternative degree granting school with individualized study for adults. Marilyn Jackson has an active interest in holistic health and has learned and taught Natural Vision Improvement. She has studied at Augustana College in Rock Island, Illinois, and at the Institute for Culture and Creation Spirituality at Holy Names College in Oakland. Marilyn Jackson has published poems in *Creation* magazine, a publication of Friends of Creation Spirituality in Oakland (9-10-86 and 7-8-87 issues), including one that was reprinted in the World Council of Churches publication, *Women in a Changing World* (Jan. 1988). Marilyn Jackson has also written articles for *Planted*, a publication of the Ecumenical Peace Institute in Berkeley (Winter/Spring 1999 and Spring 2000). Her email address is: c/o mail@wisr.edu.

Rhonda R. Janke works at Kansas State University, researching sustainable agriculture, educating Kansans about organic and sustainable agriculture (including medicinal herbs), and teaching at the University. Dr. Janke's appointment is with the Department of Horticulture, Forestry, and Recreation Resources, where she shares university knowledge with groups of adult learners in the state, who decide how to apply this knowledge to problem-solving efforts in their own regions. As part of the Cooperative Extension Service, the land-grant outreach arm of state universities, Professor Janke works closely with producers and consumers on sustainable agricultural issues. She conducts community development education on a daily basis, both at work and in her community, where she has helped to start a small-town farmer's market and promote economic development there. A pioneer in U.S. organic and sustainable agriculture, Rhonda Janke has served on the Board of Directors of Salina's Land Institute, which was recently a recipient of the global Right Livelihood award. She was one of a few leading horticulturalists who received extended training in organic agriculture at the Rodale Institute. Rhonda Janke's experiences are broadening as she learns more about sustainable agriculture in Latin America, and as she conducts research on her own farm, where her diverse agricultural practices have taken her into sheep and turkey raising, organic vegetable gardening, and bee-keeping.

Shomarka Omar Keita was born in South Carolina and grew up in Florida. He was educated in both public and private schools. His post-high school education was obtained at Williams College, Howard University College of Medicine, SUNY-Binghamton, and Oxford University. Research interests include: skeletal biology; early African history; human variation and how it is conceived and misconceived; paradigms in understanding population history; the history of ideas; racism in historical and anthropological writing; the biology of poverty; and the phenomenon of the discussions about "race," "culture," and genetics. He takes the position that the biological history of modern humans did not lead to a structuring of *Homo sapiens sapiens* into sub-species ("races") based on current genetic data, and is concerned about the misuse of terminology. There is a geographical variation but it does not rise to the level of race in its correct sense.

Dr. Keita is concerned about the feverish attempts to find a gene for everything (except curiously the racism of the last 300 years), and bothered by the lack of such fire to make sure that all children have nutritious meals, a sense of security and belonging, and life experiences which are made equivalent in fact (by any means necessary), thus giving a true equal chance at a good life in which full potential is reached.

Dr. Keita is currently Medical Officer for the Mental Retardation and Developmental Disabilities Administration for the District of Columbia; he holds research associate appointments with the anthropology departments in the Field Museum in Chicago and the Smithsonian Museum of Natural History.

Cynthia Lawrence received her B.S. in Education, Massachusetts State Teachers College at Boston, 1960; her M.A. in Multicultural Education, Pepperdine College, 1977; and her Ph.D. in Higher Education and Social Change, WISR, 1987. Cynthia is a former school teacher and is expert in the areas of multicultural education, alternative education, and the teaching and learning of language skills. She is a retired faculty member in Teacher Education at the University of California at San Diego. She continues to develop materials and training sessions to heighten teachers' sensitivity to multicultural issues. She frequently conducts workshop sessions on interracial issues for such groups as the Family Stress Center and the National Organization for Women (NOW). Cynthia Lawrence was appointed in 1991 to the San Diego Human Relations Commission.

Cynthia has been a core faculty member at WISR for 12 years. At WISR, Cynthia devotes considerable attention to leading an ongoing feminist social theory studies circle, to leading seminars on social change theory and issues of multiculturality, and to nurturing intellectual autonomy through collaborative knowledge-building activities among learners. In all of her work with students, she instructs and supports their efforts to write clearly, meaningfully, and in their own voice.

Sharon Murphy completed her Ph.D. in Education at Claremont Graduate University and San Diego State University in 2001. Her dissertation was entitled: "Informing Our Practice: A Case Study to Interrogate and Seek Critical Foundations for Community-Based Education." Dr. Sharon Murphy's professional experiences include positions in formal and informal K-16 education and non-profit organizations. She has been an educational administrator, researcher, and teacher. Her academic and personal interests center on justice and oppression studies, and on equity in education. She is currently a lecturer at California State Polytechnic University in Pomona, where she teaches "Community Service Learning." Sharon Murphy's publications include contributing to *Queering Elementary Education: Advancing the Dialogue about Sexualities and Schooling* (edited by J. Sears and W. Letts, 1999, Rowman and Littlefield). Readers are welcome to contact Dr. Murphy at glamur123@yahoo.com.

Mechthild E. Nagel is a scholarly activist who has been engaged in abolitionism as it affects prisons, prisoners, and those in communities affected by racism. She received her Ph.D. from the University of Massachusetts at Amherst and her undergraduate degree from the Albert-Ludwigs University in Freiburg, Germany. Currently Dr. Nagel is Associate Professor of Philosophy at SUNY-College at Cortland, New York, where she now serves as Chair of the Center for Multicultural and Gender Studies. In her recent past, Mechthild Nagel taught for the Department of Women's Studies at Minnesota State University, Mankato, which has one of the most respected Women's Studies and applied social-change programs in the United States. Mechthild Nagel has been very involved in teaching in prisons, and in learning from these social-change classrooms. Her publications include: *Masking the Abject: A Genealogy of Play* (Lexington Books, forthcoming) and (eds., Nagel and Light) *Race, Class and Community Identity* (Prometheus Press, 2000). Mechthild Nagel has mentored various U.S. faculty members who have an interest in researching prison education, and who want to volunteer to teach in prisons.

Joyce Rothschild is Professor of Sociology at Virginia Tech. For many years, she has studied grassroots collectives and co-operatives, culminating in many articles and her book, with J. Allen Whitt, *The Co-operative Workplace: Potentials and Dilemmas of Organizational Democracy and Participation* (Cambridge University Press). This book won the C. Wright Mills Award in 1987 as the most significant book in the general discipline of Sociology. In recent years, Dr. Rothschild has been studying whistleblowers and the suppression of dissent in the large bureaucratic organizations, both public and private. Feel free to communicate with her at: joycevt@aol.com or at: joycer@vt.edu.

Michael E. Rotkin, Ph.D., has been a leading force in the development of the Community Studies Department at the University of California, Santa Cruz (UCSC). His publications include the co-edited volume *Revolutionary Theory*. Currently Mike Rotkin is Lecturer and Director of Field Studies in the Community Studies Department at UCSC. Mike Rotkin has been a lecturer in Community Studies since 1974, and Director of the Field Program since 1979.

Mike Rotkin has a Ph.D. in the History of Consciousness from UCSC and teaches courses in community organizing, Marxist theory, and mass and alternative media. In addition to vicariously experiencing global social change through reading his students field notes, Mike was recently elected to his fifth term on the Santa Cruz City Council. He has also served three terms as Mayor of Santa Cruz.

Yoshiro Sanbonmatsu sees "Michelangelo / Dorothea Lange" as his signature piece. His interest in art began with his early explorations of Renaissance art, but it was through Edward Steichen's book *The Family of Man* that he learned to measure humanity, i.e., in terms of social realism and not elitist idealism. Dorothea Lange's photo of a migrant family from Steichen's book remained especially indelible because he had watched, as a youngster, migrant workers, driven out of the South by the dust bowl, camping out on the edge of town and moving on to look for work up north. He writes, "When younger, I had grown up with a Mexican lad whose father worked for my father doing physical labor in the sweating sun—we lived in a big white house and they, in a shack with an earthen floor. And later, living through the internment, serving in WWII, witnessing the tumultuous sixties, especially with respect to duplicitous US foreign policy, would come the realization that Western civilization and its culture was built on myths, lies and cruel inhumanity." And after teaching American literature and culture—and Black literature and culture for a short period—to high school students for forty years, Yoshiro Sanbonmatsu embarked on a second career as a social/political painter to rage against the social injustices past, present and the likely future.

The Gallery of Social/Political Art, co-founded by Yoshiro Sanbonmatsu, is located at 565 Boyleston Street (in residence at the Community Church of Boston), Boston, Massachusetts 02116, geocities.com/gallery_gspa.

Teresa Schmidt, an Associate Professor at Kansas State University (KSU), received her BA and MA from Central Washington University, Ellensburg in 1969 and 1970. She received her MFA from Washington State University, Pullman in 1972. Listed with *Who's Who in American Art*, Professor Schmidt teaches drawing and printmaking at KSU; she has also taught guest classes in Washington State; Arbroath, Scotland; and Norwich, England.

Teresa Schmidt's art has been included in solo and invitational exhibits. She has received awards in international, national, regional, state and local exhibitions by such jurors as: author and critic Barbara Rose; internationally known artist Salvatore Scalora; the Curator of Twentieth Century Art, the Philadelphia Museum of Art, Susan Rosenberg; Associate Curator, Solomon R. Guggenheim Museum of Art, Tracy Bashkoff; Associate Curator, The Metropolitan Museum of Art, New York City, Michiel Pomp; Associate Curator, The Phillips Collection, Washington, D.C., Stephen B. Phillips; Professor Bernard Chaet, Yale University; Curator, Chicago Art Institute, Mark Pascale; Director, O.K. Harris Gallery, New York City, Ivan Karp; and Curator of Prints, The Whitney Museum of American Art, New York City, David Kiehl.

Teresa Schmidt's work is found in permanent collections, including: The Albrecht-Kemper Museum of American Art, St. Joseph, Missouri; The Norwich School of Art and Design, Norwich, England; The Fogg Art Museum, Cambridge, Massachusetts; The Springfield Art Museum, Springfield, Missouri; Minot State University, North Dakota; Appalachian State University, Boone, North Carolina; Western Washington University, Bellingham, Washington; Evergreen State College, Olympia, Washington; The Helen Spencer Museum of Fine Arts, Lawrence, Kansas; Nicolet College, Rhinelander, Wisconsin; Hays State University Art Department, Fort Hays, Kansas; The Marianne Beach Art Museum, Manhattan, Kansas; and The Savannah School of Art and Design, Savannah, Georgia.

Teresa Schmidt's artwork has been included in the 1997 Rockport publication: *The Best of Printmaking: An International Collection* (hardbound). She has illustrated a book, *Fast Forward: Work, Gender and Protest in a Changing World*, written by Torry Dickinson and Robert Schaeffer and published by Rowman and Littlefield in 2001. Images of Teresa Schmidt's artwork appear in *Community and the World*, along with a statement about what inspires her.

Rashad Shabazz is currently a PhD student in the History of Consciousness program at the University of California, Santa Cruz. He has a Masters degree from Arizona State University and a B.S. from Minnesota State University, Mankato. Rashad's publications include (2001) "Exercise, Training and Getting Rid of the Fat" in *bad subjects Bad Subjects*; (2000) "A Taste of Freedom" in *The Cobbler Magazine*; (1998) "Hotel Civilization" in the *Minnesota State University Magazine*; and (1998) book review, *Journal of Philosophy and*

Technology. His activism includes acting as: president for the Coalition for the Abolition of Prisons, Co-founder of the Anti-Oppression Action Alliance at Minnesota State University, Mankato, and currently an editor for the *Journal of Prisoners on Prisons*. Also, he works with local Bay Area anti-prison organizations such as the California Prison Moratorium Project and Jericho. Rashad Shabazz can be contacted at: rashad_Shabazz@hotmail.com.

Wendy Terry has made the history of workers' educational associations a subject of her academic studies since 1983. As President of the Ontario Association for Continuing Education, she became aware of the 1950's decline of this community model for liberal arts learning in North America, and its continued vitality in Nordic, some Commonwealth, and European countries. The subject of her current studies and community development work is the role of community access to liberal arts learning in fostering active citizenship, particularly in relation to the development of global citizenship. As an adult, Wendy Terry returned to school, initially seeking additional job training and then becoming engaged in liberal arts learning. She became a community activist for adult learners and an advocate for the popularization of liberal arts learning.

In 1997 Wendy Terry earned a M.Ed. in International Education at Harvard's Graduate School of Education. She was the founding Coordinator of the Continuing Education Students' Association of Ryerson (CESAR) and in 1980 received a Honourary Award from Ryerson University. In 1995 members of the Ontario Association for Continuing Education selected her to receive their Norman High Award for outstanding leadership in the field of adult and continuing education. From 1992 to 2000 she was a member of the Executive Committee of the International Federation of Workers' Educational Associations and IFWEA's Liaison to UNESCO.

Wendy Terry currently is President of the Workers' Educational Association (WEA) of Canada. The WEA of Canada produces a community magazine for adults returning to school in Toronto and the Greater Toronto area, called *Learning Curves*. For the past five years she has been the Coordinator for a Co-op Program for foreign-trained immigrants held at Overland Learning Centre, a community learning centre of the Toronto District School Board. Her publications include *Unravelling the Tangle, Learning Information Services for Adults in Canada,* Learnxs Press 1991, and "The Learners' View of Community Based Training Program," published in *The Learners' View of Community Based Training: A Field Guide*, Ontario Network of Employment, Skills Training and Education Programs, ONESTEP 1989. She may be reached at WEA's email learningcurves@hotmail.com.

INDEX

R

S